Early Children's Books
and Their Illustration

EARLY CHILDREN'S BOOKS AND THEIR ILLUSTRATION

The Pierpont Morgan Library
Oxford University Press
1975

OXFORD UNIVERSITY PRESS, ELY HOUSE, LONDON, W.1

GLASGOW MELBOURNE WELLINGTON

CAPE TOWN IBADAN NAIROBI DAR ES SALAAM LUSAKA ADDIS ABABA

DELHI BOMBAY CALCUTTA MADRAS KARACHI LAHORE

KUALA LUMPUR SINGAPORE HONG KONG TOKYO

ISBN 0 19 211565 0

29 EAST 36 STREET, NEW YORK, N.Y. 10016

PHOTOGRAPHS BY CHARLES V. PASSELA

PRINTED IN THE UNITED STATES OF AMERICA

LIBRARY OF CONGRESS CATALOGUE CARD NUMBER 75-15020

To Miss Elisabeth Ball

Contents

Preface

This book attempts to show us, by word and by picture, how and where children's literature originated and which kinds of stories were chosen *for* children—and *by* children—over the centuries. We follow the tales which became popular and see how they were often initially illustrated by crude woodcuts, and how they might later be transformed by the drawings, watercolors, or engravings of great artists. This is not a history of children's literature; it is a selection of masterpieces or milestones from the past two thousand years of books and pictures which either were intended for children or which before long became their special property. From the two hundred twenty-five examples presented in this volume you should be able to get a sense of the evolution of the various types of children's literature.

We show you what the text of the most celebrated children's stories looked like in its earliest known form, how it was first printed and illustrated, and then the development of the illustrated text. We begin with fragments of the third century and we end with books and pictures at the beginning of the twentieth century. You are led up to our own time, we show you all of the antecedents, but we do not cross over into the world of contemporary children's books.

The book is intended for everyone who loves illustrated children's books; it is more particularly for the student and the collector of these stories and pictures. Prospective collectors must be warned at the outset, however, that there is little chance of forming a library of the most significant early children's stories as they were first published. Many of these works are unique—not only the manuscripts and the drawings, of course, but the first or early printed books; or these books are today nearly unique, for they were literally read and looked at and fingered and torn until they were used up and disappeared. For a large number of the printed works described here you will read that they are one of two or three copies known, or that the first edition is rare or very rare, that only a few copies are known, or that less than a handful survive. Whenever possible we have indicated the number of known copies, but there is still so little bibliographical information about many of the early children's books that we can often give only an approximate statement which indicates that less than five, or that not more than ten copies are believed to exist today. As long as there are attics and cupboards we can hope that more early children's books will come to light; and, in fact, we trust that this volume may call forth a few others from dusty, forgotten shelves.

Here you will find fables and tales, courtesy books, ABC's and nursery rhymes, primers and readers, grammars and schoolbooks, Bibles and religious books, hymns, emblem books, proverbs, fairy tales, moral tales, and cautionary tales, street cries, broadside ballads, almanacs, puzzles and riddles and jests, sports and games, fantasy and fiction. There are hornbooks and battledores, and other kinds of literature for children which have long since disappeared. There are the books for adults which were adapted for children: above all, Aesop, the bestiaries, and mediaeval romances; *Pilgrim's Progress*, *Robinson Crusoe*, and *Gulliver's Travels* but also Lord Chesterfield's *Letters*, Samuel Richardson's *Clarissa*, and Fielding's *Tom Jones*. Some of the stories, authors, or publishers receive special attention, whether *A Christmas Carol*, Baron Munchausen, the Brothers Grimm, Hans Christian Andersen, Edward Lear, Beatrix Potter, or Thomas Boreman. There are more than thirty divisions of the book, arranged approximately in chronological order, and within each of these the works are listed according to their first publication.

It should already be apparent that the emphasis is Anglo-American, not only because this volume is intended first of all for that world, but chiefly because the English contribution to the writing, illustrating, and publishing of children's literature was so very great. The first flourishing of books for children came in England about the middle of the eighteenth century, with booksellers like Thomas Boreman in the seventeen forties; then John Newbery and his successors, the two Francis Newberys and Elizabeth Newbery; John Marshall; the firm of Darton and Harvey; and John Harris, who had been the manager of Elizabeth Newbery's shop. At the end of that century in England we find Thomas Bewick, the first man in modern times to earn his living by illustrating books, many of them for children; and the artist and poet William Blake, who first yoked picture and poem in his own inimitable way in *Songs of Innocence*.

The development of the children's book in this period and the new achievement in illustration are so important that we have had a special essay written for this volume by Professor J. H. Plumb of Cambridge University concerning the social history of children, their books and their schools, and of the publishing of their books, during the eighteenth century in England. For many of the types of literature discussed in our text you will find that the English books from 1740 to 1820 are pivotal works in the change from primitive fable or romance to the modern children's story and twentieth-century illustration. This revolution in children's literature in England in the eighteenth century, as Professor Plumb writes, created a union of easy comprehension and delightful contents, and the marriage of text and illustration, which, "like all true marriages, has proved indissoluble."

In the very beginning was Aesop, or someone like Aesop, telling fables. And so we begin with the earliest known papyrus fragment (third or early fourth century) of the story of the farmer who set fire to a raiding fox's tail and thereby destroyed his own field of grain; next the earliest and most nearly complete collection of Aesopian fables as presented in Latin verse by Phaedrus (ninth century); then the earliest known manuscript in Greek prose (late tenth century) of the collections of Aesop by Babrius and the Aesopian collection called the Augustana, together with the earliest known translation into Greek of the fables of Bidpai and the earliest illustrated life of Aesop.

Two of the bestiaries, magnificently illuminated, come from the twelfth century when these stories about real and fabulous animals first changed from the ancient *Physiologus* to the form now known as the bestiary. There are as well monuments of early printing and illustration, like the Zainer Aesop of 1476, *Der Ritter vom Turn* (1493) with woodcuts by Dürer, the first illustrated printed edition of the *Gesta Romanorum* (in Dutch, 1481) and *Valentin et Orson* (Lyon, 1489)—each of these books is unique in America. From works like these, the earliest children's fables and romances and courtesy books are drawn.

After that there is the unique copy of what is thought to be the first edition of the earliest known book printed for children: *Les Contenances de la table* (Lyon, about 1487). You will see also what is probably the single most famous work in all of children's literature, the only manuscript known (1695) of the Perraults' *Contes de ma Mere L'Oye* ("Mother Goose"), that one presented to Mademoiselle, the spirited young niece of Louis XIV. There are the first printed ABC's and grammars, the first miniature Bible and the first English miniature Bible for children—each of these a nearly unique copy. There is the only extant copy of the first book about Tom Thumb, which seems to be the earliest surviving printed English nursery tale.

The chief treasures of later children's literature go on and on, frequently with original manuscripts and drawings as well as the first edition of the printed book: *A Christmas Carol*, Lear's *Book of Nonsense*, Saint-Exupéry's *Le Petit Prince*. We shall see illustrated letters in which Beatrix Potter conceived the story of Peter Rabbit. There is a legendary rarity like the first edition (1865) of *Alice's Adventures in Wonderland*, with some of the original drawings. Frank Baum's *Wizard of Oz* is shown, and *Pinocchio*, as it first appeared in a periodical. The work of Hans Christian Andersen has been selected from a complete set of the first editions of his fairy tales and from several manuscripts of these tales, his poems, and dozens of his autograph letters.

You will not, however, find every favorite children's story, nor all of the major illustrators of children's literature before World War I. But we have striven to indicate the variety of children's literature in all of Europe, England, and America, and the achievement over the centuries in writing and illustrating such stories. As you go through this book you will also detect the feud, particularly in Great Britain and America, from the seventeenth century well into the nineteenth, between the Puritans or the moralists and the romancers, ballad lovers, and weavers of fairy tales. In the early period we find someone like Bunyan writing "A Caution to Stir Up to Watch against Sin"; later we have Hannah More, Mrs. Trimmer, Mrs. Barbauld, and others, mostly gentlewomen, producing moral tales of unctuous edification. It took many years before the point of view of a man like Dr. Johnson triumphed over the millions of stern parents and teachers. One of Johnson's conversations is recorded (in 1780) in which

> Lady Rothes spoke of the advantages children now derived from the little books published purposely for their instruction. Johnson controverted it, asserting that at an early age it was better to gratify curiosity with wonders than to attempt planting truth, before the mind was prepared to receive it, and that therefore, *Jack the Giant-Killer*, *Parismus and Parismenus*, and *The Seven Champions of Christendom* were fitter for them than Mrs. Barbauld and Mrs. Trimmer.

About twenty years later, Charles Lamb, himself a writer of delightful stories for children, wrote to Samuel Taylor Coleridge (23 October 1802):

> "Goody Two Shoes" is almost out of print. Mrs. Barbauld's stuff has banished all the old classics of the nursery; and the shopman at Newbery's hardly deigned to reach them off an old exploded corner of a shelf, when Mary [Charles Lamb's sister] asked for them. Mrs. B.'s and Mrs. Trimmer's nonsense lay in piles about. Knowledge insignificant and vapid as Mrs. B.'s books convey, it seems, must come to a child in the *shape* of *knowledge*, and his empty noddle must be turned with conceit of his own powers when he has learnt that a Horse is an animal, and Billy is better than a Horse, and such like; instead of that beautiful Interest in wild tales which made the child a man, while all the time he suspected himself to be no bigger than a child. Science has succeeded to Poetry no less in the little walks of children than with men. Is there no possibil-

ity of averting this sore evil? Think what you would have been now, if instead of being fed with Tales and old wives' fables in childhood, you had been crammed with geography and natural history?

Damn them!—I mean the cursed Barbauld Crew, those Blights and Blasts of all that is Human in man and child.

The conflict between "the cursed Barbauld Crew" and "old wives' fables," between fearsome religious tracts and wonderful tales, and then between science and poetry is constantly part of the development of children's literature. But, as we know, fantasy and fable win out.

A full range of books on both sides of the feud is shown here. The development from Aesop to Saint-Exupéry can be illustrated in this volume because of the riches of The Pierpont Morgan Library. We are especially fortunate because the Founder of the Library and his son, J. P. Morgan, brought together so many remarkable early manuscripts and printed books, and a number of the Trustees of the Library have distinguished collections of children's books and manuscripts: Miss Julia P. Wightman, Mr. Arthur A. Houghton, Jr., Mr. Francis Kettaneh, and Dr. Gordon N. Ray. We have supplemented our collections with items on loan from their libraries. (All works not otherwise identified in the following pages were purchased for the Library by J. Pierpont Morgan, by his son, J. P. Morgan, or from general funds.)

Above all we are grateful to Miss Elisabeth Ball who brought together the major part of the large collections of children's literature now at the Morgan Library. Since the disposal of the late Edgar Oppenheimer's library, considered to be the finest collection of children's books of all nations, there can be no question of the supremacy of that formed by Miss Ball. Others, like the Osborne Collection of early English children's books (in Toronto), or the Rosenbach Collection of early American children's books (in Philadelphia), may have greater completeness for a given country. But the various collections now at the Morgan Library, and those promised to it, make an incomparable source for the study and enjoyment of children's books and their illustration, from their ancient beginnings to the early part of the twentieth century.

In 1954 and 1955 the Library presented a catalogue and an exhibition devoted to *Children's Literature*; Herbert Cahoon, Curator of Autograph Manuscripts, prepared these, chiefly through loans; the result was one of the most important milestones in our knowledge of children's books. Now twenty years later, we are publishing a far larger volume, and this time extensively illustrated, which, because of the generosity of Miss Ball, can be based for the most part on our own collections. Gerald Gottlieb, our new Curator of Early Children's Books, has written an engaging narrative to accompany our selection of books, manuscripts, and drawings. We are deeply indebted to him for this work, and to Charles V. Passela, the chief photographer of the Library, for his superlative photographs for this volume.

Charles Ryskamp
DIRECTOR

Foreword

It is an aim of this work to suggest sources and influences that may have played a part in the long development of books for children. Perhaps nowhere in the world could this aim have been carried out so well as here, amid the truly extraordinary holdings of The Pierpont Morgan Library. It has been profoundly gratifying to be able to draw upon such resources. It will be even more gratifying if this work stimulates others to look into the matter further.

In the descriptive material that is presented along with the discussion of items in the text, considerations of utility—whether for scholars, collectors, or the general reader—have been allowed to take precedence over consistency. Thus, collations and paginations are fuller for some items than for others; and information on bindings has been given only where it is deemed significant. For page sizes, in most cases only the height is provided; where two dimensions are given, the height is the first. It is an unfortunate fact that at present bibliography in the area of early children's books is often frustratingly inadequate. Accordingly, bibliographical references have been supplied only where it is thought that they will contribute information of real value.

We are especially grateful to the Trustees of The Andrew W. Mellon Foundation for creating a fund at the Library for facilitating the use of our collections by qualified scholars. The Andrew W. Mellon Fund will help to enable scholars to use the early children's books and other collections at the Library which previously were uncatalogued and inaccessible. Now through this book and the exhibition at the Morgan Library, 2 September through 30 November 1975, the general public as well as the scholars will have an opportunity to see many treasures hitherto largely unknown.

During the process of selecting and discussing the material presented here I have enjoyed the benefit of valuable advice and much other assistance from my colleagues at the Morgan Library. I should like to express my gratitude first of all to the Director of the Library, Charles Ryskamp, not only for his imaginative counsel but as well for his unfailing enthusiasm and support throughout the entire project. I should also like to thank Curt Bühler, Research Fellow for Texts Emeritus; Herbert Cahoon, Curator of Autograph Manuscripts; Paul Needham, Curator of Printed Books; his assistant, Thomas V. Lange; Robert Riggs Kerr, Supervisor of the Catalogue; William M. Voelkle, Associate Curator of Mediaeval and Renaissance Manuscripts; Alexander Jensen Yow, Conservator; Mrs. Patricia Reyes, Associate Conservator; Miss Deborah Evetts, Bookbinder; Miss Priscilla Barker, Assistant to the Director; Miss Doris Hamburg, Secretary for the Fellows; Mrs. Evelyn Semler, Supervisor of the Reading Room; Miss Christine Stenstrom, Supervisor of Photographic Records; Mrs. Susan Vosk, Secretarial Assistant; and Mrs. Laura Voorhies, my assistant.

A number of persons outside the Morgan Library have also helped in various ways. I should like to thank Michael Papantonio, John Fleming, Justin Schiller, Mrs. Lola Szladits, Milton Reissman, Mrs. Ludwig Ries, Miss Judith St. John, Walter Schatzki, Milton Glick, Miss Elizabeth Riley, Mrs. Vivien Noakes, and Charles Lewsen.

Finally, let me record my debt to my wife, Robin Gottlieb, sometime bibliographical consultant to the Morgan Library and permanent consultant to her grateful husband.

Gerald Gottlieb

The First Flourishing of Children's Books

A new attitude to children developed in England during the eighteenth century, a new attitude which spread as easily to Boston, New York, and Philadelphia as it did to Birmingham, Leeds, and Glasgow. Greater emphasis was placed on their education in respect to its usefulness for their future life in society. Although a knowledge of the classics was still regarded as the mark of a gentleman, more and more small schools, run for a profit, provided a far more practical education—in bookkeeping, clerical handwriting, English language, foreign languages, mathematics, navigation, surveying, geography, and the use of the globes; and it was this type of education, not the grammar schools, which flourished so vigorously in the eighteenth century. One hundred and twenty-five schoolmasters offering this type of education, in evening classes as well as day schools, advertised in the Philadelphia newspapers between 1740 and 1776, which is very comparable to what was happening at the same time in England, where between 1720 and 1760 one hundred schools advertised in the *Northampton Mercury*, and sixty-three advertised in the *Norwich Mercury* during the decade 1749–1759. Nor were these schools confined to boys; some provided education for girls, a few took both sexes. In addition to commercial education, the schools also provided lessons in social deportment, music, dancing, drawing, and fencing for boys.

As well as a new and widespread form of education flourishing in the eighteenth century, so, too, did a new and much more humane system of teaching develop, springing from the ideas of John Locke, which he had set out in his *Some Thoughts Concerning Education* in 1693. This was by far his most popular book, for it was reprinted nineteen times before 1761 and was as well known in America as it was in England. Locke believed in arousing the child's interest in education by a system of esteem for those who did well, and of shame for those who were reluctant to learn. He disapproved of the time-honoured method of flogging boys into learning, a sentiment which was already widespread, but to which his authority gave added force. Children were to be beguiled into learning; or ridiculed if they would not learn, a method employed by David James Dove of Philadelphia, an English schoolmaster (he had taught for sixteen years at Chichester) much admired by Benjamin Franklin. By 1740, therefore, perhaps before, there was a new attitude to children. No longer were they regarded as sprigs of Old Adam, whose wills had to be broken by the rod, nor was education regarded as a genteel accomplishment; boys and girls were being educated in order to play an effective and successful role in an aggressive commercial society. And because commercial opportunities everywhere abounded, parents were willing to invest, as never before, in the education of their children. Naturally enough this had a profound influence on the production of children's books.

Books by which children could be taught had existed from the first days of printing—alphabets, grammars, and the like—but few were designed specifically for children. Authors and publishers made very little attempt to entice the young mind with attractive and compelling illustrations and typography. And it should be remembered that fairy stories, ballads, riddles, and fables were intended as much for adults as for children. Indeed, Aesop was not specifically adapted for children in England until 1692, when Roger l'Estrange produced his edition.

As with so many cultural and educational developments, the late seventeenth and early eighteenth centuries saw the beginnings of a changed attitude toward children's literature, and methods of learning to read. In 1694, "J.G." published *A Play-book for children, to allure them to read as soon as they can speak plain. Composed of small pages, on purpose not to tire children, and printed with a fair and pleasant letter. The matter and method plainer and easier than any yet extant*, which was, for once, a true statement in a blurb. The book has wide margins, large type; its language is simple and concrete and mostly within the compass of a child's experience. The author states in his preface that he wished to "decoy Children into reading." It did well enough to be reprinted in 1703, by which time a few other authors, noticeably William Ronksley, were attempting to find methods and materials more suitable for very young children. Ronksley believed in teaching by verse according to the metre of the Psalms—first week, words of one syllable, the next week words of two syllables, and so on. And he used jokes, riddles, and proverbs to sugar his pills. Even so, his and other innovative children's books of Queen Anne's reign were designed, quite obviously, to be chanted, to be learnt by the ear rather than by the eye. They were more for teachers and parents to teach with than books meant for a child's own enjoyment. Similar books were slow to appear, and it is not until the seventeen forties that the change in style of children's literature becomes very marked. The entrepreneurial noses of Thomas Boreman and John Newbery twitched and scented a market for books that would be simple in production, enticing to the eye, and written specifically for children. Of course, it was not quite as simple as that. Children do not buy books; adults do.

So the new children's literature was designed to attract adults, to project an image of those virtues which parents wished to inculcate in their offspring, as well as beguile the child. These alphabet and reading books, by their simplicity, also strengthened the confidence of parents in their ability to teach their children to read in the home. The new children's literature was aimed at the young, but only through the refraction of the parental eye.

By the seventeen forties and fifties, as in so many aspects of English life, the market was there, ready to be exploited, and no man was quicker to seize the opportunity than John Newbery, whose *Little Pretty Pocket-Book*, in 1744, captured the public imagination. Until the early nineteenth century Newbery's family produced vast quantities of children's literature. Each decade the number of titles grew, and the most popular books were reprinted over and over again. His range was exceptional—from simple books for reading, writing, and arithmetic, to *The Newtonian System of Philosophy Adapted to the Capacities of young Gentlemen and Ladies, . . . by Tom Telescope*. It is crystal-clear, the examples exceptionally apposite, and its attitude to the universe, to philosophy, to humanity, and to the natural sciences would have drawn prolonged cheers from the Encyclopaedists. Hence it is not only a brilliantly produced book for adolescent children, but it also gives us a novel insight in how the ideas of the Enlightenment were being disseminated through society. The way ideas become social attitudes is one of the most complex problems that face a social historian, and almost all have neglected the influence of children's literature in changing the climate of ideas. Therefore *Tom Telescope* deserves a closer study.

There are six lectures. The first is on matter and motion, quite brilliantly explained. The second deals with the universe, particularly the solar system, and also with the velocity of light. Tom Telescope then moves on to atmosphere and meteors, and so to mountains, particularly volcanoes, and earthquakes, and so to rivers and the sea. Minerals, vegetables, and animals follow, and the final lecture is on the natural philosophy of man—his senses, the nature of his understanding, and the origin of ideas, with a great deal on optics, including the prism; Tom also deals with pleasure and pain. The book is relatively brief—only 126 pages—nevertheless it is wide-ranging, giving a simple outline of the most advanced attitude to the universe and to man's place in it. God is present, but only as divine wisdom which reason will, if pursued, ultimately reveal to mankind.

The philosophic attitude is purely Lockeian, as the science is entirely Newtonian. "All our ideas, therefore," says Tom Telescope, "are obtained either by *sensation* or *reflection*, that is to say, by means of our five senses, as *seeing*, *hearing*, *smelling*, *tasting*, and *touching*, or by the *operations of the mind* [upon them]." Although packed with lucid scientific information, the book has many asides, allegories, and stories that plead for a compassionate humanity, particularly toward animals. Cruelty to animals is improper, although cruelty between animals is necessary to sustain the life of the animal creation; hence cruelty, in this aspect, is a part of divine wisdom, but such necessity alone permits cruelty in the shape of killing and eating. Wanton cruelty is reprehensible, particularly to young animals and, above all, young birds. Most detestable of all is cruelty to a mother bird by the taking or destruction of eggs. (This is an exceptionally common theme in children's books.) Tom has no patience, however, with those who put kindness to animals before that to their fellow men. Tom's lecture reminds his hostess, Lady Caroline, of one of her neighbours, Sir Thomas, whom young Tom has seen treat animals well if they please, "but rave, at the same time, in a merciless manner, at poor children who were shivering at his gate, and send them away empty handed." Another neighbour, Sir William, "is also of the same disposition; he will not sell a horse, that is declining, for fear he should fall into the hands of a master who might treat him with cruelty; but he is largely concerned in the slave trade (which, I think, is carried on by none but *we good Christians*, to the dishonour of our *coelestial Master*) and makes no difficulty of separating the husband from the wife, the parents from the children, and all of them . . . from their native country, to be sold in a foreign market, like so many horses, and often to the most merciless of the human race." Kindness to animals, yes, but greater kindness to human beings is the burden of Tom's final lecture.

Hence, perhaps, we may discern one way by which ideas became social attitudes, that is, through the education of young and impressionable minds. For Tom's book, I would say, was aimed to be read in the home—it was partly directed, like many children's books, in its sentiments to mothers (this is very marked in the passage about animals, cruelty to birds, and the like)—and read, I would have thought, to, or by, children between twelve and fourteen, the impressionable years. Certainly it had an extraordinary success. Within a few weeks of publication in 1761, it was on sale in Norwich and was being advertised there in the newspapers. A new edition was required in 1762, a third edition in 1766, and a fourth in 1770. All together there were at least ten editions by 1800. It is difficult to be in any way certain of the size of the edition of Newbery's books. He printed 1,500 copies of his juvenile edition of Dr. Johnson's *Idler*; but editions of 10,000 were made of his very popular *Little Pretty Pocket-Book*. Doubtless the editions of *Tom Telescope* varied, the second probably being much larger than the first, which, following Newbery's usual practice, would be small to test the market. A conservative estimate would be that the book enjoyed a sale of 25,000 to 30,000 copies between 1760 and 1800, but the number could be far higher. Hence Lockeian and Newtonian ideas, combined with a compassionate humanity, were being widely disseminated amongst the middle-class young, and must have influenced their attitude to life.

And it must be stressed that *Tom Telescope* was not a unique book. For example, *A Museum*, published probably for the first time in 1750 or earlier, contained essays on the solar system, on volcanoes and earthquakes, and on natural history. This work was aimed at a somewhat younger audience than *Tom Telescope*, but it was equally successful, running to fifteen editions by 1800, and nineteen in all. *A Museum* also contained, very much in the spirit of the *Encyclopaedia*, a description of the manners, customs, and habits of foreign countries.

Newbery and *Tom Telescope*'s success, naturally, did not go unnoticed, and the range of cheap books on science, designed for children, grew. The Reverend Samuel Ward produced twelve such volumes on *The Modern System of Natural History* in 1776. In the same year *Mr. Telltruth's Natural History of Birds and of Animals* was written for very young children—but again it was full of the reasonableness of nature. And it cost only sixpence. In 1800 one publisher, not Newbery, advertised thirty-eight books for children, covering the arts and sciences; of these, fifteen were scientific and only two dealt with religion. Geography, history, and the classics were adapted to juvenile readers. Newbery and other publishers also produced quantities of moral tales, more beloved, one suspects, by the parents than by the children. Through Edward Augustus Kendall, the Newberys produced new types of fable, derived from the ballad of Cock Robin, in which birds develop human attributes, converse freely among themselves, and offer their own criticisms of human failure and shortcomings. Kendall wrote *The Swallow*, *The Wren*, *The Canary*, *The Sparrow*; and their themes are simple —cruelty to birds, taking eggs, breaking up nests, caging finches is the mark of an evil boy. The new sensitivity to birds and animals is best conveyed by the Robin Redbreast's song in *The Swallow* (1800):

Here, if heedless childhood plays,
Here, if truant schoolboy strays,
Let him, ere he hie along,
Stop, and hear the Robin's song!

To please *his* ears, I'll frame my lays,
Deeds of ruthless sport to praise;
I'll chuse the theme his heart approves:
I'll sing the joys that most he loves;

Bliss to the wild unthinking bands
Who nobly seize, with eager hands,
The downy nest, in gallant train,
And triumph in a parent's pain!

May thread-strung eggs still swell your store!
Deride, as ever, pity's lore!
For plunder, still, thro' spring-time rove,
And revel in the pangs of love!

Or, snare the bird, and starve its nest,
Nor care what anguish rends its breast! . . .
Ah! stay, forgive, thou peaceful shade!
That these rude notes your bow'rs invade!

And, schoolboy! if you dare refuse
A cruel sport, yet want excuse,
Stop, when you're ask'd to hie along,
And say: "I've heard the Robin's song!"

Cruelty is wicked, humane behaviour entirely laudable. Charity and benevolence will not only make a child happy but bring him the proper social rewards. A similar burden is echoed in the potted biographies of eminent children or in the examples of historic characters held up for the edification of youth. There is no space to describe these in detail, but the themes of most of them are avoidance of cruelty, violence, brutality, and the development of innocent virtues which are obedience, sensitivity, a love of nature, and therefore of reason, which naturally leads to industry, benevolence, and compassion. Nothing was regarded as more edifying than the death of a model child. Between 1780 and 1800, the moral note gets stronger. Mrs. Trimmer, the most formidable of children's writers at that time, dominates, and Mrs. Trimmer was not light of heart. There had always been a savage, macabre streak in the attitude to children. Corpse viewing—practised at Wesley's school at Kingswood—had been thought of as salutary. Before Mrs. Trimmer the desire to entertain, delight, and instruct children had disguised, if not obliterated, much of the heavy moralising. The Evangelical Revival, however, made a great deal of children's literature darker and gloomier as the century drew to a close.

Nevertheless, the contrast of, say, 1800 and 1700 in the range of what was available for children, is vivid. By 1800 there was no subject, scientific or literary, that had not its specialised literature designed for children—often beautifully and realistically illustrated, at times by really great book illustrators such as Thomas Bewick. The simpler textbooks—for reading, arithmetic, and writing—were carefully designed, with large lettering, appropriate illustration, and a small amount of print on a large page; and there were books for very young children, such as *A Pretty Play-thing for Children*. Novels specifically written about children for children began with *Sandford and Merton*, by Thomas Day. And the arts, as well as letters, were catered for—Master Michael Angelo's *The Drawing School for Little Masters and Misses* appeared in 1773, and there are books designed to teach children the first steps in music. And, as with adult books, less prosperous children could buy their books a part at a time. Nor was it necessary to buy the books; they could be borrowed. By 1810, there was a well-established juvenile library at 157 New Bond Street, run by Tabart. Some owners of circulating libraries kept a special juvenile section, as did James Woollen in Sheffield.

And children's books, as well as becoming far more plentiful, also became cheaper. John Newbery had used every type of gimmick to extend his market. With the *Little Pretty Pocket-Book* he had offered—for an extra twopence—a ball for the son or a pincushion for the daughter. He had used new types of binding that did not stain, and he had even tried giving a book away so long as the purchaser bought the binding. He advertised his books in every possible way—rarely did a parent finish one of his books without finding in the text a recommendation to read others. He sensed that there was a huge market ready for exploitation. He was right. Within twenty years, children's books were a thriving part of the Newcastle printer's trade; indeed, educational books attracted a very large number of provincial printers in the late eighteenth century, for they were well aware of the hunger of shopkeepers, tradesmen, and artisans such as weavers for education, not only for themselves, but also, and most emphatically, for their children. The printers of Philadelphia did not lag behind those of the English provinces; indeed they were some of the earliest in the field of children's literature outside London. In 1768 Shorhawk and Anderton, principally a firm of druggists (John Newbery was also the proprietor of the famous Dr. James's Fever Powder, which he plugged remorselessly in his books: the relationship between children's books and patent medicines was always close), advertised "a very great choice of books adapted for the instruction and amusement of all the little masters and mistresses in America." Some of these books may, of course, have been imports. By 1800, children's books had become very cheap; those at a penny were plentiful and this was a time when books in general, because of inflation, had increased in price by twenty-five percent. Nevertheless, Oliver and Boyd of Edinburgh turned them out by the score, under the title of *Jack Dandy's Delight*. They published forty at sixpence, twenty-six at twopence, forty at one penny, and ninety at a halfpenny. The penny books were well printed and delightfully illustrated. Only the very poorest families of unskilled labourers could not afford a halfpenny. Like Tom Paine's *Rights of Man*, children's literature was within the range of the industrious working class, and particularly of those families where social ambition had been stirred by the growing opportunities of a new industrialising society—more and more clerical jobs were available, and more and more parents were willing to make sacrifices to secure them for their children. Middle-class parents had begun to buy children's books in quantity.

From 1700 onwards, the intellectual and cultural horizons of the middle-class child, and indeed of the lower-middle-class child, had broadened vastly. About a great deal of his reading there was an air of modernity, a sense that he belonged to a new and exciting world. The same was true of his education, both the formal, so long as he avoided the grammar school, and the informal. Informal education, too, grew very rapidly in the English-speaking world of the eighteenth century. Itinerant lecturers in science, usually accompanied by a complex electrical apparatus, were exceptionally popular. Although they designed their courses principally for adults, more often than not they offered cheap tickets for children. Indeed this became a common practice for public amusements that were also partly educational. The range and variety of such amusements may be demonstrated by looking at what was available at Leeds, a prospering industrial and commercial city of Yorkshire, during the summer months of 1773. In April, families at Leeds were regaled by Mr. Manuel of Turin with his display of automata which, as well as having an Indian lady in her chariot moving around the table at ten miles an hour, also contained the "Grand Turk, in the Seraglio dress, who walks about the table smoaking his pipe in a surprising manner." All, of course, to the accompaniment of mechanical musical instruments. After Mr. Manuel, Mr. Pitt arrived with his principal marvel, a self-moving phaeton which traveled at six miles an hour, climbed hills, and started and stopped with the touch of a finger. He also brought along his electrifying machine, his *camera obscura*, his miraculous door which opened inside, outside, left, or right by the turn of a key. All for one shilling. The phaeton either wore out, broke down, or at 5 cwt. proved too expensive to move, for it was dropped by Pitt, who continued for some years to travel the Midland circuit, Nottingham, Leicester, Coventry, etc., but only with his scientific apparatus. Quite obviously he made a tolerable living.

On 10 August the attraction at Leeds was geographical, rather than mechanical, when the model of the city and suburbs of Paris arrived at the Town Hall. It was extremely elaborate and eighteen feet square. Viewing started at nine in the morning and closed at eight in the evening. In September a spectacular, double-column advertisement with woodcuts announced the arrival of Astley's circus, prices as usual a shilling for front seats, sixpence back, but Astley warned that boys trying to climb in would be taken care of by guards. He now also brought along with him his famous "Chronoscope"; an apparatus for measuring the velocity of projectiles.

The emphasis was on marvels, curiosities that were new and remarkable and usually mechanical or optical; hence many children were given a keen sense of a new, developing, and changing world in which mechanical ingenuity and electricity and science in general played an active part—a totally different cultural atmosphere to that which their grandfathers had lived in. Their cultural horizons, too, were widened by the availability of music to listen to in festivals and concerts, the cheapness of musical instruments, and the plentiful supply of music teachers. The same is true of art. Art materials were to be found in every provincial town, and so were drawing masters, who taught in the home as well as in the school. Prints of old masters and modern artists were a commonplace of provincial as well as London life. Visually it was a far more exciting age for children than ever before.

However, through most of the amusements ran the theme of self-improvement and self-education. The same is true of indoor games, as well as outdoor excursions. Playing-cards had long been used to inculcate knowledge—largely geographical, historical, or classical. One of the earliest packs of about 1700 taught carving lessons—hearts for joints of meat, diamonds for poultry, clubs for fish, and spades for meat pies. But more often than not these were importations, usually from France. The eighteenth century witnessed a rapid increase in English educational playing-cards, so that almost every variety of knowledge or educational entertainment could be found imprinted on their faces. The majority of booksellers, provincial as well as metropolitan, stocked them. Some cards were designed for the education of adults, or at least adolescents, but there were packs, very simply designed, for young children to play with and learn at the same time. One pack taught the first steps in music.

After playing-cards, one of the earliest educational games to be developed was the jigsaw puzzle, seemingly an English invention by the printer-bookseller and young entrepreneur John Spilsbury who, in 1762, produced dissected maps for the teaching of geography. These enjoyed an immediate, perhaps a phenomenal, success, and by the mid-seventeen-sixties he had thirty different maps in jigsaw form for sale. Unfortunately Spilsbury died young—at twenty-four—but what he had launched quickly proliferated not only in the teaching of history, geography, classics, or morals, but also purely for fun, though even these puzzles tended to have a moral overtone. The principal publisher of educational games became John Wallis, whose firm began to flourish in the seventeen eighties and lasted until 1847, during which time, with the Dartons, it held the field of educational games, some of which were extremely complex. All such games were not jigsaws. In the seventeenth century, Pierre du Val had used the painted-board, dice gambling games for teaching geography and history; indeed it has been said that Louis XIV learnt his lessons in this way, for the French court and aristocracy of the seventeenth century had no inhibitions about children gambling. The first dice game in England played on a painted board for instruction seems to have been invented by John Jefferys in 1759. His game was called *A Journey through Europe or The Play of Geography*, and the players moved along a marked route according to the throw of their dice. This proved very popular, and spawned a host of similar games, some of extreme complexity, such as Walker's *Geographical Pastime exhibiting a Complete Voyage Round the World in Two Hemispheres*, which must have taken hours to play. As well as board games, there were card games—often employing the rebus—which were extremely popular for teaching spelling and extending the vocabulary, as well as quickening wits, in the manner of Scrabble. By the early nineteenth century, in spite of the fulminations of Maria Edgeworth about the uselessness of these toys, there were almost as many educational toys available as there are today. For boys, there were complex mechanical toys—water mills, printing presses, looms, etc., which could be assembled and made to work. There were also cheap inflatable globes, complicated perspective views, and toy theatres with moveable scenery and actors, on which whole plays could be acted and re-acted from the scripts provided; and there were scientific toys, *camera obscura* and the like, made cheaply for children. And by that time too there were large quantities of toys on the market whose educational value was present, if secondary—Noah's arks, animal farms, soldiers and forts of every variety for the potential soldier, and, of course, dolls' houses and dolls. These varied from the extremely cheap—cut-outs in paper with brightly coloured interchangeable clothes—to elaborate models with wax or earthenware faces, jointed bodies, and complete wardrobes. And in London there were, by 1800 at least, two shops that specialised in making rocking-horses. In 1730, there were no specialised toy shops of any kind, whereas by 1780 toy shops everywhere abounded, and by 1820 the trade in toys, as in children's literature, had become very large indeed.

Children, in a sense, had become luxury objects upon which their mothers and fathers were willing to spend larger and larger sums of money, not only for their education but also for their entertainment and amusement. In a sense they had become superior pets—sometimes spoilt excessively, like Charles James Fox, sometimes treated with indifference or even brutality, but usually, as with pets, betwixt and between. Whatever the attitude of parents, children had become a trade, a field of commercial enterprise for the sharp-eyed entrepreneur.

The competition was fiercest, the ingenuity greatest, in the field of children's literature, and in those indoor games which taught as well as amused. Both fields were remarkably inventive and their most important feature was that they encouraged teaching in the home. They were so skilfully designed, so beautifully illustrated, that they gave confidence to parents as well as children by the ease with which they could be used. Ease of comprehension was as important as the delight of the contents, and books that married both had an enduring success generation after generation, as did Newbery's great little books—*Little Goody Two-Shoes* or *A Little Pretty Pocket-Book*. The most permanent effect of this revolution in children's literature was to marry text and illustration and, like all true marriages, that has proved indissoluble.

J. H. Plumb

Early Children's Books and Their Illustration

ILLUSTRATIONS

Items marked with an ornament [❧] are represented by full-color illustrations, which are distributed at intervals throughout the volume. All other items are illustrated with halftones placed at the end of each section. Each illustration is identified by its item number.

Aesop's Fables

Perhaps no book has been more read by children than Aesop's Fables. Certainly no book for children has been illustrated so frequently. Aesop himself is a personage about whom very little is known. According to information pieced together from ancient writers (principally Herodotus and Eugeon of Samos), Aesop was born in Thrace in the early sixth century B.C. and later was a slave on the island of Samos. There he won renown for telling clever stories in the form of pointed fables, chiefly about foxes and geese and lions and other animals. Aesop probably never wrote his fables down. But in the late fourth century B.C. Demetrius of Phalerum, a Greek politician and orator who was also a scholar, collected and wrote down Aesop's fables in Greek prose. Demetrius' intention, in all likelihood, was merely to make available to other speakers or writers a collection of fables they might use as illustrations in their discourses. No manuscript of this collection, known as *Aesopia*, has survived (though there does exist a papyrus fragment that may contain some passages from it). In the first half of the first century A.D., however, Demetrius' book was still extant in its entirety; and at that time a Roman poet named Phaedrus, who probably had access to the book, wrote a collection of fables in Latin verse. It is believed that Phaedrus' principal source was the *Aesopia* of Demetrius, but it is also believed that Phaedrus made changes in the fables, added fables drawn from various other sources, and invented new fables. Phaedrus' verse collection, in short, was a literary composition with almost as much of Phaedrus in it as of Aesop.

A little after the time of Phaedrus, or about the second half of the first century A.D., another collection of Aesopian fables was produced by a Greek poet named Babrius. This collection, like that of Phaedrus, was a literary production in verse (but Greek verse). Like Phaedrus, Babrius probably drew upon the prose *Aesopia* collection of Demetrius, and he may also have drawn upon other sources and upon his own invention. Babrius' work is the earliest collection known to us of Aesopian fables in Greek verse, just as Phaedrus' work is the earliest known collection of Aesopian fables in Latin verse.

About the second century A.D. there was also written down, in Greek prose, anonymously, another collection of Aesopian fables. This collection is called the Augustana. It was not known to Phaedrus, and probably not to Babrius.

From these three collections—Phaedrus, Babrius, and the Augustana—have come most of the fables known today as Aesop's, the fables that still captivate children as they have for so many centuries.

1 Babrius

FABLES 11, 16, AND 17. [*Greek-Latin.*]

[*? Egypt: Third or fourth century.*]
Amherst Greek Papyrus 26.
26 × 21.5 cm.
Newberry, Amherst, *26.* *Perry,* Aesopica.

The Morgan Library's Amherst Greek Papyrus 26, which was unearthed in Egypt, dates from the third or early fourth century. These papyrus fragments (26.1 and 26.2) contain portions of three of the fables of Babrius, numbers 11, 16, and 17. The fables are written in Greek and are accompanied by Latin (very bad Latin) translations. These are the earliest surviving Greek texts of the three fables.

Fable 11 concerns a farmer who caught a fox that had been raiding his garden. As a punishment he set fire to the fox's tail. The fox then ran into a field of the farmer's grain, which caught fire and burned to the ground—illustrating the moral that a great anger can bring a great retribution.

2 Phaedrus

FABULARUM AESOPIARUM. [*Latin.*]

[*Reims, France: Ninth century.*]
M.906. [*Codex Pithoeanus.*]
19.5 cm. 87 f.
Perry, Loeb.
Purchased on the Belle da Costa Greene Fund.

This manuscript is the earliest surviving collection of the Aesopian fables presented in Latin verse by Phaedrus. "Aesop is my source," Phaedrus writes in his prologue. "He invented the substance of these fables, but I have put them into finished form. . . ." The manuscript was discovered in the sixteenth century, presumably in France, by François Pithou, a philologist. (His brother, Pierre Pithou, published a critical edition of the text in 1596; a first edition of that book is in the Morgan Library.) The Phaedrus manuscript is called the Codex Pithoeanus, after the Pithou brothers. It is the oldest and most nearly complete text of Phaedrus to have survived. Palaeographical investigations have established that the manuscript was written in Reims in the ninth century. The Codex Pithoeanus, owned by the descendants of the Pithou brothers since the sixteenth century, was brought to the vaults of the Morgan Library for safekeeping during World War II. It is now the property of the Library, which purchased it in 1961.

3 [Aesop]

FABLES AND THE LIFE OF AESOP. [*Greek.*]

[*South Italy: Late tenth century.*]
M.397.
21.5 cm. 112 f.
Perry, Aesopica.

The early manuscripts of Aesop's fables often included a *Life of Aesop*, much of it told in the form of fables. The manuscript shown here, Morgan Library M.397, which was written in Greek and illuminated during the late tenth century in southern Italy, contains the earliest known illustrated *Life of Aesop*. The illustrations depict Aesop in the manner that became traditional—as a deformed slave, devoid of the power of speech until the goddess Isis bestows it upon him.

In addition to the illustrated *Life of Aesop*, Morgan M.397 includes the earliest known manuscript of any substantial source for the text of the Augustana, that anonymous second-century compilation of Aesop's fables in prose. Morgan M.397 also contains one of the earliest extensive texts of Babrius' Aesopian fables, consisting of thirty-one fables (among them four that are not found anywhere else in this, their original verse form). And also included in Morgan M.397 is the earliest translation into Greek of the fables of Bidpai. These are moralized animal-tales, derived from the ancient Panchatantra fables of India. The Bidpai fables were later incorporated into printed editions of Aesop's fables, and they have since appeared in many versions of Aesop produced for children.

4 [Aesop]

VITA ET FABULAE. [*Latin-German.*] *Translated by Heinrich Steinhöwel.*

Ulm: Johann Zainer, [*about 1476*].
30.5 cm. 288 f.
Goff A-116.

The fables of Aesop were among the first books to be printed after the invention of the printing press in the mid-fifteenth century. They were also among the first printed books to be illustrated. This edition, brought out by Johann Zainer in Ulm about 1476, is not only the very earliest printed Aesop to carry pictures, but it is also one of the finest examples of the early German illustrated book. The strong, effective woodcuts are the work of several hands, all unknown. The Zainer Aesop was immediately popular, being reprinted soon and often. The woodcuts were frequently copied for editions put out by other printers in the fifteenth century. The text of this Aesop was written in German by Heinrich Steinhöwel, a physician and classical scholar who also contributed financially to Zainer's printing establishment. Steinhöwel drew his version of the fables from several sources, including Phaedrus, Babrius, and the Bidpai fables. Probably because of its attractive illustrations, the Steinhöwel version became the standard one of late mediaeval Europe, and it was widely translated into other languages. The anonymous illustrations have had a strong influence on almost all the illustrated Aesops that followed, down to those given to children in the twentieth century. The Morgan Library copy of the Zainer Aesop is the only copy in America.

5 [Aesop]

AESOPUS MORALIZATUS. [*Latin-Italian.*] *Translated by Accio Zucco.*

Verona: Giovanni Alvise, 26 June 1479.
21 cm. 120 f.
Goff A-148.

The first edition of a fifteenth-century translation, by Accio Zucco, of the fables of Aesop into Italian verse. The vigorous woodcuts in this copy have been rather crudely colored by hand. The fable illustrated here is the familiar one of the dog who drops his piece of meat to grasp at its reflection in the water.

6 [Aesop]

ESOPO HISTORIADO. [*Latin-Italian.*] *Translated by Accio Zucco.*

Venice: Manfredus de Bonellis, 25 February 1503.
15 cm. 80 f.
Gift of the Fellows.

This copy of a 1503 printing of the Accio Zucco Italian Aesop appears to be the only one to survive from its edition. It is the earliest edition of the Zucco Aesop to be published in octavo, or "pocket" format, far smaller than the more usual quarto or folio size of the period (and of course easier for children to handle). The sixty-four woodcut illustrations are full of character and charm, although they are simple in the extreme. Illustrated here is the fable of the frog who wished to be as big as the ox and swelled himself until he burst.

7 [Aesop]

ESOPET EN FRANCOYS. [*French.*] *Translated by Julien Macho.*

Paris: Alain Lotrian, [*about 1525*].
17.5 cm. 70 f.
Purchased on the Lathrop C. Harper Fund.

Aesop's fables in an early French edition, published in Paris about the year 1525. The Morgan Library copy is believed to be the sole surviving copy of this edition. The translator, Julien Macho, based his version of the fables on the widely known Latin-German Aesop of Heinrich Steinhöwel, published about 1476. Macho's French translation (which first appeared in 1480 in a Lyon edition) is of particular interest because it was used by William Caxton, who in 1484 produced the first Aesop in English. Caxton's Aesop, which became the basis for countless Aesops written for English-speaking children, was a faithful translation of Macho's French translation of Steinhöwel's Latin-German Aesop. And, similarly, the woodcuts with which Caxton's English Aesop was illustrated followed those in Macho's French version, and ultimately derived from those in the Steinhöwel Aesop. A total of ninety woodcuts, some of them repeated, illustrate the unique Morgan Library copy of this French Aesop. The woodcut shown illustrates the fable of the dog in the manger.

8 [Aesop]

LES FABLES. [*French.*] *Translated by Gilles Corrozet.*

Paris: Denys Janot, 1544.
16 cm. 104 f.
Brunet, I, 94. Catalogue J. de Rothschild, I, 639 (+ correction: V, p. 189). Hofer-Mortimer 4.
Gift of the Fellows.

The one hundred fine woodcuts that illustrate this French collection of Aesop's fables, published in Paris in 1544, are anonymous, but scholars have seen in them stylistic parallels with the work of Geofroy Tory, who died in 1533. This Aesop provides an important and influential example of the illustrated books issued by Denys Janot. The unknown artist (or artists) responsible for the woodcuts also provided a considerable number of illustrations for other books from the same press. The first edition of Corrozet's translation was published by Janot in 1542; the edition shown here is the second. Both are of the greatest rarity.

9 [Aesop]

AESOP'S FABLES WITH HIS LIFE: IN ENGLISH, FRENCH & LATIN. The English by Tho. Philipott Esq; The French and Latin by Rob. Codrington M.A. Illustrated with one hundred and twelve sculptures by Francis Barlow.

London: Printed by William Godbid for Francis Barlow, 1666.
29.5 cm. [12], 1–40, 1–31, [1], 1–17, 2–221, [3] p.
Wing A-696. Hofer.
Gift of Mrs. G. W. P. Heffelfinger.

This seventeenth-century polyglot (English-French-Latin) Aesop is handsomely illustrated with engravings after designs by Francis Barlow (?1626–1702), an English painter renowned for his pictures of country life and field sports. (He was perhaps the finest English draughtsman of animal scenes in the seventeenth century.) Barlow, who published the book at his own expense, explains in his preface that he intends the work to contribute to the education of young people. This is the first edition; the relatively few copies known are all survivors of the Great Fire of London, which swept over the printer's premises in 1666.

10 [Aesop]

AESOP'S FABLES, IN ENGLISH AND LATIN, INTERLINEARY, FOR THE BENEFIT OF THOSE WHO NOT HAVING A MASTER, WOULD LEARN EITHER OF THESE TONGUES. [*?Edited by John Locke.*]

London: A. and J. Churchil, 1703.
18.5 cm. [6], 1–337, [9] p. + plates.
Darton, p. 17. Thwaite, p. 34.
Purchased for the Elisabeth Ball Collection.

The educational theories of the English philosopher John Locke (1632–1702) had a considerable influence on eighteenth-century writers who produced books for children, and this copy of Aesop's fables, with Latin and English in alternating lines, may well be a work in which Locke himself put his theories to practice. In his *Some Thoughts Concerning Education* (1693), Locke had suggested that an illustrated Aesop would be desirable for children to read—and this 1703 Aesop, with illustrations carefully keyed to the text, appears to have been prepared by Locke himself. Although the first edition, which is shown here, does not carry his name a subsequent (1723) issue by Locke's publishers bears on its title page the line "By John Locke, Gent." This statement may or may not be accepted at face value (Locke had then been dead nearly twenty years, and publishers have been known to stretch the truth), but the book does indeed practice what the eminent philosopher preached. Only a few copies of the first edition are known.

11 Gabrielle Faërno

LES FABLES DE FAËRNE, TRADUITS EN VERS FRANÇOIS PAR M. PERRAULT.

Amsterdam: Gerard Onder de Linden, 1718.
15.5 cm. [24], 192 p.
Brunet, II, 1160. Tchemerzine, IX, 187.
Purchased for the Elisabeth Ball Collection.

Gabrielle Faërno, a Latin poet who died in 1561, based his collection of Aesop's fables on Phaedrus. The first edition of Faërno's fables, published in 1565, had the distinction of bearing illustrations engraved after drawings attributed to the painter Titian. (The Morgan Library possesses a copy of that edition.) The French translation shown here, which is illustrated with engravings copied from those in the 1565 first Latin edition, is noteworthy for still another reason. It was translated by Charles Perrault, who gave the world the fairy tales of Mother Goose. This is the second edition; the first was published in Paris in 1699. Of both editions there is but a handful of copies in America. The Aesopian fable illustrated is that of the fox and the grapes.

12 [Robert Dodsley]

SELECT FABLES OF ESOP AND OTHER FABULISTS.

Birmingham: Printed by John Baskerville, for R. and J. Dodsley, 1761.
17.5 cm. [2], iii, lxxviii, 204, [28] p.
Gaskell 14.
Gift of Miss Julia P. Wightman.

An Aesop written by the bookseller-publisher-writer Robert Dodsley (1703–1764), friend and publisher to Dr. Johnson and his circle. Dodsley, who earlier had written a celebrated book for children (*The Preceptor*), addressed his fable collection to children as well as their elders. It won considerable popularity with both, and was widely read until at least the end of the century. Dodsley had the first edition of *Select Fables* printed by John Baskerville, one of the greatest of English printers. Baskerville's pages were extraordinarily attractive and readable, and the book was adorned with plates engraved by Grignon after designs by the artist Samuel Wale. The Morgan Library copy, a first edition, has laid into it some of Wale's original pen-and-ink-and-watercolor drawings for the engravings, as well as early states of the plates.

13 [Aesop]

YOUNG AESOPS FABLES, WITH INSTRUCTIVE MORALS.

London: H. Turpin, [about 1775].
8.5 cm. [25] f. Dutch flowered boards.
Elisabeth Ball Collection.

Twenty-four fables are presented in this anonymous eighteenth-century collection, which is apparently for rather young children. Each leaf, printed on one side only, contains a complete verse fable and its moral, a rhymed couplet. The entire book, text as well as pictures, is made up of copperplate engravings and—what is more unusual—is printed in red.

14 [Aesop]

SELECT FABLES, IN THREE PARTS.

Newcastle: T. Saint, 1784.
17 cm. xii, 308, ii p.
Roscoe, Bewick, *p. 149.*
Gift of Mrs. Samuel C. Chew.

This version of Aesop's fables draws upon earlier collections, notably those of Robert Dodsley and Samuel Croxall. The real importance of this 1784 edition, published by Thomas Saint of Newcastle, lies in the fact that it is illustrated by Thomas and John Bewick. For the Bewick brothers, whose new "white line" technique of wood-engraving virtually revolutionized the art, the illustrations in this book did much toward establishing a reputation. In brief, instead of employing the traditional woodcut method of cutting with a knife into the side grain of a relatively soft wooden plank, Thomas Bewick worked on the polished end-grain (which meant no grain at all) surface of very hard wood. Instead of the knife that woodcutters had used since the Middle Ages, he used the graver, or burin, of the copperplate-engravers. What he (and subsequently his younger brother John) produced from the responsive wood was a sensitive engraving, detailed yet fluid, that often took the form of a principally white drawing against a dark ground. The Morgan Library copy of *Select Fables* is the rare first edition.

15 [Aesop]

ENTERTAINING FABLES FOR THE INSTRUCTION OF CHILDREN.

Worcester, Massachusetts: Isaiah Thomas, 1794.
9.5 cm. [6], 9–27, [4] p. Green printed wrappers.
Welch 336.2. Rosenbach 173.
Elisabeth Ball Collection.

This collection of seventeen verse fables was brought out in Worcester, Massachusetts, by the printer and antiquarian Isaiah Thomas, one of America's very earliest publishers of books for children. Like a great many of Thomas' children's books, it is a close imitation of a work first published in England. Only a few copies of this book are recorded.

16 [Richard Scrafton Sharpe]

OLD FRIENDS IN A NEW DRESS; OR, FAMILIAR FABLES IN VERSE.

London: Harvey and Darton, and William Darton, 1820.
13.5 cm. [3], 6–46 p. Buff printed wrappers (bound in).
Osborne, p. 7.
Elisabeth Ball Collection.

"This present little publication," declares its author in his preface, "is humbly offered to parents, and other superintendents of the education of youth." He goes on to explain that he has written these Aesopian fables "in a simple and unadorned style" so that they may easily be memorized by children, who will thus profit from the moral he has woven into each fable. The author, though he is not named on the title page, was Richard Scrafton Sharpe, to whom has been attributed *Anecdotes and Adventures of Fifteen Gentlemen* (a far less earnest work). Some, if not all, of the engravings in this Aesop may be by one of its publishers, William Darton (1755–1819).

17 Charles H. Bennett

THE FABLES OF AESOP AND OTHERS, TRANSLATED INTO HUMAN NATURE.

London: W. Kent & Co., [1857].
25 cm. [3], 21 f. + frontispiece + 21 plates.
Loaned by Gordon N. Ray.

The first edition of an unusual, rather biting adaptation of Aesop's fables. It has a sophistication that makes it perhaps best suited to older children (and adults). The engravings are by Joseph Swain, after designs drawn on the wood by Charles Bennett, who also wrote the text. Bennett was a mid-nineteenth-century illustrator whose highly original work has not received the attention it deserves.

18 [Aesop]

AESOP'S FABLES. A NEW TRANSLATION BY V. S. VERNON JONES WITH AN INTRODUCTION BY G. K. CHESTERTON AND ILLUSTRATIONS BY ARTHUR RACKHAM.

London: William Heinemann, 1912.
29 cm. [4], v–xxix, [1], 1–223, [1] p. + frontispiece + 12 plates. Buff boards gilt.
Hudson, p. 94, 169.
Loaned by Miss Julia P. Wightman.

The first edition of a version of Aesop illustrated by the marvelously imaginative artist Arthur Rackham. This Aesop, which contains sixty-five illustrations in color and in black-and-white, proved to be an extremely popular one and had a large sale. The copy illustrated here is from a limited issue of the first edition; it is signed by Rackham.

1

45
melos. augurium coruo. leua cornix homi
na. omnesque propriis sunt contentę uoci
bus noli adfectare. quod tibi non ē datum
delusa ne spes ad querelam recidat.
AESOPUS. R̄P. GARRULO
Aesopus domino solus cum esset familia pa
rare cenā iussus ē maturius. ignem ergo
querens aliquot lustrauit domus tandem
que inuenit ubi lucernā accenderet. tum
circū eunti fuerat quod iter longius effecit
breuius. namq. recta p forū coepit redire.
& quidam e turba garrulus: eso pe medio
sole quid tu cum lumine. hominem inquit quę
ro. & abit festinans domū. hoc si molestus
ille ad animum rettulit. sensit profecto
se hominem non uisū seni. intempestiue
qui occupato adluserit. PHEDRI AUG
LIBERTI. LIBER. III. EXPL. INCIPIT
LIBER. IIII. ASINUS. ET GALLINA.

2

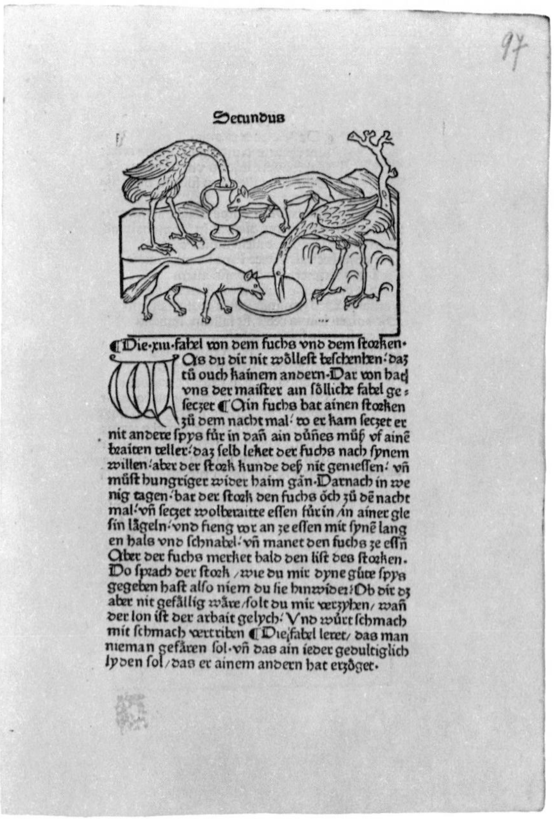

97

Secundus

¶ Die·xiii·fabel von dem fuchs vnd dem storken·
Was du dir nit wöllest beschehen· daz
tů ouch kainem andern· Dar von hat
vns der maister ain sölliche fabel ge=
seczet ¶ Ain fuchs bat ainen storken
zů dem nachtmal· wo er kam seczet er
nit andere spys für in dañ ain dünes můß vf ainē
braiten teller· daz selb leket der fuchs nach synem
willen· aber der stork kunde deß nit geniessen· vñ
můst hungriger wider haim gān· Darnach in we
nig tagen· bat der stork den fuchs öch zů dē nacht
mal· vñ seczet wolberaitte essen für in / in ainer gle
sin lägeln· vnd fieng vor an ze essen mit synē lang
en hals vnd schnabel· vñ manet den fuchs ze essñ
Aber der fuchs merket bald den list des storken·
Do sprach der stork / wie du mir dyne gůte spys
gegeben hast also niem du sie hinwider· Ob dir dz
aber nit gefällig wäre / solt du mir verzyhen / wañ
der lon ist der arbait gelych· Vnd würt schmach
mit schmach vertriben ¶ Die fabel leret / das man
nieman gefären sol· vñ das ain ieder gedultiglich
lyden sol / das er ainem andern hat erzöget·

4

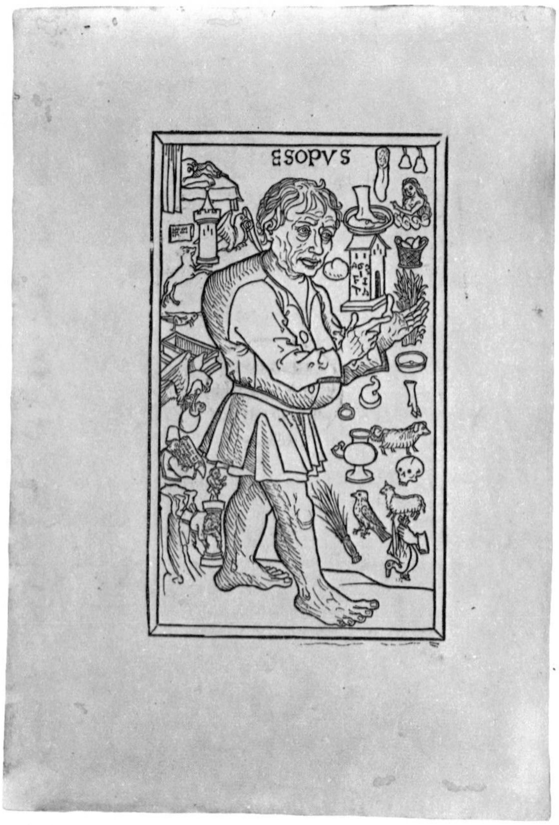

4

SONETO MORALE.

5

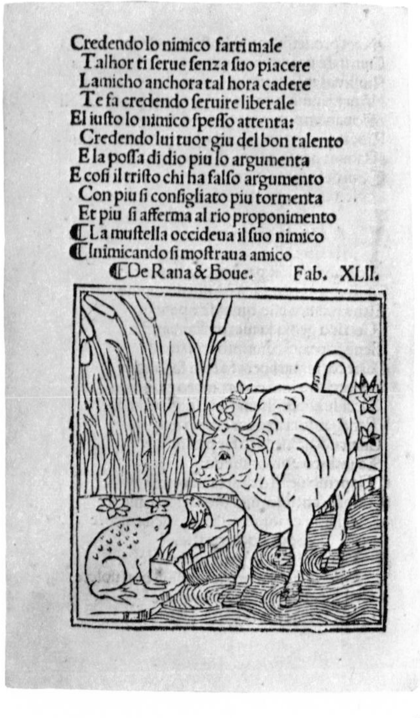

Credendo lo nimico farti male
Talhor ti serue senza suo piacere
Lamicho anchora tal hora cadere
Te fa credendo seruire liberale
El iusto lo nimico spesso attenta:
Credendo lui tuor giu del bon talento
E la possa di dio piu lo argumenta
E cosi il tristo chi ha falso argumento
Con piu si consigliato piu tormenta
Et piu si afferma al rio proponimento
¶ La mustella occideua il suo nimico
¶ Inimicando si mostraua amico
¶ De Rana & Boue. Fab. XLII.

6

3

18

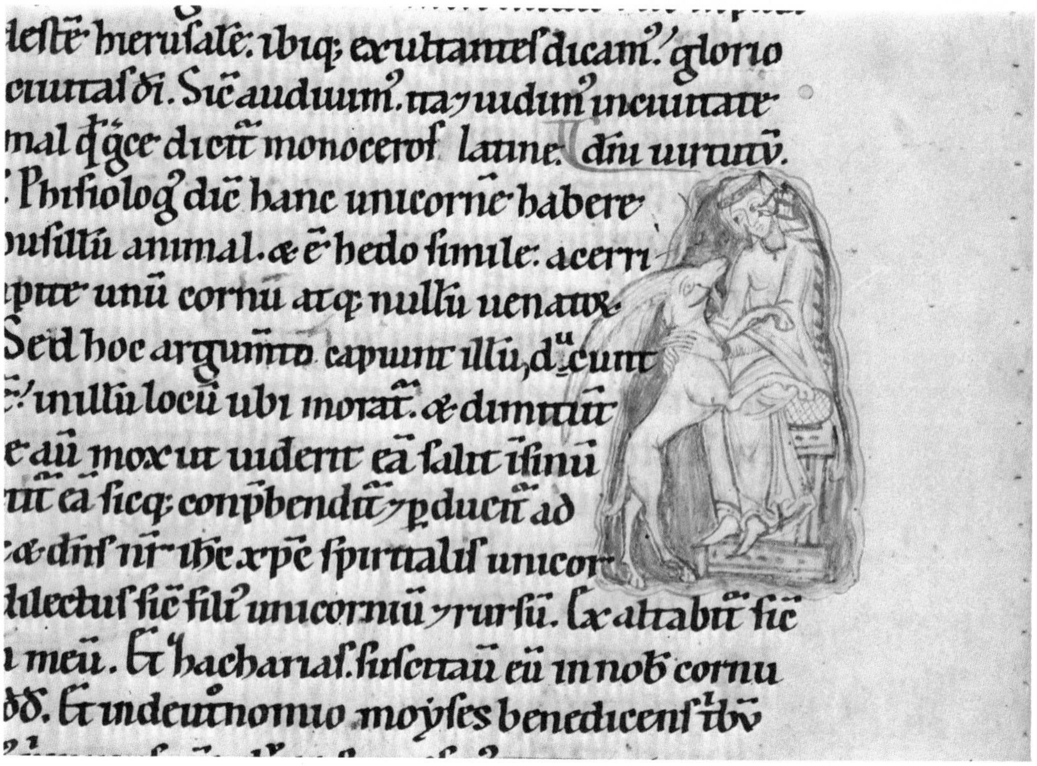

19

19

ce sen courut au boys tout ainsi na
ture quil estoit/et la se rendit en pl⁹
grāde humilite que iamaisnauoit
este. Par ceste fable chascun peult
veoir que moult reste de ce que fol
pense/car lon ne retourne pasquāt
on veult. Et ce demonstre que on
ne se doibt point vanter ne ingerer
de chose que on ne scet faire/ mais
chascun se doit gouuerner selon sa
faculte et selon son estat.

¶La.vi.fable est du
chien enuieulx.

Nul ne doit a-
uoir enuye du
biendaultruy ne du
prouffit/ lequel ne
luy peult proffiter
Ainsi que dit ceste
fable/ Dung chien
enuieulx qui estoit
en vne estable de
beufz q estoit plai-
ne de foig/& le chiē
gardoit les beufz
dentrer en leur esta
ble/pource quilz ne
mengeassent de ce
foing.Les beufz lui
dirent. Tu es bien mauluais da-
uoir enuye du bien/ lequel nous est
necessaire et tu nen as que faire/
car ta nature nest pas de menger
du foing. Ainsi faisoit il dūg gros
os que il tenoit en sa gueulle& ne le
vouloit laisser a vng aultre. Et
pourtant garde toy de la compai-
gnie des enuieulx/car auoir affaire a eulx est chose moult perilleuse
comme il appert de lucifer.

¶La.vii.fable est du
chien affame.

Tel cuyde aulcunefoys gai-
gner qui pert bien souuent:cō
Esope.
me il apert par ceste fable/ car lon
dit cōmunement que plus despent
chiche que large Ainsi quil appert
par ceste fable, dung homme qui a
uoit vng grand parc de brebis/& a
uoit vng chien quil tenoit auec ses
brebis pour les deffēdre des loupz
Mais il ne dōnoit point a demy a
mēger au chien qui gardoit sesbre
bis:pour la grāt auarice qui estoit
enluy/& pource vng iour le loup sē
vint au chien & puis luy demanda
la cause pourquoy il estoit ainsi po
ure et maigre/ Je voy bien que tu
meurs de fain/ Car ton maistre ne
te donne point a menger/ Mais se

7

Le bien perdu faict à l'ingrat.

Il n'est rien plus mal employé
Que de faire à l'ingrat du bien,
Quiconques l'aura essayé
Vne aultresfoys s'en garde bien.

8

The Lyon and Mouse. 47

A Lion was Entangled in a Snare,
Nor could his teeth or paws ye ambush teare
Since his wilde Struglings more engag'd him in
The treacherous foldings of ye ruder Gin.

When a kinde Mouse by gnawing did vntwine
The Snarled Cordage of the raveld line
So did the Lion Life and freedome gett,
Infranchis'd from ye Prison of his Nett.

Doe not ye humble tho neglect dispise.

A Mouse a Lion rescu'd from Surprize.

FAB. XXIII. *De Leone & Mure.*

LEO æstu, cursuq; defessus in umbra quiescebat, Murium autem grege tergum ejus percurrente expergefactus unum è multis comprehendit, Supplicat misellus, clamitans Indignum se esse cui irascatur; Leo reputans nihil laudis esse in Nece tantillæ bestiolæ captivum dimittit; Non multo post, Leo dum per segetes currit incidit in plagas, rugire licet, exire non licet, Rugientem Leonem Mus audit, vocem agnoscit, repit in cuniculos, & quæsitos laqueorum nodos invenit, corroditque, quo facto Leo è plagis evadit.

MORALE.

INterdum & ipsi potentes egent ope servorum humilimorum, Vir prudens igitur etiamsi potest, timebit tamen, vel vilissimo homuncioni nocere; Nibil est quod magis commendat Reges quam clementia, & annexa potestati Moderatio.

R 2 FAB.

9

10

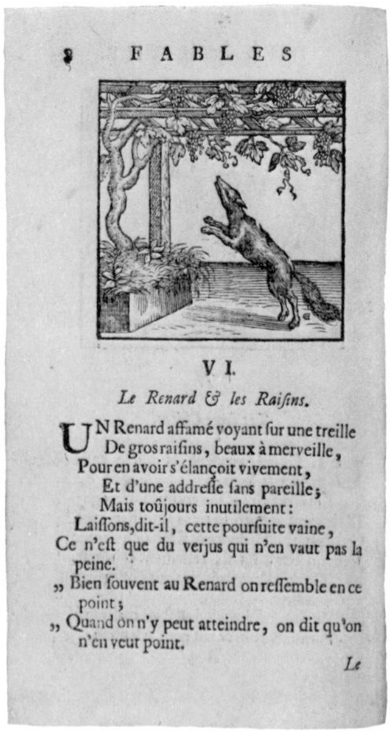
8 FABLES

V I.

Le Renard & les Raisins.

UN Renard affamé voyant sur une treille
De gros raisins, beaux à merveille,
Pour en avoir s'élançoit vivement,
Et d'une addresse sans pareille;
Mais toûjours inutilement:
Laissons, dit-il, cette poursuite vaine,
Ce n'est que du verjus qui n'en vaut pas la peine.
„ Bien souvent au Renard on ressemble en ce point;
„ Quand on n'y peut atteindre, on dit qu'on n'en veut point.

Le

11

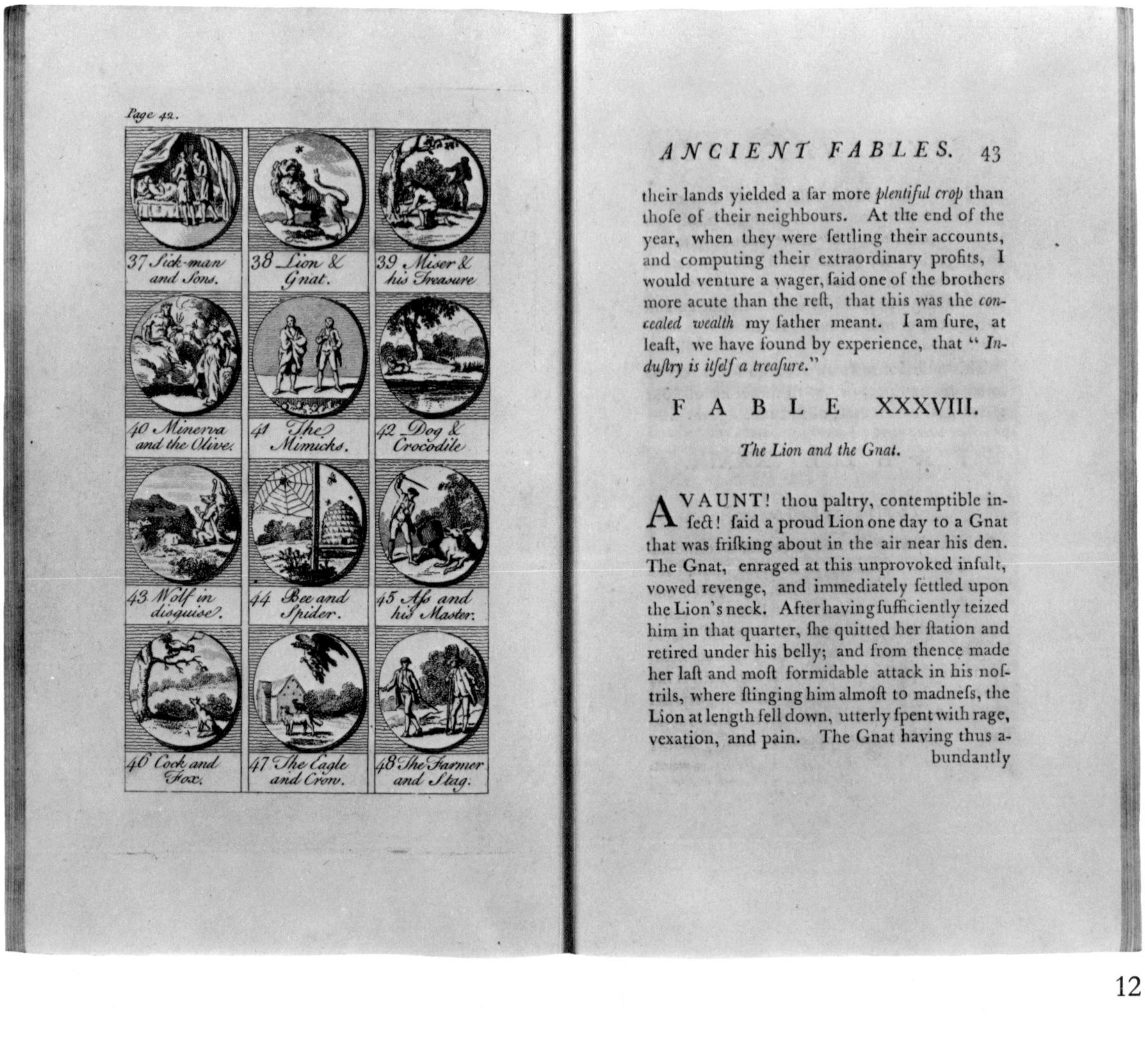

ANCIENT FABLES. 43

their lands yielded a far more *plentiful crop* than those of their neighbours. At the end of the year, when they were settling their accounts, and computing their extraordinary profits, I would venture a wager, said one of the brothers more acute than the rest, that this was the *concealed wealth* my father meant. I am sure, at least, we have found by experience, that "*Industry is itself a treasure.*"

FABLE XXXVIII.

The Lion and the Gnat.

AVAUNT! thou paltry, contemptible insect! said a proud Lion one day to a Gnat that was frisking about in the air near his den. The Gnat, enraged at this unprovoked insult, vowed revenge, and immediately settled upon the Lion's neck. After having sufficiently teized him in that quarter, she quitted her station and retired under his belly; and from thence made her last and most formidable attack in his nostrils, where stinging him almost to madness, the Lion at length fell down, utterly spent with rage, vexation, and pain. The Gnat having thus abundantly

12

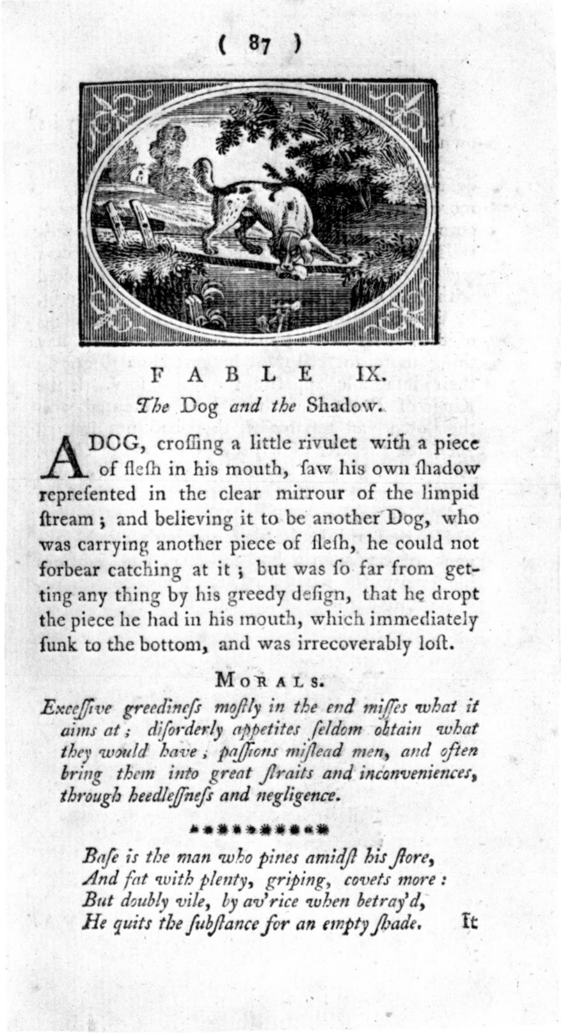

(87)

FABLE IX.

The Dog *and the* Shadow.

A DOG, croſſing a little rivulet with a piece of fleſh in his mouth, ſaw his own ſhadow repreſented in the clear mirrour of the limpid ſtream; and believing it to be another Dog, who was carrying another piece of fleſh, he could not forbear catching at it; but was ſo far from getting any thing by his greedy deſign, that he dropt the piece he had in his mouth, which immediately ſunk to the bottom, and was irrecoverably loſt.

MORALS.

Exceſſive greedineſs moſtly in the end miſſes what it aims at; diſorderly appetites ſeldom obtain what they would have; paſſions miſlead men, and often bring them into great ſtraits and inconveniences, through heedleſſneſs and negligence.

****

Baſe is the man who pines amidſt his ſtore,
And fat with plenty, griping, covets more:
But doubly vile, by av'rice when betray'd,
He quits the ſubſtance for an empty ſhade.

It

14

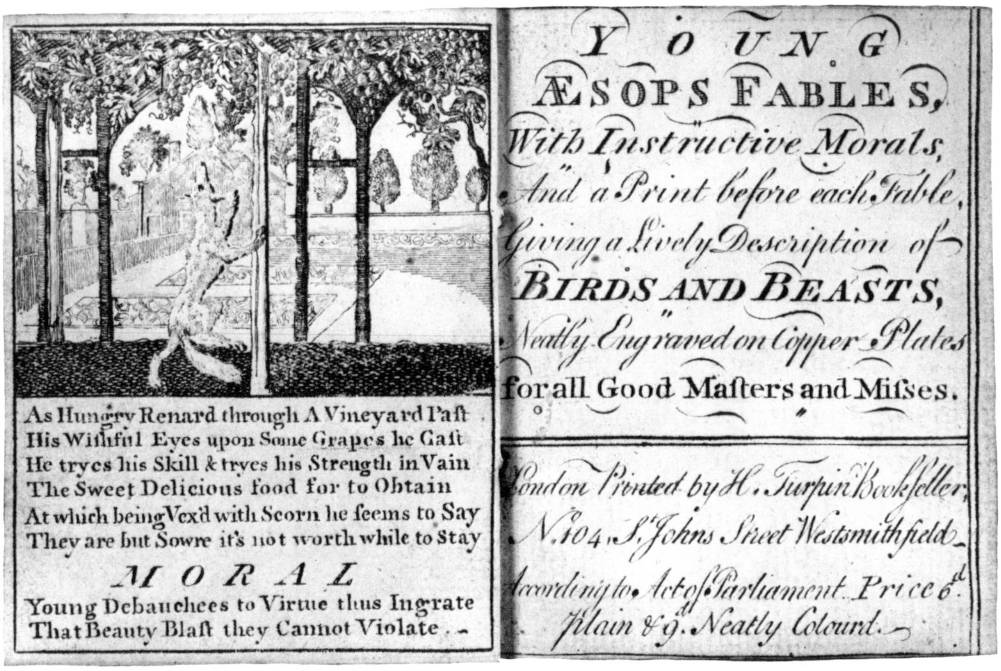

As Hungry Renard through A Vineyard Paſt
His Wiſhful Eyes upon Some Grapes he Caſt
He tryes his Skill & tryes his Strength in Vain
The Sweet Delicious food for to Obtain
At which being Vex'd with Scorn he ſeems to Say
They are but Sowre it's not worth while to Stay

MORAL

Young Debauchees to Virtue thus Ingrate
That Beauty Blaſt they Cannot Violate.

YOUNG
ÆSOPS FABLES,
With Instructive Morals,
And a Print before each Fable,
Giving a Lively Description of
BIRDS AND BEASTS,
Neatly Engraved on Copper Plates
for all Good Maſters and Miſses.

London Printed by H. Turpin Bookſeller,
No. 104 St. Johns Street Westsmithfield
According to Act of Parliament Price 6d.
Plain & 9d. Neatly Colourd.

13

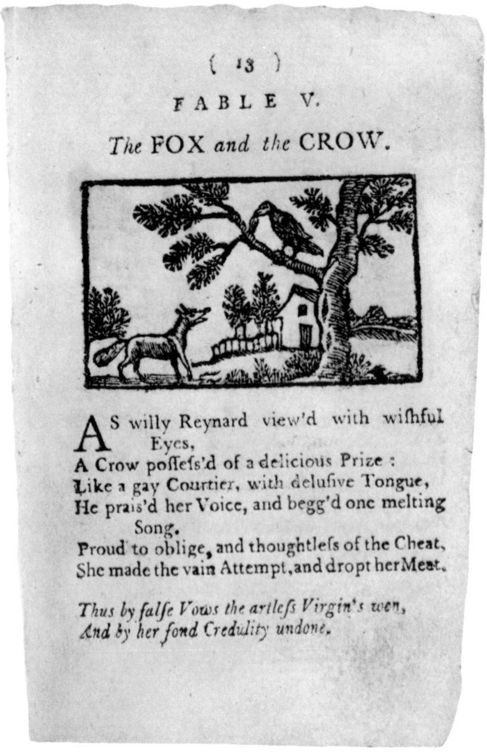
(13)

FABLE V.

The FOX *and the* CROW.

AS willy Reynard view'd with wiſhful Eyes,
A Crow poſſeſs'd of a delicious Prize:
Like a gay Courtier, with deluſive Tongue,
He prais'd her Voice, and begg'd one melting Song.
Proud to oblige, and thoughtleſs of the Cheat,
She made the vain Attempt, and dropt her Meat.

Thus by falſe Vows the artleſs Virgin's won,
And by her fond Credulity undone.

15

The Farmers Boy
See Page 34
and the Goose with Golden Eggs.
The Shepherds Boy & the Wolf.

OLD FRIENDS

IN A NEW DRESS;

OR,

FAMILIAR FABLES

IN VERSE.

See page 15

LONDON:

HARVEY AND DARTON, 55, GRACECHURCH STREET,

AND WILLIAM DARTON, 58, HOLBORN HILL.

16

THE DOG IN THE MANGER.

Bestiaries and Natural History

The mediaeval manuscripts known to us as bestiaries—descriptions of animals, usually with pictures—had as their principal source an anonymous Greek work called the *Physiologus*, or the *Naturalist*. This work, which itself drew upon a number of earlier works, was probably written in Egypt, perhaps in the fourth century A.D. It was divided into more than forty chapters, each describing a fabulous (or almost always fabulous) animal whose life, habits, or characteristics offered some moral or religious lesson. (The Morgan Library possesses what is probably the earliest known Greek manuscript of the *Physiologus*, written down in the late tenth century A.D.) The *Physiologus* became enormously popular and was translated into many languages, among them Latin. During the twelfth century the Latin *Physiologus* was modified and enlarged and took the form that we know as the bestiary.

Bestiaries were originally made for use in monasteries, but for the children who were fortunate enough to see them these books must have been quite irresistible, filled as they were with marvelous legend and lore and pictures of animals—often strange, phantasmagorical animals.

19 DE NATURIS BESTIARUM.

[Austria: First half of the twelfth century.]
M.832.
28.5 cm. 10 f.
Harrsen 13. McCulloch.
Purchased with the assistance of the Fellows.

The earliest of the three mediaeval bestiaries illustrated here, Morgan manuscript M.832, was written and illuminated in the first half of the twelfth century at the Benedictine monastery of Göttweig in Austria. On one of its vellum leaves (fol. 3r) the illuminator has drawn a unicorn resting its head in a virgin's lap, a depiction of the legend that a unicorn will come and do so if a virgin enters the forest where it lives. On another leaf (fol. 4v) the artist has drawn three elephants at the gates of Paradise. Beneath the elephant at the right is a smaller elephant. This may be its newborn young, or it may be a depiction of the legend that when an elephant falls down it cannot rise again unassisted, for it has no joints in its legs. But a smaller elephant can burrow under it and lift, helping it to regain its feet.

20 ❧ THE WORKSOP BESTIARY.

[England: ? Lincoln, before 1187.]
M.81.
21.5 cm. 120 f.
De Ricci, Census, *II, p. 1381. Kauffmann 106.*

Long celebrated for its striking illustrations, this Latin manuscript was written and illuminated in England, probably at Lincoln, some time before 1187, when it was presented by Philip, Canon of Lincoln, to the Augustinian Priory of Radford (now Worksop). The upper picture on the left-hand leaf (fol. 36v) shows the fabulous beast known as a griffin, which has the torso of a lion and the head and upper body of an eagle. The griffin is immensely strong; here it is carrying off a boar in its talons. Below are two more representations of boars, both fairly realistic. On the facing leaf (fol. 37r) is the fabulous bonacon, a lion-like beast with a mane, cloven hooves, and curling horns; it has fallen prey to a group of hunters.

21 THE FOUNTAINS ABBEY BESTIARY.

[England: Second quarter of the fourteenth century.]
M.890.
23 cm. 18 f.
James, Roxburghe, *34. McCulloch.*
Gift of Alastair Bradley Martin.

This manuscript was written and illuminated in England before the middle of the fourteenth century, perhaps by a Cistercian monk at the monastery of Fountains Abbey. An interesting feature of this book is that its illustrator, instead of always following stylized models for his pictures of animals, occasionally relies on personal observation. For example, the picture of canis, the dog (fol. 7r), shows it with bells on its collar—no doubt a detail observed on one of the monastery's sheep-dogs.

22 LES DICTZ DES OISEUAX [*sic*] ET DES BESTES.

Châlons-sur-Marne: Étienne Bally, [? about 1493].
19.5 cm. [8] f.
Goff D-271. Brunet, II, 764.
Purchased as the gift of the Fellows.

During the late fifteenth century there appeared on the continent of Europe various small and rather crudely printed versions of bestiaries. These little pamphlets were of course only the palest shadows of the great mediaeval bestiaries, but they came into the hands of a far larger number of folk—and their children—than the sumptuous handwritten bestiaries of the Middle Ages ever had. The texts that were used for these printed books included a *Dits des Oiseaux* (*Sayings of the Birds*) and a *Dits des Bêtes* (*Sayings of the Beasts*), in which the various animals gave little moralized descriptions of themselves. The leaves shown here are from an incomplete copy of a pamphlet printed by Étienne Bally at Châlons-sur-Marne in France. It is almost certainly the first book to be printed in that city, and it is the only book known to have come from Bally's press. This book, which combines a bird-text with a beast-text, is the earliest known version of the *Dits* to contain illustrations. The eight leaves of the Morgan Library copy, which is the only copy known, were discovered (together with four duplicate leaves now at the Bibliothèque Nationale) in the nineteenth century. They had been used as binder's waste in the construction of the leather binding of a Book of Hours in the library of the Duc d'Arenberg. The two birds depicted here are the *épervier*, or sparrow hawk, and the pelican. Neither is a fabulous creature, but the pelican is shown illustrating the belief that the adult birds pluck feathers from their own breasts to cause blood to flow and thus nourish their young.

23 Edward Topsell

THE HISTORY OF FOUR-FOOTED BEASTS AND SERPENTS.

London: G. Sawbridge, 1658.
35 cm. [22], 586, [4], 591–1130, [10] p.
DNB, "Topsell, Edward."

Edward Topsell, an English clergyman, published his first work about the animal world, fabulous and real, in 1607. Entitled *The Historie of Foure-footed Beastes*, it was drawn largely from the *Historia Animalium* of the early-sixteenth-century Swiss encyclopedist and bibliographer Konrad Gesner, and it displayed the sixteenth century's awe, curiosity, and credibility about the world of nature. Topsell published a second volume in 1608;

and in 1658 the two books were brought together, edited by a physician named John Rowland, and published in the form shown here. The remarkable illustrations, firm and apparently precise in their depiction of beasts only some of which ever existed, were pored over by many a seventeenth-century child both before and after learning to read the moralizing text. The animals illustrated here are, left, the fabulous hydra and, right, the familiar lizard.

24 JACKEY DANDY'S DELIGHT; OR, THE HISTORY OF BIRDS AND BEASTS: IN VERSE AND PROSE.

London: John Marshall and Co., [about 1783].
10 cm. [3], 5–31 p. Dutch flowered wrappers.
Elisabeth Ball Collection.

A distant but clearly recognizable descendant of the mediaeval bestiary, this rare eighteenth-century children's chapbook offers crude, reasonably accurate woodcut illustrations of animals. Each is accompanied by a bit of moralizing, in both prose and verse. The copy shown here is the earliest known of this anonymous work. It is from the Aldermary Churchyard establishment of John Marshall, one of the most important publishers for children in the latter part of the eighteenth century.

25 [Thomas Bewick] A GENERAL HISTORY OF QUADRUPEDS.

Newcastle upon Tyne: S. Hodgson, R. Beilby, & T. Bewick, 1790.
24cm. [4], v–viii, [1], 2–452, [1], 454–456 p.
Roscoe, Bewick, *1a (Variant A).*

The English wood-engraver Thomas Bewick, whose work gave a new direction and vitality to the art of wood-engraving in the eighteenth century, was a zealot in the cause of accurate natural history for children. "My principal object," he wrote, "was directed to the mental pleasure and improvement of youth . . . to lead them on till they become enamoured of this innocent and delightful pursuit." In bringing out his *General History of Quadrupeds* and the later *History of British Birds* (1797–1804) he was motivated by his strong views about the proper education of children in natural history, and also by "the great pleasure I felt in imitating nature." Deploring the inadequate illustrations in the available books on natural history, he set himself to improving the situation, and he did so through the use of the "white line" wood-engraving technique he brought to such perfection. The copy shown is the first edition.

26 THE CHILDREN'S CABINET: OR, A KEY TO NATURAL HISTORY.

London: Laurie and Whittle, 1798.
11 × 14.5 cm. [*4*], *4–32 f.*, [*5*], *6–33*, [*4*], *38–47*, [*1*] *p. + plates.*
Pink printed wrappers.
Elisabeth Ball Collection.

The anonymous engravings in this English work published just before the close of the eighteenth century are accompanied by texts that bear no moral messages whatever. The whole book is a straightforward work of natural history, of a kind quite familiar to any twentieth-century child.

27 [Georges-Louis Leclerc de Buffon]
LE PETIT BUFFON DES ENFANS.

Paris: Pigoreau, 1806.
16 cm. [*6*], *103 p.*
Gumuchian 952.
Elisabeth Ball Collection.

In the forty-four volumes of his *Histoire naturelle, générale, et particulière*, the great French naturalist Georges-Louis Leclerc de Buffon (1707–1788) attempted to organize all the current knowledge about natural history. The results of his monumental efforts have frequently found their way into children's books, in one form or another. The little volume shown here was intended to serve as a guide for children visiting the natural history museum in the Jardin des Plantes in Paris.

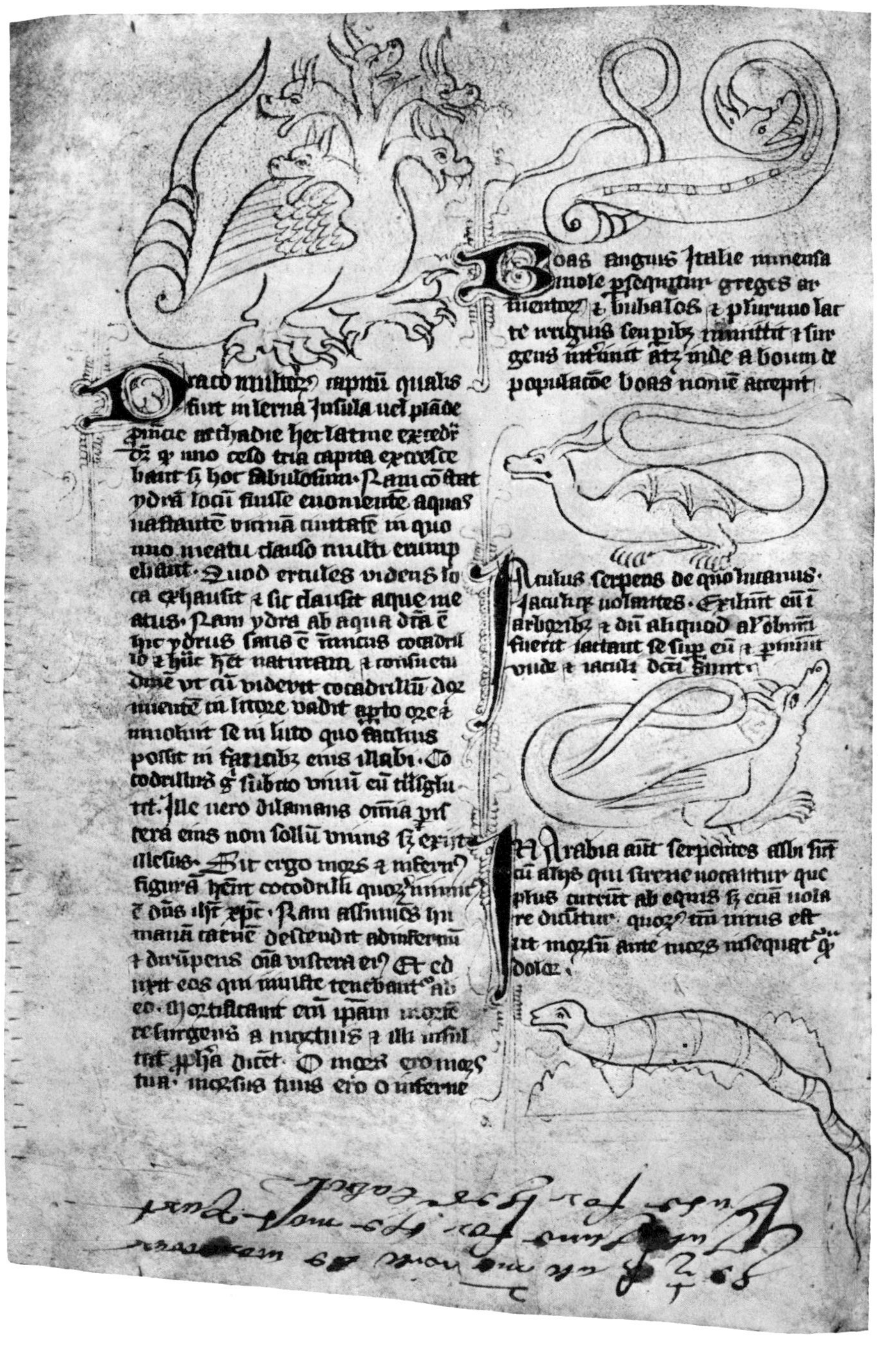

Draco multorum capitum qualis fuit in lerna insula vel palude provincie archadie hec latine excedra dicitur quod uno ceso tria capita excresce bant sed hoc fabulosum. Nam constat ydram locum fuisse evomientem aquas vastantem vicinam civitatem in quo uno meatu clauso multi erump ebant. Quod ercules videns loca exhausit et sic clausit aque meatus. Nam ydra ab aqua dicta est. Hic ydrus satis est inimicus cocodrillo et hunc habet naturam et consuetu dinem ut cum viderit cocodrillum dormientem in litore vadit et primo ore et inmoluit se in luto quo facilius possit in faucibus eius illabi. Cocodrillus igitur subito vivum eum transglutit. Ille vero dilanians omnia viscera eius non solum vivus sed et exit illesus. Sic ergo mors et infernus figuram habent cocodrilli quorum inimicus est dominus ihesus christus. Nam assumens humanam carnem descendit ad infernum et dirumpens omnia viscera eius et eduxit eos qui iniuste tenebantur ab eo. Mortificavit enim ipsam mortem resurgens a mortuis et illi insultat propheta dicens. O mors ero mors tua. morsus tuus ero o inferne

Boas anguis italie inmensa mole persequitur greges armentorum et bubalos et plurimo lacte irriguis se uberibus inmittit et sugens interimit atque inde a boum depopulatione boas nomen accepit.

Iaculus serpens de quo lucanus iaculique volantes. Exiliunt enim in arboribus et dum aliquid obvium fuerit iactant se super eum et perimunt unde et iaculi dicti sunt.

In arabia autem serpentes albi sunt cum alis qui sirene vocantur que plus currunt ab equis sed etiam volare dicuntur. quorum tantum virus est ut morsum ante mors insequatur quam dolor.

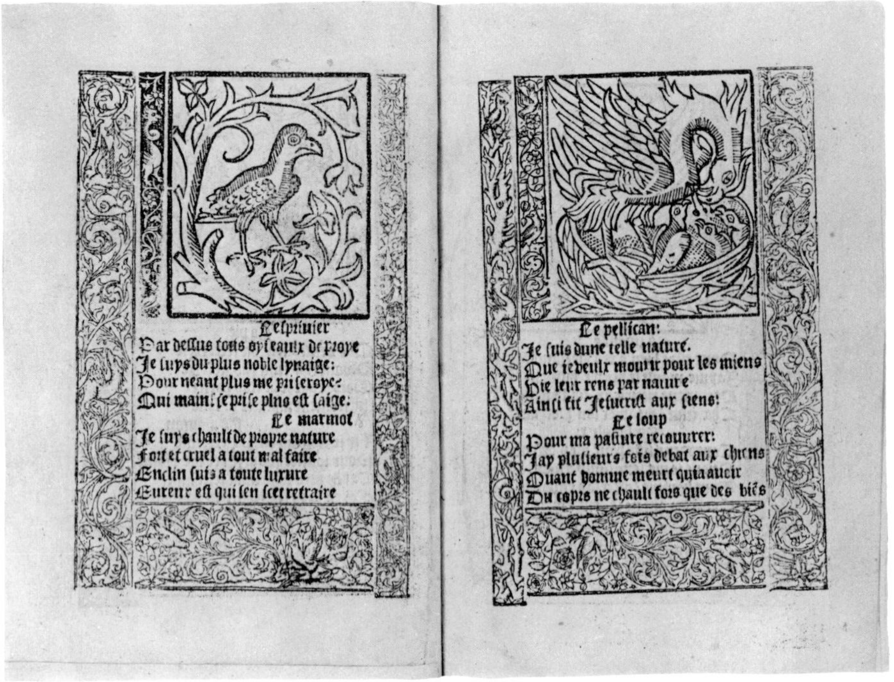
Lespriuier
Par dessus tous oyseaulx de proye
Je suys du plus noble lynaige:
Pour neant plus me priseroye:
Qui main: se prise plus est saige:
Le marmot
Je suys chault de propre nature
Fort et cruel a tout mal faire
Enclin suis a toute luxure
Eureux est qui sen scet retraire
Le pellican:
Je suis dune telle nature.
Que ie veulx mourir pour les miens
Vie leur rens par nature
Ainsi fit Jesucrist aux siens:
Le loup
Pour ma pasture recouurer:
Jay plusieurs fois debat aux chiens
Quant homme meurt quia aueir
Du corps ne chault fors que des biēs

22

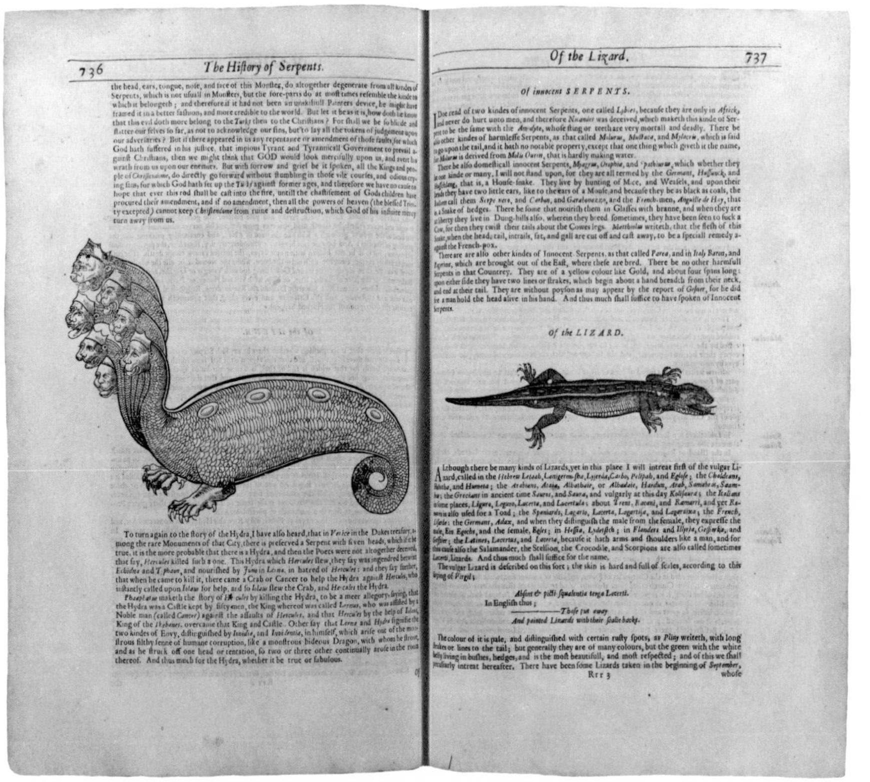
736
The History of Serpents.
Of the Lizard.
737
Of innocent SERPENTS.
Of the LIZARD.

23

31. Grifes uocatur quod sit animal pennatum et quadrupes. hoc genus ferarum in hyperboreis nascitur locis uel montibus. omni parte corporis simile leoni. alis et facie aquilis simile. equis uehementer infestum. nam et homines uisos discerpit.

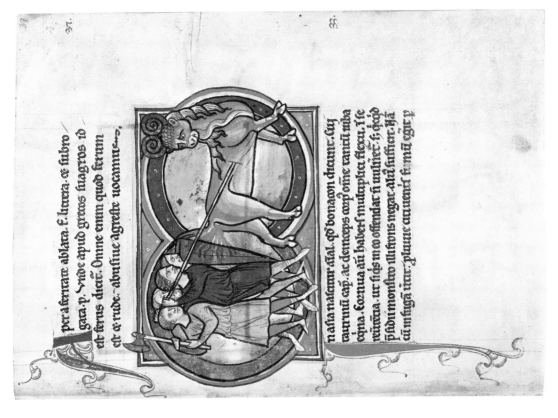

37. Aper a feritate ablata F. littera et subrogata p. Unde apud grecos suagros id est ferus dicitur. Omne enim quod ferum est et rude. abusiue agreste uocamus.

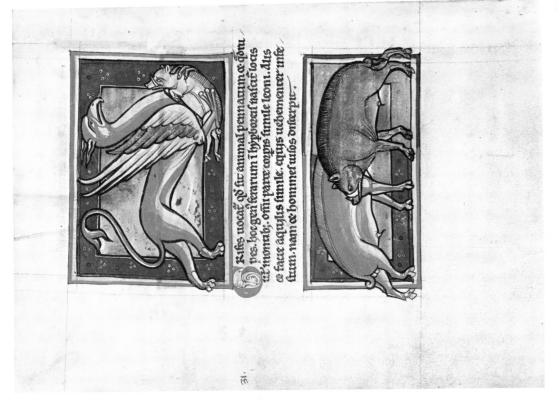

33. In asia nascitur animal. quod bonacon dicunt. Cui taurinum caput. ac deinceps corpus omne tantum iuba equina. Cornua autem habens multiplici flexu. in se recurrentia. ut si quis in eo offendat non uulneret. sed quod presidium monstro illi frons negat. aluus sufficit. Nam cum in fugam iteritur. pluuie citiuentis fimum egit p

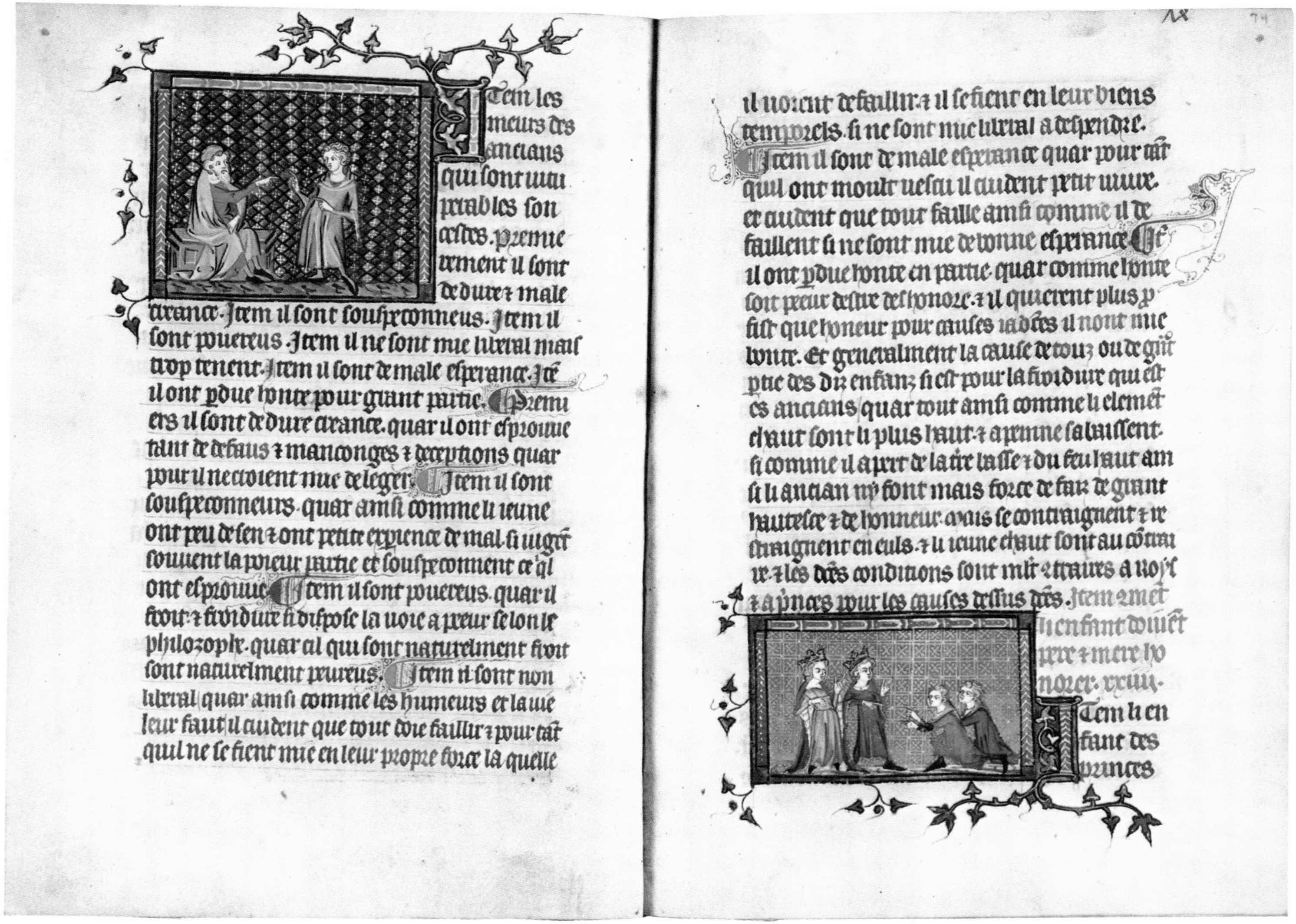

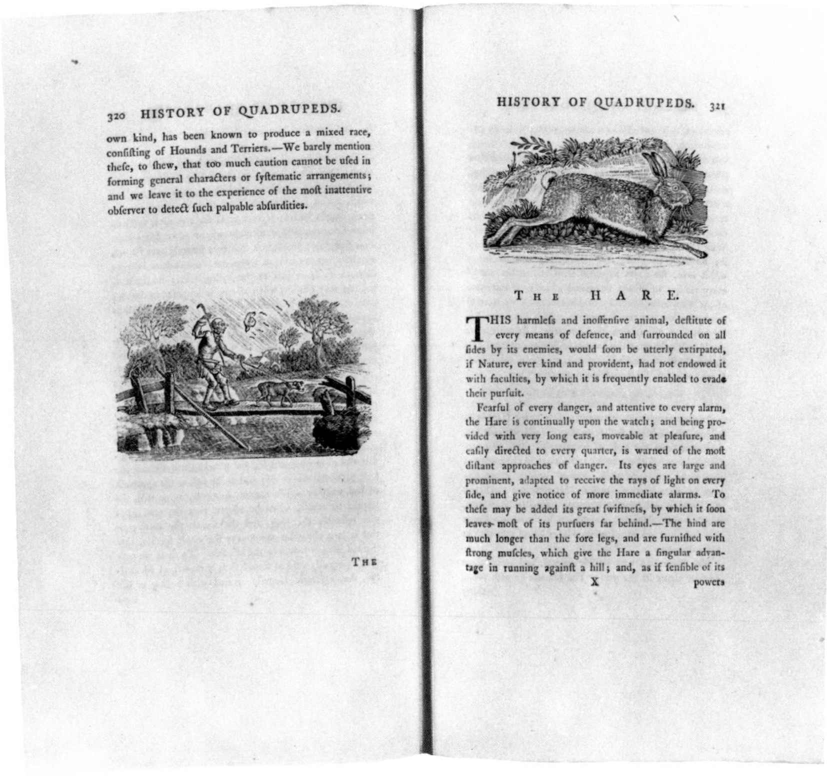
320 HISTORY OF QUADRUPEDS.

own kind, has been known to produce a mixed race, conſiſting of Hounds and Terriers.—We barely mention theſe, to ſhew, that too much caution cannot be uſed in forming general characters or ſyſtematic arrangements; and we leave it to the experience of the moſt inattentive obſerver to detect ſuch palpable abſurdities.

THE

HISTORY OF QUADRUPEDS. 321

THE HARE.

THIS harmleſs and inoffenſive animal, deſtitute of every means of defence, and ſurrounded on all ſides by its enemies, would ſoon be utterly extirpated, if Nature, ever kind and provident, had not endowed it with faculties, by which it is frequently enabled to evade their purſuit.

Fearful of every danger, and attentive to every alarm, the Hare is continually upon the watch; and being provided with very long ears, moveable at pleaſure, and eaſily directed to every quarter, is warned of the moſt diſtant approaches of danger. Its eyes are large and prominent, adapted to receive the rays of light on every ſide, and give notice of more immediate alarms. To theſe may be added its great ſwiftneſs, by which it ſoon leaves moſt of its purſuers far behind.—The hind are much longer than the fore legs, and are furniſhed with ſtrong muſcles, which give the Hare a ſingular advantage in running againſt a hill; and, as if ſenſible of its

X powers

25

JACKEY DANDY's

DELIGHT;

OR,

The HISTORY of

BIRDS and BEASTS:

IN

VERSE and PROSE.

Theſe are my theme, am I to blame
If men in morals are the ſame?
I no man call an Ape or Aſs,
'Tis his own conſcience holds the glaſs.

LONDON,

Printed and Sold by JOHN MARSHALL and Co. No. 4, *Aldermary Church-Yard*, Printers to the Society of LILLIPUTIANS, and Bookſellers in ordinary to the GOOD CHILDREN of *Great Britain* and *Ireland*.

[Price ONE PENNY, bound and gilt.]

24

26

L'AUTRUCHE.

Pag. 20.

27

L E

PETIT BUFFON DES ENFANS,

C O N T E N A N T

UNE Description des Animaux les plus intéressans à connaître, et que l'on voit au Jardin des plantes,

ORNÉ DE ONZE FIGURES.

A PARIS,

Chez PIGOREAU, Libraire, place Saint-Germain-l'Auxerrois.

ET A EVREUX,

Chez ANCELLE, Imprimeur-Libraire.

1806.

27

Courtesy Books

They began to appear on the Continent in the fourteenth century—solemn books written in the hope of teaching children the principles of proper behavior. The earliest of these books of polite and pious conduct, which we call courtesy books, were directed at the young sons of the nobility, and were in effect manuals of conduct for high-born children who were being sent off to be pages at court. The courtesy books were intended to inculcate breeding and courtly etiquette along with religious piety and moral excellence, if not perfection.

28 ❧ AVIS AUS ROYS.

France: [? Paris, about 1360].
M.456.
18 cm. 136 f.
De Ricci, Census, *II, p. 1452. Bell.*

The anonymous courtesy book known as the *Avis aus Roys* has a loftier purpose than most of its kind. It is a courtesy book for sovereigns, being addressed to princes who might one day rule in France. The *Avis aus Roys*, which embraces the romantic and chivalrous ideals of the fourteenth century in France, lists the qualities the ideal prince should possess (as well as the vices he must avoid). It treats of the prince's duties as a good son and his obligations and responsibilities, in peace and in wartime, as the sovereign. The text and miniature on the left-hand page shown (fol. 37v) deal with some traits of the elderly (such as timidity and pessimism) which the young should shun. In the facing miniature (fol. 74r), a king and queen stand while two of their children kneel before them; the text discusses the respect that children owe their parents. The Morgan Library *Avis aus Roys*, with its 136 vellum leaves containing 140 miniatures, is the most superbly illustrated example known of this text.

29 LES CONTENANCES DE LA TABLE.

[Lyon: Printer of the "Champion des Dames" (? Jean Du Pré), about 1487.]
18 cm. 6 f.
GW 7447.
Purchased for the Elisabeth Ball Collection.

Issued a few decades after the invention of printing, this French rhymed treatise on table manners is a courtesy book addressed to children of humble as well as noble rank. It has been argued that this is the first printed book (apart from elementary Latin grammars) intended to be read specifically by children. The unknown author of *Les Contenances* offers his advice in the form of quatrains, each beginning "*Enfant. . . .*" The name of the printer does not appear, but typographical evidence suggests that the book comes from the Lyon press of Jean Du Pré. It was evidently a popular book, for seven fifteenth-century editions survive (each in a single exemplar), and there may well have been others. The Morgan Library copy is thought to be the first edition, of which it is the only copy known.

30 Geoffroy de la Tour-Landry

DER RITTER VOM TURN. [*German.*] *Translated from the French by Marquart von Stein.*

Basel: Michael Furter for Johann Bergmann, 1493.
28 cm. 73 f.
Goff L-73. NGA, Dürer, *209. Panofsky 436c.*

This courtesy book is directed to girls of the upper classes. It was translated into German from a French original—*Livre pour l'enseignement de ses filles* (*Book for the Instruction of his Daughters*)—written about 1371 by Geoffroy de la Tour-Landry, a member of the provincial nobility of France. La Tour-Landry wrote the work as a guide to conduct for his young daughters, incorporating into it examples of proper behavior from ancient literature, the Scriptures, and his contemporary world. This is the first edition of Marquart von Stein's translation. It is illustrated with woodcuts by Albrecht Dürer. *Der Ritter vom Turn* has been called the greatest illustrated book of its day, and the finest produced up to that time. The Morgan Library copy is the only one in America.

31 Philip Dormer Stanhope, 4th Earl of Chesterfield

[AUTOGRAPH LETTER TO HIS SON, PHILIP STANHOPE. 5 November 1739.]

22×18.5 cm. 3 p.

In 1737 Philip Dormer Stanhope, 4th Earl of Chesterfield, embarked on a project to supplement the formal education of his illegitimate son, Philip Stanhope, by instructing him in the ways and graces of elegant society in the eighteenth-century world. Lord Chesterfield delivered his witty, cogent, coolly realistic lessons in the form of a series of personal letters, the fame of which outshines his considerable achievements as a statesman. Posterity's image of Chesterfield seems to be that of an amoral, calculating cynic. But the letter shown here, written 5 November 1739, when young Stanhope was seven, says in part: "One should do well, for the sake of doing well, and vertue is it's [*sic*] own reward. That is, the consciousness of having done right, makes one happy enough even without any other reward."

32 Philip Dormer Stanhope, 4th Earl of Chesterfield

LETTERS WRITTEN BY THE EARL OF CHESTERFIELD TO HIS SON, PHILIP STANHOPE, TOGETHER WITH SEVERAL OTHER PIECES ON VARIOUS SUBJECTS, PUBLISHED BY MRS EUGENIA STANHOPE.

London: J. Dodsley, 1774.
28.5 cm. 2 vols.: [5], ii, [1], iv–vii, [2], 2–568 + frontispiece; [5], 2–606, [2] p.
Rothschild 596.
Gift of Eugene R. Black.

Lord Chesterfield never intended that his letters should be viewed by anyone but the single youth to whom they were addressed, in affectionate confidence. But by 1774 both Chesterfield and his son were dead, and the carefully preserved letters were in the possession of the son's widow. That lady, Mrs. Eugenia Stanhope, turned them over to the publisher James Dodsley for the then very handsome sum of £1500. Dodsley's two-volume edition of the letters swiftly became a best-seller, being reprinted four times in its first year. Many an eighteenth- and nineteenth-century child was read to at length from these imposing quarto volumes, and some may even have been interested enough

—Chesterfield has an absorbing style—to take up the book themselves. The copy shown here, with its frontispiece portrait of Chesterfield by J. Vitalba, is the first edition.

33 Philip Dormer Stanhope, 4th Earl of Chesterfield

LORD CHESTERFIELD'S MAXIMS . . . BEING THE SUBSTANCE OF THE EARL OF CHESTERFIELD'S LETTERS.

London: F. Newbery, 1774.
13.5 cm. [4], iii–xii, 90, [6] p. Dutch flowered boards.
Roscoe J53(1).
Elisabeth Ball Collection.

In the same year that saw the first printing by Dodsley of Chesterfield's *Letters*, another publisher hastened to bring out a condensed version designed to be put into children's hands. This enterprising character was Francis Newbery, John Newbery's nephew and successor in his famous children's-book-publishing endeavors. As frontispiece the Newbery book bears a careful, child's-size imitation of the Vitalba portrait of Chesterfield which graced Dodsley's publication. This copy of the Newbery *Chesterfield* is one of perhaps three that are known to survive from the first edition.

34 "Solomon Winlove" [i.e., ?Oliver Goldsmith]

MORAL LECTURES.

London: F. Newbery, 1769.
11 cm. [2], iv, [2], 95, [5] p. Dutch flowered boards.
Gumuchian 2765. Roscoe J382(1).
Elisabeth Ball Collection.

This little book of sage advice to the young, arranged under twenty-eight headings, has been attributed to Oliver Goldsmith. It certainly has passages evocative of Goldsmith's humorous optimism; the chapter "Of Application," for example, begins with the rhyme

> Submit not to despair, tho' baffled once;
> Necessity gives Genius to a Dunce.

One of three recorded copies of the earliest known edition, probably the first.

35 THE COLUMBIAN READING BOOK, OR HISTORICAL PRECEPTOR.

Philadelphia: Mathew Carey, 30 November 1799.
17.5 cm. [5], 6–120 p.
Mrs. Sherman Post Haight Collection.

This rare American courtesy book was issued by the early Philadelphia printer and publisher Mathew Carey. Its subtitle reads: "A collection of authentic histories, anecdotes, characters, &c. &c. calculated to incite in young minds a love of virtue, from its intrinsic beauty, and a hatred of vice, from its disgusting deformity." The book's 164 inspirational pieces, illustrated with oval woodcut vignettes, offer moral and ethical lessons drawn from ancient history and from contemporary life in eighteenth-century England and America. This edition, which is in all likelihood the first, appears to be unrecorded.

36 [R. Ransome]

THE GOOD BOY'S SOLILOQUY; CONTAINING HIS PARENTS' INSTRUCTIONS RELATIVE TO HIS DISPOSITION AND MANNERS.

London: W. Darton, Junr., 1811.
12 cm. [3], 4–16 p. + [16] f.
NBL 254.
Elisabeth Ball Collection.

A book of manners aimed at children of comfortable station in Regency England. It carefully describes and illustrates many forms of misbehavior, in the expectation—touchingly naïve—that these acts will then be avoided by the young. No doubt it was a very useful manual of mischief for any child worth his salt. This is the first edition.

37 [Stacey Grimaldi]

A SUIT OF ARMOUR FOR YOUTH.

London: Published for the Proprietor [i.e., Stacey Grimaldi], 1824.
18 cm. [5], vi–vii, [7], 3–92 p. + 12 plates.
Gumuchian 1995. Heath 93.
Loaned by Miss Julia P. Wightman.

An ingenious guide, or moral preceptor, in the form of an allegorical description of knightly armor. Each piece of equipment, whether helmet, breastplate, or lance, is illustrated in a hand-colored engraving that may be folded up to uncover a depiction of the ideal character trait it symbolizes. "The Strongest Breast Plate" is thus seen to be "Virtue," and so on. Accompanying each pair of plates is a text that is inspirational but imparts much historical information as well. The author, Stacey Grimaldi, was an English antiquary and solicitor who was descended from the seventeenth-century doges of Genoa. This is believed to be the first edition, but there may have been a trial issue in 1823.

38 LA CIVILITÉ EN ESTAMPES.

Paris: P. Blanchard, [about 1825].
11 × 16.5 cm. [23] f.
Loaned by Miss Julia P. Wightman.

The hand-colored copperplate engravings of this early-nineteenth-century French courtesy book illustrate eleven little lessons in polite behavior. Children are warned never to yawn in public, never to spit, never to rest their elbows on the table when eating. They are exhorted to stand politely aside when others wish to pass, to show respect for the aged, and to be quick to offer a visitor a chair. To do otherwise, they are told solemnly by the anonymous author, will cause their parents to be deeply mortified, and the children themselves to die of shame.

39 Gelett Burgess

GOOPS AND HOW TO BE THEM. A MANUAL OF MANNERS FOR POLITE INFANTS INCULCATING MANY JUVENILE VIRTUES BOTH BY PRECEPT AND EXAMPLE.

London: Methuen & Co., 1900.
21 cm. [48] f.
Loaned by Gordon N. Ray.

The strange little goops, with their globular heads and antisocial manners, have struck a spark of gleeful rapport in children ever since their first appearance. (No one seems to know quite why, unless it is that they engender a feeling of superiority in children.) Interestingly, in his *Goops* the American author and artist Gelett Burgess is returning to the reverse approach that was used in an English courtesy book produced nearly a century earlier, *The Good Boy's Soliloquy* (see above). The copy of *Goops* illustrated here is the first English edition, published in the same year as the first American edition.

Es
contenances & la table.

29

Sensuyuent les contenãces & la
table

e   Nfant qui veult estre courtoys
Et a toutes gens agreable
Et principallement a table
Garde ces rigles en francoys

Enfant soit de coupper soigneux
Ses ongles et oster lordure
Car sil y est ort de nature
Quant il se grate il est roigneux

Enfant donneur laue tes mains
A ton leuer et au disner
Et puis a soupper sans finer
Ce sont troys foys a tout le moins

Enfant dy benedicite
Et fais le signe de la croix
Ains que prendre se tu me croix
Ce qui test de necessite

Enfant quãt tu seras aux places
Ou aucun prelat deglise est

a ii

29

verbergen/syns nechsten schand vnnd laster/mag alles gütt bekomen/ Wie dann das die ewangelia vnnd die bücher der wysen thünt jnn halten vnnd bewysen.

wie der Ritter vom Thurn sy-
nen döchtern dyß büch zü jren handen über antwurt.

Also vnnd hie mitt mynen lieben döchtern so ich dann dyß myn büchlin üch jn exempel vnnd vorbyld wyße mit anzeigungen der güten vnnd wolthünden frowen/ Deßglich der bößen vnnd belümdeten/regimentz vnnd thaten / Wie die güten zü eren / vnnd die bößen zü schanden vnnd laster komen syent/mit mancherley andern meynungen/ Wie jr üch dann halten vnnd wo vor jr üch hüten söllenn / Alles mitt kurtz vergriffnen vßlegungen zü samen gelesen/vnd setzen lassen hab/ So vil vnnd ich dero dyßer zyt nach kleyne myner verstentnyß hab zü wegenn bryngen vnnd wyssen mögen / Will ich abbrechen vnnd dyß büchlyn also

72

30

Dear Boy.   Bath Nov: ye 5th 1739

I am glad to hear that you went to see the Lord Mayor's show, for I suppose it amus'd you, and besides, I would have you see every thing. It is a good way of getting knowledge, especially if you enquire carefully (as I hope you always do) after the meaning, and the particulars of every thing you see. You know then, to be sure, that the Lord Mayor is the Head of the City of London, and that there is a new Lord Mayor chosen every year: That the city is govern'd by the Lord Mayor, the Court of Aldermen, and the common councill. There are six and twenty Aldermen, who are the most considerable tradesmen of the City; the Common councill is very Numerous, and consists likewise of Tradesmen. who all belong to the several companys, that you saw march in the procession, with their colours and Streamers. The Lord Mayor is chosen every year out of the Court of Aldermen. There are but two Lord Mayors in England; one for the city of London, and the other for the city of York. The Mayors of other Towns, are only call'd Mayors, not Lord Mayors. People who have seen little, are apt to stare sillily, and wonder at every new thing they see, but a Man, who [redacted] has been bred in the world, looks at every thing with coollness and sedateness, and makes proper observations, upon what he sees.

PHILIP DORMER STANHOPE
EARL OF CHESTERFIELD.
From a Painting by Mr. Hoare, in the Possession of Solomon Dayrolles Esq.

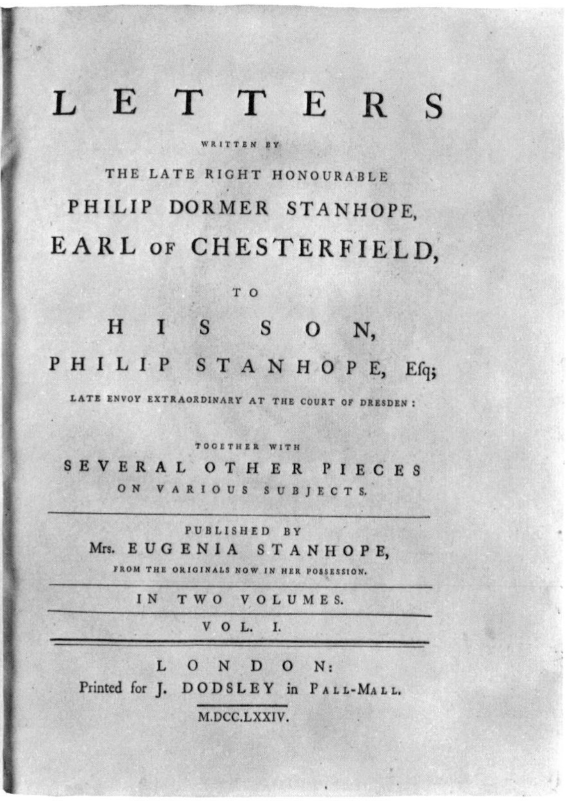

LETTERS
WRITTEN BY
THE LATE RIGHT HONOURABLE
PHILIP DORMER STANHOPE,
EARL OF CHESTERFIELD,
TO
HIS SON,
PHILIP STANHOPE, Esq;
LATE ENVOY EXTRAORDINARY AT THE COURT OF DRESDEN:
TOGETHER WITH
SEVERAL OTHER PIECES
ON VARIOUS SUBJECTS.
PUBLISHED BY
Mrs. EUGENIA STANHOPE,
FROM THE ORIGINALS NOW IN HER POSSESSION.
IN TWO VOLUMES.
VOL. I.
LONDON:
Printed for J. DODSLEY in PALL-MALL.
M.DCC.LXXIV.

32

PHILIP DORMER STANHOPE
EARL OF CHESTERFIELD.

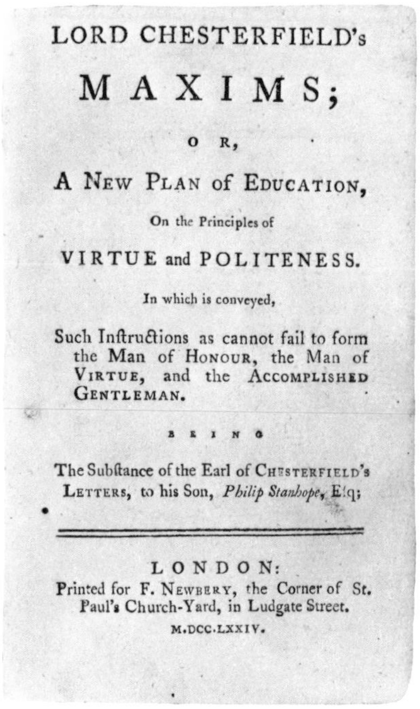

LORD CHESTERFIELD's
MAXIMS;
OR,
A NEW PLAN of EDUCATION,
On the Principles of
VIRTUE and POLITENESS.
In which is conveyed,
Such Instructions as cannot fail to form the Man of HONOUR, the Man of VIRTUE, and the ACCOMPLISHED GENTLEMAN.
BEING
The Substance of the Earl of CHESTERFIELD's LETTERS, to his Son, *Philip Stanhope*, Esq;
LONDON:
Printed for F. NEWBERY, the Corner of St. Paul's Church-Yard, in Ludgate Street.
M.DCC.LXXIV.

33 33

MORAL LECTURES,

ON THE

FOLLOWING SUBJECTS.

Pride,	Induſtry,
Envy,	Wiſdom,
Avarice,	Indolence,
Anger,	Application,
Hypocriſy,	Beauty,
Charity,	Advice,
Generoſity,	Company,
Compaſſion,	Splendor,
Ill-Humour,	Happineſs,
Good-Humour,	Friendſhip,
Affectation,	Mankind,
Truth,	Credulity,
Falſhood,	Contempt,
Education,	Modeſty.

By SOLOMON WINLOVE, Eſq;

Embelliſhed with twenty-eight curious CUTS.

LONDON:

Printed for F. NEWBERY, at the Corner of St Paul's Church Yard, 1769.

Price Six-pence.

34

(25)

CHAP. X.

Of GOOD-HUMOUR.

When the loud laugh prevails, at your expence,
All want of temper is but want of ſenſe;
Would you diſarm the ſnearer of his jeſt,
Frown not, but laugh in concert with the reſt.

GOOD HUMOUR is ſo eſſential a requiſite to all agreeable converſation, that it never fails to endear the poſſeſſors of it to their friends and acquaintance. Beſides which, it creates a perpetual tranquility in

D the

34

THE

Columbian Reading Book,

OR

HISTORICAL PRECEPTOR:

A COLLECTION OF AUTHENTIC

HISTORIES, ANECDOTES, CHARACTERS, &c. &c.

CALCULATED TO INCITE IN YOUNG MINDS

A LOVE OF VIRTUE,

FROM ITS INTRINSIC BEAUTY,

AND

A HATRED OF VICE,

FROM ITS DISGUSTING DEFORMITY.

PHILADELPHIA:

PRINTED FOR MATHEW CAREY.

November 30th, 1799.

[*Copy ſecured according to Law.*]

35

(110)

CXLI.

No Diſtinction in the Grave.

ALEXANDER the Great, ſeeing Diogenes looking attentively at a large collection of human bones, piled one upon another, aſked the philoſopher what he was looking for? "I am ſearching," ſays Diogenes, "for the bones of your father; but I cannot diſtinguiſh them from thoſe of his ſlaves."

CXLII.

Undaunted Spirit.

PETER, count of Savoy, a ſovereign prince, preſenting himſelf before Otho, emperor of Germany, to receive inveſtiture from him of his dominions, came dreſſed in a very odd manner. One ſide of him was cloathed in very rich attire, and

35

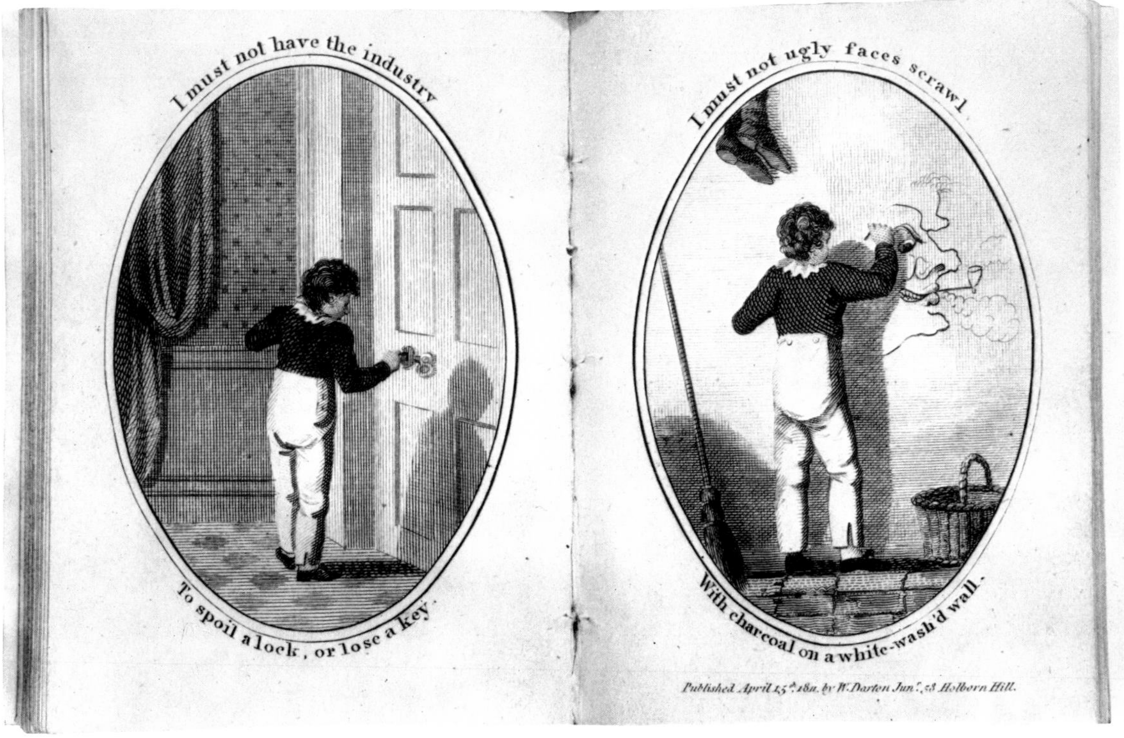
I must not have the industry
To spoil a lock, or lose a key.
I must not ugly faces scrawl
With charcoal on a white-wash'd wall.
Published April 15th 1811. by W. Darton Junr. 58 Holborn Hill.

36

TABLE MANNERS.—I.

The Goops they lick their fingers,
And the Goops they lick their
knives;
They spill their broth on the table-
cloth—
Oh, they lead disgusting lives!
The Goops they talk while eating,
And loud and fast they chew;
And that is why I'm glad that I
Am not a Goop—are you?

39

Early Tales

40 ☙ GESTA ROMANORUM. [*Dutch.*]

Gouda: Gerard Leeu, 30 April 1481.
26 cm. 242 f.
Goff G-298.

Various collections of *exempla*, or tales carrying attached morals, circulated during the Middle Ages, but none enjoyed so great a popularity or was so influential as the *Gesta Romanorum* (*Deeds of the Romans*). The origins of the *Gesta* are obscure, but it appears to have been first compiled, in Latin, soon after the year 1300, probably in an English Franciscan or Dominican friary. The tales, which were used in instruction or to enliven sermons, purported to be accounts of events in the history of the Roman Empire. In fact, however, the *Gesta Romanorum* as it has come down to us is a compilation of fantastic stories blending history with myth, fable, and religion. Some of the sources from which the material is drawn are very far from Rome; many of the tales come from Oriental or Sanskrit originals, such as the fables of Bidpai. Chaucer and Shakespeare and a host of other writers drew incidents and themes from the *Gesta*. It contains the anecdotes of the three caskets and the pound of flesh, both of which are used in *The Merchant of Venice*. The original of Shakespeare's King Lear is in it, as well as the original of Chaucer's Man of Law, and it also contains a synopsis of the mediaeval romance, *Guy of Warwick*. The appeal of these tales to children is obvious; and the moral lessons appended to them led to their being given to the young by parents and other hopeful adults.

This Dutch edition of the *Gesta Romanorum*, issued in Gouda by Gerard Leeu, is the first printed edition of the tales to contain illustrations (the artist is unknown). It is also the first version in any vernacular language. The Morgan Library copy is one of just six perfect copies that have survived. It is the only one in America.

41 B. P.

GESTA ROMANORUM: OR, FIFTY-EIGHT HISTORIES ORIGINALLY (AS 'TIS SAID) COLLECTED FROM THE ROMAN RECORDS. WITH APPLICATIONS OR MORALS FOR THE SUPPRESSING VICE, AND ENCOURAGING VIRTUE AND THE LOVE OF GOD.

London: G. Conyers, [? about 1720].
14 cm. [4], 5–131, [1] p.
Esdaile, p. 61.
Elisabeth Ball Collection.

An early-eighteenth-century version of the *Gesta Romanorum*. The identity of "B. P." is not known, although it has been surmised that he was one Bartholomew Pratt. He first issued this version, in a somewhat shorter form, in 1703, claiming to have translated it from a 1514 Latin edition published in Paris. Both the 1703 edition and the present one are extremely rare. The three separate woodcuts composing the frontispiece are repeated individually as illustrations in the text. This copy once belonged to a celebrated English classical scholar and bibliophile, Archdeacon Francis Wrangham (1769–1842); his signature, dated 1815, can be seen atop the title page.

42

[GUY OF WARWICK.] CY COMMENCE GUY DE VVARUICH. . . .

Paris: Anthoine Couteau pour François Regnault, 12 March 1525.
25.5 cm. [80] f.
Brunet, II, 1832.

The mediaeval romance recounting the story of the legendary English hero Guy of Warwick was a rousing tale that became enormously popular. It was drawn upon by Elizabethan chroniclers and dramatists, and it persisted in various forms, many of them produced for children, well into the nineteenth century. The romance was first written down, in Anglo-Norman French verse, in the early thirteenth century. A prose version, also in French, was composed in the fifteenth century; this first appeared in print in Paris in 1525. A copy of the rare first edition, which is illustrated with woodcuts, is shown here. The Morgan Library also possesses (M.956) a sixteenth-century illustrated manuscript that, in the form of a genealogical tree, traces the descent of Guy of Warwick from the tenth to the thirteenth century.

43 A PLEASANT SONG OF THE VALIANT DEEDS OF CHIVALRY, ATCHIEVED BY THAT NOBLE KNIGHT SIR GUY OF WARWICK. . . .

[? London: ? about 1700.]
19.5×33.5 cm.
Simpson, p. 283.

This broadside ballad about the wondrous deeds of Guy of Warwick begins, "Was ever Knight for Lady's sake, / so tost in love as I Sir Guy?" and goes on to recount the hero's travels and his triumphs, in the name of "fair Phillis," over giants, dragons, and "a monstrous wild and cruel Beast / Called the Dun-Cow of Dunsmore Heath." Single sheets like this one first appeared in England in the sixteenth century; a ballad entitled "A pleasant songe of the valiant actes of Guy of War wicke. to the tune of, Was ever man soe tost in love" was entered in the Stationers' Register on 5 January 1592 (the entry survives, but both the broadside and the tune have been lost). Crudely printed and illustrated, these ballads were addressed primarily to adults rather than to children, but they nevertheless provided the young with an exciting change from the religious and educational works that were their normal fare.

44 [G. L.]

THE NOBLE AND RENOWNED HISTORY OF GUY EARL OF WARWICK.

London: A. Bettesworth, [1711].
15 cm. [8], 157, [3] p.
Esdaile, p. 234.
Elisabeth Ball Collection.

An early-eighteenth-century version of the romance of Guy of Warwick, written in prose and illustrated with vigorous woodcuts. The dedication is signed "G. L.," presumably the initials of the author. Nothing is known of him, other than that his version of the tale was first published in 1706 and went through numerous editions. The fifth edition, a copy of which is shown here, was printed in 1711. It is rare, as are all the early editions of this prose version of the romance.

45 VALENTIN ET ORSON.

Lyon: Jacques Maillet, 30 May 1489.
27 cm. 136 f.
Goff V-11. Dickson.

The tale of Valentine and Orson was one of the most popular—and has proved to be one of the most long-lived—of all the romances that circulated on the continent of Europe and in England during the late Middle Ages. The story concerns a pair of royal twins who are lost in infancy and then separated; one of the brothers, Orson, is suckled by a bear and becomes a wild man of the forest, while his brother Valentine is brought up at court. The brothers, ignorant of their relationship, clash in an epic fight, after which they become friends and embark on adventures together. It is a violent, romantic, and rather jumbled tale, with elements of chivalry and the supernatural. Although it was not written for children, they undoubtedly read it from the very first, and by the latter part of the eighteenth century it had become almost exclusively theirs. In Laurence Sterne's *Tristram Shandy*, published 1760–1767, Uncle Toby recalls reading it as a boy; and in Charles Dickens' *A Christmas Carol* (1843) Scrooge, having visions of his childhood, cries, "And Valentine . . . and his wild brother Orson, there they go!" The tale is still in print at the present day. The romance is believed to have been originally composed in French verse in the early fourteenth century. That version does not survive. The earliest text we have is a French prose romance, *Valentin et Orson*, which was printed in 1489 in Lyon. From this printed text have come all the subsequent versions of the tale, in French, English, and all the other many languages in which it has appeared. The Morgan Library copy, the frontispiece of which is shown here, is one of the three surviving copies of the first edition. It is the only copy in America.

46 THE HISTORY OF VALENTINE AND ORSON.

[*London:*] *Printed for the Company of Walking Stationers,* [*about 1790*].
16 cm. 16 p.
Elisabeth Ball Collection.

A late-eighteenth-century chapbook version of *Valentine and Orson*. It is a descendant of the first English version, printed in 1510 by Wynkyn de Worde, in an edition of which only a fragmentary copy survives. The ancestor of Wynkyn de Worde's version, and of course of all other known versions including this one, was the 1489 French edition. This sixteen-page chapbook, printed on a single sheet that was then folded but not stitched or cut, was sold in the city and countryside by the itinerant peddlers known as chapmen—the "walking stationers" mentioned on the title page.

47 THE HISTORY OF FRIER RUSH . . . BEING FULL OF PLEASANT MIRTH AND DELIGHT FOR YOUNG PEOPLE.

London: Thomas Vere, 1649.
18 cm. [20] f.
NCBEL, I, 2028.

"Frier Rush" is really the Devil, who takes the form of a friar in order to enter a monastery and bring wild disorder into the lives of its prior and monks. The tale is indeed "full of pleasant mirth and delight," as its subtitle claims, but today it would probably be considered rather strong meat for "young people." The story can be traced back to Teutonic folklore of the Middle Ages, to the doings of the character known as Bruder Rausch. An English version of the tale was entered in the Stationers' Register in 1568; no copy of that edition is known to survive. The Morgan Library copy is the only one known of its edition. There are two earlier recorded editions, of 1620 and 1626; each, like the Morgan Library 1649 edition, is known by a single copy.

48 THE FAMOUS HISTORY OF FRIER BACON.

London: W. Thackery and C. Bates, [?1695].
20.5 cm. [24] f.
Esdaile, p. 17.

The scientific writings of the learned English monk Roger Bacon (1214–1292) caused his name to be surrounded by much superstitious lore and legend during the later Middle Ages and for a long time afterward. Bacon was the subject of a play by Robert Greene, *The Honourable History of Friar Bacon and Friar Bungay*, which was staged at least as early as 1594. To the popular mind Bacon was a magician and necromancer. In the seventeenth-century tale illustrated here he produces mists, mysterious music, and lavish banquets at the wave of a wand; he causes people to appear out of thin air and vanish again; and he fashions a bronze head that has the power of speech. The story of Friar Bacon was a staple item in the chapmen's stock, and it was read avidly by children and the more credulous of their elders all through the eighteenth century.

49 THE HISTORY OF SIR RICHARD WHITTINGTON, THRICE LORD MAYOR OF LONDON.

[London:] Aldermary Church-Yard, [about 1750].
15.5 cm. 24 p.
DNB, "Whittington, Richard." *Wheatley.*

The sources of this famous tale of a London apprentice whose cat makes his fortune may be looked for in folklore, but the original of the hero was a real Richard Whittington. He did indeed become Lord Mayor of London three times, in 1397, 1406, and 1419. An important merchant who supplied wedding outfits for the daughters of Henry IV (the invoices survive to this day), he was a public-spirited subject of his king, giving money freely for such things as hospital, church, and library buildings. Why and how the cat entered the story remains unclear—it may come from a fourteenth-century term for a kind of coal-barge ("catte"), or from a French word used in commerce ("achat")—but pictorial representations of a cat with Whittington go back to the time of Sir Richard's death in 1423. This mid-eighteenth-century chapbook version came from Aldermary Churchyard, which was a busy center of the London chapbook trade in the eighteenth century.

50 WHITTINGTON AND HIS CAT.

London: John Harris, [1827].
18 cm. [3], 2–54, [2] p. Buff printed wrappers.
Gumuchian 5833.
Elisabeth Ball Collection.

By the nineteenth century more than one English publisher was doing a thriving business in children's books. John Harris was probably the foremost in the field during the early decades of the century. His version of the Whittington tale employed the format of the early chapbooks, if not their vigorous style of illustration.

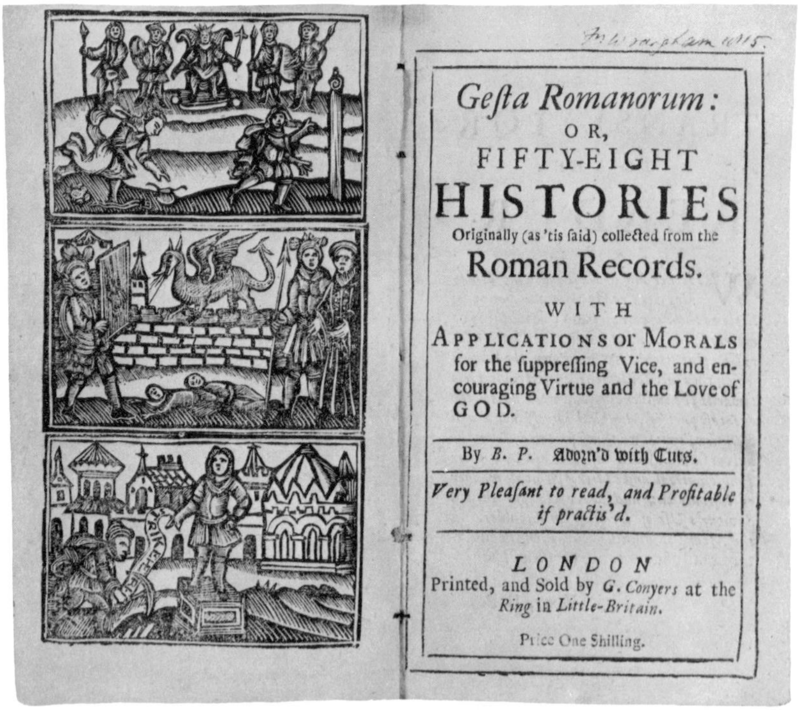

Gesta Romanorum:
OR,
FIFTY-EIGHT
HISTORIES
Originally (as 'tis said) collected from the
Roman Records.
WITH
Applications or Morals
for the suppressing Vice, and encouraging Virtue and the Love of
GOD.

By B. P. Adorn'd with Cuts.

Very Pleasant to read, and Profitable if practis'd.

LONDON
Printed, and Sold by *G. Conyers* at the *Ring* in *Little-Britain.*

Price One Shilling.

41

Fueillet premier.

Cōment le conte Roalt auoit vne belle fille nōmee Felipe surmontant en beaulte toutes autres dames et damoiselles/ et enuoya querir Guyōnet filz de son seneschal pour demeurer en sa court.

En icelle honnorable saison ꝛ regne dudit roy Athelstā estoit ou royaulme dangleterre vng tres puissant conte nomme Roalt leql auoit la seigneurie de la conte de warwich et des contes de Exensfordi et de wringchim et de plusieurs autres seigneuries/grāt ꝛ puissant seigneur estoit entre les plus grans du royaulme/et moult se contenoit richement ꝛ en bel estat/ de gens/de mesgnee et de tous autres appareilz sur tous autres De propos aymoit et exaulcoit le noble nom de cheualerie Et trop se delectoit a veoir et honnorer tous bons cheualiers et moult leur estoit secourable cōme celluy qui auoit este et encores estoit tresbon cheualier de sa main. De tous enfās nauoit celluy conte fors vne seulle fille nommee Felipe: mais de beaulte/sens et gracieusete elle passoit toutes les damoyselles de son aage que len scauoit en nulle part Et tant couroit delle grant renōmee quon la tenoit la plus belle du monde: et pour sa beaulte ꝛ doulce maniere estoit moult desiree de plusieurs grans seignrs/et moult en auoit son pere de prieres et requestes/ ꝛ souuent luy en touchoit Mais elle cōme pucelle de ieune aage nentendoit que peu a telle affaire: de toutes bonnes meurs estoit pleine et de science / a toutes dames conuenable bien enseigner. Et cōbien que aucuns acteurs au deuant de ce temps se

B i

42

A Pleaſant Song of the valiant Deeds of Chivalry, Atchieved by that Noble Knight Sir *GUY* of *Warwick*; Who for the Love of fair *Phillis*, became a Hermit, and dy'd in a Cave of a Craggy Rock, a Mile diſtant from *Warwick*. *Tune was ever Man, &c.*

WAS ever Knight for Lady's ſake,
so toſt in Love as I Sir Guy?
For *Phillis* fair that Lady bright,
as ever Man beheld with Eye.
She gave me leave my ſelf to try,
the valiant Knight with Shield and Spear,
E'er that her Love ſhe would grant me,
Which made me venture far and near,
The proud Sir *Guy* a Baron bold,
in deeds of Arms the doubtful Knight,
That every Day in *England* was
with Sword and Spear in Field to fight.
An Engliſh-man I was by *Birth*,
in Faith of Chriſt a Chriſtian true,
The wicked Laws of Infidels,
I ſought by Power to ſubdue.
Two hundred twenty Years and odd,
after our Saviour Chriſt his Birth,
When King *Athelſton* wore the Crown,
I lived here upon the Earth,
Sometimes I was of *Warwick* Earl,
and as I ſaid on very Truth,
A Lady's love did me conſtrain,
to ſeek ſtrange Ventures in my Youth.
To try my Fame by feats of Arms,
in ſtrange and ſundry *Heathen* Lands,

Where I atchieved for her ſake,
right dangerous Conqueſts with my hands
For firſt I ſail'd to *Normandy*,
and there I ſtoutly won in Fight,
The Emperor's Daughter of *Almain*,
from many a valiant worthy Knight.
Then paſſed I the Seas of *Greece*,
to help the Emperor to his Right,
Againſt the mighty Souldan's Hoſt,
of puiſſant *Perſians* for to fight,
where I did ſlay of *Sarazens*,
and Heathen Pagans many a Man,
And ſlew the Souldan's Couſin dear,
who had to Name Doughty *Colbryn*.
Ezeldered, that famous Knight,
to Death likewiſe I did purſue;
And *Almain*, King of *Tyre* alſo,
moſt terrible too in height to view.
I went into the Souldan's *Hoſt*,
being thither on Ambaſſage ſent,
And brought away his *Head* with me,
I having ſlain him in his *Tent*.
There was a Dragon in the Land,
which I alſo my ſelf did ſlay,
As he a Lion did purſue,
moſt fiercely met me by the way.

From thence I paſt the Seas of *Greece*,
and came to *Pavyland* aright,
where *I* the Duke of *Pavy* kill'd,
his heinous Treaſon to requite.
And after that came into this Land,
towards fair *Phillis* Lady bright,
For love of whom I travell'd far,
to try my Manhood and my might.
But when I had eſpouſed her,
I ſtaid with her but forty Days;
But there I left this Lady fair,
and then I went beyond the Seas,
All clad in Gray in Pilgrim ſort,
my Voyage from her, I did take
Unto that bleſſed holy Land,
for *Jeſus Chriſt* my Saviour's ſake:
where I Earl *Jonas* did redeem,
and all his Sons, which were Fifteen;
who with the cruel *Sarazens*,
in Priſon for long Time had been,
I ſlew the Giant *Amarant*,
in Battle fiercely Hand to Hand;
And Doughty *Barknard* killed I,
the Mighty Duke of the ſame Land.
Then I to England came again,
and here with *Colbren* fell I fought,

An Only Giant which the *Danes*,
had for their Champion hither brought,
I overcame him in the Field,
and ſlew him Dead right valiantly;
where I the Land did then redeem,
from *Daniſh* Tribute utterly:
And afterwards I offered up
the uſe of weapons ſolemnly,
At *Winchester*, whereas I fought,
in fight of many far and near.
In *Windſor Forreſt* I did ſlay
a *Boar* of paſſing might and ſtrength,
The like in England never was,
for hugeneſs both in *Bredth* and Length.
Some of his Bones in *Warwick* yet,
within the Caſtle there doth lie;
One of his Shield *Bores* to this Day,
hangs in the City of *Coventry*.
On *Dunſmore Heath* I alſo ſlew,
a monſtrous wild and cruel *Beaſt*,
Call'd the *Dun-Cow* of *Dunſmore Heath*,
which many People had oppreſt.
Some of her Bones in *Warwick* yet,
ſtill for a Monument doth lye,
which unto every Looker's view,
as wondrous ſtrange they may eſpy.
And the *Dragon* in the Land,
I alſo did in Fight deſtroy,
which did both Men and Beaſts oppreſs,

and all the Country ſore annoy,
And then to *Warwick* came again,
like Pilgrim poor, and was not known;
And there I liv'd a *Hermet's* Life,
a Mile and more out of the Town.
where with my Hand I hew'd a *Houſe*
out of a Craggy Rock of Stone;
And lived like a *Palmer* poor,
within that Cave my ſelf alone:
And daily came to beg my Food
of *Phillis* at my Caſtle-Gate.
Nor known unto my loving wife,
who daily mourned for her Mate,
Till at the laſt I fell ſore ſick,
ye. Sick ſo ſore that *I* muſt die,
I ſent to her a Ring of Gold,
by which ſhe knew me preſently
Then ſhe repaired to the Cave,
before that I gave up the Ghoſt,
Her ſelf cloſ'd up my dying Eyes.
my *Phillis* fair whom I lov'd moſt,
Thus dreadful Death did me arreſt,
to bring my Corps unto the Grave,
And like a *Palmer* died I,
whereby I hope my Soul to ſave.
My *Body* in *Warwick* yet doth lye,
though now it is conſum'd to Mould,
My Statute was engraven in Stone,
this preſent Day you may behold.

43

See here brave Guy in all his Warlike Pride,
With a Fierce Lion *walking by his Side,*
Which from a monſtrous Dragon *he deliver'd;*
At whoſe fell Rage the Princely Lion *quiver'd.*

Nor was there any monſtrous Giant, *who*
He did not both Engage, *and* Conquer *too:*
For Giants, Dragons, Boar, *and* Dunſmore-Cow
To Guy's *all conquering Arm were forc'd to bow.*

The Noble and Renowned

HISTORY
OF
GUY Earl of *Warwick*:

CONTAINING

A Full and True Account of his many Famous and Valiant Actions, Remarkable and brave Exploits, and Noble and Renowned Victories.

Alſo his Courtſhip to fair *Phælice*, Earl *Roband*'s Daughter and Heireſs; and the many Difficulties and Hazards he went thorow, to obtain her Love.

Extracted from Authentick Records; and the Whole Illuſtrated with Cuts ſuitable to the Hiſtory.

The Fifth Edition.

LONDON:
Printed for *A. Betteſworth*, at the Red Lion in *Pater-noſter-row*.

44

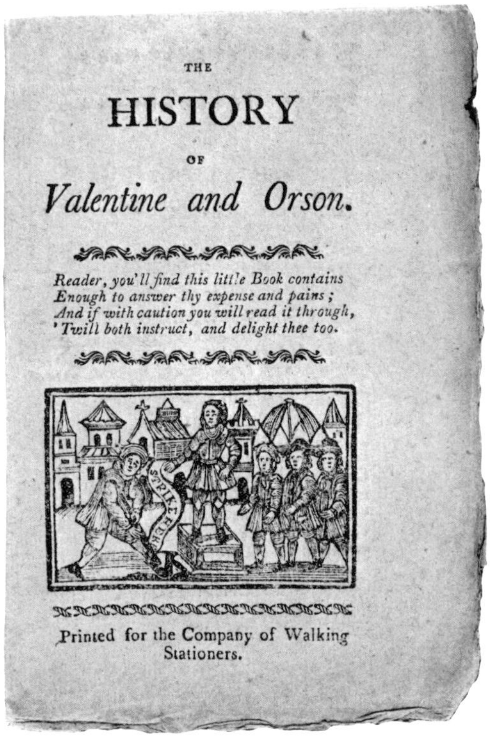

THE

HISTORY

OF

Valentine and Orson.

Reader, you'll find this little Book contains
Enough to answer thy expense and pains;
And if with caution you will read it through,
'Twill both instruct, and delight thee too.

Printed for the Company of Walking Stationers.

46

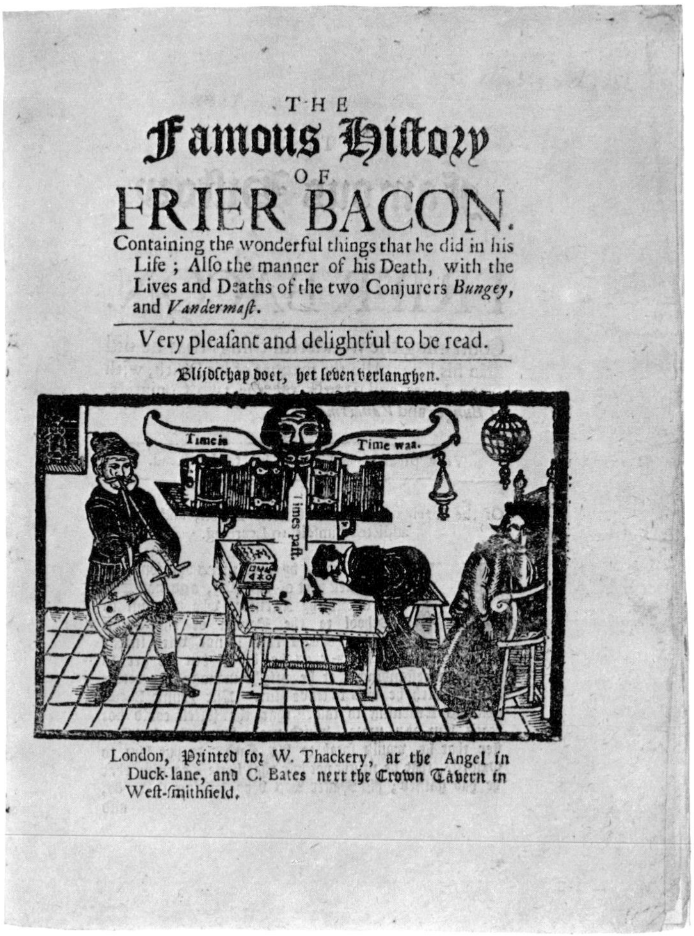

THE

Famous Hiſtory

OF

FRIER BACON.

Containing the wonderful things that he did in his Life; Alſo the manner of his Death, with the Lives and Deaths of the two Conjurers *Bungey*, and *Vandermaſt*.

Very pleaſant and delightful to be read.

Blijdſchap doet, het leven verlanghen.

London, Printed for W. Thackery, at the Angel in Duck-lane, and C. Bates next the Crown Tavern in Weſt-ſmithfield.

48

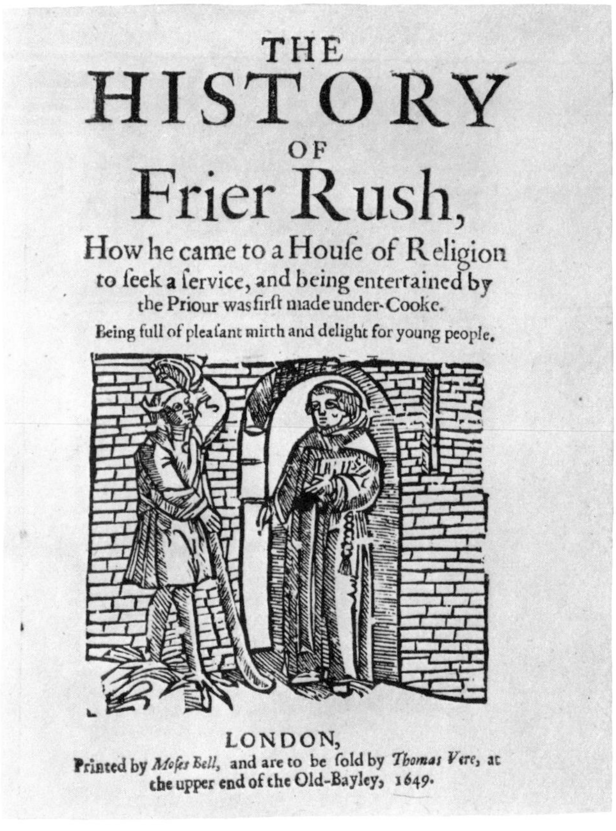

THE

HISTORY

OF

Frier Rush,

How he came to a Houſe of Religion to ſeek a ſervice, and being entertained by the Priour was firſt made under-Cooke.

Being full of pleaſant mirth and delight for young people.

LONDON,
Printed by *Moſes Bell*, and are to be ſold by *Thomas Vere*, at the upper end of the Old-Bayley, 1649.

47

(2)

The Hiſtory of
Sir Richard Whittington.

CHAP. I.

Of Whittington's obſcure Birth and hard Fortune; and of his being drove to London.

ONE Richard Whittington, ſuppoſed to have been an outcaſt, for he did not

49

WHITTINGTON

AND

HIS CAT.

LONDON:
JOHN HARRIS, ST. PAUL'S CHURCH-YARD.

The ABC's

51 ABECEDARIUM. [*French.*]

Paris: [*about 1520*].
15 cm. [*4*] *f.*

This group of four leaves, printed—in red and black—in Paris in the early sixteenth century, probably formed part of a prayer book. But this first page, with alphabet (preceded by a cross) and Paternoster, is remarkably like the pages that later would be printed up for use in hornbooks.

52 TABULAE ABCDARIAE PUERILES.

[*Leipzig: Valentin Bapst, about 1544.*]
34×21 cm.
Gumuchian 1.
Elisabeth Ball Collection.

This printed alphabet-instruction sheet for children is one of the earliest known. Its text, thought to have been arranged by Petrus Plateanus, Rector of the School of Zwickau, contains three alphabets set in both Roman and Gothic type, together with lists of vowels, diphthongs, and consonants, and a Paternoster. The identity of the printer was traced through a study of the woodcut ornaments, some of which occur in other items printed by Valentin Bapst.

53 [A SHEET OF HORNBOOKS.]

Aberdeen: E[*dward*] *Raban,* [*1622*].
28.5×18.5 cm.
STC 13813. Tuer, I, p. 126.

The four different pages printed on this sheet were designed to be cut apart and used in hornbooks. The printer, Edward Raban, set up the first printing press in the city of Aberdeen, Scotland. He produced this little sheet during his first year of printing there.

54 [A SILVER HORNBOOK.]

[? England: ? Late seventeenth century.]
Frame 8×5.5 cm.
Tuer, I, p. 95.

A silver hornbook bearing a text printed on paper and covered with a sheet of transparent horn. The printing was probably done in England; the engraved bird and stylized foliage on the silver back, however, are characteristic of Dutch or Flemish work of the late seventeenth century. The hole in the handle was designed to receive a thong by which the hornbook was attached to a child's waist. This convenient handle, as might be expected, inspired children to turn their hornbooks into paddles—or "battledores"—in games of battledore and shuttlecock. The usual hornbook was made of wood and served very well indeed as a paddle; this silver example is an elegant variation. The hornbook was in use through the end of the eighteenth century. Thereafter it was supplanted by a cardboard folder known as a battledore, a name reminiscent of the happy use to which the earlier hornbook had been put so frequently.

55 ABC. [*German.*]

Hamburg: J. D. Reise, [about 1735].
17 cm. 16 p.
Loaned by Miss Julia P. Wightman.

This German ABC is a sixteen-page chapbook, folded but not stitched, and uncut. The first and last pages, which are shown here, are partly colored in red; this was achieved not by hand-coloring but by two successive printings from different types and woodcut blocks, the first printing in black ink and the second in red. The rooster was a symbol of diligence; it appeared frequently in German children's books of the early eighteenth century.

56 [A PICTURE ALPHABET.]

London: William Darton, 13 December 1799.
15 cm. 56 f.
James, p. 33.
Elisabeth Ball Collection.

The fifty-six plates in this volume depict 336 objects and activities, from an alligator and a microscope to a yacht, flowers, and children's games. The plates also give present-day children and adults an absorbing glimpse of everyday life in the England of 1799. On the plates illustrated here, the "Machine" pictured is a bathing machine, from which bathers descended to the water after a horse had drawn the machine from the beach out into the sea. "Tunnel" was in use in England into the nineteenth century as a term for the device we now know as a funnel.

57 R. R[ansome]

THE INVITED ALPHABET, OR, THE ADDRESS OF A TO B; CONTAINING HIS FRIENDLY PROPOSAL FOR THE AMUSEMENT AND INSTRUCTION OF GOOD CHILDREN.

London: W. Darton, Jun., [?about 1804].
12 cm. 4, [28], 2 f.
NBL 8. Muir, p. 220.
Elisabeth Ball Collection.

A to Z in sign language, together with verses inviting the twenty-six letters to assemble "In what is call'd the ALPHABET," by means of which good little girls and boys shall "with speed, Both elegantly spell and read." For the purchase price of eighteen pence, buyers got not only the alphabet and accompanying verses but also a rather scholarly preface and notes—as well as two pages of music in the form of a "Glee for Three Voices" based on the newly learned letters. This is the first edition. Very little is known about the author other than his surname and the fact that he also wrote the courtesy book entitled *The Good Boy's Soliloquy*.

58 "Z"

THE HISTORY OF THE APPLE PIE.

London: J. Harris, 25 June 1808.
10.5 cm. [27] f. Buff printed wrappers.
ODNR 1.
Elisabeth Ball Collection.

A cheerful variation of a venerable "A was an apple-pie" rhymed alphabet that first appeared in print in 1671 but was apparently well known for some time before that. The poetical justification for this version of the apple pie's adventures is given in the final plate: "Z, zealous that all good boys & girls should be acquainted with his family, sat down & wrote the History of it." This is the first edition.

59 MARTIN'S NEW BATTLEDOOR OF NATURAL HISTORY.

London: G. Martin, [about 1810].
16 cm. [3] f.
Elisabeth Ball Collection.

Along with the alphabet, this English "battledoor" of the early nineteenth century offers some instruction in natural history. This is a battledore of the more elaborate type, comprising three stiff leaves and a flap. Simpler battledores (which were often smaller; this is a large one) had only two leaves and a flap.

60 ☙ MAMMA'S PICTURES, OR THE HISTORY OF FANNY AND MARY.

London: Darton, Harvey, and Darton, [about 1818].
12.5 cm. [23] f.
Elisabeth Ball Collection.

Beneath the hand-colored stipple engravings of this alphabet book are engraved verses that occasionally offer moral lessons—and beneath the verses an early owner has added sardonic comments, such as these on plates F and G: "What a set of noodles"; and "Give his messmate his shoes & legs. That's better." (Honest George and his unfortunate shipmate are of course former British tars home from the Napoleonic Wars.)

61 ☙ THE ALPHABET ANNOTATED FOR YOUTH AND ADULTS IN DOGGEREL VERSE BY AN OLD ETONIAN. Illustrated and etched by G. W. Terry.

London: Ackermann & Co., [about 1853].
33 cm. [5], vi–x, 11–63, [1] p. Gray printed wrappers.
Loaned by Miss Julia P. Wightman.

A whimsical, fanciful alphabet book designed to amuse older children and also adults. It is illustrated with hand-colored etchings. Each page has a different, but always elaborate, border design; the treatment of the letter T is shown here. This is the first edition. The publisher is Ackermann, a firm celebrated for its fine color-plate books. The founder of the firm, Rudolph Ackermann (1764–1834), pioneered the use of lithography in England.

62 Kate Greenaway

KATE GREENAWAY'S ALPHABET.

London: George Routledge & Sons, [?1885].
7 cm. [16] f. Yellow printed boards.
Spielmann and Layard, p. 287.
Mrs. Sherman Post Haight Collection.

These capital letters and their graceful young acrobatic adornments were first drawn by Kate Greenaway for William Mavor's *English Spelling-Book* in 1885. That edition, in which the Greenaway illustrations were reproduced in brown ink, did not sell well. The publisher thereupon decided to issue the capital letters alone in this small volume, printed in full color by Edmund Evans. The result was gratifying to both Miss Greenaway and her publisher; the alphabet in this form achieved a sale of 24,500 copies, including 2,000 to the French publisher Hachette in Paris. The first edition is shown here.

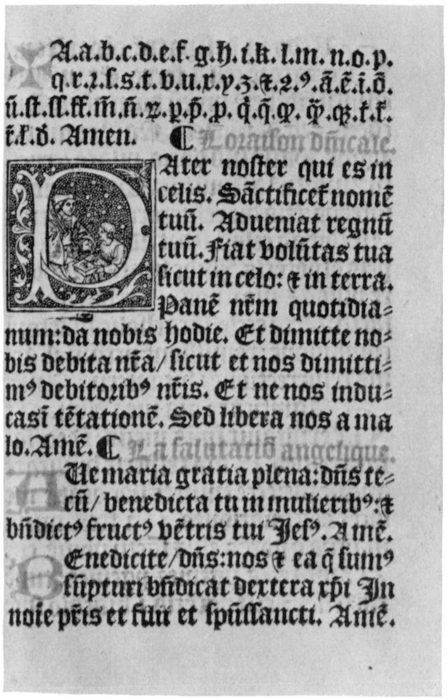

A.a.b.c.d.e.f.g.h.i.k.l.m.n.o.p.
q.r.ꝛ.ſ.s.t.v.u.x.y.z.&.ꝛ.ꝰ.ā.ē.ī.ō.
ū.ſt.ſſ.ff.m̄.n̄.ꝑ.ꝓ.ꝑ̄.p.q̇.q̄.ꝙ.ꝙ̄.ꝗ.k.k.
k.k.ꝺ. Amen. ¶ Loraison dñicale.
Pater noster qui es in
celis. Sãctificet nomē
tuū. Adueniat regnū
tuū. Fiat volūtas tua
sicut in celo: ⁊ in terra.
Panē nr̄m quotidia-
num: da nobis hodie. Et dimitte nobis debita nr̄a / sicut et nos dimitti-
mꝰ debitoribꝰ nr̄is. Et ne nos indu-
cas ī tētationē. Sed libera nos a ma
lo. Amē. ¶ La salutatio angelique.
Ave maria gratia plena: dn̄s te-
cū / benedicta tu in mulieribꝰ: ⁊
bn̄dictꝰ fructꝰ vētris tui Jesꝰ. Amē.
Benedicite / dn̄s: nos ⁊ ea q̄ sumꝰ
sūpturi bn̄dicat dextera xp̄i In
noīe pr̄is et filii et spūssancti. Amē.

51

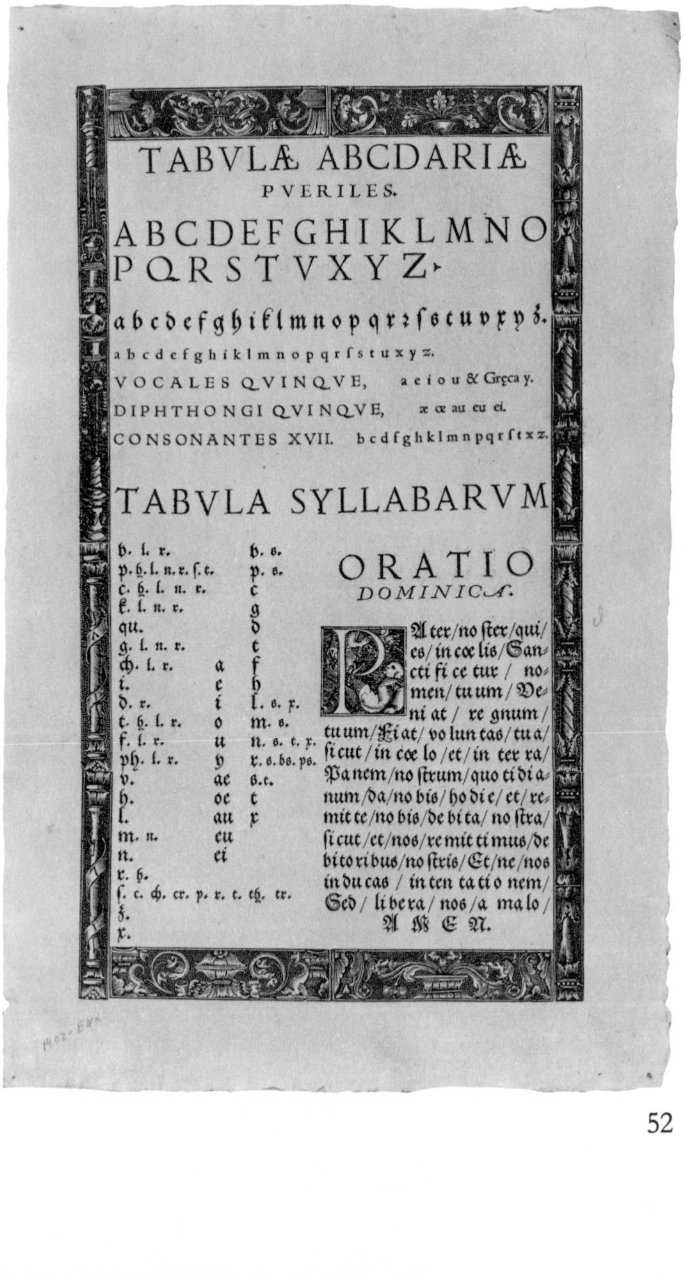

TABVLÆ ABCDARIÆ
PVERILES.

ABCDEFGHIKLMNO
PQRSTVXYZ.

abcdefghiklmnopqrꝛſstuvxyz.

abcdefghiklmnopqrſstuxyz.

VOCALES QVINQVE, a e i o u & Græca y.

DIPHTHONGI QVINQVE, æ œ au eu ei.

CONSONANTES XVII. bcdfghklmnpqrſtxz.

TABVLA SYLLABARVM

b. l. r.		b. s.
p. h. l. n. r. ſ. t.		p. s.
c. h. l. n. r.		c
k. l. n. r.		g
qu.		d
g. l. n. r.		t
ch. l. r.	a	f
i.	e	h
d. r.	i	l. s. x.
t. h. l. r.	o	m. s.
f. l. r.	u	n. s. t. x.
ph. l. r.	y	r. s. bs. ps.
v.	ae	s. t.
h.	oe	t
l.	au	x
m. n.	eu	
n.	ei	
r. h.		
ſ. c. ch. cr. p. r. t. th. tr.		
z.		
x.		

ORATIO
DOMINICA.

Pater / no ster / qui / es / in coe lis / San- cti fi ce tur / no- men / tu um / Ve- ni at / re gnum / tu um / Fi at / vo lun tas / tu a / si cut / in coe lo / et / in ter ra / Pa nem / no strum / quo ti di a- num / da / no bis / ho di e / et / re- mit te / no bis / de bi ta / no stra / si cut / et / nos / re mit ti mus / de bi to ri bus / no stris / Et / ne / nos in du cas / in ten ta ti o nem / Sed / li be ra / nos / a ma lo /
A M E N.

52

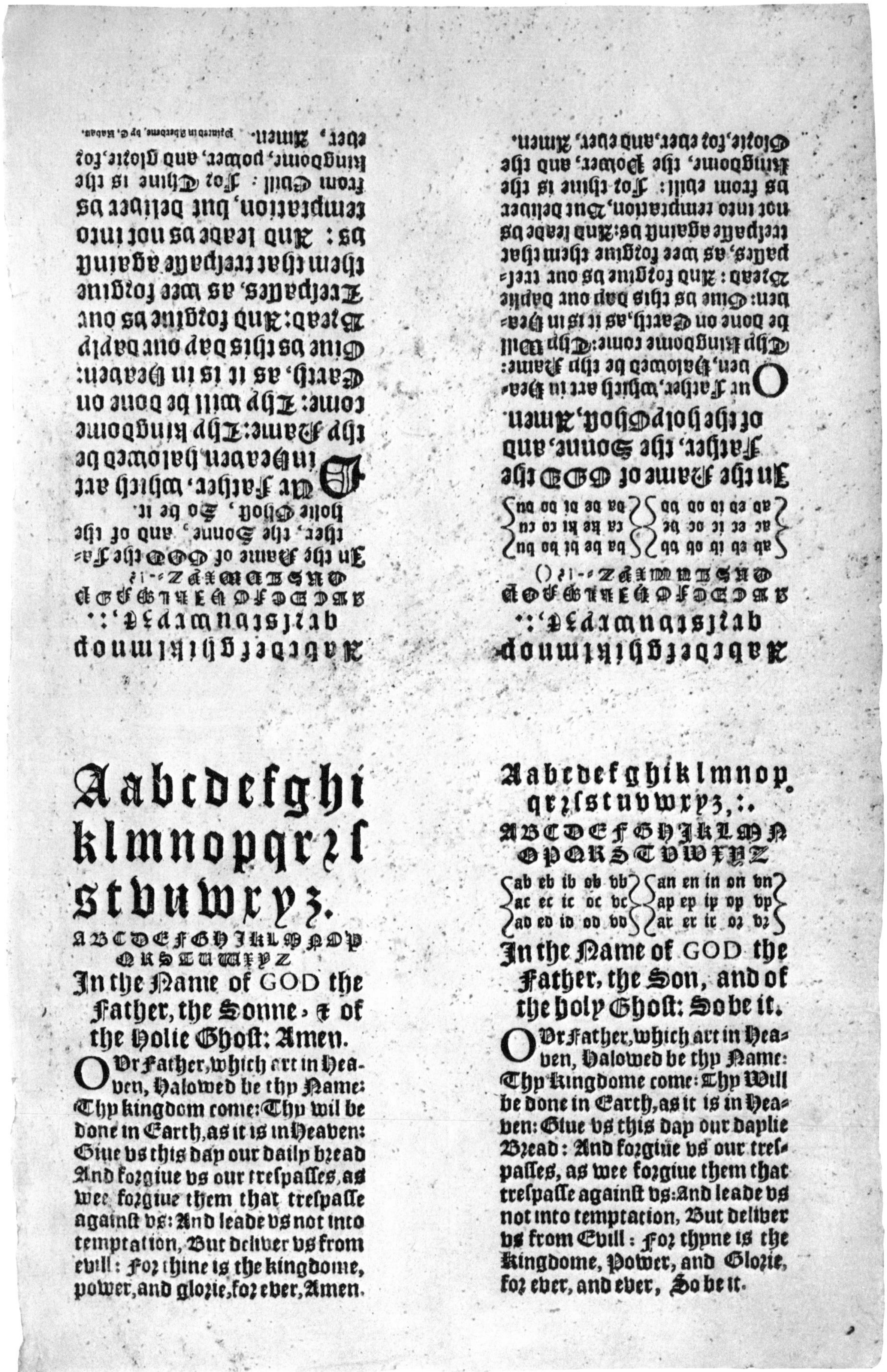

Aabcdefghi
klmnopqr ꝛ ſ
stuvwxyz.
ABCDEFGHIKLMNOP
QRSTUWXYZ

In the Name of GOD the
Father, the Sonne, & of
the Holie Ghost: Amen.

OUr Father, which art in Heaven, Halowed be thy Name: Thy kingdom come: Thy wil be done in Earth, as it is in Heaven: Giue vs this day our daily bread And forgiue vs our trespasses, as wee forgiue them that trespasse against vs: And leade vs not into temptation, But deliver vs from evill: For thine is the kingdome, power, and glorie, for ever, Amen.

Aabcdefghiklmnop
qrꝛſstuvwxyz,:.
ABCDEFGHIKLMN
OPQRSTUWXYZ

ab	eb	ib	ob	ub	an	en	in	on	un
ac	ec	ic	oc	uc	ap	ep	ip	op	up
ad	ed	id	od	ud	ar	er	ir	or	ur

In the Name of GOD the
Father, the Son, and of
the holy Ghost: So be it.

OUr Father, which art in Heaven, Halowed be thy Name: Thy kingdome come: Thy Will be done in Earth, as it is in Heaven: Giue vs this day our daylie Bread: And forgiue vs our trespasses, as wee forgiue them that trespasse against vs: And leade vs not into temptation, But deliver vs from Evill: For thyne is the Kingdome, Power, and Glorie, for ever, and ever, So be it.

Aabcdefghiklmnop
qrꝛſstuvwxyz&,:.
ABCDEFGHIKLMNOP
QRSTUWXYZ-!?()

ab	eb	ib	ob	ub	ba	be	bi	bo	bu
ac	ec	ic	oc	uc	ca	ce	ci	co	cu
ad	ed	id	od	ud	da	de	di	do	du

In the Name of GOD the
Father, the Sonne, and
of the holy Ghost, Amen.

OUr Father, which art in Heaven, Halowed be thy Name: Thy kingdome come: Thy Will be done on Earth, as it is in Heaven: Giue vs this day our daylie Bread: And forgiue vs our trespasses, as wee forgiue them that trespasse against vs: And leade vs not into temptation, But deliver vs from evill: For thine is the kingdome, the Power, and the Glorie, for ever, and ever, Amen.

Aabcdefghiklmnop
qrꝛſstuvwxyz&,:.
ABCDEFGHIKLMNOP
QRSTUWXYZ-!?

In the Name of GOD the Father, the Sonne, and of the holie Ghost, So be it.

OUr Father, which art in Heaven, halowed be thy Name: Thy kingdome come: Thy will be done on Earth, as it is in Heaven: Giue vs this day our dayly Bread: And forgiue vs our Trespasses, as wee forgiue them that trespasse against vs: And leade vs not into temptation, but deliver vs from Evill: For Thine is the kingdome, power, and glorie, for ever, Amen. Printed in Aberdene, by E. Raban.

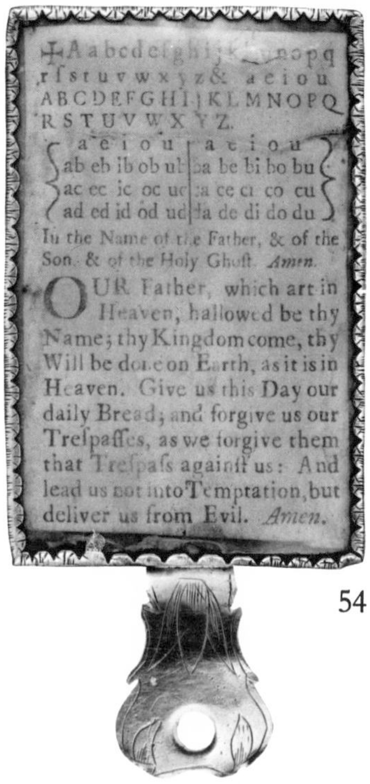

54

54

16 Abcdefffghiklmnopqrsſſßſtuvwxyz.

Auf, auf, ihr Kinder, und zieht euch an,
Die Glock ſchlägt Sechs, euch weckt der Hahn.

Der Hahn hat oft gekrähet heut,
Steh auf, mein Kind, es iſt ſchon Zeit,
Zur Schul zu gehn. O! lerne wohl,
Was Lebenslang dir nützen ſoll.

A a b
c d e f
ff ſi ſl
g h ch i k ck l ll m
n o p q r r ſ ſſ s ß
ſt t u v w x y z tz.

A B C D E F G H I K L M N
O P Q R S T U V W X Y Z.

Die lauten Buchſtaben:
a e i o u y.

Die ſtummen Buchſtaben:
b c d f g h k l m n p q r ſ s t v w x z.

Hamburg,
zu haben bey J. D. Neiſe.

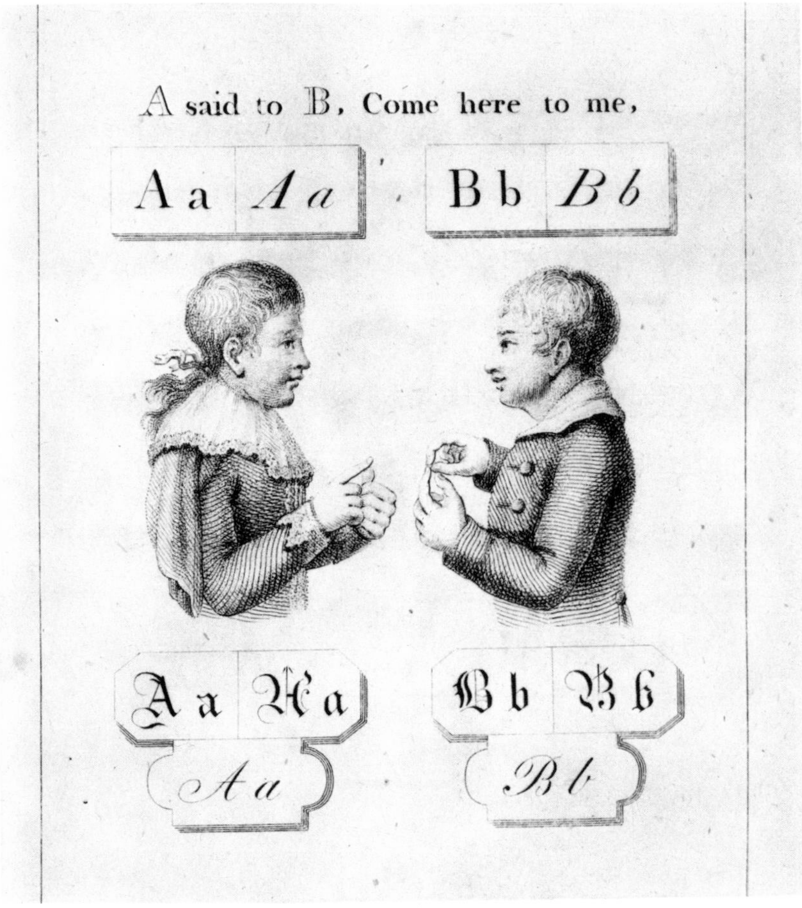
A said to B, Come here to me,
Aa Aa
Bb Bb
Aa Aa
Bb Bb
Aa
Bb

57

J jump'd over it. j

58

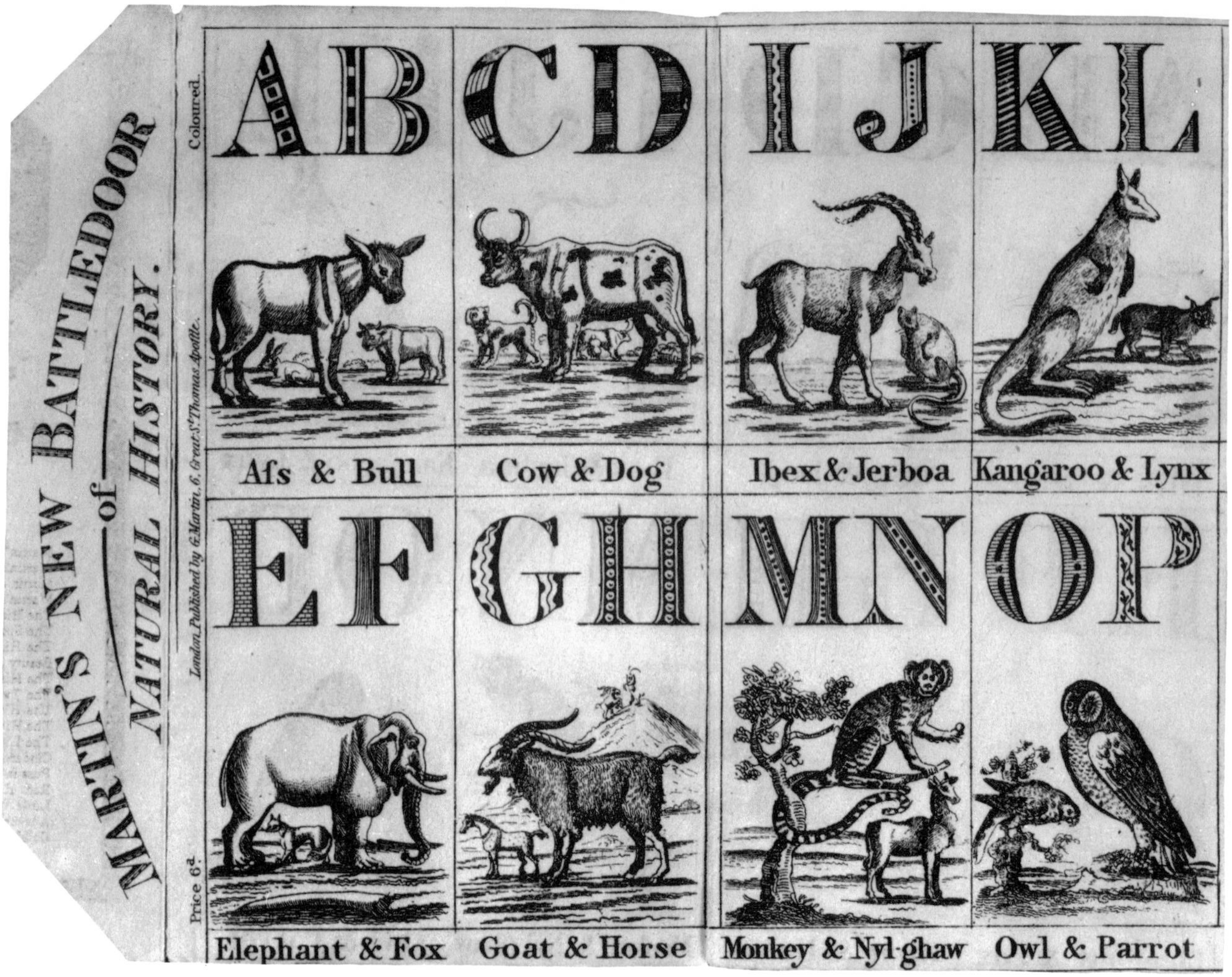
MARTIN'S NEW BATTLEDOOR
of
NATURAL HISTORY.
London, Published by G. Martin, 6, Great St Thomas Apostle.
Coloured.
Price 6d.
A B C D I J K L
Afs & Bull
Cow & Dog
Ibex & Jerboa
Kangaroo & Lynx
E F G H M N O P
Elephant & Fox
Goat & Horse
Monkey & Nyl-ghaw
Owl & Parrot

59

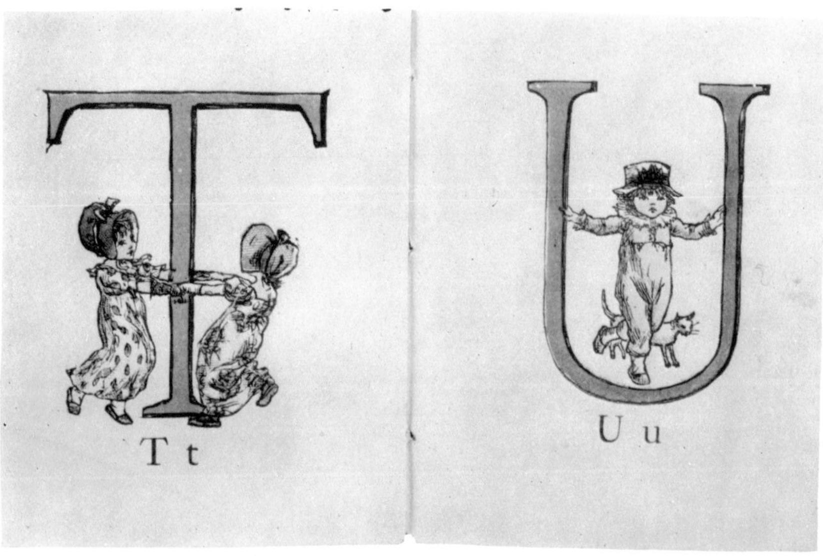
T t
U u

62

Primers and Readers

The children's books known as primers have a very long history. As early as the fourteenth century in England the term "primer" was applied to Books of Hours in which the text was at least partly translated from Latin into English. These were of course devotional books, but they were well suited to the instruction of children in reading. By the sixteenth century, alphabets and lists of vowels, consonants, and syllables were being incorporated into the primers along with their religious contents. These contents were increasingly English rather than Latin; and the word "children" was appearing more frequently on the title pages. It would be centuries before the primer would be entirely transmuted from a devotional manual to a secular alphabet-and-reading book, but the process was under way.

63 THE PRYMER IN ENGLYSHE FOR CHILDREN, AFTER THE USE OF SALISBURYE.

London: [? John Day], 1556.
13.5 cm. 80 f.
STC 16075. Hoskins 222. Butterworth.*

A type-ornament border that incorporates human figures surrounds the title page of this mid-sixteenth-century English primer for children. It is believed that this book was produced by the celebrated John Day, one of the greatest of English printers. This is the sole known copy of the book.

64 [?Benjamin Harris]

THE NEW-ENGLAND PRIMER ENLARGED: FOR THE MORE EASY ATTAINING THE TRUE READING OF ENGLISH. TO WHICH IS ADDED, THE ASSEMBLY OF DIVINES AND MR. COTTON'S CATECHISMS.

Boston: T. and J. Fleet, 1763.
9.5 cm. [*31*] *f.*: [*A*]^{8}, *B*^{6}, *C*^{6}, *D*^{8}, *E*^{4}. (*Incomplete: first leaf wanting.*) *Brown calf over wooden boards.*
Heartman 20.

One of the relatively few surviving early copies of *The New England Primer*, a work probably first published about 1686 but of which no copy is extant before 1727. The influence of this early American children's book can hardly be overestimated. It went into thousands of American homes, where for generations it was, next to the Bible, probably the book most frequently given to children. It became a powerful factor in the education of countless young Americans.

The authorship, and the printing and publishing as well, of *The New England Primer* have generally been attributed to the London printer Benjamin Harris, a rabid anti-Catholic who came to Boston from England in 1686 after having fallen afoul of the authorities in London. In 1679, while still in London, Harris produced *The Protestant Tutor*, which contained many elements—alphabet, Lord's Prayer, the burning of the martyr John Rogers—later found in *The New England Primer*. There is an entry in the Stationers' Register of London, dated 5 October 1683, for a *New England Primer* in the name of one "John Gain"; but almost nothing is known of this person, and it has been speculated that the name Gain might have been an alias used by Harris. In this connection, it is interesting to note the similarity between the tiny woodcut illustrations in *The New England Primer* shown here and those in the 1724 *Holy Bible in Verse* (see item 74), a work also attributed to Benjamin Harris.

65 [?John Newbery]

THE ROYAL PRIMER: OR, AN EASY AND PLEASANT GUIDE TO THE ART OF READING.

London: J. Newberry [sic], [*between 1750 and 1767*].
10 cm. [*3*], *4–78*, [*2*] *p.* *Dutch flowered wrappers.*
Roscoe J324. *Heartman*, Non-New England Primers, *157.* *Merritt.*
Purchased for the Elisabeth Ball Collection.

Il présente une chaise.

38

On ne baille pas en compagnie

38

R. L. Wright sculp.

A NOBLE HELMET.

37

R. L. Wright sculp.

A NOBLE HELMET.

37

The most famous early publisher of children's books, John Newbery, was probably the author of this primer, which represents a softening of the stern (not to say harsh) theological character of *The New England Primer*. The very subtitle, "An easy and pleasant guide to the art of reading," announces an approach and a goal quite different from those of *The New England Primer*. First published about 1750, *The Royal Primer* won great popularity on both sides of the Atlantic and was steadily reprinted and emulated. It is thought to have had a humanizing influence on later versions of *The New England Primer*. The publishing history of the Newbery editions of *The Royal Primer* is obscure, and establishing the year of publication in the case of an undated copy such as the one illustrated here is extremely difficult, if not impossible. Consequently, all that can safely be said about the date of this copy of *The Royal Primer* is that it was published some time between 1750 and 1767, the year of John Newbery's death. It is one of perhaps two known copies of this edition.

66 [Thomas Bewick]

A NEW LOTTERY BOOK OF BIRDS AND BEASTS, FOR CHILDREN TO LEARN THEIR LETTERS BY AS SOON AS THEY CAN SPEAK.

Newcastle: T. Saint for W. Charnley, 1771.
10 cm. [30] f. Dutch flowered boards.
Weekley, p. 106. Hugo 4.
Purchased as the gift of the Viscount Astor.

The English wood-engraver Thomas Bewick did not finish his apprenticeship until 1774, but before then, in 1771 at the age of eighteen, he produced this little primer. Its illustrations are significant not only because they are the first animal pictures engraved by the man who would go on to become the greatest of all English wood-engravers. The illustrations also represent a break with the tradition of crude, slapdash woodcut pictures in books for children. Thomas Bewick's increasingly skillful work—and that of his younger brother John, who soon joined him—would create new and far higher standards for the illustration of children's books. *A New Lottery Book of Birds and Beasts* contains the beginnings of the artistry that would characterize all the subsequent books Thomas Bewick produced for the young. Each recto page, such as that illustrated here, presents a bird-vignette above a beast-vignette. Some word-exercises and short sentences from the Scriptures complete the primer. This is the first edition.

67 "Toby Ticklepitcher"

THE HOBBY-HORSE, OR CHRISTMAS COMPANION: CONTAINING . . . THE SONG OF A COCK AND A BULL, A CANTERBURY STORY, AND A TALE OF A TUB. FAITHFULLY COPIED FROM THE ORIGINAL MANUSCRIPT, IN THE VATICAN LIBRARY.

London: E. Newbery, 1784.
10.5 cm. [2], 5–61, [2] p. (Last leaf is a pastedown.) Red and gold flowered wrappers.
Roscoe J354 (Dutch flowered boards).
Elisabeth Ball Collection.

The alphabet that occupies the first page of this primer begins "A was an Arch Boy" and ends as the illustration shows. Also included are some Moral Sentences to memorize. The opening lines of "A Tale of a Tub" contain what may be an allusion to Oliver Goldsmith. The author of *The Vicar of Wakefield* is of course known to have written frequently for the Newbery publishing enterprises, and it is quite possible that he produced this little primer. Goldsmith died in 1774, but this work was advertised in the *London Chronicle* as early as 1771. No copy survives, however, of any edition before 1784. The Morgan Library copy, which is unique, is the earliest known.

68 A PRIMER, FOR THE USE OF THE MOHAWK CHILDREN, TO ACQUIRE THE SPELLING AND READING OF THEIR OWN, AS WELL AS TO GET ACQUAINTED WITH THE ENGLISH, TONGUE; WHICH FOR THAT PURPOSE IS PUT ON THE OPPOSITE PAGE.

London: C. Buckton, 1786.
13 cm. [2], 2–98 p.
Sabin 65547–65548. James, p. 32.
Elisabeth Ball Collection.

The first London edition of the very rare first Mohawk-English primer. This is the second edition of the primer; the first edition was printed in Montreal in 1781 and is known today in but a single copy. The frontispiece depicts Indian children in school. It is by James Peachey, an English artist who is believed to have spent some time working in North America.

69 LE GUIDE ASSURÉ DE L'ENFANCE.

Le Locle: Girardet, [about 1789].
20.5 cm. [1], 27 p.
Gumuchian 137.
Elisabeth Ball Collection.

A rare and artistic reading-book intended for French-speaking Swiss children—rather sophisticated children, it would appear—of the late eighteenth century. The engravings that accompany the moralizing descriptive text are by Girardet, the publisher of the work. The book is one of the earliest examples known of printing in Le Locle, in the Swiss canton of Neuchâtel. The Morgan Library copy is the first edition.

70 [Thomas Dobson]
FIRST LESSONS FOR CHILDREN.

Philadelphia: T. Dobson, 1797.
15.5 cm. [2], 3–36 p. Gray wrappers.
Welch 275.1. Evans 32054.
Gift of Charles Ryskamp, in honor of Miss Elisabeth Ball.

The printer of this eighteenth-century American primer was also its author. (A separate title page of the book is in the collection of the Library of Congress in Washington, D.C., with the following inscription on its verso: "deposited 6. March 1797 by T. Dobson as Author.") The copy illustrated here, one of a very few that are recorded, is in remarkable condition, some of its leaves still being unopened. This fact makes it an item of particular interest, for on the pages within the unopened folds there are colored woodcuts—indicating that the coloring was done by the printer before the book's sheets were folded and stitched, and not by a later child-owner of the book. This would therefore appear to be an extremely early example of an American children's book issued with colored illustrations.

71 THE YOUNG CHILD'S ABC, OR, FIRST BOOK.

New York: Samuel Wood, 1806.
9.5 cm. [2], 3–16 p. Gray printed wrappers.
Hamilton 235. Rosenbach 325.
Gift of Charles Ryskamp, in honor of Miss Elisabeth Ball.

A pleasantly illustrated alphabet runs across the tops of the pages of this early-nineteenth-century American primer, the first children's book to be published by Samuel Wood of New York. The cuts are thought to be the work of America's foremost early wood-engraver, Alexander Anderson. Samuel Wood subsequently published a large number of children's books, and he is known to have commissioned Anderson to illustrate many of them.

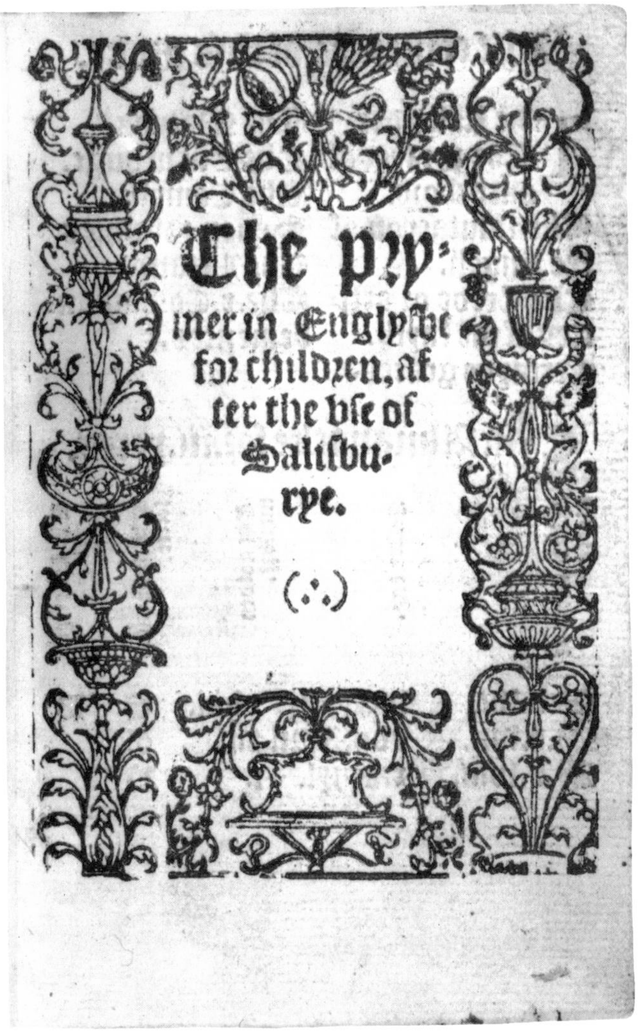

The pry-
mer in Englyshe
for chyldren, af-
ter the vse of
Salisbu-
rye.

(.·.)

63

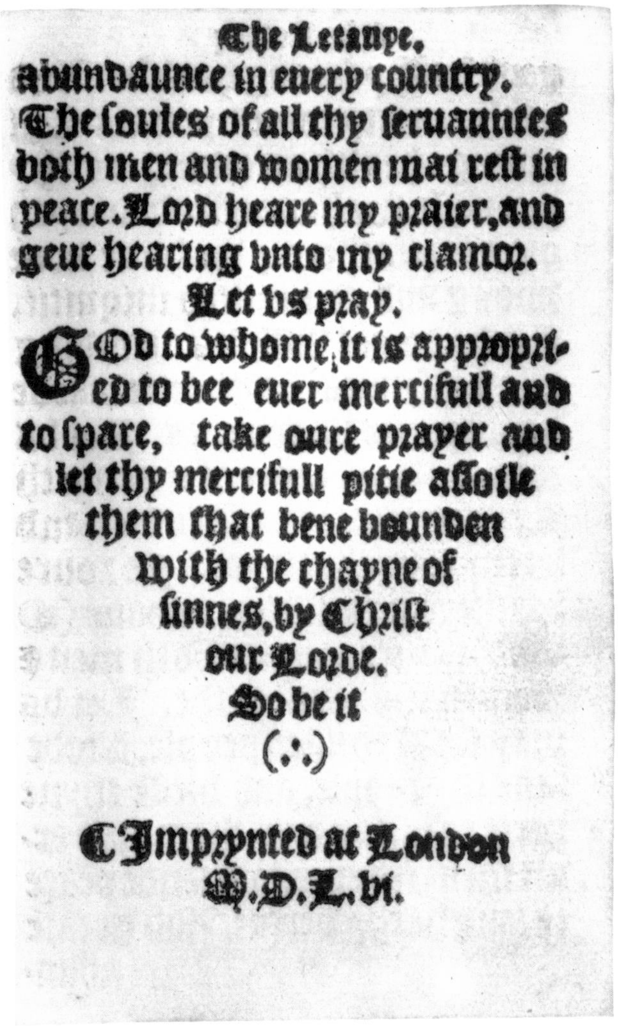

The Letanye.
abundaunce in euery country.
The soules of all thy seruauntes
both men and women mai rest in
peace. Lord heare my praier, and
geue hearing vnto my clamor.
Let vs pray.
GOd to whome it is appropri-
ed to bee euer mercifull and
to spare, take oure prayer and
let thy mercifull pitie assoile
them that bene bounden
with the chayne of
sinnes, by Christ
our Lorde.
So be it
(.·.)

¶ Imprynted at London
M.D.L.vi.

63

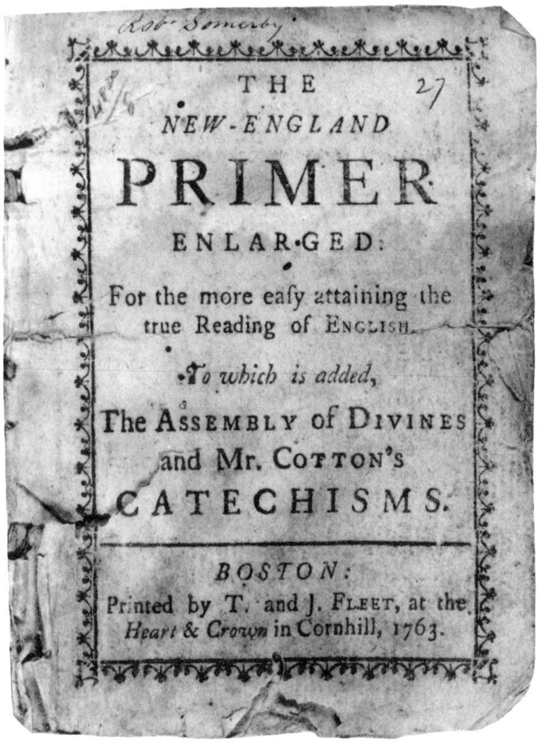

THE
NEW-ENGLAND
PRIMER
ENLARGED:
For the more eaſy attaining the
true Reading of ENGLISH.
To which is added,
The ASSEMBLY of DIVINES
and Mr. COTTON's
CATECHISMS.

BOSTON:
Printed by T. and J. FLEET, at the
Heart & Crown in Cornhill, 1763.

64

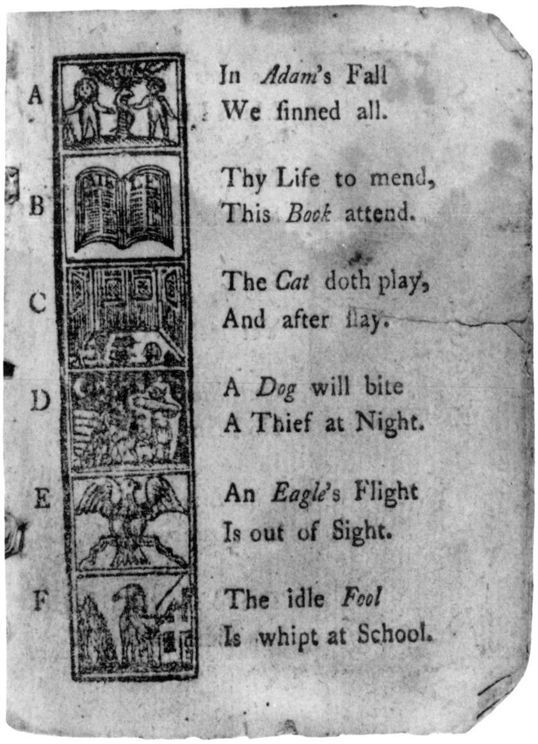

A In *Adam's* Fall
We ſinned all.

B Thy Life to mend,
This *Book* attend.

C The *Cat* doth play,
And after ſlay.

D A *Dog* will bite
A Thief at Night.

E An *Eagle's* Flight
Is out of Sight.

F The idle *Fool*
Is whipt at School.

64

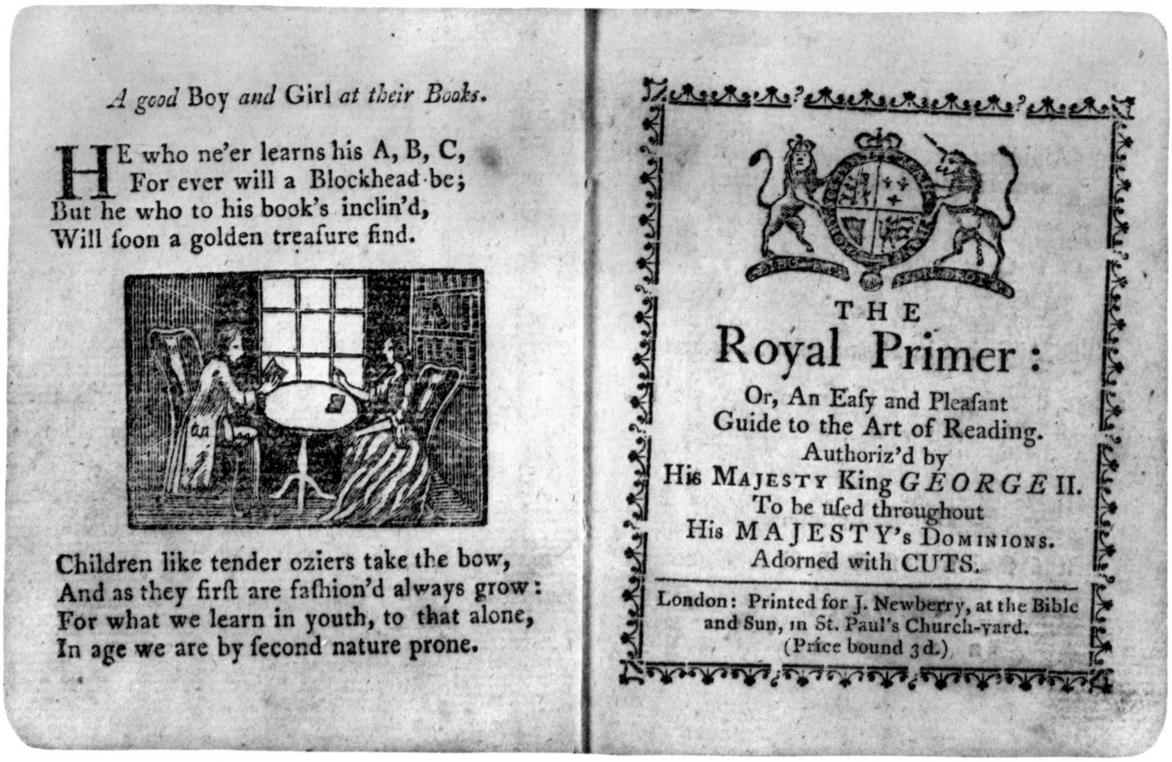
A good Boy *and* Girl *at their Books.*

HE who ne'er learns his A, B, C,
For ever will a Blockhead be;
But he who to his book's inclin'd,
Will ſoon a golden treaſure find.

Children like tender oziers take the bow,
And as they firſt are faſhion'd always grow:
For what we learn in youth, to that alone,
In age we are by ſecond nature prone.

THE
Royal Primer:
Or, An Eaſy and Pleaſant
Guide to the Art of Reading.
Authoriz'd by
His MAJESTY King *GEORGE* II.
To be uſed throughout
His MAJESTY's DOMINIONS.
Adorned with CUTS.

London: Printed for J. Newberry, at the Bible
and Sun, in St. Paul's Church-yard.
(Price bound 3d.)

65

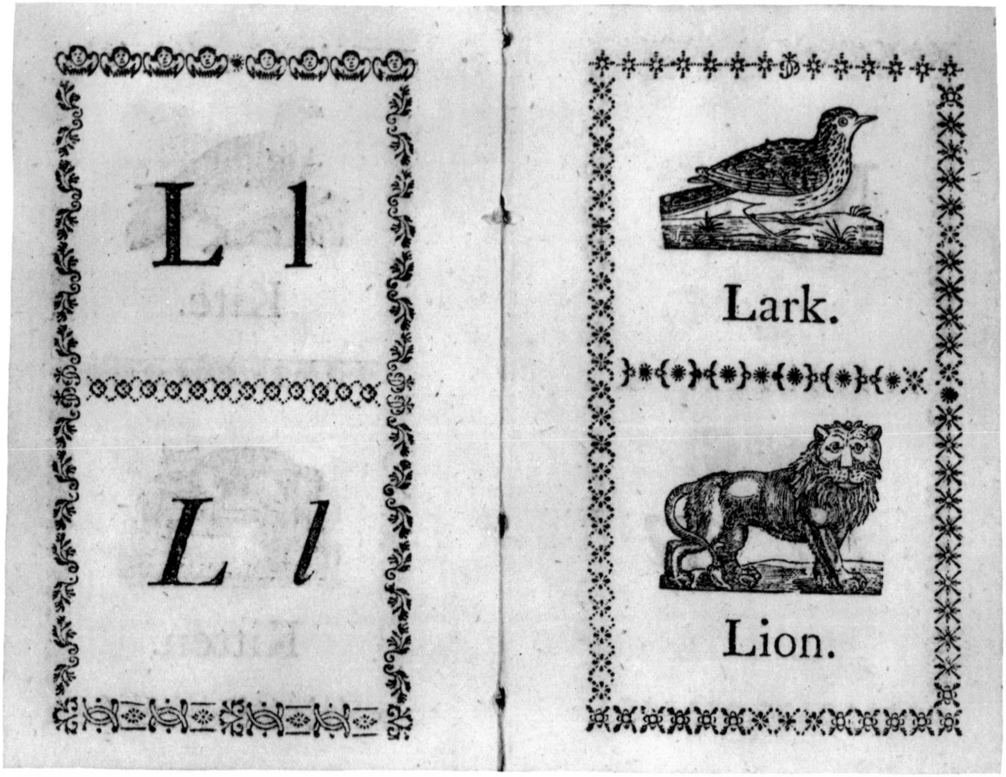
L l

L l

Lark.

Lion.

66

THE

HOBBY-HORSE,

OR

CHRISTMAS COMPANION:

CONTAINING

Among other interefting Particulars,

The Song of a COCK and a BULL,

A

CANTERBURY STORY,

AND

A TALE OF A TUB.

Faithfully copied from the original Manu-
fcript, in the Vatican Library.

By TOBY TICKLEPITCHER.

Embellifhed with elegant Cuts.

LONDON:

Printed for E. NEWBERY, at the Corner of
St. Paul's Church-Yard. 1784.

[Price Two-pence.]

67

Y.

A Youth well-fhaped and tall.

Z.

Whips up the Rear.

67

A

TALE OF A TUB.

I.

THE Wakefield vicar's verfes fhow,
To all who mark his Song,
Man wants but little here below,
Nor wants that little long.

II.

A Scrip with vegetables fill'd,
A mat whereon to reft,
A Cell, a Garden half untill'd,
May make a man full bleft.

III.

If then a Cell content can give,
While thro' this life we rub,
Why may not I contented live,
And happy in a TUB.

E 3 The

67

A

PRIMER,

FOR THE USE OF THE

MOHAWK CHILDREN,

To acquire the SPELLING and READING of their OWN, as well as to get acquainted with the ENGLISH, Tongue; which for that Purpoſe is put on the oppoſite Page.

WAERIGHWAGHSAWE IKSAONGOENWA

Tſiwaondad-derighhonny Kaghyadoghſera; Nayondeweyeſtaghk ayeweanaghnòdon ayeghyàdow Kaniyenkehàga Kaweanondaghkouh; Dyorheaſ-hàga oni tſinihadiweanotea.

LONDON,

PRINTED BY C. BUCKTON, GREAT PULTNEY-STREET.

1786.

69

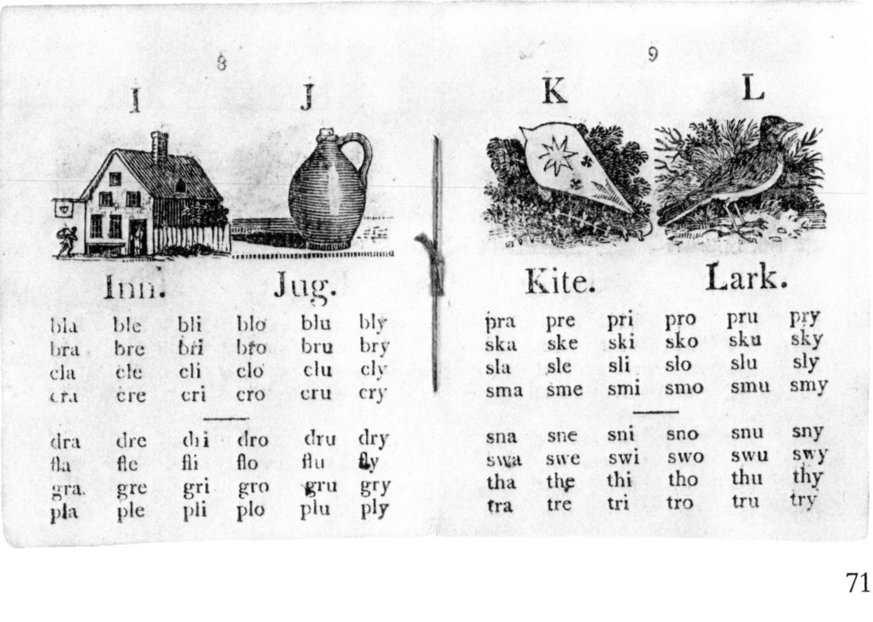

8

I J

Inn. Jug.

bla	ble	bli	blo	blu	bly
bra	bre	bri	bro	bru	bry
cla	cle	cli	clo	clu	cly
cra	cre	cri	cro	cru	cry
dra	dre	dri	dro	dru	dry
fla	fle	fli	flo	flu	fly
gra	gre	gri	gro	gru	gry
pla	ple	pli	plo	plu	ply

9

K L

Kite. Lark.

pra	pre	pri	pro	pru	pry
ska	ske	ski	sko	sku	sky
sla	sle	sli	slo	slu	sly
sma	sme	smi	smo	smu	smy
sna	sne	sni	sno	snu	sny
swa	swe	swi	swo	swu	swy
tha	the	thi	tho	thu	thy
tra	tre	tri	tro	tru	try

71

Religious Books

72 John Foxe

ACTES AND MONUMENTS . . . TOUCHING MATTERS OF THE CHURCH.

London: John Day, 1562, 1563.
32 cm. 2 vols.: [25], 2–888 (i.e., 944); 889–1741, [39] (i.e., 1898) p. + plates.
STC 11222.

In sixteenth-century England there were no children's books even remotely resembling those of the present day. But neither, in a sense, were there any children like those today. Adults beheld the young (and the young were forced to behold themselves) through the dark glass of Original Sin. Children were "brands of Hell." Almost the only books directed at them were designed to save them from the Devil. Bibles, lives of the Christian martyrs, works of religious exhortation, a few courtesy books, some grammars—there were virtually no other books for children. But children have always, as soon as they could read (and even before), picked up whatever book might be within reach. In the absence of children's books as we know them today, many improbable works served the young. These included bestiaries, of course—what child could resist the pictures?—but also such works of lofty intent as Foxe's Book of Martyrs. This book (its real title was *Actes and Monuments . . . Touching Matters of the Church*) was frequently given to children. It was adored by the young in a way its author never intended. What attracted children—what they thrilled to—were the flame-filled pictures of martyrs and their tormentors. Principally because of these horrific illustrations, the work became a favorite of children from the nursery age onward. The first edition in English is illustrated here; this is the version of the work that was most familiar in England, although it had first appeared in a Latin version published in Basel in 1559.

73 John Weever

AN AGNUS DEI.

London: Val. Sims for Nicholas Lyng, 1601.
3.5 cm. [128] f.
STC 25220. Roscoe, Bibles, *1.*
Loaned by Miss Julia P. Wightman.

This miniature volume, produced at the very beginning of the seventeenth century, is an abridged New Testament in rhymed couplets. (The frontispiece is a crowned Tudor rose.) The pages, each containing one couplet, are set in a pleasantly spaced type and are quite readable. With its minuscule but easily legible format and its simple text, lending itself to memorizing, Weever's book must have been a natural choice to give to children in an age when the Bible was practically the only acceptable reading matter for the young. In the mid-eighteenth century Thomas Boreman, one of the earliest publishers to pay serious attention to children's books, would adopt a format much like Weever's. But even before then would come a series of miniature Bibles, called "Thumb Bibles," all clearly inspired by this *Agnus Dei*. The copy illustrated here is the first edition; it is one of two recorded copies.

74 [Benjamin Harris]

THE HOLY BIBLE IN VERSE.

[? Boston: ? John Allen], 1724.
9 cm. Fragment: [15] f.
Welch 452.3.
Elisabeth Ball Collection.

An abridged, rhyming version of the Bible. The author, Benjamin Harris, was a firebrand whose anti-Catholicism was so virulent that it drew him into trouble with the authorities in Protestant England. He fled to America in 1686 and there wrote the renowned *New England Primer* for children. Later Harris returned to England, where in 1698 he brought out *The Holy Bible in Verse*. The book was first published in America in 1717, by John Allen of Boston, with whom Harris, who was a publisher as well as a writer, had been in partnership briefly during his American sojourn. The fragmentary copy shown here is from an edition (probably the third) brought out by Allen in Boston in 1724. It is the only copy of this edition known to survive.

75 BIBLIA OR A PRACTICAL SUMMARY OF YE OLD AND NEW TESTAMENTS.

London: R. Wilkin, 1727.
4 cm. [4], 278, [6] p.
Spielmann 15B. Roscoe, Bibles, *22.*
Purchased for the Elisabeth Ball Collection.

The first English miniature Bible for children. The anonymous text of this abridgment was used later in a series of miniature Bibles brought out by various children's-book publishers, Elizabeth Newbery among them, from 1771 on. Known as "Newbery Bibles," these later miniature books were illustrated with tiny engravings copied from, but much inferior to, the engravings in this Wilkin publication. The copy illustrated here is from the very rare first issue of the first edition; Wilkin subsequently issued the book with the 1727 on the title page altered in ink to 1728.

76 THE CHILDRENS BIBLE.

London: Printed, And, Dublin: Re-printed by Ann Law, 1763.
12 cm. [5], vi–xiv, [1], 16–224 p. Brown calf.
Gumuchian 1709.
Elisabeth Ball Collection.

A simplified version of the Old and New Testaments, "reduced to the tender Capacities of the little Readers, by a lively and striking Abstract." The title page's frank—and for this period still relatively uncommon—declaration of an intention to entertain children while administering the Bible to them is diluted somewhat by the author in his preface, wherein he points out that "the BIBLE is no fit PLAY-THING FOR CHILDREN." This is an augmented edition of a work first published in 1759. The "Divine of the Church of England" mentioned on the title page has not been identified, although the dedication is signed "N. H."

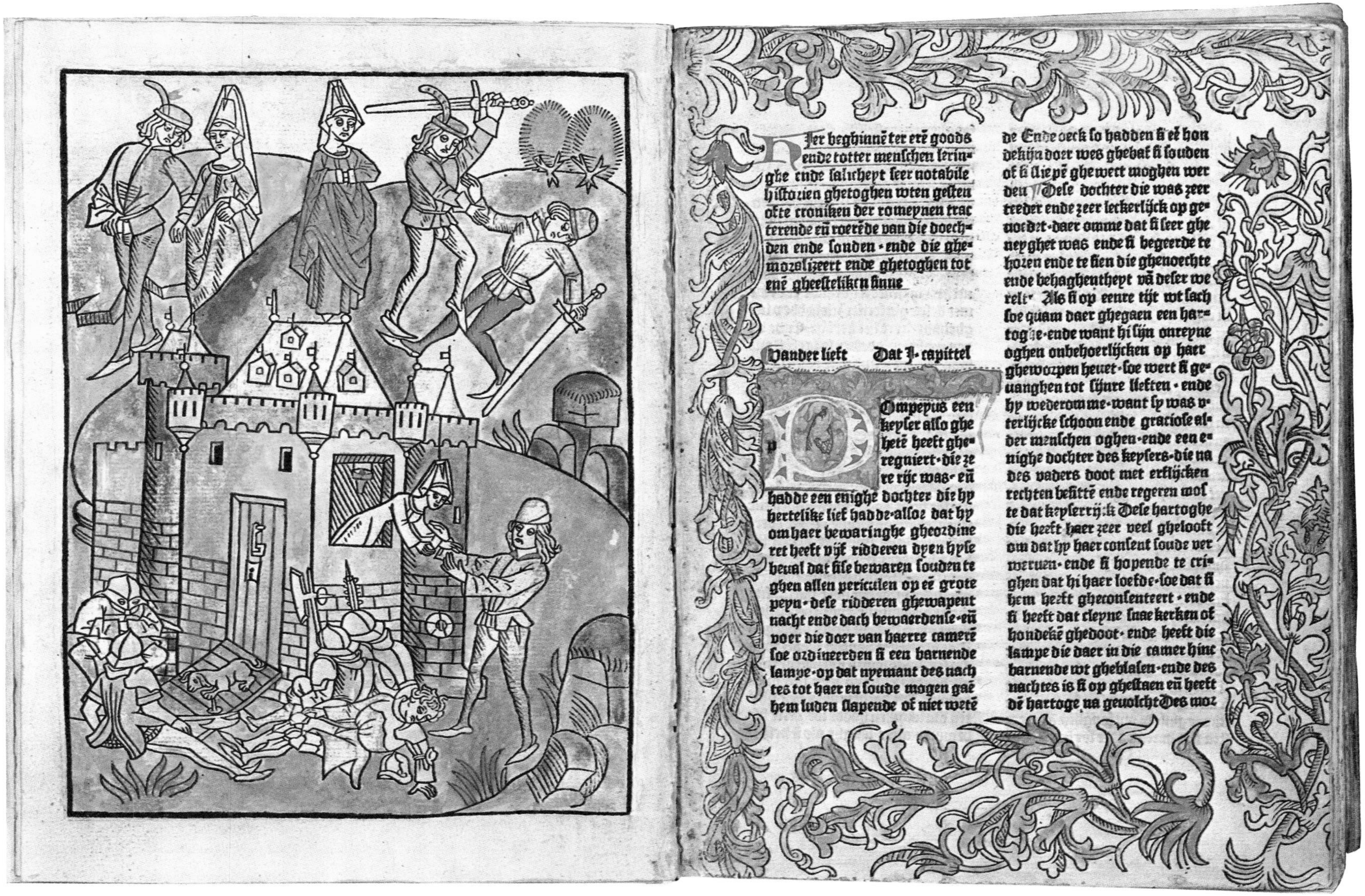

Her beghinnẽ ter erẽ goods
ende totter menschen lerin-
ghe ende salichept seer notabile
historien ghetoghen wten gesten
ofte croniken der romeynen trac
terende eñ roerẽde van die doech-
den ende sonden · ende die ghe-
morsliseert ende ghetoghen tot
enẽ gheestelikẽ sinne

Vander liefte Dat .I. capittel

Ompeyus een
keyser also ghe
hetẽ heeft ghe-
regniert · die ze
re rijc was · eñ
hadde een enighe dochter die hy
hertelike lief hadde · alsoe dat hy
om haer bewaringhe gheordine
ret heeft vijf ridderen dyen hyse
beual dat sise bewaren souden te
ghen allen pericullen op eẽ grote
peyn · dese ridderen ghewapent
nacht ende dach bewaerdense · eñ
voer die doer van haerre camerẽ
soe ordineerden si een barnende
lampe · op dat nyemant des nach
tes tot haer en soude mogen gaẽ
hem luden slapende of niet wetẽ
de Ende oeck so hadden si eẽ hon
dekijn doer wes ghebar si souden
of si sliepẽ ghewect moghen wer
den Dese dochter die was zeer
teeder ende zeer leckerlijck op ge-
voedet · daer omme dat si seer ghe
neyghet was ende si begeerde te
horen ende te sien die ghenoechte
ende behaghenthept vã deser we
relt · Als si op eenre tijt wt sach
soe quam daer ghegaen een hartoghe · ende want hi sijn onreyne
oghen onbehoerlijcken op haer
ghewozpen heuet · soe wert si ge-
uanghen tot sijnre liefter · ende
hy wederomme · want sy was v-
terlijcke schoon ende gracIose al-
der menschen oghen · ende een e-
nighe dochter des keysers · die na
des vaders doot met erflijcken
rechten besittẽ ende regeren mos
te dat keyserrijck Dese hartoghe
die heeft haer zeer veel ghelooft
om dat hy haer consent soude ver
weruen · ende si hopende te cri-
ghen dat hi haer loefde · soe dat si
hem heeft gheconsenteert · ende
si heeft dat cleyne snae kerken of
hondekẽ ghedoot · ende heeft die
lampe die daer in die camer hinc
barnende wt gheblasen · ende des
nachtes is si op ghestaen eñ heeft
dẽ hartoge na geuolcht Des mor

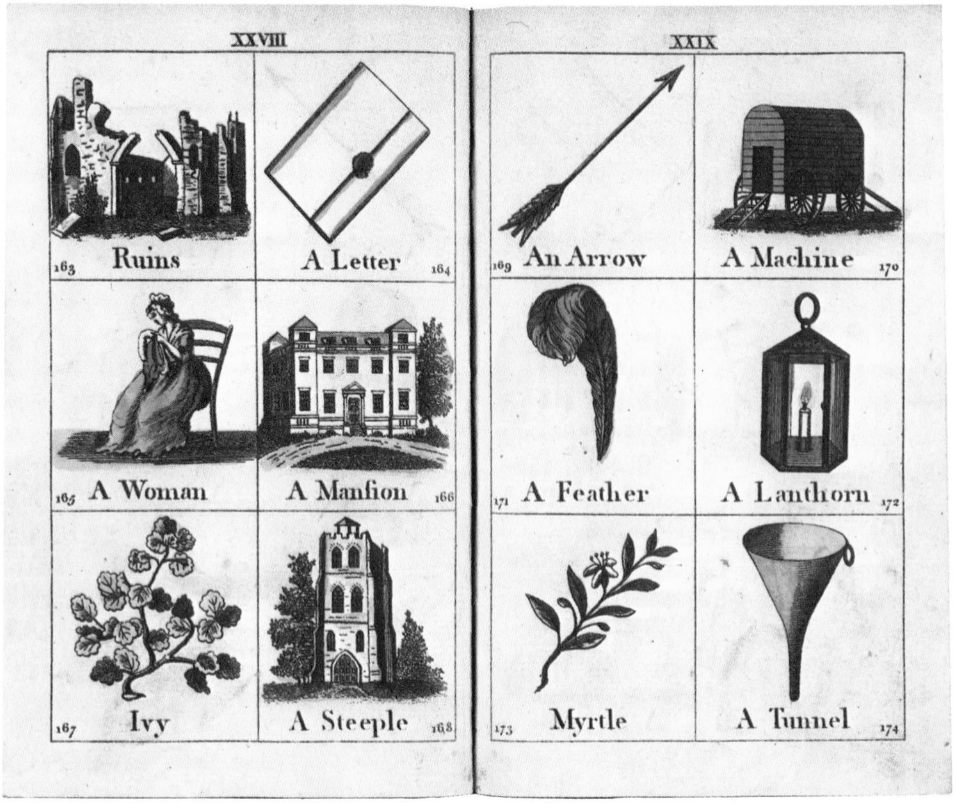
XXVIII
XXIX
163 Ruins
A Letter 164
169 An Arrow
A Machine 170
165 A Woman
A Manfion 166
171 A Feather
A Lanthorn 172
167 Ivy
A Steeple 168
173 Myrtle
A Tunnel 174

56

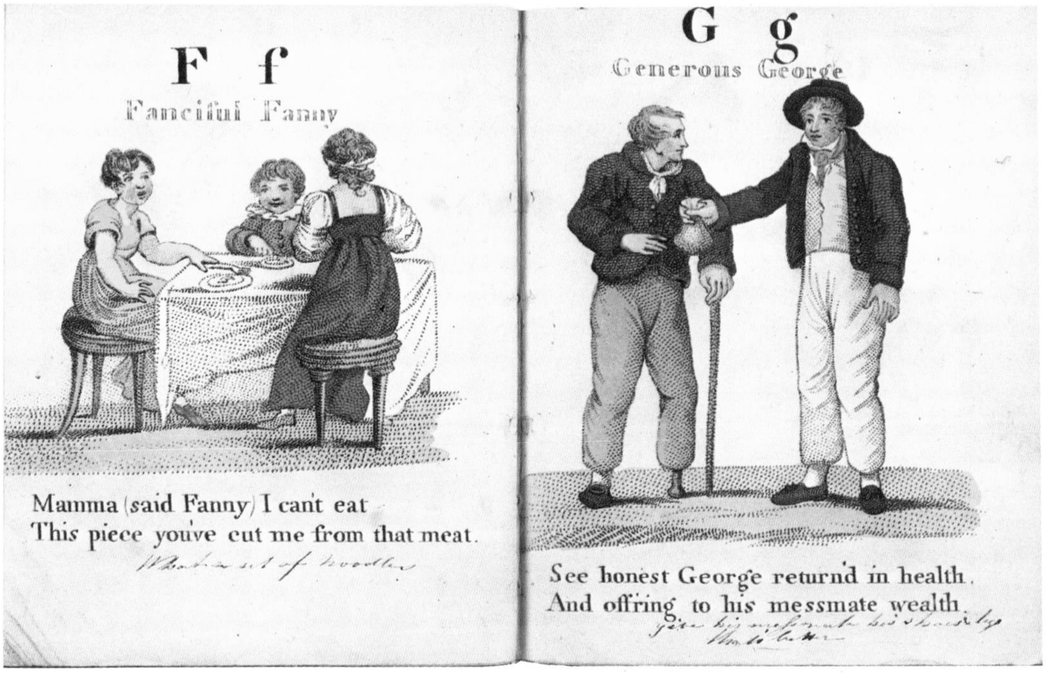
F f
Fanciful Fanny
Mamma (said Fanny) I can't eat
This piece you've cut me from that meat.
G g
Generous George
See honest George return'd in health,
And off'ring to his messmate wealth.

60

77 [Oliver Goldsmith]

AN HISTORY OF THE LIVES, ACTIONS, TRAVELS, SUFFERINGS, AND DEATHS OF THE MOST EMINENT MARTYRS, AND PRIMITIVE FATHERS OF THE CHURCH.

London: J. Newbery, 1764.
9.5 cm. [4], 228 p. Buff printed boards.
Roscoe J148 (Dutch flowered boards). NBL 124.
Elisabeth Ball Collection.

This little work, written by Oliver Goldsmith for the publisher John Newbery, bears a strong resemblance in its subject matter to Foxe's Book of Martyrs. Unlike Foxe's work, however, this book was published specifically for children. Newbery apparently intended it to be one of the volumes (Number IV) in a series of religious books called The Young Christian's Library, advertisements for which are found in issues of the *London Chronicle* and *Lloyd's English Post* during 1764. The Morgan Library copy of the Goldsmith book is the first edition, one of two recorded copies.

78 A CURIOUS HIEROGLYPHIC BIBLE . . . FOR THE AMUSEMENT OF YOUTH.

Worcester, Massachusetts: Isaiah Thomas, 1788.
14 cm. Incomplete: [2], 9–142 p.
Welch 468. Rosenbach 128. Hamilton 122.
Elisabeth Ball Collection.

"Hieroglyphics," or rebuses, have been long employed in books for the young. This book uses these pictorial devices to entice children into reading the Bible (and provides the clear text at the bottom of the page). Such Bibles became quite popular in the eighteenth century. The volume illustrated here is from the press of the renowned American printer Isaiah Thomas. It is the first edition of the first hieroglyphic Bible to be printed in America.

79 [Hannah More]

MOSES IN THE BULRUSHES: A SACRED DRAMA.

Worcester, Massachusetts: I. Thomas, Jun., June 1802.
10 cm. [4], 6–31 p. (First and last leaves are pastedowns.) Green flowered wrappers (bound in).
Welch 809.2.
Elisabeth Ball Collection.

Hannah More's collection of short plays, *Sacred Dramas, Chiefly Intended for Young Persons*, was first published in England in 1782. These plays were among the earliest to be written specifically for children to stage themselves. The purpose, as with all Hannah More's writings for children, was religious uplift; all the plays were on Biblical themes. This rare separate edition of *Moses in the Bulrushes* was brought out in America by Isaiah Thomas, Junior, who continued the Thomas practice of publishing American children's books from English originals.

truely, and to kepe faithfully, charitably, and continually all the commaundementes of God, and so than to pray deuoutly to al the blessed trinitie, that I may haue grace with wisdom & prudence from aboue, to end my life here in this forsaid truthe and for this cause, in true fauth and stedfast hope, and persit charitie. Amen.

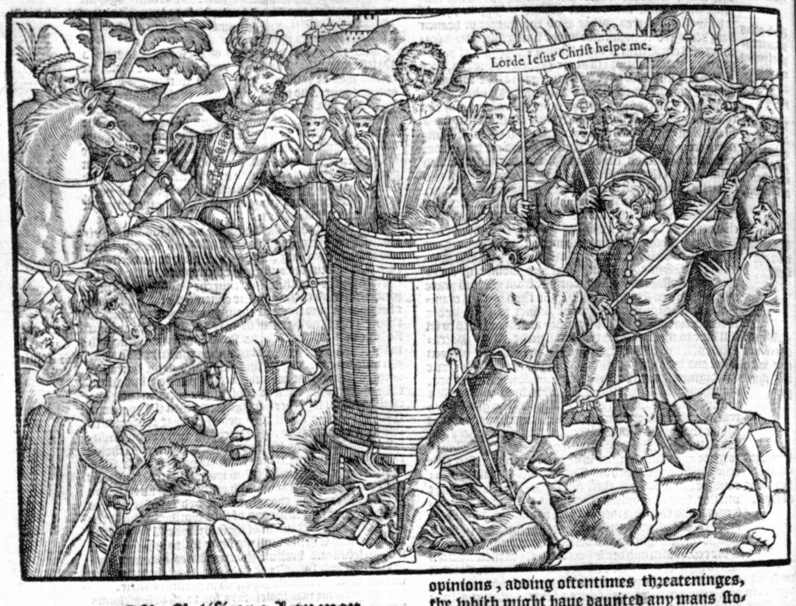
Lorde Iesus Christ helpe me.

¶ An Artificer a Lay man.

1410. After this priest folowed an handecraftes mā, in the yeare of our Lorde M. iiii. C. x. he held this opinion, that it was not the body of Christe really, the whiche was sacramentally vsed in the churche: when as he could by no meanes be perswaded from the constancie of this opinion, but that he had wholy determined with him self to die therin, he was deliuered ouer to the seculer power. And when as the sentence of his condemnatiō was geuen against him, and that this valiaūt Martyr of Christ should be caried into a market place without the citie to be included in a pype or tunne, for so muche as Cherillus Bul was not then in vre amongst the byshops, as it happened the prince the eldest sonne of kyng Henry was there present: this man as a good Samaritane, indeuored him selfe to saue the life of him, whome the vnshamefast Leuites & Phariseis sought to put to death: he admonished and counseled him that hauing respect vnto him selfe, he should spedely withdrawe him selfe out of these daungerous Laberynthes of opinions, adding oftentimes threateninges, the which might haue daunted any mans stomack. But this valiaunt champion of Christe neglecting the princes fayre wordes and vanquishing all mens deuises, fully determined, rather to suffer any kinde of tormente were it neuer so greuous, then so great Idolatry and wickednes. whereupon being inclosed in the pype or tonne, he was tormēted by the raging flame. The innocent soule moste miserably roring and criyng out in the middest of the fier. With whiche horrible crie the Prince beynge moued, he cometh agayne vnto the man to reclaime hym vnto life (that pytie and mercye whyche commen sence of nature wrought in him, the same by this cruel new deuyse or new crueltie of so straūge death, was double in him augmēted) he cōmaunded ẏ fyer to be drawen backe and takē away, he comforted him which was tormēted, promysing him yet hope of his lyfe, if he would consent vnto his counsels: adding moreouer that he should haue certayne yearly stipend geuē him out of the kynges treasury, asmuch as shold suffise for his sustētatiō. But againe he refused the offer of wordly promyses, without al doubt being more vehemētly inflamed with the spirite of God then with any earthly desire. Wherfore when as yet he continued vnmouable in his former mynde, the prince commaunded him straight to be put againe into the Pype or Tunne, and that he should not afterward loke for any grace or fauour. But as he could be allured by no rewardes, euen so was he nothing at al abashed at their tormentes, but as a valiaunt champiō of Christe, he perseuered inuincible vnto the ende. Notwithout a great and mooste cruell battaile, but with muche more greater triumphe of victory, the spirite of Christ hauing all wayes the vpperhande in his members, maugre the fury rage & power of ẏ whole world. — A maruelous example of constancy

¶ Here cometh in the story of Syr John Oldcastel knight, Lord Cobhā, who in this year of our lord M. iiii. C. xiii. was apprehendid and cast into the towre, also examined & condemned by the bishops, but for so muche as he suffred not vntill the yeare of our Lorde M. iiii. C. xviii. we will prosecute our Story with Sir Roger Acton & others, which suffered in the meane tyme.

¶ Sir Roger Acton knight, Maister John Browne Gentilman, John Beuerle a preacher, with many other more in this yeare. M. iiii. C. xiii. in the moneth of January, they were put to death for the syncere and pure Religion.

1413. As sone as kyng Henry the fift, had begon his raigne euē at the same time when the Lord Cobham was caste into the towre, the bishoppes and the Diuines with importunate supplications and cries, renued a greuous complaint vnto the kinge as touchingthe state of the churche, whiche was then like to decaye. For so muche said they, as the byshops and ecclesiasticall rulers, begin now to be had in contempt, no man will scarsely obey the suffragans, Archedeacons, Chaūcelors, doctors & comissaries, so that the lawes and ordinaunces of the holy churche ar nowe anihilate the Christiā faith with the true worshiping of God is in daunger. Little reuerēce or none is atributed vnto their spiritual iurisdiction autoritie, rytes, censures, keyes, and canonicall decrees, so that finally all do tende to vtter rewine and decay. Al these thinges come of none other cause then of the ouermuche sufferaunce of heretikes, which holde their assembles in secret places & corners, to wryte bokes and teache in Medowes, Woodes, & dennes, the which thinges if they were any longer suffered wold at the last vtterly subuert and ouer throwe the whole common wealth. — The complaint of the clergye.

Where vpon the king holding a parliament at Lecester (the whiche peraduenture had not bene so wel holden at Londō, because of the fauourers of the Lorde Cobham) he set forth an act wherein he decreed most cruell punishment vnto such as hereafter would folow that kind of doctrine, yea he was so seuere against them that he decreed them not only to be heretikes,

O Lord receiue my spirite.

but also traitours. And therfore he ordeined ẏ they should be tormented with a double kynde of torment. That is to say, with the Galloes & fier. And that neither ẏ hallowed sanctuaries neither any priuileges, should be any ayde or succor for them. in suche sorte had he bent his whole force and reason against the Wickliefistes: for in those dayes whosoeuer did reade ẏ scriptures of god in their mother tongue were so called. The byshops being armed with this decree, exercised wonderful great crueltie and tyrannie against many good and giltles men, among the whiche nomber besides the Lorde Cobham whose story we haue differred, are to be remembred sir Roger Acton, knight of the same order, M. John Broun Gentleman, and John Beuerle a precher of ẏ gospel, who were put to death at ẏ same time. But before I wyll speake any more of them, it is necessary that I talke a litle with Pollidore Virgill, wryter of the storye of Englande, who in the. xxii. boke of his history accuseth the Lord Cobham — The cruell decre of the king. — Walden to Pope Martin in his. 2 boke. 46. chapiter.

R.iii. and

Maries birth.
A Bright Starre
riseth which
a Sun will bring,
Heauens fairest
floure vppon the
earth doth spring.
A 3 To

73

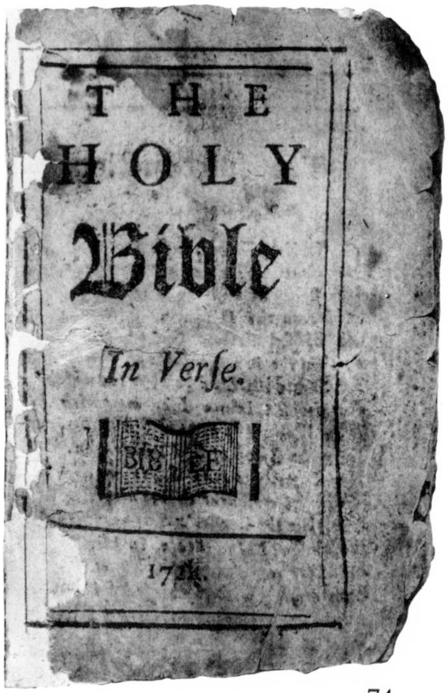
THE
HOLY
Bible
In Verse.

74

Genesis.
THis book contains a full relation
Of God Almighty's wise Creation.

74

BIBLIA
or a Practical
Summary
of ye Old & New
TESTAMENTS
LOND. Printed For
R.WILKIN,
in St. Pauls-Church
Yard 1727.

75

P.122
Joshua.
B.III. 121
CHAP. I.
Moses and A-
ron dying
last years of the
Israelites sojourn-
ning

75

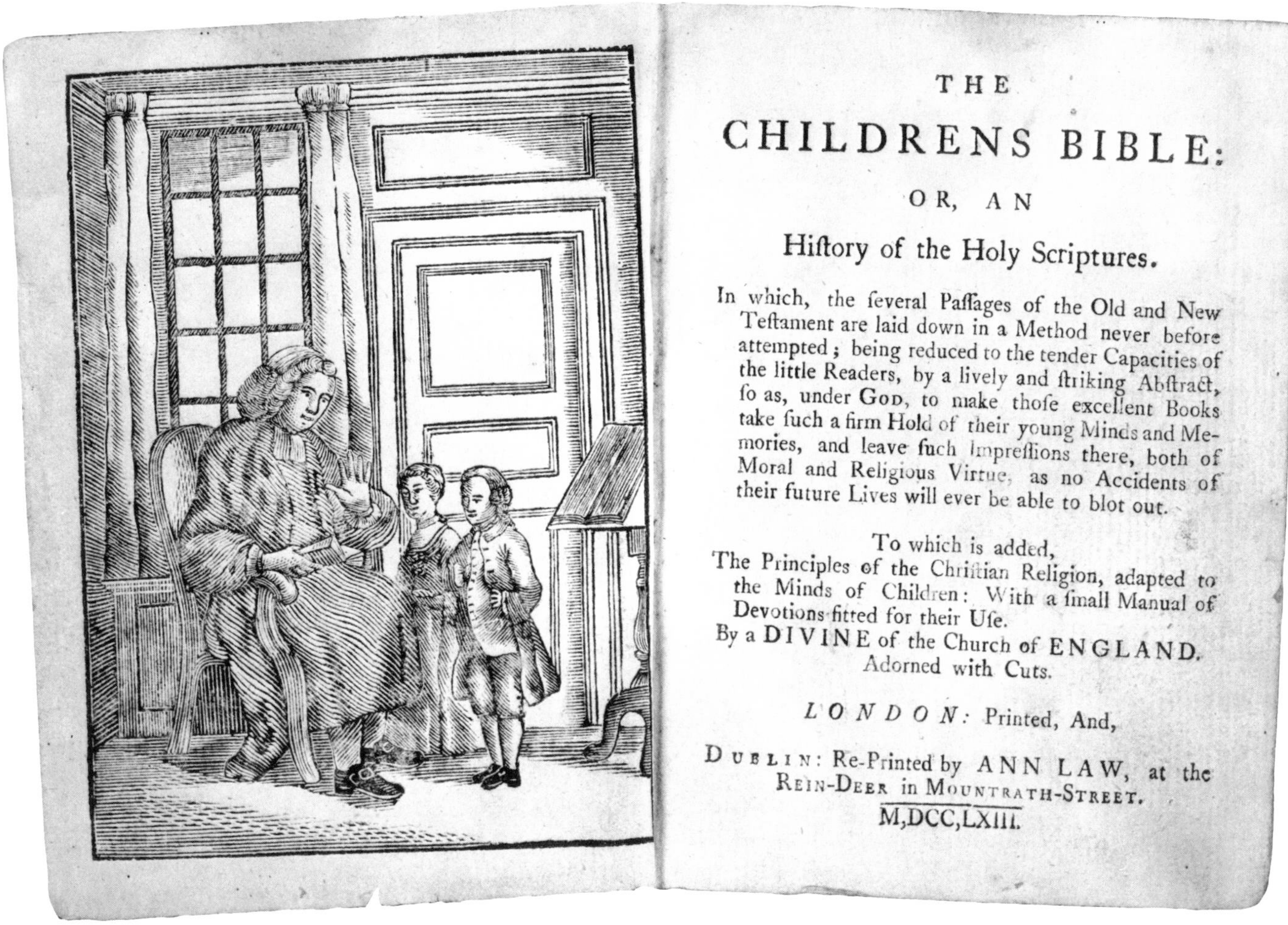

THE

CHILDRENS BIBLE:

OR, AN

Hiſtory of the Holy Scriptures.

In which, the ſeveral Paſſages of the Old and New Teſtament are laid down in a Method never before attempted; being reduced to the tender Capacities of the little Readers, by a lively and ſtriking Abſtract, ſo as, under GOD, to make thoſe excellent Books take ſuch a firm Hold of their young Minds and Memories, and leave ſuch Impreſſions there, both of Moral and Religious Virtue, as no Accidents of their future Lives will ever be able to blot out.

To which is added,
The Principles of the Chriſtian Religion, adapted to the Minds of Children: With a ſmall Manual of Devotions fitted for their Uſe.
By a DIVINE of the Church of ENGLAND.
Adorned with Cuts.

LONDON: Printed, And,

DUBLIN: Re-Printed by ANN LAW, at the REIN-DEER in MOUNTRATH-STREET.

M,DCC,LXIII.

76

St. Polycarp burning at a stake.

77

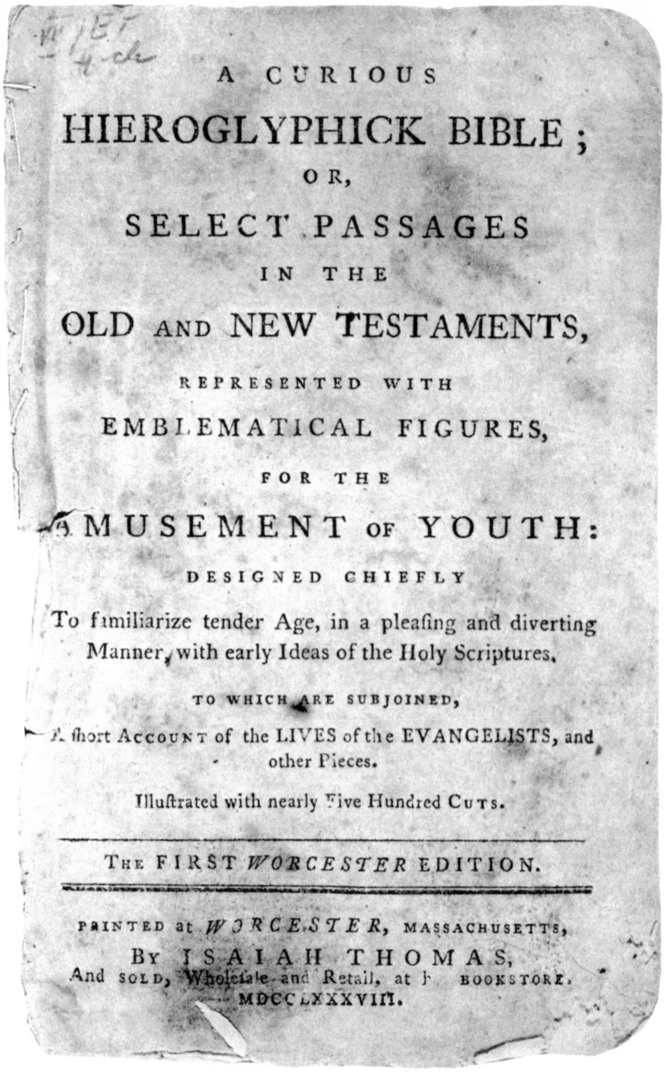
A CURIOUS
HIEROGLYPHICK BIBLE;
OR,
SELECT PASSAGES
IN THE
OLD AND NEW TESTAMENTS,
REPRESENTED WITH
EMBLEMATICAL FIGURES,
FOR THE
AMUSEMENT OF YOUTH:
DESIGNED CHIEFLY
To familiarize tender Age, in a pleasing and diverting Manner, with early Ideas of the Holy Scriptures.
TO WHICH ARE SUBJOINED,
A short Account of the LIVES of the EVANGELISTS, and other Pieces.
Illustrated with nearly Five Hundred Cuts.

THE FIRST *WORCESTER* EDITION.

PRINTED at *WORCESTER*, MASSACHUSETTS,
BY ISAIAH THOMAS,
And SOLD, Wholesale and Retail, at h BOOKSTORE.
MDCCLXXXVIII.

78

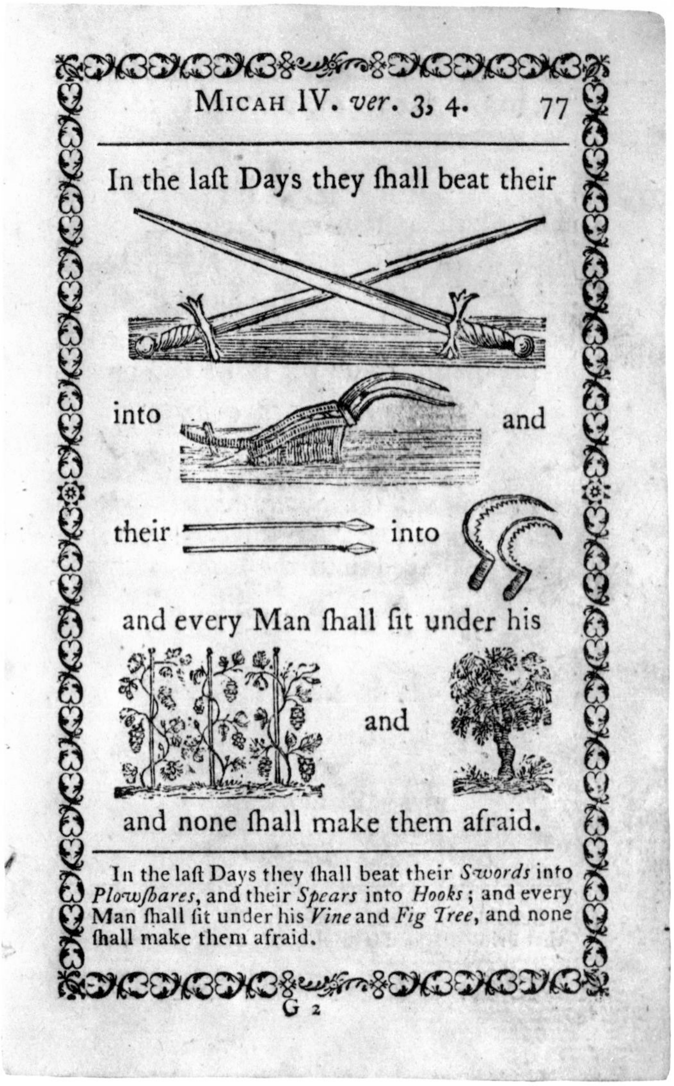
MICAH IV. *ver.* 3, 4. 77

In the laſt Days they ſhall beat their

into and

their into

and every Man ſhall ſit under his

and

and none ſhall make them afraid.

In the laſt Days they ſhall beat their *Swords* into *Plowſhares*, and their *Spears* into *Hooks*; and every Man ſhall ſit under his *Vine* and *Fig Tree*, and none ſhall make them afraid.

G 2

78

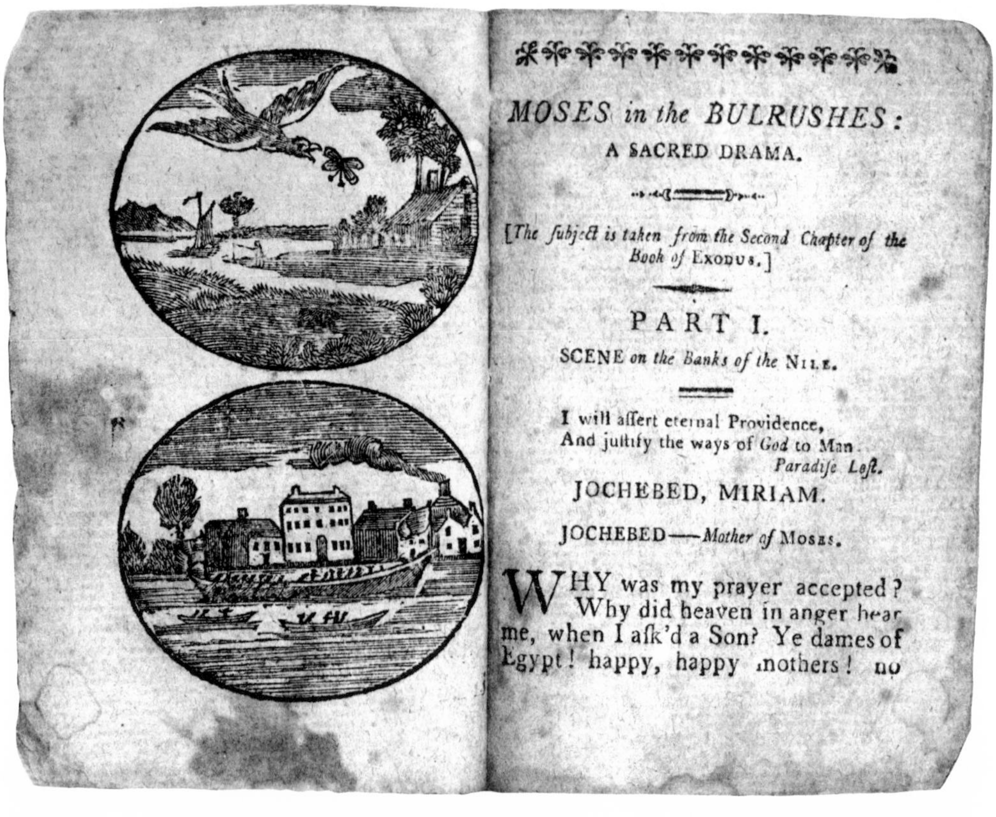
MOSES in the BULRUSHES:
A SACRED DRAMA.

[*The Subject is taken from the Second Chapter of the Book of* EXODUS.]

PART I.
SCENE *on the Banks of the* NILE.

I will aſſert eternal Providence,
And juſtify the ways of *God* to Man.
Paradiſe Loſt.

JOCHEBED, MIRIAM.

JOCHEBED—*Mother of* MOSES.

WHY was my prayer accepted? Why did heaven in anger hear me, when I aſk'd a Son? Ye dames of Egypt! happy, happy mothers! no

79

Emblem Books

80 Andrea Alciati

EMBLEMATA

Augsburg: Heinrich Steiner, 28 February 1531.
15 cm. [44] f.
Brunet, I, 147. Graesse, I, 62. Green 2.
Gift of the Fellows.

Andrea Alciati (1492–1550), a Milanese jurist, created the first emblem book, in which pictures chosen for their symbolic meaning were combined with text to present brief moral or religious lessons. Alciati's *Emblemata* enjoyed great popularity and was soon widely imitated by other writers. These early emblem books, rich in pictures and piety, were—like Aesop—given to the young for their moral betterment long before there were any emblem books (or indeed many books at all) written expressly for children. The copy of Alciati's *Emblemata* shown here is from the first issue of the first edition. The woodcuts are by Hans Schaüfelein, a follower of Albrecht Dürer who achieved some fame as a painter and engraver. The lower of the two emblems on the page derives from an ancient popular legend: that when storks become too old to fly they are carried on the backs of their dutiful young.

81 Geoffrey Whitney

A CHOICE OF EMBLEMES

Leiden: Francis Raphelengius in the house of Christopher Plantin, 1586.
21.5 cm. [20], 230 p.
STC 25438. Praz. Freeman.

The first edition of the first English emblem book, printed in the Low Countries at the celebrated press of Christopher Plantin. Inspired by the many emblem books circulating on the Continent, Whitney, an Englishman, wrote this while a student at the newly founded University of Leiden. He drew heavily upon Alciati and his successors, but he also added new emblems. Whitney's English verses have a felicity that helped to make the book popular. William Shakespeare had a knowledge—as is evident from his works—of the great Continental emblem writers of the sixteenth century, and it was principally from Whitney's book that he acquired his knowledge.

82 Jacob Cats

SILENUS ALCIBIADIS.

Middleburg: Iohannis Hellenij, 1618.
23 cm. [41], 2–120, [3], 4–111, [4], 4–107, [5] p. + fold-out plate (23×31 cm.).
Landwehr 81.
Purchased for the Elisabeth Ball Collection.

A Dutch emblem book, of the type that circulated widely on the Continent during the sixteenth and seventeenth centuries (and nowhere more than in Holland, where they attained a great popularity). The emblems and their accompanying verses are taken from Latin, French, Italian, Spanish, and Dutch proverbs. The engraved plate shown here depicts, in a manner somewhat reminiscent of the famous painting by Pieter Brueghel the Elder, children playing various games. The engraving is (probably) by J. Swelinck after Adriaen Pietersz van de Venne, and the setting is the courtyard of the Abbey of Middelburg, in Holland. It was at Middelburg that the poet Jacob Cats and the artist Adriaen van de Venne began a collaboration that was to last nearly forty years; this book was their first joint effort. Shown here is the second edition, published in the same year as the first.

83 Bunyan, John

DIVINE EMBLEMS: OR TEMPORAL THINGS SPIRITUALIZED. CALCULATED FOR THE USE OF YOUNG PEOPLE.

London: T. Bennett . . . , [about 1790].
12 cm. [5], 6–88 p.
Purchased on the Lathrop C. Harper Fund.

The first emblem book for children. It is the only book John Bunyan ever wrote expressly for children, although his earlier *Pilgrim's Progress*, which demonstrated his supreme genius for allegory, became one of the great "adopted" children's books. *Divine Emblems* was first published by Bunyan—under the title *A Book for Boys and Girls; or, Country Rhimes for Children*—in 1686, two years before his death (it was one of his "post-imprisonment" works). The first edition is of formidable rarity, with only the British Museum and Harvard University possessing copies; in fact, all editions of this book published before 1800 are very rare today. Oddly enough for an emblem book, the first edition was not illustrated, nor was any edition before 1707. In 1724 a somewhat shortened version of the work was published bearing a changed title, *Divine Emblems*, and woodcut illustrations. Most subsequent editions of Bunyan's emblem book for children have appeared under this title, with this text, and with illustrations. The Morgan Library copy of the work, which is from an edition published about 1790, is engraved throughout; i.e., the entire text is engraved, as well as the illustrations.

84 EMBLEMS, FOR THE ENTERTAINMENT AND IMPROVEMENT OF YOUTH: CONTAINING HIEROGLYPHICAL AND ENIGMATICAL DEVICES, RELATING TO ALL PARTS AND STATIONS OF LIFE.

London: R. Ware, [about 1750].
19.5 cm. [63] f.
NBL 744.
Loaned by Miss Julia P. Wightman.

The first edition of a mid-eighteenth-century English emblem book, intended "for the Entertainment and Improvement of Youth," and thus demonstrating in its title that entertainment of the young had become an accepted technique in their moral education. The book contains more than 900 engraved emblems, with accompanying mottoes.

85 [John Huddlestone Wynne]

CHOICE EMBLEMS, NATURAL, HISTORICAL, FABULOUS, MORAL AND DIVINE, FOR THE IMPROVEMENT AND PASTIME OF YOUTH.

London: George Riley, 1772.
15 cm. [2], iii–xii, [1], 2–192 p. + frontispiece.
DNB, "Wynne, John Huddlestone."
Purchased for the Elisabeth Ball Collection.

One of the most famous emblem books ever written for young people. The author, John Huddlestone Wynne, was a hack writer and minor poet who is said to have promised his mother on her deathbed that he would forever after shun boats, belfries, and horses. His adherence to this vow in eighteenth-century England, where boats, belfries, and especially horses figured so large in daily life, gained him a reputation as an eccentric. In keeping with the more enlightened approach to children and children's books which was now prevailing, Wynne intended his emblem book "to convey the golden Lessons of Instruction under a new and more delightful Dress." The book later became known as Riley's Emblems, after its publisher, and was frequently reprinted in the eighteenth and nineteenth centuries. This is the first edition.

86 [Hans Holbein]

EMBLEMS OF MORTALITY; REPRESENTING, IN UPWARDS OF FIFTY CUTS, DEATH SEIZING ALL RANKS AND DEGREES OF PEOPLE. . . . INTENDED AS WELL FOR THE INFORMATION OF THE CURIOUS, AS THE INSTRUCTION AND ENTERTAINMENT OF YOUTH.

London: T. Hodgson, 1789.
17 cm. [5], ii–xxviii, 51, [1] p.
Praz II, p. 54. Hugo 35.

Not, strictly speaking, emblem books but closely allied to them, versions of Hans Holbein's Dance of Death were often produced for—as the title page of this work announces—"the Instruction and Entertainment of Youth." The illustrations in this eighteenth-century edition are by Thomas and John Bewick, the pioneer English wood-engravers. The rarity of the engravings is enhanced by the fact that the original wooden blocks were destroyed in a fire soon after this work was published.

87 "Miss Thoughtful"

INSTRUCTIVE AND ENTERTAINING EMBLEMS, ON VARIOUS SUBJECTS, IN PROSE AND VERSE.

Hartford: J. Babcock, 1795.
10 cm. [3], 5–31 p. Pink gilt wrappers.
Welch 1155.1 (imperfect).
Elisabeth Ball Collection.

An emblem book for children in the form of a tiny chapbook illustrated with woodcuts. The printer, John Babcock of Hartford, Connecticut, was an early publisher of children's books in America. The emblem of the filial stork, employed by Alciati in the very first emblem book, became an obvious choice for many later writers of emblem books intended for children.

Romanũ postquàm eloquium Cicerone perempto
Perdiderat patria pestis acerba suæ
Inscendit currus victor uinxitq; leones
Compulit & durũ colla subire iugum
Magnanimos cessisse suis Antonius armis
Ambage hac cupiens significare duces.

GRATIAM REFERENDAM

80

24 *Latet anguis in herba.*

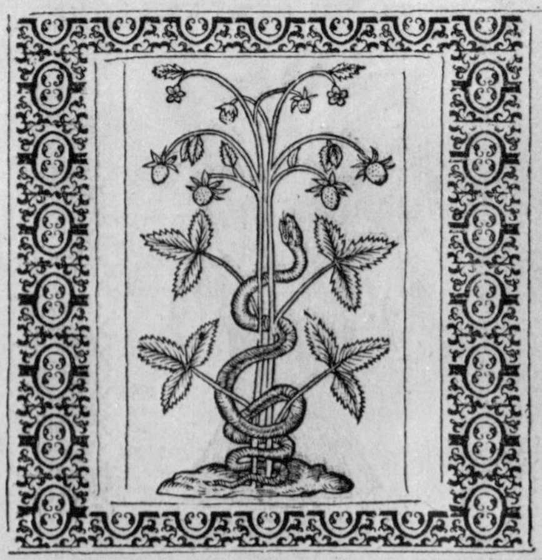

Of flattringe speeche, with sugred wordes beware,
Suspect the harte, whose face doth fawne, and smile,
With trusting theise, the worlde is clog'de with care,
And fewe there bee can scape theise vipers vile:
With pleasinge speeche they promise, and protest,
When hatefull hartes lie hidd within their brest.

The faithfull wight, dothe neede no collours braue,
But those that truste, in time his truthe shall trie,
Where fawning mates, can not theire credit saue,
Without a cloake, to flatter, faine, and lye:
No foe so fell, nor yet soe harde to scape,
As is the foe, that fawnes with freindlie shape.

Ouid 1. Art. *Tuta, frequensq; via est, per amici fallere nomen.*

Idem 1. Fast. *Sic iterum, sic sæpe cadunt, vbi vincere apertè*
Non datur: insidias, armaq; tecta parant.

Curis

81

Kinder spel ghedûydet tot Sinne-beelden ende Leere der Seden.
Ex nugis seria.
Part 2.
Pag. 107.

84 Mr. JOHN BUNYAN's

Of Man by Nature.

FROM God he's a back-flider,
Of ways he loves the wider;
With wickednefs a fider,
More venom than a fpider.
In fin he's a confider,
A make-bate and divider;
Blind reafon is his guider,
The devil is his rider.

DIVINE EMBLEMS. 85

Upon the Difobedient Child.

CHILDREN, when little, how do they delight us!
When they grow bigger, they begin to fright us.
Their finful nature prompts them to rebel,
And to delight in paths that lead to hell.
Their parents love and care they overlook,
As if relation had them quite forfook.
They take the counfels of the wanton, rather
Than the moft grave inftructions of a father,
They reckon parents ought to do for them,
Though they the fifth commandment do contemn.
They fnap, and fnarl, if parents them controul,
Although in things moft hurtful to the foul,
They reckon they are mafters, and that we
Who parents are, fhould to them fubject be.
If parents fain would have a hand in chufing,
The children have a heart ftill in refufing.

G

83

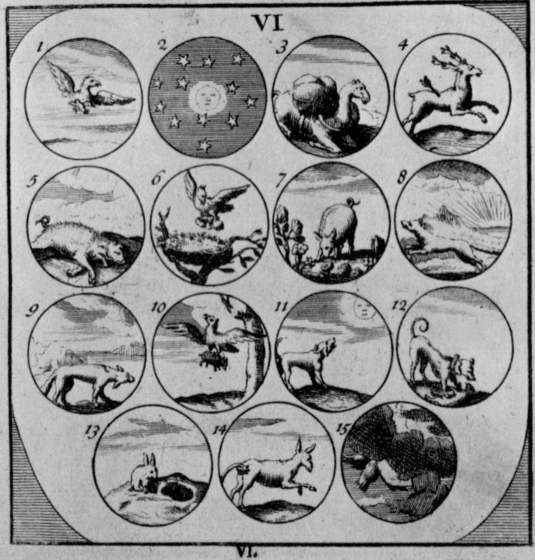

VI.

4. An Eagle mounting the Air with a Wren. *Non ufitata vebor.* I am not ufed to go fo high.

2. A Moon in the midft of the Stars. *Una piu che mille.* One Moon is more to me than a thoufand.

3. A Cammel fallen under its Burthen. *Nil ultra vires.* Nothing fhould be undertaken beyond one's Strength.

4. A Stag wounded with an Arrow. *Hinc dolor inde fuga.* My Pain caufes my Flight.

5. A Boar on the Ground with a Knife in his Throat. *Haud aliter prodeft.* He brings no profit but by his Death.

6. An Eagle carrying a Stone to its Neft. *In tempore munit.* She fortified it againft Time of Need.

7. A Hog among Flowers. *Non bene conveniunt.* They do not fuit well.

8. A Wolf flying, and the Sun rifing above him. *Hoc oriente fugio.* I fly when that appears.

9. A Fox liftning on a River that he is paffing over. *Fide & diffide.* I do not confide in it, nor wholly diftruft it.

10. An Eagle carrying its Prey and beholding the Sky. *Dum detonet imber.* It is my Provifion for the worft Times.

11 A Moon and a Dog barking beneath it. *Defpicit alta feras.* Her Station makes her defpife Fools.

12. A Hound having a Hare under its Feet *Gloria fi vis.* He confiders only the Glory. Or Victory.

13. A Rabbit on the Edge of its Burrough. *Vigilandum.* 'Tis good to watch.

14. An Afs ftung by a Fly. *Et parvis fua vis.* The leaft Thing may be troublefome.

15. An Eagle that hides herfelf in the Clouds. *Non captu facilis.* It is not eafy to take me.

84

(157)

E M B L E M XL.

O F V A I N G L O R Y.

BEHOLD that filly bird, how proudly vain,
Of the bright colours of his gaudy train!
Ev'n to a proverb grown his idle pride
By outward fhew alone in worth fupply'd,
For no harmonious found, no chearful note,
Muft ever iffue from that hideous throat,
Nor of the hundred eyes that grace his tail,
Can one for fight, or real ufe avail.

O fon of vanity be wife in time!
Apply the moral of this homely rhyme,
To *real worth* alone fhould praife be giv'n,
And *real worth* inherits it from Heav'n.

JUNO

85

[39]

The CHILD.

Man that is born of a Woman, is of few Days, and full of Trouble. He cometh forth like a Flower, and is cut down: He fleeth alſo as a Shadow, and continueth not.

JOB xiv. 1.

Man, who conceiv'd in the dark Womb,
Into the World is brought,
Is born to Times with Miſery,
And various Evil fraught.

And as the Flow'r ſoon fades and dies,
However fair it be,
So ſinks he alſo to the Grave,
And like a Shade does flee.

E 2

[45]

The BLIND MAN.

If the Blind lead the Blind, both ſhall fall into the Ditch.

MATTHEW xv. 14.

The blind Man to a Guide as blind
Himſelf does here commit;
Both wanting Sight, they here deſcend
Into the fatal Pit.

For, while the Man does vainly hope
Succeſs his Steps attends,
Into the Darkneſs of the Grave
He ſuddenly deſcends.

86

INSTRUCTIVE

AND

ENTERTAINING

EMBLEMS,

On Various Subjects,

IN PROSE AND VERSE,

By Miſs THOUGHTFUL.

HARTFORD:

PRINTED BY J. BABCOCK.

1795.

EMBLEM II.

Of Filial Duty and Affection.

SEE the young ſtork his duteous wing prepare
His aged ſire to feed with conſtant care;
O'er hills and dales his precious load conveys,
And the great debt of filial duty pays.
Grateful return! by nature's ſelf deſign'd,
A fair example ſet to human kind.
Should'ſt thou refuſe thy parent's needful aid,
The very ſtork might the foul crime upbraid:
Be mindful how they rear'd thy tender youth,
Bear with their frailties; ſerve them ſtill with truth:
So may'ſt thou with long life and peace be bleſt,
Till Heaven ſhall call thee to eternal reſt.

Proverbs

88 John Trusler

PROVERBS EXEMPLIFIED.

London: Literary-Press, 1 May 1790.
16 cm. [2], iii–viii, 196 p.
Gumuchian 5647. NBL 481.
Loaned by Miss Julia P. Wightman.

Proverbs, maxims, adages, old wives' tales have always played an important part in the education of the young. This collection of some eighty sayings popular in the eighteenth century contains many that are still current today—"Birds of a feather flock together," "A friend in need is a friend indeed," "Rome was not built in a day"—but also a great many more that are quite unfamiliar in the twentieth century. The Reverend John Trusler had previously enjoyed success with his "moralized" edition of the engravings of William Hogarth; here his similarly moralized proverbs are illustrated with wood-engravings by the renowned John Bewick. Shortly before this John Bewick had engraved, together with his older brother Thomas, some emblems after Hans Holbein's Dance of Death. The influence of those works by Holbein can often be discerned in John Bewick's engravings for Trusler's proverbs. This is the first edition.

89 [Benjamin Franklin]

MAXIMS AND MORALS FROM DR. FRANKLIN.

London: Darton and Harvey, 1807.
15.5 cm. [3], 4–47, [1] p. Buff printed wrappers.
Elisabeth Ball Collection.

Benjamin Franklin's words of wisdom had an enormous appeal for early-nineteenth-century Englishmen, and they were administered regularly to the young. This volume of extracts from Franklin's writings is illustrated by the talented engraver-author-publisher William Darton.

90 PETER PRIM'S PRIDE, OR PROVERBS THAT WILL SUIT THE YOUNG, OR THE OLD.

London: J. Harris, 26 December 1810.
12.5 cm. [3], 2–16 p. + 15 plates. Buff printed wrappers (bound in).
NBL 755.
Elisabeth Ball Collection.

Handsome stipple engravings—the artist is unknown—together with brief texts by an avuncular "Peter Prim," also unidentified. This is the first edition of the work.

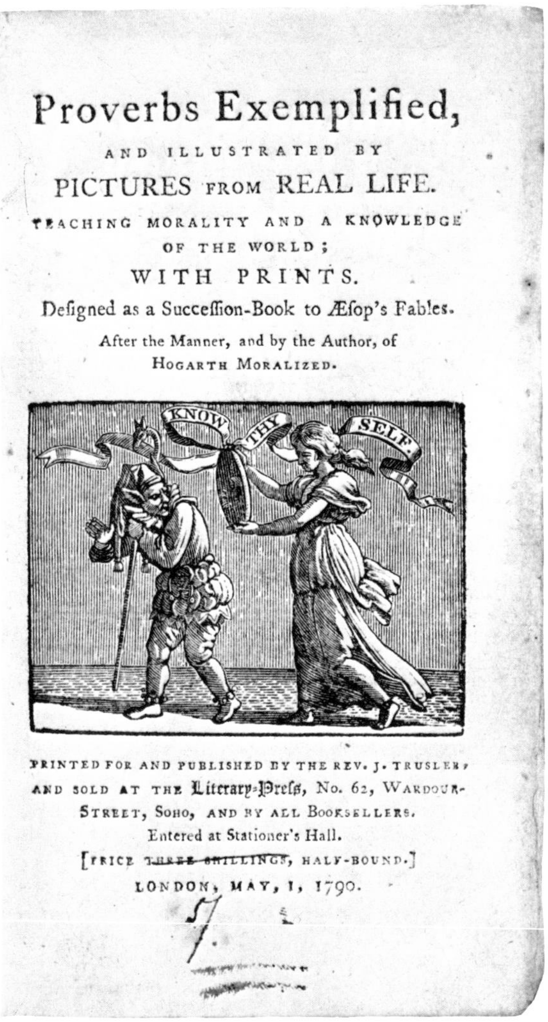

Proverbs Exemplified,

AND ILLUSTRATED BY

PICTURES FROM REAL LIFE.

TEACHING MORALITY AND A KNOWLEDGE OF THE WORLD;

WITH PRINTS.

Deſigned as a Succeſſion-Book to Æſop's Fables.

After the Manner, and by the Author, of HOGARTH MORALIZED.

PRINTED FOR AND PUBLISHED BY THE REV. J. TRUSLER, AND SOLD AT THE Literary-Preſs, No. 62, WARDOUR-STREET, SOHO, AND BY ALL BOOKSELLERS.

Entered at Stationer's Hall.

[PRICE ~~THREE SHILLINGS~~, HALF-BOUND.]

LONDON, MAY, 1, 1790.

88

Out of the Frying-Pan into the Fire.

FROM the deſperate ſituation of a poor fiſh, thrown alive into the water, to be boiled, and jumping in that water for life, and its having no alternative in eſcaping, but falling into the fire, this Proverb would teach us, not to give up one ſituation for another, let the firſt be ever ſo diſagreeable, if the ſecond be not a better. We are too apt to think our own ſituation

L of

88

MAXIMS AND MORALS

FROM

Dr. FRANKLIN:

BEING

INCITEMENTS TO INDUSTRY, FRUGALITY AND PRUDENCE.

He who by the plough would thrive,
Himself should either hold or drive.

LONDON:

PRINTED FOR DARTON AND HARVEY, GRACECHURCH-STREET.

1807.

89

If you would have your business done, go yourself; if not, send another.

This is not to be taken literally; a master cannot go every where himself; but he may be said to be at the elbow of his servants, when he keeps them under proper subjection. The master of this porter seldom rose before eleven o'clock, and then he bid Harry go and find James to carry the letter. James, by that time, was half tipsy, and, instead of going on his errand, called at a favourite public-house, where he fell asleep and lost the letter.

For

89

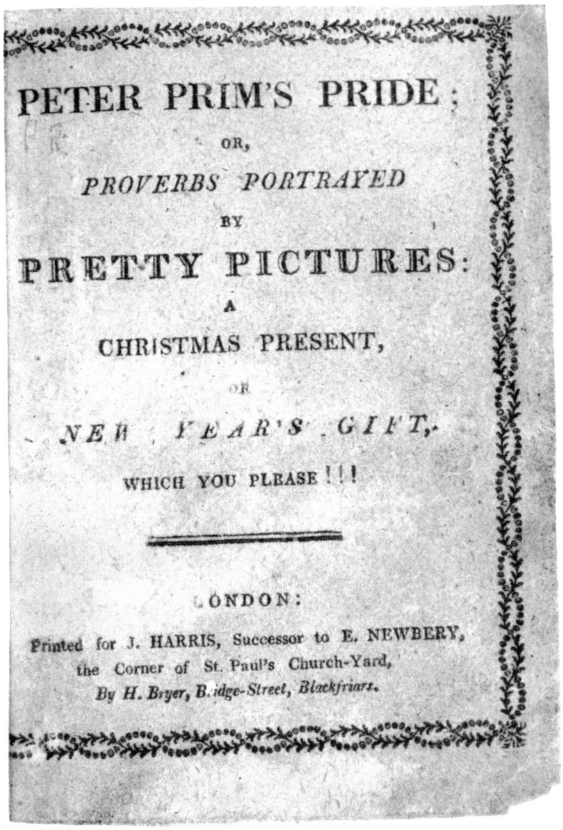
PETER PRIM'S PRIDE;
OR,
PROVERBS PORTRAYED
BY
PRETTY PICTURES:
A
CHRISTMAS PRESENT,
OR
NEW YEAR'S GIFT,
WHICH YOU PLEASE!!!

LONDON:
Printed for J. HARRIS, Successor to E. NEWBERY,
the Corner of St. Paul's Church-Yard,
By H. Bryer, Bridge-Street, Blackfriars.

90

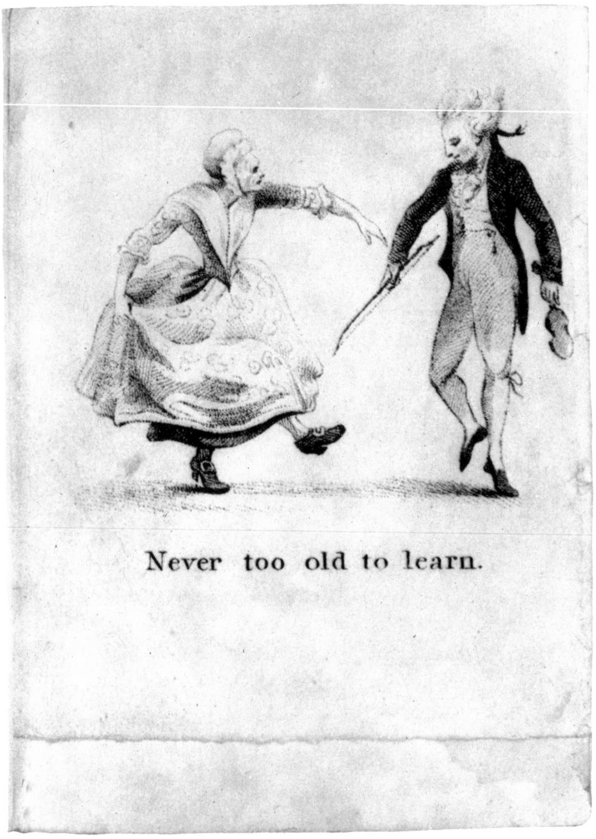

90

Grammars and Schoolbooks

91 INFORMATIO PUERORUM.

[London:] Richard Pynson, [about 1500].
18 cm. 19 f.
Goff I-78.

Although the second half of the fifteenth century—the five "incunabula" decades after the invention of printing—saw a great proliferation of books, very few were intended in any way for children. And of these few, undoubtedly most were schoolbooks. The volume shown here was printed in London by the celebrated English printer Richard Pynson, about the year 1500. It is an elementary Latin grammar, written in English. The book is anonymous, but internal evidence suggests that the work may have been prepared for use at Winchester College. Three editions of this book, all undated, were issued by Pynson. The Morgan Library copy, which is probably from the second edition, is the only copy in America. One other copy is known of the second edition, in the Bodleian Library at Oxford; and of the first edition but a single copy has survived, in the Pepysian Library at Cambridge.

92 Udalricus Ebrardi
MODUS LATINITATIS.

Nuremberg: Hieronymus Hölzel, 1500.
20 cm. [1], ii–xlvii, [1] f.
Gumuchian 5199.
Elisabeth Ball Collection.

A Latin grammar in German and Latin, this schoolbook was extremely popular in the late fifteenth century. It was first published in 1487 and appeared in more than two dozen editions in at least ten German cities during the next thirteen years. The copy illustrated here is from the last of the fifteenth-century editions. The woodcut of a teacher and pupils indicates that the young on the Continent in the fifteenth century were just as familiar with the birch rod of the schoolmaster as were their counterparts in England.

93 L. C. D. E. M. [i.e., Louis Couvay, Docteur en Medecine]

MÉTHODE NOUVELLE ET TRÈS-EXACTE, POUR ENSEIGNER ET APPRENDRE LA PREMIERE PARTIE DE DESPAUTERE.

Paris: Jean Gaillard, 1649.
18 cm. [22], 52, [4] p.
Brunet, II, 639. Gumuchian 5195.
Elisabeth Ball Collection.

Scholars have long pondered the question of which book deserves to be called the earliest picture-book for children. An alphabet book with pictures illustrating the letters was published in England as early as 1570, but not until some time later would anyone combine a substantial text with pictures in such a way as to create a genuine illustrated book for children, a book that would be an authentic prototype of the modern illustrated textbook. The first such book has generally been considered to be the *Orbis Sensualium Pictus*, a Latin vocabulary book brought out in 1658 by the Moravian educator Johann Comenius. In 1649, however, there appeared in Paris the volume illustrated here. It is a Latin grammar, with a text that is superbly and imaginatively augmented by a large number of engravings, many of them illustrating rather sophisticated concepts in the text. The author of the book was Louis Couvay, a physician and writer from the city of Arles in southern France. The copperplate engravings in the book were done by Louis' brother Jean Couvay, an artist of some fame. Louis Couvay's text is based on a work by the Belgian scholar Johann Despauterius, or Jean Despautère, whose textbooks were widely used on the Continent in the sixteenth and seventeenth centuries. The Morgan Library copy of *Méthode nouvelle* is a first edition; three other copies are recorded. After their first appearance in 1649, the Jean Couvay engravings were published again, together with additional engravings by the same artist, in an expanded edition of the work. This was published in 1668; a copy is in the Morgan Library.

94 Johann Amos Comenius

JOH. AMOS COMMENII ORBIS SENSUALIUM PICTUS. . . . JOH. AMOS COMMENIUS'S VISIBLE WORLD. OR, A PICTURE AND NOMENCLATURE OF ALL THE CHIEF THINGS THAT ARE IN THE WORLD; AND OF MENS EMPLOYMENTS THEREIN. A WORK NEWLY WRITTEN BY THE AUTHOR IN LATINE, AND HIGH-DUTCH (BEING ONE OF HIS LAST ESSAYS, AND THE MOST SUITABLE TO CHILDRENS CAPACITIES OF ANY THAT HE HATH HITHERTO MADE): & TRANSLATED IN[T]O ENGLISH, BY CHARLES HOOLE.

London: J. Kirton, 1664.
14.5 cm. [15], 2–309, [9] p.
Wing 5505. Sadler, p. 438.
Loaned by Miss Julia P. Wightman.

Johann Comenius' *Orbis Sensualium Pictus*, of which the Couvay work above is a precursor, or perhaps even a parent, was first published in 1658, in Nuremberg. Its text was in Latin and German. Comenius was an educator of considerable influence and renown, and his book was translated into English almost immediately, in 1659. This first Latin-English edition adhered closely to the text of the original Nuremberg edition, adding only a preface by the translator, Charles Hoole. But the woodcuts of the Nuremberg edition, which had been done by Paul Kreutzberger, were now replaced with anonymous copperplate engravings that rather improved the visual usefulness of the book. The *Orbis Pictus* in this English translation by Hoole was destined to enjoy a very long life. It was given to children in the English-speaking world until well into the nineteenth century. The rare volume illustrated here is the second edition of Charles Hoole's translation. It is a close reprint of the 1659 first edition, with merely some slight changes in the preliminary matter.

95 [Elisha Coles]

NOLENS VOLENS: OR, YOU SHALL MAKE LATIN WHETHER YOU WILL OR NO.

London: T. Basset, 1675.
16.5 cm. [8], liv, [2], 156 p.
NBL 228.
Elisabeth Ball Collection.

The first edition of an extremely popular (and today extremely rare) seventeenth-century Latin-English grammar and vocabulary book. Coles' book is really in large part an adaptation of the *Orbis pictus* of Comenius. It contains a section entitled "The Youths Visible Bible" which uses pictures to illustrate—in the manner of Comenius, or of Couvay before him—concepts taken from Biblical passages. The harsh point of view expressed in the subtitle is typical of the seventeenth-century attitude toward learning, and indeed toward children in general.

96 Johann Amos Comenius

ORBIS SENSUALIUM PICTUS. TRANSLATED BY CHARLES HOOLE, M.A., FOR THE USE OF YOUNG LATIN SCHOLARS. THE FIRST AMERICAN, FROM THE TWELFTH LONDON EDITION, CORRECTED AND ENLARGED.

New York: T. & J. Swords, 1810.
17 cm. [3], 4–213, [5] p.
Sadler, p. 441.
Gift of Mrs. Samuel C. Chew.

The first American edition of Johann Comenius' *Orbis Pictus.* It is based on the twelfth London edition of 1777. The translation is still Charles Hoole's seventeenth-century English rendering of Comenius' German. The illustrations, however, are new in this edition. They are the work of the celebrated American engraver Alexander Anderson, a follower of Thomas Bewick.

97 [Thomas Love Peacock]

SIR HORNBOOK: OR, CHILDE LAUNCELOT'S EXPEDITION. A GRAMMATICO-ALLEGORICAL BALLAD.

London: Sharpe and Hailes, 1814.
13 cm. [7], 4–29, [3] p. Gray printed wrappers.
NBL 660.
Elisabeth Ball Collection.

Grammatical instruction for children in the form of an allegorical poem set in the Age of Chivalry. Peacock produced this before any of the satirical novels (such as *Headlong Hall* and *Nightmare Abbey*) that were to make him, along with Maria Edgeworth, Sir Walter Scott, and Jane Austen, one of the principal English novelists of the early nineteenth century. The volume illustrated here is from the rare first edition. It is noteworthy for its illustrations, which represent a very early use of lithography (black-and-white lithography, hand-colored) in a book for children.

98 Lemuel Gulliver, Jun. [i.e., Elizabeth Susannah Graham]

VOYAGE TO LOCUTA; A FRAGMENT.

London: J. Hatchard, 1818.
17 cm. [5], vi–vii, [2], 10–47, [5] p. + frontispiece + plates.
Gumuchian 2788.
Elisabeth Ball Collection.

After the end of the seventeenth century in England, a change began to take place in the way adults viewed education and children. It was John Locke who perhaps most eloquently sounded the keynote for the altered thinking. In 1693, in *Some Thoughts Concerning Education*, he had written: "'Tis impossible children should learn anything whilst their thoughts are possessed and disturbed with any passion, especially fear, which makes the strongest impression on their tender and weak spirits. Keep the mind in an easy calm temper, when you would have it receive your instructions or any increase of knowledge. 'Tis as impossible to draw fair and regular characters on a trembling mind as on a shaking paper." Humanity and pleasure were now to replace force and fear. And this approach was mirrored in the illustration of children's books, which began to show clear signs of an effort to entertain while educating. A good example of the sort of book this new, more humane style would one day culminate in is the volume shown here. It is an English grammar, attractively illustrated with etchings, and cast in the form of an imaginary voyage modeled on the Voyage to Laputa in Jonathan Swift's Gulliver's Travels. The author of this pleasant instructional fantasy, Elizabeth Susannah Graham, was far from alone in appropriating Swift's hero, Lemuel Gulliver, for her own purposes. Many writers after Swift made free use, in one form or another, of his creations. The choice of Laputa is somewhat unusual, however; Lilliput and its miniature population were more often used by children's-book writers, for obvious reasons. Under another pseudonym, Theresa Tidy, this author also wrote a courtesy book for children, *Eighteen Maxims of Neatness and Order*. The Morgan Library copy of *Voyage to Locuta* is the first edition.

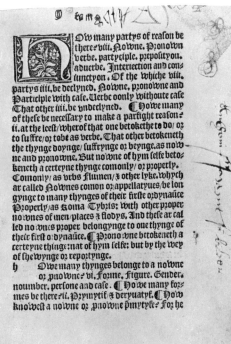

How many partys of reason be there? viii. Nowne. Pronown verbe. partyciple. prepositwritten aduerbe. Interiection and coniunctyon. Of the whiche viii. partys iiii. be declyned. Nowne, pronowne and Participle with case. Verbe oonly withoute case That other iiii. be undeclyned. ¶ Howe many of these be necessary to make a parfight reason? ii. at the leest / wherof that one betokethe to do / or to suffre / or tobe as verbe. That other betokeneth the thynge doynge / suffrynge or beynge. as nowne and pronowne. But nowne of hym selfe betokeneth a certeyne thynge comonly / or properly. Comonly / as vrbs Flumen / & other lyke. whych ar called Nownes comon or appellatyues / be longynge to many thynges of their firste ordynaūce Properly / as Roma Tybris: with other proper nownes of men / places & flodys. And these ar called nownes proper belongynge to one thynge of their first ordynaūce. ¶ Pronowne betokeneth a certeyne thinge: nat of hym selfe: but by the wey of shewynge or reportynge.

h How many thynges belonge to a nowne or pronowne? vi. Forme. Figure. Gender. noumber. persone and case. ¶ Howe many formes be there? ii. Prymytif & deryuatyf. ¶ How knowest a nowne or pronowne prymytyfe? For he

Liber Primus

Qum ego animaduertissem vos in cōi & familiari sermone nimiū oberrare: ita vt oēs fere vocabulorū pbatissimas differētias cōfunderetis et cōmitteretis barbarismos admodū magnos: mulus p ore: me friget p ego frigeo: ire domi p ire domū: & silia p ferēdo: vr̄is ineptis & agrestibus sermonibus subueniendū mecū duxi attendēs nihil cōducere posse grāmaticā nisi ea ad dicendum pmpti fieremus Nec ego nunc id ago q̄ his tantulis p̄ceptis eruditos imbuere vellem: sed vos qui infantes magis videmini q̄ loquētes: q̄ si que iam traditurus sum cōfuse vigili attentaq̄ mēte sectaturos vos videro. Deinceps altissimo annuēte vobis cōscribam distinctiora: grauiora: & elegantiora.

Ein guten tag. Bona dies. aut forte elegātius. Bonus dies. Nā dies in masculino genere determinatū tpus fcat. In feminino vo genere confusum. Dicimus em̄. Multa dies dat magnā hoibus rerū experientiā. Et inde habemus dieculū p paruo tpe. Et forte elegātius dr̄: h die legā q̄ hac die. Et itē hesterno die potius q̄ hesterna die. — Dies / Dieculū

Ein guten abent. Bonū sero. aut potius elegātius Bonū vesper. Naz vesp fcat tp̄s q̄ sol occidit. Aliqui tn̄ increpāt h vbū. Bonu sero: sed illud mihi nō oino displicet. Sero em̄ trib modis accipi solet. Primo p vespere. Scdo p tpe q̄d est post lucē solis. Tercio p tarde. — Sero / Vesper

Vil heyl. Salus plurima.
Vil heyl vnd freud. Et salus & gaudium.
Sey gegrußt. Salue.
Sey gegrußt liber bruder. Salue mi frater.
Seyt gegrusset. Saluete.
Seyt gegrusset liben gesellen. Saluete mi socij.
Ein gut nacht. Beata nox.
Schlafft wol. Quiescatis dulciter. vel dormiatis dulciter vel suauiter.
Sey gesegnet libe swester. Vale mi soror. Et in tali vel consimili oratione mi aduerbium est blandientis. — Mi
Seyt gesegnet liber meyster. Valete mi magister.
Seyt gesegnet. Valete
Seyt gesegnet lieben freund. Valete amici dulcissimi. Item discedētes nō apte dicimus. pficiat vobis. Tūc em̄ hac orōe vobis vti possum quotiēs aliq̄d alteri pdesse optam vt assequēti sacerdotiū: magistratū: aliā ve dignitatē: dicere possumus: pficiat vobis Item decedētes nō dicimus. cū licentia: nisi apud eos sine quorū — Proficiat vobis

a ij

Modus latinitatis.

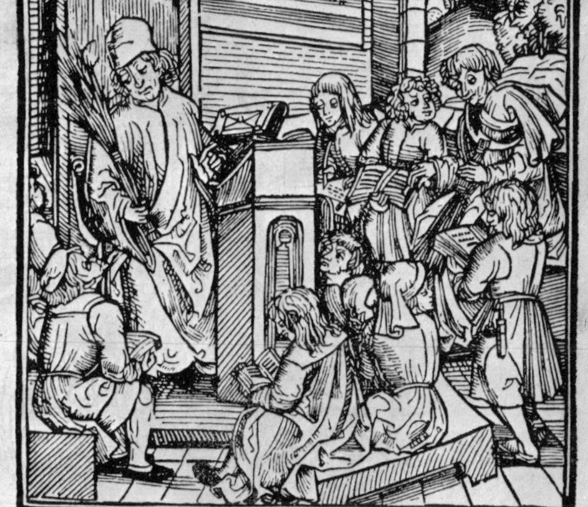

Ordo
Comme l'accord des lettres fait les mots, ainsi le rapport du commencement auec la fin establit l'ordre, qui depend proprement de la sagesse increée, laquelle dit ie suis A, & Ω, le commencement & la fin.

Icon
Pourquoy la statuë d'Amour non vne autre? parce qu'il faut aimer les lettres.

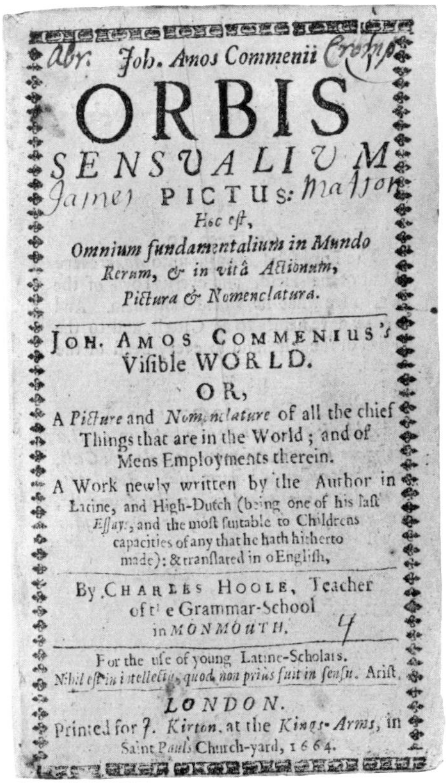

Joh. Amos Commenii

ORBIS SENSUALIUM PICTUS:

Hoc est,

Omnium fundamentalium in Mundo Rerum, & in vitâ Actionum, Pictura & Nomenclatura.

JOH. AMOS COMMENIUS's Visible WORLD.

OR,

A Picture and Nomenclature of all the chief Things that are in the World; and of Mens Employments therein.

A Work newly written by the Author in Latine, and High-Dutch (being one of his last Essays, and the most suitable to Childrens capacities of any that he hath hitherto made): & translated into English,

By CHARLES HOOLE, Teacher of the Grammar-School in MONMOUTH.

For the use of young Latine-Scholars.

Nihil est in intellectu, quod non prius fuit in sensu. Arist.

LONDON.

Printed for J. Kirton, at the Kings-Arms, in Saint Pauls Church-yard, 1664.

94

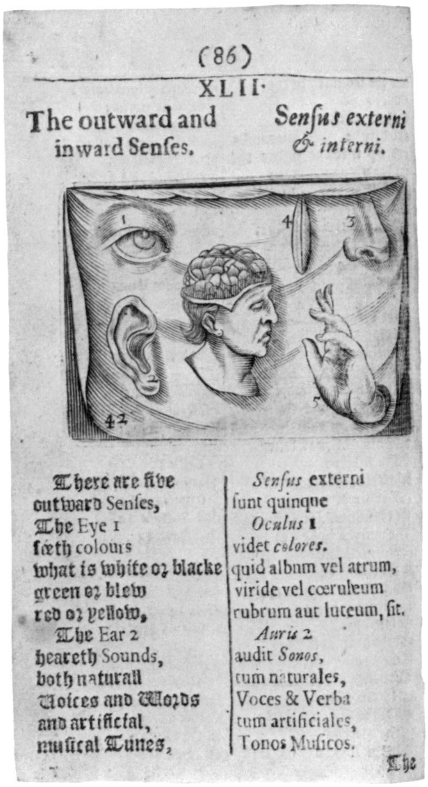

(86)

XLII.

The outward and inward Senses. | Sensus externi & interni.

There are five outward Senses,	Sensus externi sunt quinque
The Eye 1	Oculus 1
seeth colours	videt colores,
what is white or black	quid album vel atrum,
green or blew	viride vel cœruleum
red or yellow,	rubrum aut luteum, sit.
The Ear 2	Auris 2
heareth Sounds,	audit Sonos,
both naturall	tum naturales,
Voices and Words	Voces & Verba
and artificial,	tum artificiales,
musical Tunes,	Tonos Musicos.

The

94

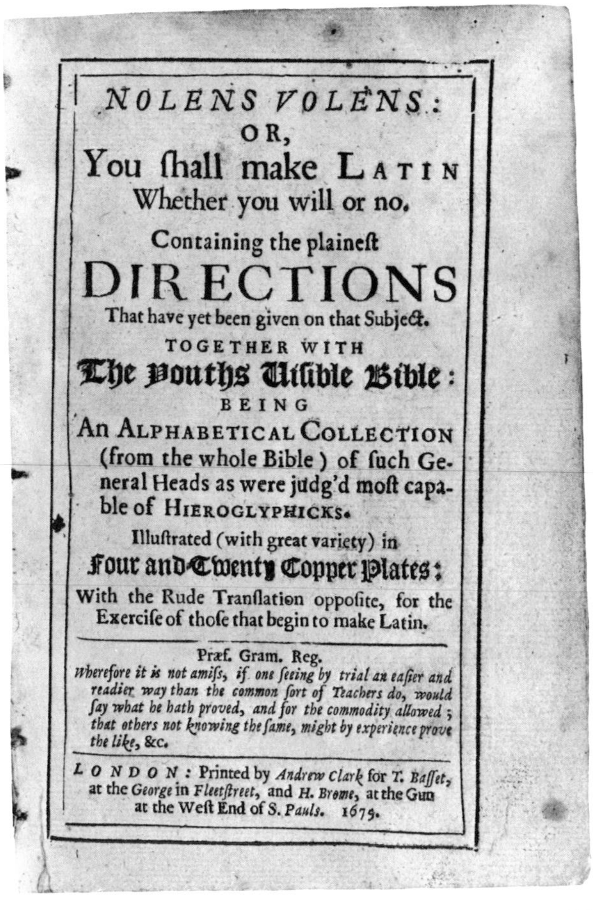

NOLENS VOLENS:

OR,

You shall make LATIN Whether you will or no.

Containing the plainest

DIRECTIONS

That have yet been given on that Subject.

TOGETHER WITH

The Youths Visible Bible:

BEING

An ALPHABETICAL COLLECTION (from the whole Bible) of such General Heads as were judg'd most capable of HIEROGLYPHICKS.

Illustrated (with great variety) in

Four and Twenty Copper Plates:

With the Rude Translation opposite, for the Exercise of those that begin to make Latin.

Præf. Gram. Reg.

Wherefore it is not amiss, if one seeing by trial an easier and readier way than the common sort of Teachers do, would say what he hath proved, and for the commodity allowed; that others not knowing the same, might by experience prove the like, &c.

LONDON: Printed by *Andrew Clark* for *T. Basset*, at the *George* in *Fleetstreet*, and *H. Brome*, at the Gun at the West End of S. *Pauls*. 1675.

95

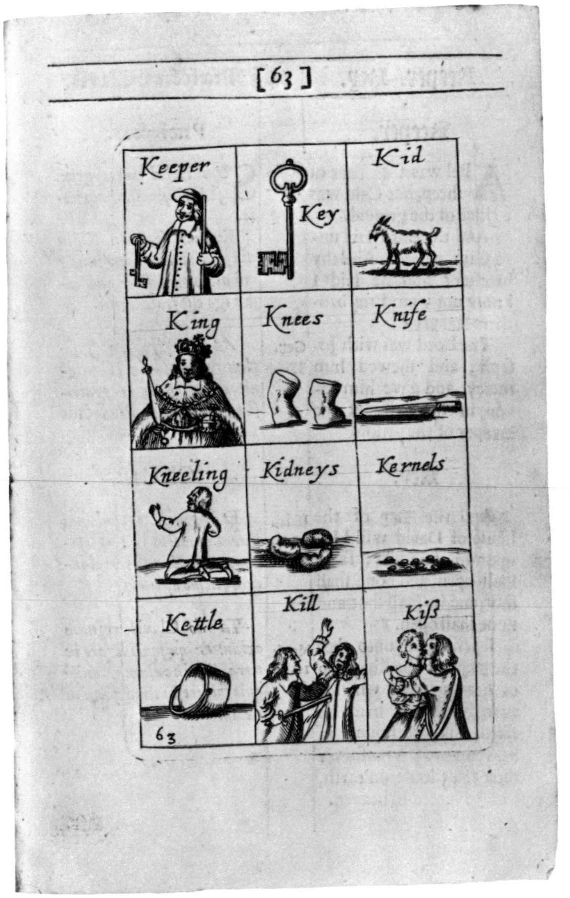

[63]

95

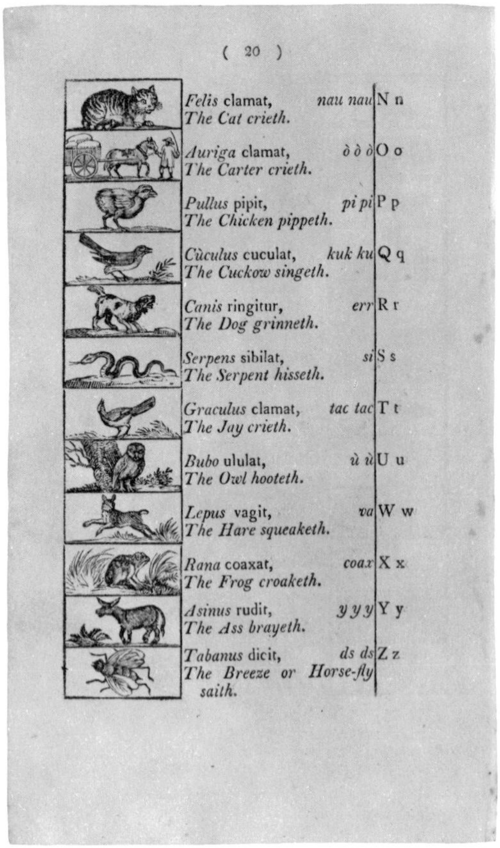
(20)

	Felis clamat, *The Cat crieth.*	*nau nau*	N n
	Auriga clamat, *The Carter crieth.*	*ò ò ò*	O o
	Pullus pipit, *The Chicken pippeth.*	*pi pi*	P p
	Cùculus cuculat, *The Cuckow singeth.*	*kuk ku*	Q q
	Canis ringitur, *The Dog grinneth.*	*err*	R r
	Serpens sibilat, *The Serpent hisseth.*	*si*	S s
	Graculus clamat, *The Jay crieth.*	*tac tac*	T t
	Bubo ululat, *The Owl hooteth.*	*ù ù*	U u
	Lepus vagit, *The Hare squeaketh.*	*va*	W w
	Rana coaxat, *The Frog croaketh.*	*coax*	X x
	Asinus rudit, *The Ass brayeth.*	*y y y*	Y y
	Tabanus dicit, *The Breeze or Horse-fly saith.*	*ds ds*	Z z

96

(31)

The Fruits of the Earth. XI. *Terræ Fœtus.*

A Meadow, 1. *yieldeth* Grass *with* Flowers *and* Herbs, *which being cut down, are made* Hay. 2.	*Pratum*, 1. fert *Gramina*, cum *Floribus & Herbis*, quæ desecta fiunt *Fœnum*, 2.
A Field, 3. *yieldeth* Corn, *and* Pot-herbs. 4.	*Arvum*, 3. fert *Fruges*, & *Olera*. 4.
Mushrooms, 5. Straw-berries, 6. Myrtle-trees, *&c. come up in* Woods.	*Fungi*, 5. *Fraga*, 6. *Myrtilli*, &c. Proveniunt in *Sylvis*.
Metals, Stones, *and* Minerals *grow under the* Earth.	*Metalla, Lapides, Mineralia* nascuntur sub *terra*.

96

to face page 27
Huzza!
Ah! that I should see him again.
Alack a day!
Oh Me!

98

Pilgrim's Progress

99 John Bunyan

THE PILGRIM'S PROGRESS FROM THIS WORLD, TO THAT VVHICH IS TO COME.

London: Nath. Ponder, 1678.
14.5 cm. A-P⁸, Q⁴. (Incomplete: leaves A_1 [blank] and Q_4 [blank] wanting, Q_2 and Q_3 supplied in facsimile.) [10], 1–232 (pagination irregular), [2] p.
Wharey, p. xxii.

The first edition of the most famous allegory in the English language, and a work that, although it was not written for children, was enthusiastically seized upon by them and became one of the great "adopted" classics among children's books. John Bunyan (1628–1688) was a tinker and a largely self-taught Puritan preacher. Steeped in the Bible, he was capable of writing remarkably vivid, dramatic prose. He wrote this work in prison, where he had been sent for preaching illegally in Restoration England. *Pilgrim's Progress* is a powerful religious allegory—a pilgrimage, fraught with temptation and trial, to a celestial city. From the beginning the book was pressed on children for their spiritual betterment, but children have also found it to be an exciting adventure story, and for that reason they have made it their own.

100 [John Bunyan]

THE CHRISTIAN PILGRIM: CONTAINING AN ACCOUNT OF THE WONDERFUL ADVENTURES AND MIRACULOUS ESCAPES OF A CHRISTIAN, IN HIS TRAVELS FROM THE LAND OF DESTRUCTION TO THE NEW JERUSALEM. FIRST AMERICAN EDITION.

Worcester: Isaiah Thomas, Jun., October 1798.
10 cm. 2 vols.: [7], 8–112; [3], 116–219, 3 p. Silvered paper over wooden boards.
Welch 131.1.
Elisabeth Ball Collection.

This abridgment of John Bunyan's *Pilgrim's Progress* was published in Worcester, Massachusetts, by Isaiah Thomas, Junior, who continued his famous father's custom of publishing English children's books in American editions. The title page of this shortened version for the young stresses the aspects of *Pilgrim's Progress* that have most endeared it to children—"Wonderful Adventures And Miraculous Escapes." This is the first edition; it is one of a small handful of recorded perfect copies of the two-volume work.

THE

Pilgrim's Progress

FROM

THIS WORLD,

TO

That which is to come:

Delivered under the Similitude of a

DREAM

Wherein is Discovered,
The manner of his setting out,
His Dangerous Journey; And safe
Arrival at the Desired Countrey.

I have used Similitudes, Hos. 12. 10.

By *John Bunyan.*

Licensed and Entred according to Order.

LONDON,
Printed for *Nath. Ponder* at the *Peacock*
in the *Poultrey* near *Cornhil*, 1678.

99

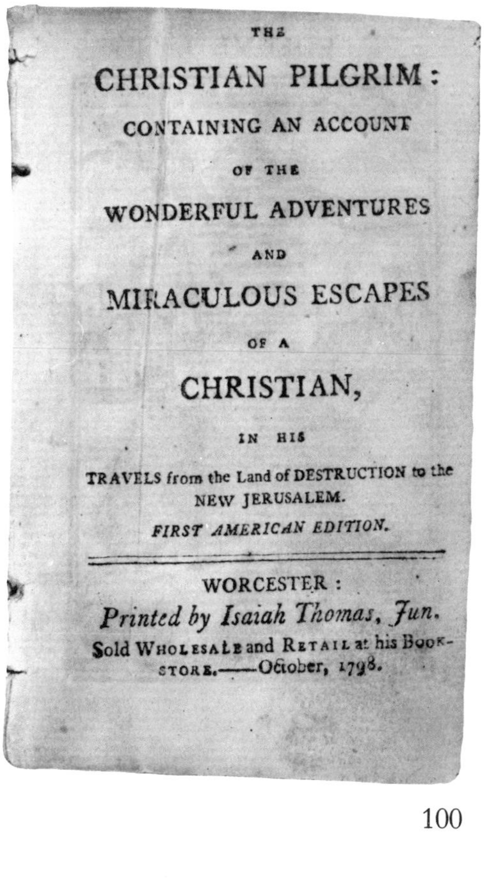

THE

CHRISTIAN PILGRIM:

CONTAINING AN ACCOUNT

OF THE

WONDERFUL ADVENTURES

AND

MIRACULOUS ESCAPES

OF A

CHRISTIAN,

IN HIS

TRAVELS from the Land of DESTRUCTION to the NEW JERUSALEM.

FIRST AMERICAN EDITION.

WORCESTER:
Printed by Isaiah Thomas, Jun.
Sold WHOLESALE and RETAIL at his BOOK-STORE.—October, 1798.

100

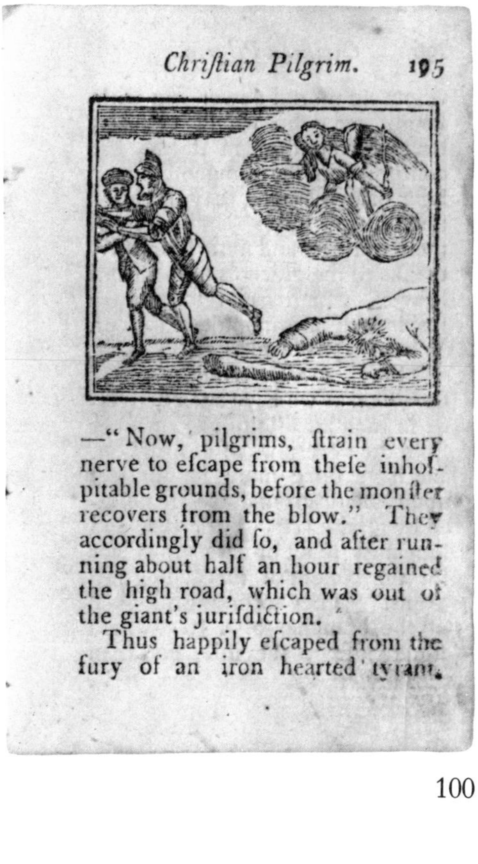

Christian Pilgrim. 195

—"Now, pilgrims, strain every nerve to escape from these inhospitable grounds, before the monster recovers from the blow." They accordingly did so, and after running about half an hour regained the high road, which was out of the giant's jurisdiction.

Thus happily escaped from the fury of an iron hearted tyrant.

100

Fairy Tales and Fables

101 Giovanfrancesco Straparola

LE TREDICI PIACEVOLISSIME NOTTI.

Venice: Marco Claseri for Alessandro de' Vecchi, 1599.
20.5 cm. [3], 4–348, [4] p.
Brunet, V, 560. Thwaite, p. 247. Opie, Classic, *p. 20.*
Purchased for the Elisabeth Ball Collection.

This is the first illustrated edition of a sixteenth-century Venetian collection of traditional tales which became a source for many later writers of children's literature. Straparola's book was first published, in two parts, in 1550 and 1553. Among the stories related by the book's protagonists (who are on the island of Murano in the lagoon of Venice during carnival time) are early forms of such fairy tales as Puss in Boots and Beauty and the Beast. It is highly likely that Charles Perrault and Mme Le Prince de Beaumont, who put these tales into the forms that children know today, drew upon Straparola's book for inspiration, for it was published in France in 1560.

102 [? Richard Johnson]

THE HISTORY OF TOM THUMBE.

London: Tho. Langley, 1621.
14 cm. [19] f.
STC 14056. Bühler.
Purchased as the gift of Robert H. Taylor.

The legend of Tom Thumb is very old. The minuscule hero first appeared in English literature in the sixteenth century, but in allusions that indicate he was already well known, and particularly well known to children. The volume shown here is the only extant copy of the earliest known book about Tom Thumb. It might well be called the earliest surviving printed English nursery tale. It has been ascribed to Richard Johnson (1573–?1659) on the basis of internal evidence, including the initials "R.I." that appear at the end of the book. Although no evidence has been found of any earlier edition than this one of 1621, the blocks from which the woodcut illustrations were printed show signs of considerable wear, indicating use—perhaps repeated use—in earlier printings. The woodcut on the title page shows a number of incidents from Tom's unusually adventurous life, all familiar to children down to the present day. His mother (who is of course of normal size) puts him under a thistle to rest, and a cow swallows him, thistle and all; he falls into a pudding his mother is mixing, and is baked in it; he tries to help his father in the fields, but a crow seizes him and carries him off.

103 [Charles Perrault]

Manuscript in a scribal hand, with illustrations, of CONTES DE MA MERE LOYE.

1695.
19×13 cm. [59] *f.*
Opie, Classic, *p. 21. Storer. Muir, p. 45.*
Purchased as the gift of the Fellows.

This is the original manuscript of five tales that have become part of our literature and indeed our consciousness. The manuscript contains the tales we know as *Sleeping Beauty, Little Red Riding Hood, Bluebeard, Puss in Boots,* and *Diamonds and Toads.* In the versions first written down here, the stories have been cherished for nearly three hundred years. These tales have their sources in folklore, and early forms of the stories were in existence long before 1695. But the achievement of the author of the tales in this manuscript is that he put them into a form that the world has accepted as final. This is the form in which the tales have been known and loved ever since 1695; no alteration has been acceptable, no improvement has seemed possible since then.

This most beloved of all fairy tale collections was put into book form in 1697, in an edition that included three additional tales, those we know as *Cinderella, Riquet with the Tuft,* and *Hop o' My Thumb.* All eight tales show the signs of a skilled literary hand at work, but they also bear the unmistakable marks of a long tradition of oral narration. Scholars still debate the identity of this person who took a set of traditional stories and, while preserving their original, familiar elements, recast them into forms that became immortal. The manuscript is dedicated to "Mademoiselle," who was Elizabeth Charlotte d'Orléans, niece of Louis XIV, and the dedication is signed "P.P." These are presumably the initials of Pierre Perrault (1678–1700), third son of the academician and poet Charles Perrault. Pierre, who later took the name Darmancour, was sixteen or seventeen at the time; it is unclear (despite various theories) whether the young man himself composed the tales, whether they were a father-son collaboration, or whether the father wrote them and, like the doting parent he is thought to have been, gave his son the credit. In support of this last theory, it has been pointed out that whereas the father was a distinguished man of letters who continued to write until his death in 1703, the son apparently wrote nothing else, and had a subsequent career as a soldier.

The seven anonymous pictures, done in gouache, with which the manuscript is illustrated have proven to be extraordinarily influential; they are repeatedly echoed in later illustrated versions of the tales. The title, *Contes de ma mere l'Oye*, seems to have been a traditional term in France; it entered the English language as *Mother Goose's Tales*, when the book was translated into English in 1729. Mother Goose as a personage entered the nursery very soon afterward.

A facsimile edition of the manuscript was published by The Pierpont Morgan Library in 1956.

104 [Charles Perrault]

HISTOIRES OU CONTES DU TEMPS PASSÉ. AVEC DES MORALITEZ. PAR LE FILS DE MONSIEUR PERREAULT DE L'ACADEMIE FRANÇOIS. SUIVANT LA COPIE, À PARIS.

[? Amsterdam: ? Jaques Desbordes], 1700.
13 cm. [8], 1–175, [1] p.
Brunet, Supplément II, 205. Gumuchian 4408.
Elisabeth Ball Collection.

One of the very earliest printed editions of the Perrault fairy tales, comprising the eight tales as they were published in the first edition of 1697. The copperplate engravings for the frontispiece and the headpieces to five of the tales are copies of those by Clouzier in the first edition, done after the gouache illustrations in the manuscript of 1695. The phrase "*Contes de ma mere l'Oye*" is retained in the frontispiece, but the collection is now entitled *Histoires ou Contes du Temps Passé* (*Stories or Tales of Bygone Times*). This edition, which is of great rarity, bears no printer's name; it was probably printed by Jaques Desbordes of Amsterdam, who brought out an unauthorized edition in 1697, the same year that the authorized first edition appeared in Paris.

SIR HORNBOOK. 20
—'Ho! who are you that dare invade
My turrets, moats, and fences?

97

176

70 Pence are 5 Shillings and 10 pence,
You have too many flounces dear Miss to your dress.

183

16 Nightingale.

N n

N n

The Nightingale ſings
ſweetly.

70

105 [Charles Perrault]

HISTOIRES OU CONTES DU TEMS PASSÉ, AVEC DES MORALITEZ. PAR M. PERRAULT. NOUVELLE EDITION AUGMENTÉE D'UNE NOUVELLE, À LA FIN. SUIVANT LA COPIE DE PARIS.

Amsterdam: La Veuve de Jaq. Desbordes, 1721.
13 cm. [8], 1–184 p.
Brunet, Supplément II, 206.
Purchased for the Elisabeth Ball Collection.

This edition of the Perrault *Histoires ou Contes* is significant for at least two reasons. It is the first edition to have an added fairy tale, *L'Adroite Princesse*, later known in English as *The Discreet Princess*, a tale written by Mademoiselle L'Heritier and included in some early editions of the Perrault fairy tales. And this 1721 edition is also important because it presents the text on which the first English translation of the tales would be based. The engravings illustrating the book are again copies—or copies of copies—of the gouache illustrations in the original manuscript of 1695. This edition survives in only three known perfect copies.

106 [Charles Perrault]

LES CONTES DE PERRAULT.

Paris: J. Hetzel, 1862.
42.5 cm. [5], vi-xxiv, 1–59, [3] p. + plates.
Brunet, Supplément II, 207.
Purchased for the Elisabeth Ball Collection.

The first edition of a sumptuous French collection of Perrault's fairy tales illustrated with spacious, romantic engravings after drawings by Gustave Doré. These Doré pictures, rich in atmosphere and fascinating detail, are probably the most famous of all the illustrations to Perrault done in the nineteenth century. About half of them were used again, a few years later, for a London edition of some of the tales in English translation.

107 THE TRIFLE-HUNTER: OR, THE ADVENTURES OF PRINCE BONBENNIN. A CHINESE TALE.

Hartford: John Babcock, 1798.
11 cm. [3], 6–28, [2] p. (Incomplete: first leaf wanting.)
Welch 1179b.1.
Elisabeth Ball Collection.

This rare early Connecticut children's chapbook is a gentle fairy tale by an anonymous author who writes with a felicity and grace not always found in books for the young during this period. The tale is taken from an anonymous collection, *The Palace of Enchantment*, which was published in England in 1788 and included fairy tales translated from the French of the Countess d'Aulnoy.

108 B. A. T.

THE HISTORY OF MOTHER TWADDLE, AND THE MARVELLOUS ATCHIEVMENTS OF HER SON JACK.

London: J. Harris, 25 April 1807.
12.5 cm. [16] f.
NBL 427.
Elisabeth Ball Collection.

The first edition of a rare version, told in rhyme, of the familiar Jack and the Beanstalk fable. This early John Harris publication employs copperplate engravings for both the text and the illustrations, which are colored by hand. "B.A.T." has not been identified.

109 [? Charles Lamb]

BEAUTY AND THE BEAST.

London: M. J. Godwin, [? 1811].
13 cm. [3], 2–32 p. + 8 plates + 2 fold-out music sheets. Buff printed wrappers.
Thomson 28 ("surprize").

The author of this agreeable version of *Beauty and the Beast* may have been Charles Lamb. The publishers (despite the "M. J. Godwin" imprint on the title page) were William Godwin and his second wife, Mary, who had begun their publishing enterprise in 1805 under the name of the firm's manager, Thomas Hodgkins. Charles Lamb wrote a number of children's books for the Godwins, either alone or in collaboration with his sister Mary. This copy of the book, which is the extremely rare first issue of the first edition, contains two-fold-out sheets of music for "Beauty's Song."

110 [Marie Le Prince de Beaumont]

Autograph manuscript, illustrated, of BEAUTY AND THE BEAST, A FAIRY TALE. [*Translated from the French by Adelaide Doyle. Illustrated by Richard Doyle.*]

1842.
25 cm. 36 f.
Purchased for the Elisabeth Ball Collection.

Richard ("Dick") Doyle (1824–1883) was one of the greatest of the illustrators who flourished in Victorian England. He produced a wide variety of art work, much of it in the form of caricatures for the satiric magazine *Punch*, and he illustrated novels by William Makepeace Thackeray and Thomas Hughes. His effortless genius, essentially warm, playful, delicate, was particularly well suited to the illustration of children's books, and it is to be regretted that he did not turn his hand to more of them than the very small number he did. The work shown here is a children's book, but it was apparently never intended for publication. Doyle's sister, Adelaide, translated the seventeenth-century tale from the French of Madame Le Prince de Beaumont, and Dick Doyle provided the illustrations (and a more appealing Beast was surely never depicted). The joint production was intended as a gift for their father, John Doyle. The Pierpont Morgan Library published a facsimile edition of this illustrated manuscript in 1973.

111 ❧ William Makepeace Thackeray

Autograph manuscript, with illustrations by the author, of THE ROSE AND THE RING.

1853 – 1855.
14 × 22 cm. 90 f.

The original manuscript of Thackeray's fairy tale, or "fire-side pantomime," with the author's own illustrations. In this case the pictures preceded the story, for Thackeray first drew them as doll-like "characters" to be used by his two young daughters and other

English children at a Twelfth Night celebration in Rome. After the party, Thackeray collected the pictures he had drawn—King and Queen, Lady and Lover, Dandy and Captain, and others—and began to write a fairy tale about them, giving them new names for the purpose. Young Edith Story, the daughter of an English friend, was convalescing from a long illness at the time and had not come to the party; Thackeray visited her often during the ensuing month, and sat at her bedside reading aloud the latest chapters he had written of *The Rose and the Ring*. At the same time he was hard at work on a novel, *The Newcomes*; but he welcomed the respite he enjoyed whenever he turned to this children's book about the improbable kingdoms of Paflagonia and Crim Tartary. Thackeray took up the tale sporadically through 1854. A March 2 entry in his diary reads: "Wrote these days in the Fairy tale. . . . It is wonderful how easy this folly trickles from the pen." He at last finished the story, added many new drawings to supplement his original figures, and prepared the illustrated manuscript of *The Rose and the Ring* to be published as a "Christmas book" in the winter of 1855.

A facsimile edition of the manuscript was published by The Pierpont Morgan Library in 1947.

112 M. A. Titmarsh [i.e., William Makepeace Thackeray]

THE ROSE AND THE RING; OR, THE HISTORY OF PRINCE GIGLIO AND PRINCE BULBO. A FIRE-SIDE PANTOMIME FOR GREAT AND SMALL CHILDREN.

London: Smith, Elder, and Co., 1855.
18 cm. [3], iv, [1], 2–128, [1], 2–16 p. + frontispiece + 7 plates. Pink printed boards.
Shepherd 126.

The first edition of *The Rose and the Ring*, as published by Smith, Elder, and Company in 1855. The wood-engraved illustrations, as well as the story, have delighted generations of children. The sad truth, however, is that when the illustrations in the printed book are compared with Thackeray's original drawings, it becomes evident that much of the author-illustrator's pictorial wit and subtlety was lost in the process of engraving the drawings on the wooden blocks.

113 Charles Kingsley

THE WATER-BABIES: A FAIRY TALE FOR A LAND-BABY.

London: Macmillan, 1863.
20.5 cm. [11], 4–350, [2] p. + 2 plates. Blue cloth gilt.
Osborne, p. 359. Gumuchian 3520.
Purchased for the Elisabeth Ball Collection.

Charles Kingsley was a rural vicar in Victorian England, and the "land-baby" of the subtitle was his youngest son, five-year-old Grenville Arthur. In writing this fairy tale about the underwater adventures of Tom, a chimney-sweep's climbing-boy, Kingsley uttered many a sermon. But along with his zeal for Anglican Christianity he also brought into play his enthusiasm for nature and his strong sense of indignation at the Victorian practice of using small children as laborers. This copy is from the rare first issue of the first edition. It contains a leaf bearing a poem, *L'Envoi*. Kingsley had second thoughts about this while the book was being printed, and he had the leaf removed, but not before a few hundred copies of the book had already gone forth. The book is illustrated by J. Noel Paton.

114 Rudyard Kipling

JUST SO STORIES FOR LITTLE CHILDREN.

London: Macmillan and Co., 1902.
23 cm. [9], 2–249, [3] p. Red pictorial cloth.
Stewart-Yeats 260.

These modern fables, principally about animals, contain elements of folklore—albeit often Rudyard Kipling's own folklore. The dozen tales include "How the Camel Got His Hump," "How the Leopard Got His Spots," and "The Beginning of the Armadilloes." The many tricks of language and sound have made the book a delight for young children when it is read aloud. Kipling himself drew the illustrations; they are largely in the *art nouveau* style of the eighteen-nineties. The *Just So Stories* were an immediate success and have enjoyed a long popularity. This is the first edition.

NOTTE DECIMA.

GIA' in ogni parte gli stanchi animali per le diurne fatiche dauano riposo alle trauagliate membra, chi su le molli piume, chi su li duri, & aspri sassi, chi su tenere herbette, & chi sopra li frõzuti alberi, quando la Signora con le sue damigelle vscì di camera, & venne in sala, doue già erano raunati i compagni, per vdir il fauoleggiare. Et chiamato vn seruente, la Signora gli commandò, che portasse lo aureo vaso, & postoui dentro di cinque damigelle il nome, il primo che vscì, fù di Lauretta, il secondo di Arianna, il terzo di Alteria, il quarto di Eritrea, & il quinto di Cateruzza. Et subito leuossi da seder la nobil Lauretta, & alla sua fauola diede principio, cosi dicendo.

FINETTA INVOLA A MADONNA VERONICA moglie di M. Brocardo Caualli da Verona, vna collana, perle, & altre gioie, & per mezo de un suo amante, non auedendosi il marito ricupera il tutto.

FAVOLA I.

MOlte uolte pensando, & ripensando alli trauagli, & angustie, che occorrono, non trouo affanno maggiore, che vedere vna donna lealmente amar il marito, & senza cagione essere vilipesa da lui: & però non si deue marauigliare alcuno, se alle volte le mise-

The History of Tom Thumbe, the Little, for his small stature surnamed, King Arthvrs Dwarfe:
Whose Life and aduentures containe many strange and wonderfull accidents, published for the delight of merry Time-spenders.
Imprinted at London for Tho: Langley. 1621.

102

contes
De ma mere
l'oye

103

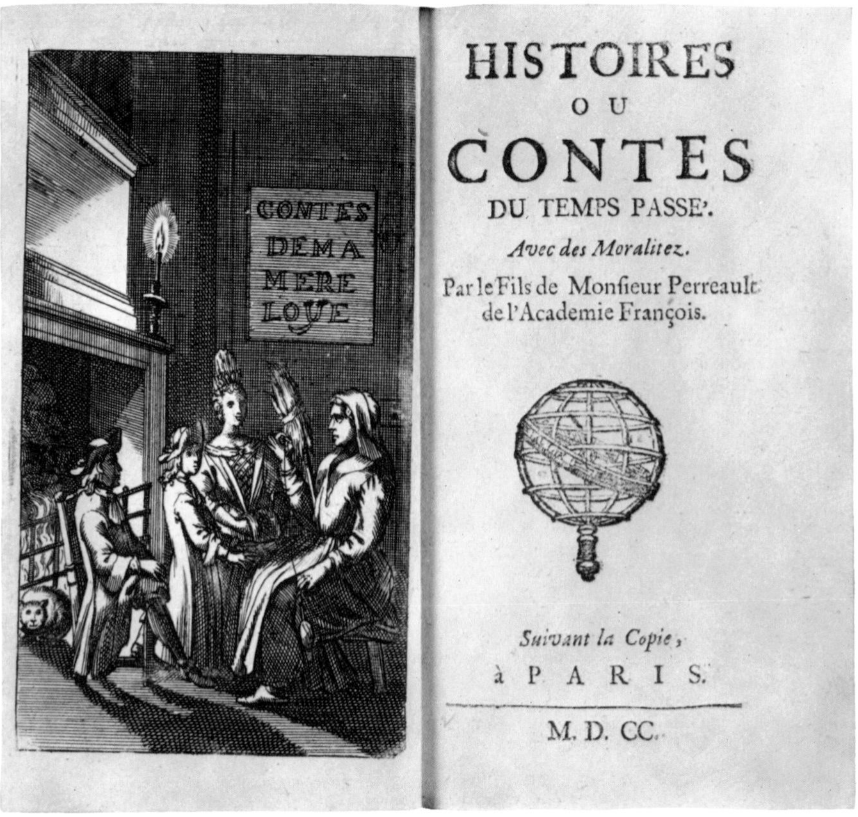

HISTOIRES
OU
CONTES
DU TEMPS PASSÉ.
Avec des Moralitez.
Par le Fils de Monsieur Perreault
de l'Academie François.

Suivant la Copie,
à PARIS.

M. D. CC.

104

35

PETIT CHAPERON
ROUGE.

CONTE.

IL estoit une fois une petite fille de Vilage, la plus jolie qu'on eut sçû voir; sa Mere en etoit folle, & sa Mere grand plus folle
B 6 en-

104

63

LE MAITRE CHAT,
OU
LE CHAT BOTTÉ.

CONTE.

UN Meusnier ne laissa pour tout biens à trois enfans qu'il avoit, que son Moulin, son Asne
&

104

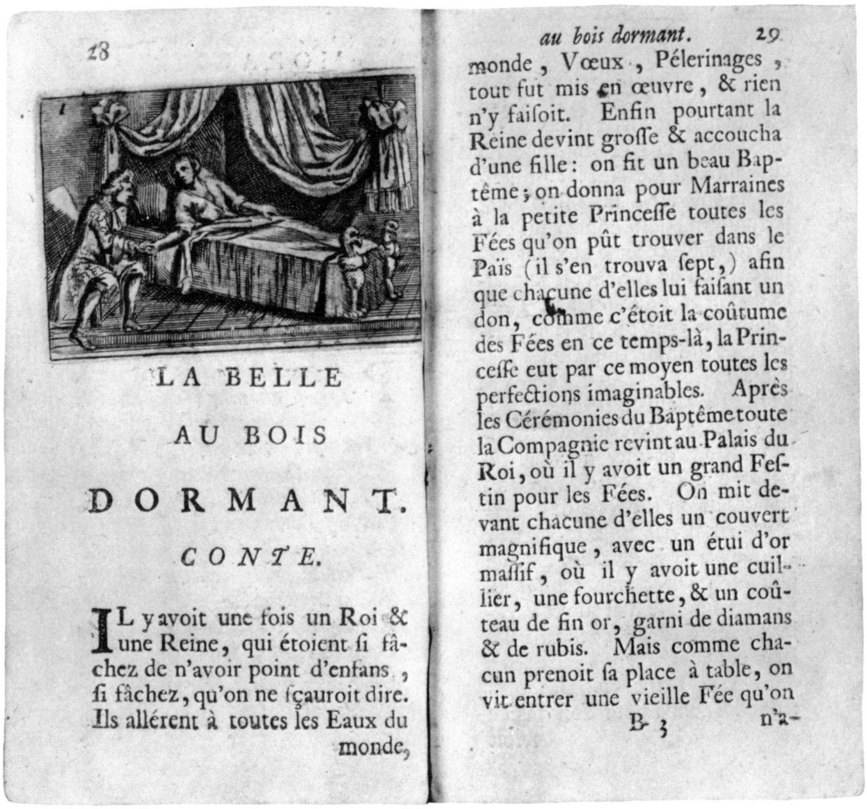

18

LA BELLE

AU BOIS

DORMANT.

CONTE.

IL y avoit une fois un Roi & une Reine, qui étoient ſi fâchez de n'avoir point d'enfans, ſi fâchez, qu'on ne ſçauroit dire. Ils allérent à toutes les Eaux du monde,

au bois dormant. 29

monde, Vœux, Pélerinages, tout fut mis en œuvre, & rien n'y faiſoit. Enfin pourtant la Reine devint groſſe & accoucha d'une fille: on fit un beau Baptême; on donna pour Marraines à la petite Princeſſe toutes les Fées qu'on pût trouver dans le Païs (il s'en trouva ſept,) afin que chacune d'elles lui faiſant un don, comme c'étoit la coûtume des Fées en ce temps-là, la Princeſſe eut par ce moyen toutes les perfections imaginables. Après les Cérémonies du Baptême toute la Compagnie revint au Palais du Roi, où il y avoit un grand Feſtin pour les Fées. On mit devant chacune d'elles un couvert magnifique, avec un étui d'or maſſif, où il y avoit une cuillier, une fourchette, & un coûteau de fin or, garni de diamans & de rubis. Mais comme chacun prenoit ſa place à table, on vit entrer une vieille Fée qu'on n'a-

B 3

105

106

106

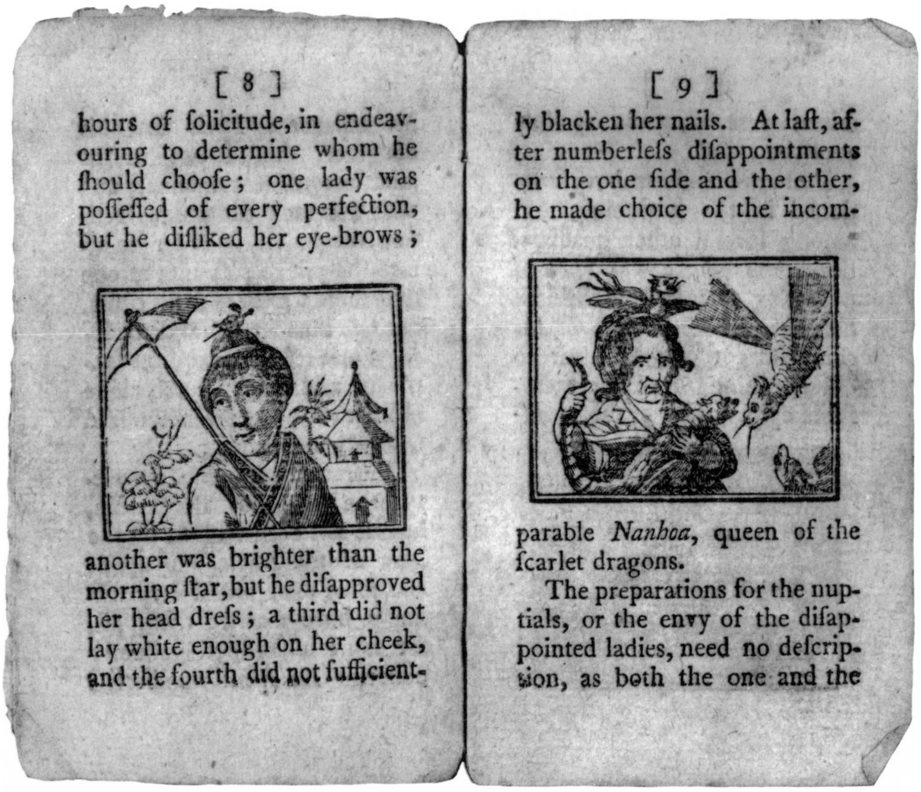

[8]

hours of ſolicitude, in endeavouring to determine whom he ſhould chooſe; one lady was poſſeſſed of every perfection, but he diſliked her eye-brows;

another was brighter than the morning ſtar, but he diſapproved her head dreſs; a third did not lay white enough on her cheek, and the fourth did not ſufficient-

[9]

ly blacken her nails. At laſt, after numberleſs diſappointments on the one ſide and the other, he made choice of the incomparable *Nanhoa*, queen of the ſcarlet dragons.

The preparations for the nuptials, or the envy of the diſappointed ladies, need no deſcription, as both the one and the

107

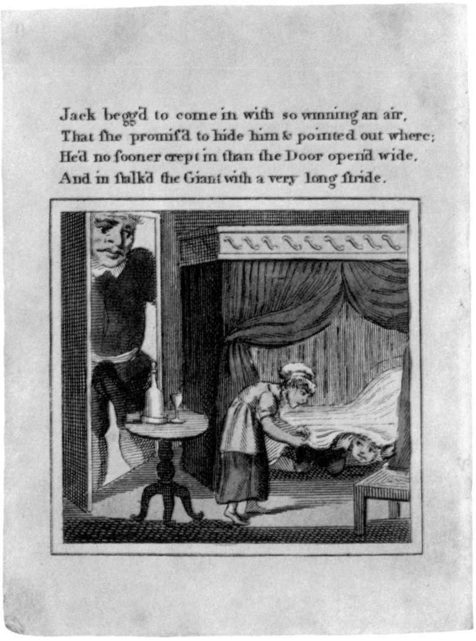
Jack begg'd to come in with so winning an air,
That ſhe promiſ'd to hide him & pointed out where;
He'd no ſooner crept in than the Door open'd wide,
And in ſtalk'd the Giant with a very long ſtride.

108

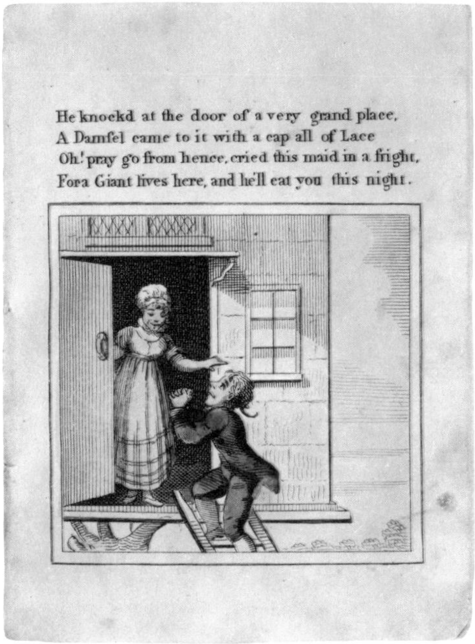
He knock'd at the door of a very grand place,
A Damſel came to it with a cap all of Lace
Oh! pray go from hence, cried this maid in a fright,
For a Giant lives here, and he'll eat you this night.

108

BEAUTY
AND THE
BEAST
A
FAIRY TALE
TRANSLATED
by
ADELAIDE
AND
ILLUSTRATED
by
DICK.

110

ANGELICA ARRIVES JUST IN TIME.

[To face p. 68.

112

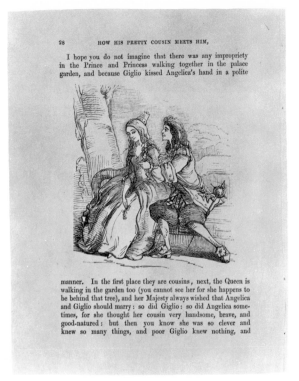

I hope you do not imagine that there was any impropriety in the Prince and Princess walking together in the palace garden, and because Giglio kissed Angelica's hand in a polite

manner. In the first place they are cousins, next, the Queen is walking in the garden too (you cannot see her for she happens to be behind that tree), and her Majesty always wished that Angelica and Giglio should marry: so did Giglio: so did Angelica sometimes, for she thought her cousin very handsome, brave, and good-natured: but then you know she was so clever and knew so many things, and poor Giglio knew nothing, and

112

WATER BABIES._ *Frontispiece*

113

162

162

An ELEGY on the GLORY of her SEX
MRS MARY BLAIZE
R. CALDECOTT's
PICTURE
BOOKS
Frederick Warne and Co.

163

There was a sick man of Tobago
Liv'd long on rice-gruel and sago;
But at last to his bliss,
The physician said this---
"To a roast leg of mutton you
may go."

217

5

OLD WOMAN OF HARROW.

There was an Old Woman of Harrow,
Who visited in a Wheel barrow,
And her servant before,
Knock'd loud at each door;
To announce the Old Woman of Harrow.

218

114

THE BUTTERFLY THAT STAMPED

THIS, O my Best Beloved, is a story—a new and a wonderful story—a story quite different from the other stories—a story about The Most Wise Sovereign Suleiman-bin-Daoud—Solomon the Son of David.

There are three hundred and fifty-five stories about Suleiman-bin-Daoud; but this is not one of them. It is not the story of the Lapwing who found the Water; or the Hoopoe who shaded Suleiman-bin-Daoud from the heat. It is not the story of the Glass Pavement, or the Ruby with the Crooked Hole, or the Gold Bars of Balkis. It is the story of the Butterfly that Stamped.

9

114

Moral Tales

Émile, the treatise on education written in 1762 by Jean-Jacques Rousseau (1712–1778), had a strong and lasting influence on those who wrote books for children. Not all the writers inspired by *Émile* embraced or even understood Rousseau's philosophy of the ideal development of a child's mind and body, but many a writer after Rousseau strove earnestly to imbue children with the love of virtue that was Rousseau's aim. These writers—they are known as the Moral School, and their work as Moral Tales—produced children's stories in which good little boys and girls won glorious rewards in direct proportion to their goodness, and bad children earned only misery and pain.

115 [?John Newbery]
[THE RENOWNED HISTORY OF GILES GINGERBREAD.]

[London: John Newbery, ?1766 or earlier.]
9.8×6.5 cm. [2], 6–30, [31] p. (First and last leaves are pastedowns.) Incomplete: title page wanting. Dutch flowered wrappers.
Roscoe J267.
Elisabeth Ball Collection.

One of the very earliest and most celebrated of all moral tales, this is also one of the most delightful. It is the story of a little boy who eats his way to learning—quite literally, for he is the son of a gingerbread baker, and he learns his alphabet from gingerbread letters which he studies and then eats. (He later graduates to whole books, on the same plan.) The anonymous tale is full of verve and wit along with its moralizing. It has been attributed to various writers, Oliver Goldsmith among them, but perhaps the most reasonable theory is that the book's author and publisher were one and the same—the ebullient, enterprising John Newbery. Although the early publishing history of *Giles Gingerbread* is somewhat obscure, it is of the same period (and achieved the same popularity) as *The*

History of Little Goody Two-Shoes, also published anonymously by Newbery and also attributed variously to him, to Goldsmith, or to others. The copy of *Giles Gingerbread* shown here, a rather battered survivor of very hard usage, has lost its title page. The date of publication must therefore be conjectural; but in its bibliographical details this copy seems to conform exactly to no other recorded copy of the book. It would appear to be one of the few extant copies of the very earliest editions. That it was indeed published by Newbery is obvious; his customary self-advertising is woven into the story.

116 [M. P. (i.e., Dorothy Kilner)]

THE LIFE AND PERAMBULATION OF A MOUSE.

London: John Marshall and Co., 1783.
11.5 cm. [7], viii–xii, [1], 14–110 p. Dutch flowered boards.
Osborne, p. 273.
Elisabeth Ball Collection.

The first edition of one of the more entertaining of English moral tales. It is the work of Dorothy Kilner, a gifted writer who laid more stress on amusing her readers than did most of her contemporaries. The device she adopted here, that of using a small animal to narrate her story, was instantly and incessantly imitated; there appeared a flood of lives and adventures of various little animals and inanimate objects, from flies and bees to threepenny coins. (Her sister-in-law, Mary Kilner, produced *The Adventures of a Pincushion* and *The Memoirs of a Peg-Top.*) Very few other writers of moral tales achieved the sprightliness, let alone the originality, of Dorothy Kilner. No name appears on the title page of this tale, but the preface is signed "M. P." The author took these initials from the village in which she lived, Maryland Point (now a part of London). So great was the popular success of *The Life and Perambulation of a Mouse* that the publisher asked its author to choose a name corresponding to "M. P."—whereupon she chose "Mary Pelham," and wrote more books for children under that name. The woodcuts illustrating *The Life and Perambulation of a Mouse* have been attributed to John Bewick.

117 Arnaud Berquin

L'AMI DES ENFANS. (*No. 4. April 1782.*)

Paris: Pissot; Theophile Barrois, 1782.
13 cm. [4], 5–143, [1] p.
Elisabeth Ball Collection.

One of the most influential of all the authors of moral tales was the French writer Arnaud Berquin (1749–1791), who in 1782 in Paris began to produce a magazine for young people entitled *L'Ami des enfans* (*The Children's Friend*). This contained tales, playlets, letters, and dialogues, all depicting the glorious triumph of virtue over assorted juvenile vices and the temptations thereunto. Berquin's tales, melodramatic and sentimental, abound in virtuous, unreal little children and equally unreal adults. Goodness triumphs inexorably over wickedness again and again, and tears of joy gush from Papa or Maman as they witness the moral excellence of their offspring. These productions cause embarrassment today, but our world is not that of the eighteenth century, which received the moral tale with approbation and much real pleasure. And Berquin's writing is often very effective. *L'Ami des enfans* was popular in France and across the Continent, and it was quickly translated and copied. The magazine began on the first of January 1782, and it appeared regularly thereafter on the first of each month. The first edition of the number for April 1782 is shown here. By the time the little journal had ceased publication, at the end of its second year, there were in print twenty-four volumes, each of 144 pages. They were soon reprinted, and they provided a rich supply of models for the numberless imitators, in French and in other languages, who followed Berquin.

118 Arnaud Berquin

THE LOOKING-GLASS FOR THE MIND; OR, INTELLECTUAL MIRROR. . . . CHIEFLY TRANSLATED FROM THAT MUCH ADMIRED WORK, L'AMI DES ENFANS, OR, THE CHILDRENS FRIEND. [*Translated by Richard Johnson.*]

London: E. Newbery, 1787.
17 cm. [6], 2–212 p.
Roscoe J25(1).
Elisabeth Ball Collection.

The first edition of the most renowned English version—really an adaptation—of Berquin's *Children's Friend.* This is probably the most enduring of the various forms by which the tales became familiar to English children. It was produced by the hack writer Richard Johnson, on assignment from the publisher Elizabeth Newbery. Johnson's name does not appear in the volume, but his account books, which have survived, record that he was paid thirty-four guineas for his labors. The copperplate-engraved frontispiece depicts the goddess Minerva presenting a copy of the book to eager children.

119 Arnaud Berquin

THE CHILDREN'S FRIEND. TRANSLATED . . . BY LUCAS WILLIAMS, ESQ. A NEW CORRECTED EDITION, WITH ADDITIONS.

London: J. Stockdale, 1793.
17.5 cm. 6 vols. in 3.
Osborne, p. 232.
Elisabeth Ball Collection.

An English collection of pieces from Berquin's *Children's Friend*, translated by Lucas Williams and brought out in an elegant six-volume edition by the publisher Stockdale. The very fine copperplate engravings are the work of the portrait-engraver and book-illustrator Thomas Cook. This is probably the largest English collection of Berquin's writings to appear in the eighteenth century; it contains much material not in other English editions.

120 [Arnaud Berquin]

DELIGHTFUL STORIES FOR GOOD CHILDREN.

London: J. Harris, 1804.
12.5 cm. [5], 4–36, [3], 4–36, [3], 4–36, [3], 4–36, [3], 4–36, [3], 4–36 p. + 17 plates. (Incomplete: 1 plate wanting.)
NBL 747.
Purchased for the Elisabeth Ball Collection.

English versions of six of Berquin's moral tales from his *L'Ami des enfans* are collected in this volume issued by the publisher John Harris in 1804. The tales included are *The Mountain Lute*, *The Little Islanders*, *The Young Robber*, *The Conjuring Bird*, *The Military Academy*, and *The Tame Goldfinch*. Each story has its own title page; Harris also issued the tales separately as individual books. The Morgan Library possesses the original drawings for all but two of the copperplate engravings with which this collection is illustrated. The artist responsible for these pen-and-ink-and-wash drawings has not been identified, nor is the engraver known. The engravings generally follow the original drawings quite closely. But a curious discrepancy can be seen in one of the illustrations for *The Mountain Lute*. The musician in the engraving, shown here, plays a lute; in the original drawing, however, he is playing a wind instrument.

121 [Thomas Day]

THE HISTORY OF SANDFORD AND MERTON.

London: J. Stockdale, 1783, 1786, 1789.
18.5 cm. 3 vols.: [3], iv–vii, [2], 2–215, [1] p.; [3], 2–306, [4] p. + frontispiece; [5], 2–308, [4] p. + frontispiece.
Gumuchian 2064.
Elisabeth Ball Collection.

This famous story probably represents a high point in the development of the moral tale. The author, Thomas Day, was deeply committed to the ideals of Rousseau, and he reaffirmed these ideals on every page of this long work. (The first volume, published in 1783, was presumably a complete story, but Day then felt the need to extend it into two more volumes.) Virtue, repeatedly and tediously described to young Harry Sandford and Tommy Merton by the clergyman-tutor Mr. Barlow, leads to happiness as inevitably as sin leads to catastrophe. The influence of John Locke can be discerned here, too, for gentleness and reason triumph throughout. Although its dense, didactic prose is quite unreadable today, *Sandford and Merton* had a very great influence in its time. It offered more narrative variety than did most of the other moral tales with which the young were being inundated in the late eighteenth century, and it became popular enough to go into many editions. It was given widely to children until late in the nineteenth century. The frontispiece to the third volume, shown here, depicts the three principals of the work. The engraving is by T. Maitland, after an original by Thomas Stothard, one of the best-known (and most prolific) illustrators of the period. The three volumes of the Morgan Library *Sandford and Merton* are a rare set of first editions.

122 [Thomas Day]

THE GRATEFUL TURK. OR THE ADVANTAGES OF FRIENDSHIP.

Boston: J. White, 1796.
8.5 cm. [3], 6–30, [2] p. (Incomplete: first leaf wanting.)
Welch 253.
Elisabeth Ball Collection.

A separate American edition of a tale that first appeared, in two parts, in Volume I of Thomas Day's *Sandford and Merton* (1783). This chapbook version, brought out by an early Boston publisher, is an abridgment of the original tale. The unknown abridger, who wrote considerably better prose than did Thomas Day, made this version far more readable than the original. The Morgan Library copy of this chapbook appears to be the only one in existence.

123 THE SISTER'S GIFT, OR THE NAUGHTY BOY REFORMED. PUBLISHED FOR THE ADVANTAGE OF THE RISING GENERATION.

London: E. Newbery, 1786.
10 cm. [3], 5–31 p. (First and last leaves are pastedowns.) Dutch flowered wrappers.
Roscoe J335.
Mrs. Sherman Post Haight Collection.

A moral tale in the form of a children's penny chapbook. It concerns a pair of well-to-do orphans, Miss Kitty Courtly, an exceedingly good little girl, and her brother Master Billy, who is much addicted to mischief—principally cruelty to animals (some of which is carefully described). His sister, observing Billy's vicious disposition, delivers a six-page lecture on his sins and the certainty of future punishment. Whereupon (to quote the last paragraph of the story) "Master Billy wept bitterly, and declared to his sister, that she had painted the enormity of his vices in such striking colours, that they shocked him in the greatest degree; and promised ever after to be as remarkable for generosity, compassion, and every other virtue, as he had hitherto been for cruelty, forwardness, and ill-nature. It is with pleasure we can add, that he faithfully kept his word, and is now one of the very best little masters in the whole universe." This anonymous Elizabeth Newbery publication is mentioned in advertisements as early as 1769, but the Morgan Library copy shown here is the earliest known, and appears to be the sole surviving copy of its edition.

124 THE BROTHER'S GIFT: OR, THE NAUGHTY GIRL REFORMED.

Hartford: Nathaniel Patten, D *[sic],* DCC, LXXX, IX *[i.e., 1789].*
9.5 cm. [3], 6–30 p. Dark blue wrappers.
Welch 126.2.
Elisabeth Ball Collection.

The writers of moral tales did not discriminate on the basis of sex; the wicked female child was just as valid a target as her erring brother. In this American children's chapbook, a rare early New England imprint, it is a girl, Miss Kitty Bland, who falls into sinful habits. She is redeemed finally by her brother Billy, who lectures her sternly. All ends well, as may be seen on the last page of the book, which is illustrated here: "The Naughty Girl become[s] Good, which makes her esteemed and beloved by everybody." This is the only recorded copy of the chapbook.

125 [Mrs. (Mary Martha Butt) Sherwood]

THE HISTORY OF LITTLE HENRY AND HIS BEARER.

Wellington: F. Houlston and Son, 1814.
15 cm. [5], 6–139, [7] p. Gray printed boards.
Cutt C1.
Purchased as the gift of Miss Julia P. Wightman.

The very rare first edition of the earliest missionary story for children, a book that in its day had an impact and a popularity not unlike that of *Uncle Tom's Cabin*. The story, set in British India, is about a six-year-old boy's conversion to Evangelical Christianity and his efforts to convert his Indian servant, Boosy. The climax of the tale is little Henry's lachrymose but inspiring end at the age of only eight. Although the work exudes sentimentality and dogma, Mrs. Sherwood's writing is simple, effective, and often vivid in the details of its exotic Anglo-Indian background. (This is the background Rudyard Kipling would evoke again for children at the end of the nineteenth century.) *The History of Little Henry* was written by Mrs. Sherwood during her stay in India as the wife of a British officer stationed there. She sent the manuscript to England, where it was published with immediate success. It helped establish the strong Evangelical trend that was to prevail for some time in English children's books, Mrs. Sherwood herself producing a long series of such works. *Little Henry* also helped bring to prominence Mrs. Sherwood's publisher, Houlston, who demonstrated his acumen when he resisted the suggestion of a critic that the Hindustani terms in the book be omitted. Recognizing that these exotic trappings gave the book enormous appeal, the publisher refused to take them out—and was of course proven right in his judgment, for *Little Henry* went on to become a great best-seller.

Mary Brackes

CHAP. I.
An Adventure of Little Giles Gingerbread.

ONE Day as *Gaffer Gingerbread* was coming from Work, he saw little *Giles*, who was as ragged as a Colt, getting up behind Sir *Toby Thompson*'s Coach;

upon which he called to him: Here, *Giles*, come hither to me! I see, says the Father,

115

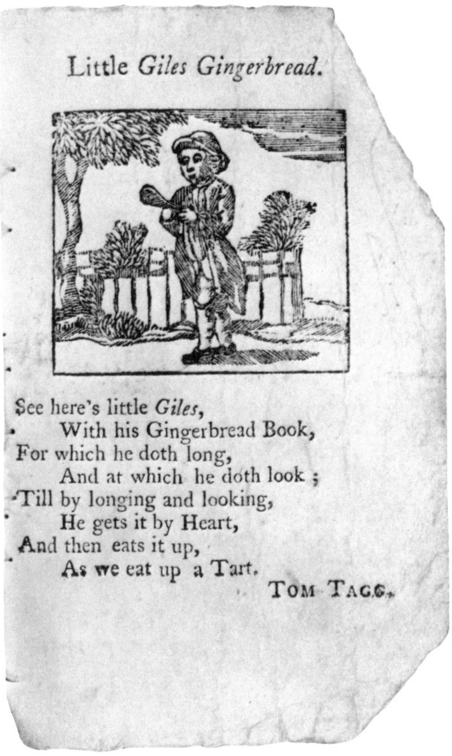
Little *Giles Gingerbread.*

See here's little *Giles*,
With his Gingerbread Book,
For which he doth long,
And at which he doth look;
Till by longing and looking,
He gets it by Heart,
And then eats it up,
As we eat up a Tart.
TOM TAGG.

115

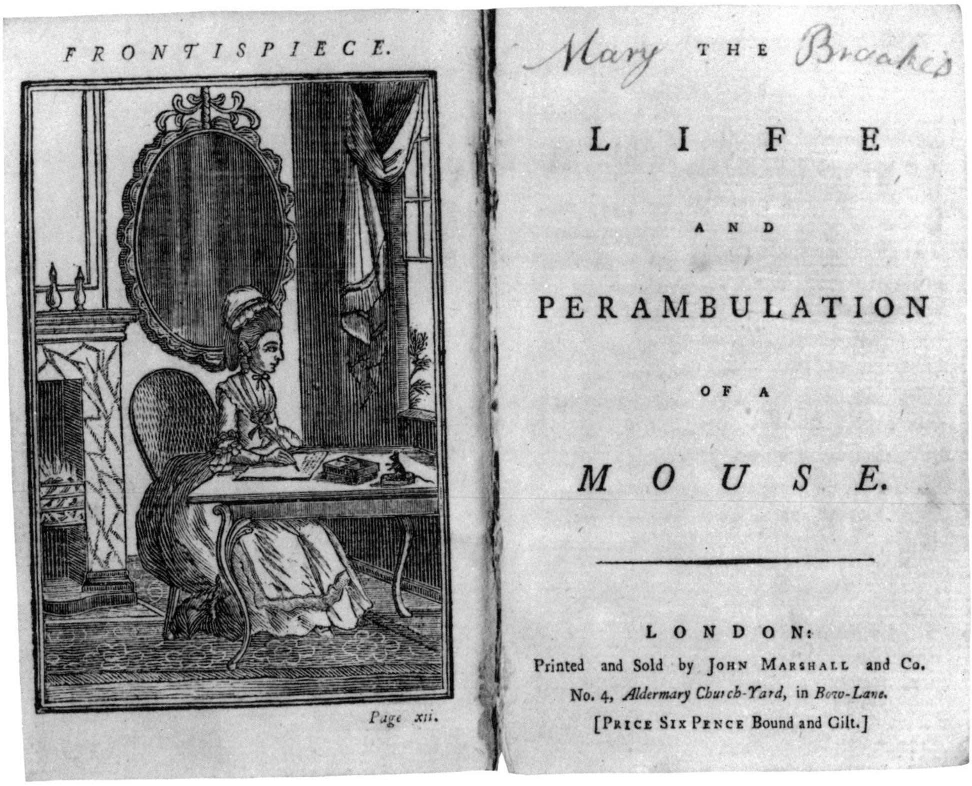
FRONTISPIECE.

Page xii.

Mary THE Brackes

LIFE

AND

PERAMBULATION

OF A

MOUSE.

LONDON:
Printed and Sold by JOHN MARSHALL and Co.
No. 4, *Aldermary Church-Yard*, in *Bow-Lane.*
[PRICE SIX PENCE Bound and Gilt.]

116

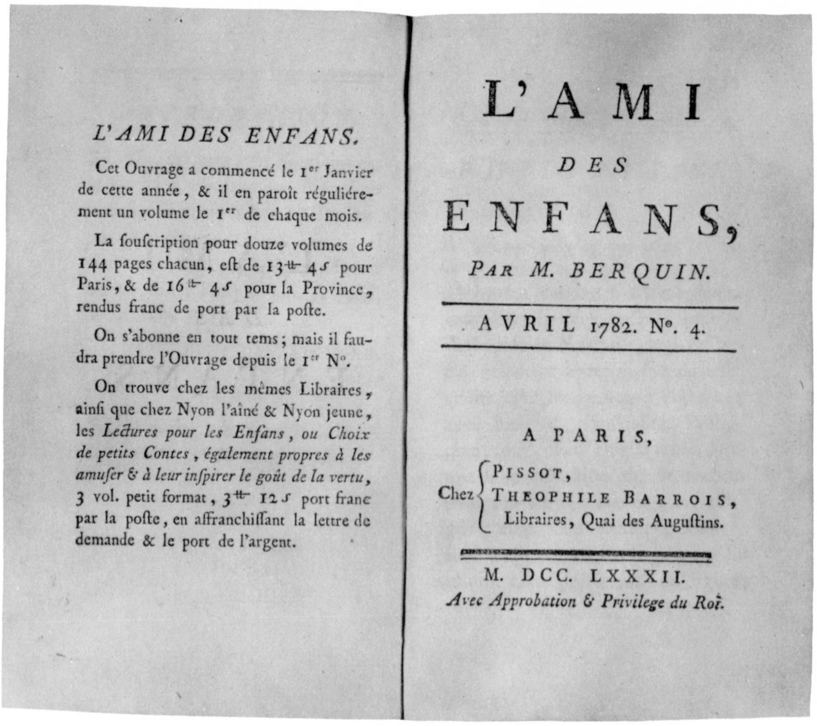

L'AMI DES ENFANS.

Cet Ouvrage a commencé le 1er Janvier de cette année, & il en paroît réguliérement un volume le 1er de chaque mois.

La souscription pour douze volumes de 144 pages chacun, est de 13# 4s pour Paris, & de 16# 4s pour la Province, rendus franc de port par la poste.

On s'abonne en tout tems; mais il faudra prendre l'Ouvrage depuis le 1er N°.

On trouve chez les mêmes Libraires, ainsi que chez Nyon l'aîné & Nyon jeune, les *Lectures pour les Enfans, ou Choix de petits Contes, également propres à les amuser & à leur inspirer le goût de la vertu*, 3 vol. petit format, 3# 12s port franc par la poste, en affranchissant la lettre de demande & le port de l'argent.

L'AMI DES ENFANS,

PAR M. BERQUIN.

AVRIL 1782. N°. 4.

A PARIS,

Chez PISSOT, THEOPHILE BARROIS, Libraires, Quai des Augustins.

M. DCC. LXXXII.

Avec Approbation & Privilege du Roi.

117

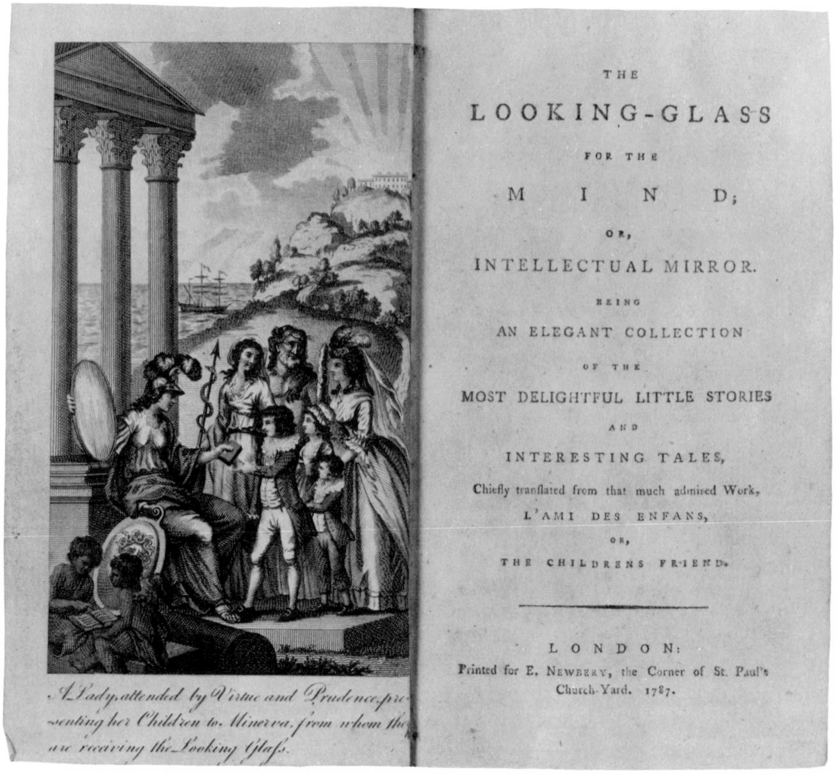

A Lady, attended by Virtue and Prudence, presenting her Children to Minerva, from whom the[y] are receiving the Looking Glass.

THE LOOKING-GLASS FOR THE MIND; OR, INTELLECTUAL MIRROR.

BEING AN ELEGANT COLLECTION OF THE MOST DELIGHTFUL LITTLE STORIES AND INTERESTING TALES,

Chiefly translated from that much admired Work, L'AMI DES ENFANS, OR, THE CHILDRENS FRIEND.

LONDON:

Printed for E. NEWBERY, the Corner of St. Paul's Church-Yard. 1787.

118

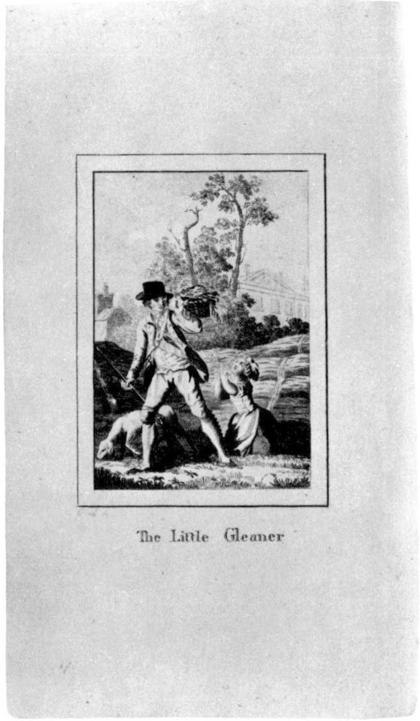

119

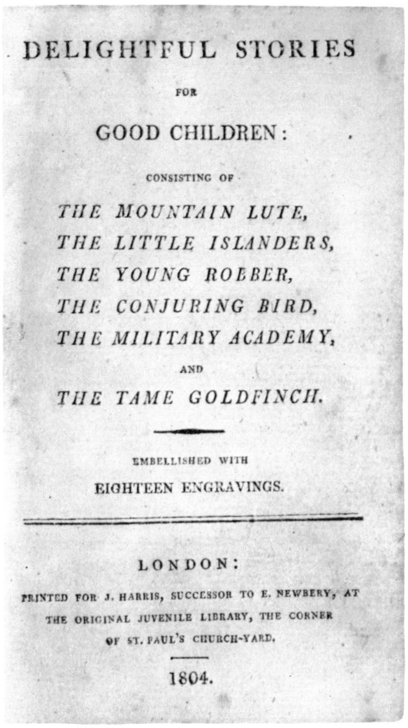
DELIGHTFUL STORIES

FOR

GOOD CHILDREN:

CONSISTING OF

THE MOUNTAIN LUTE,
THE LITTLE ISLANDERS,
THE YOUNG ROBBER,
THE CONJURING BIRD,
THE MILITARY ACADEMY,
AND
THE TAME GOLDFINCH.

EMBELLISHED WITH
EIGHTEEN ENGRAVINGS.

LONDON:

PRINTED FOR J. HARRIS, SUCCESSOR TO E. NEWBERY, AT THE ORIGINAL JUVENILE LIBRARY, THE CORNER OF ST. PAUL'S CHURCH-YARD.

1804.

120

120

120

FRONTISPIECE.

Page 158. The reconciliation was begun and completed in a moment;

Publish'd Aug. 20. 1789 by J. Stockdale

GRATEFUL

TURK.

OR

THE ADVANTAGES

OF

FRIENDSHIP.

1796

BOSTON: Printed by J. White
1796.

122

[17]

a man rushed through the crowd, and ascended the tallest ladder, seemingly determined to rescue the youth or perish in the attempt. A sudden gust of

122

Betsey Smith

Do not, unthinking Youth, too soon engage,
In all the giddy vices of the age!
For he that enters on that beaten track,
Goes on without a thought of coming back.

THE

SISTER's GIFT,

OR THE

NAUGHTY BOY REFORMED.

PUBLISHED FOR

The ADVANTAGE of the rising GENERATION.

O now, while health and vigour still remain,
Toil, toil, my lads, to purchase honest gain!
Shun idleness! shun pleasure's tempting snare!
A youth of folly, breeds an age of care.

LONDON:

Printed for E. NEWBERY, at the Corner of St. Paul's Church-yard. 1786.

[Price One Penny.]

123

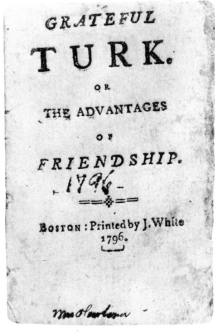

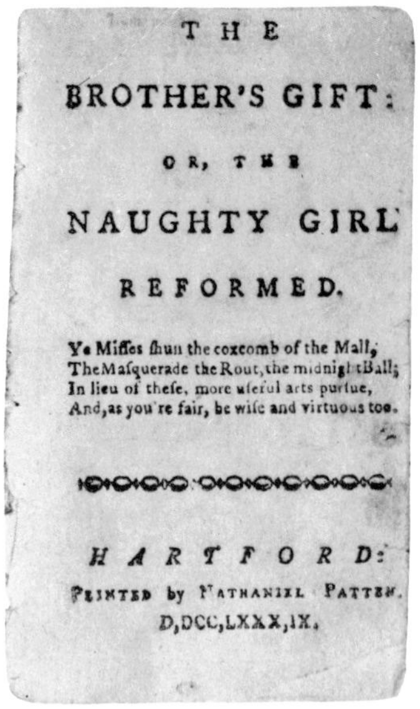
THE
BROTHER'S GIFT:
OR, THE
NAUGHTY GIRL
REFORMED.

Ye Misses shun the coxcomb of the Mall,
The Masquerade the Rout, the midnight Ball;
In lieu of these, more useful arts pursue,
And, as you're fair, be wise and virtuous too.

HARTFORD:
PRINTED by NATHANIEL PATTEN.
D,DCC,LXXX,IX.

124

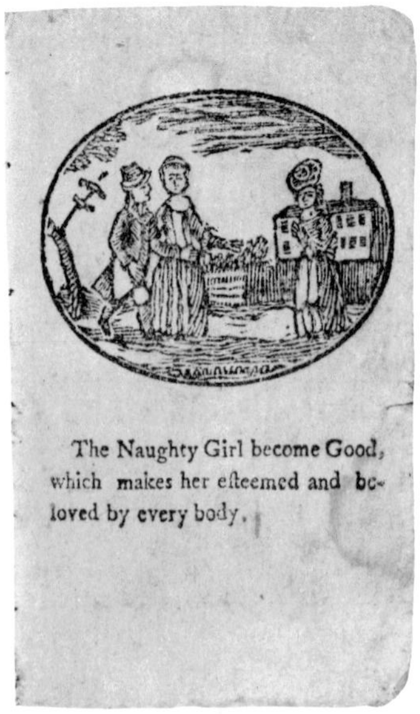
The Naughty Girl become Good, which makes her esteemed and beloved by every body.

124

THE HISTORY OF Little Henry and his Bearer.

See page 6.

WELLINGTON.
Printed by and for F. Houlston and Son 1814.
(Entered at Stationer's Hall.)

125

Cautionary Tales

126 VICE IN ITS PROPER SHAPE; OR, THE WONDERFUL AND MELANCHOLY TRANSFORMATION OF SEVERAL NAUGHTY MASTERS AND MISSES INTO THOSE CONTEMPTIBLE ANIMALS WHICH THEY MOST RESEMBLE IN DISPOSITION.

London: E. Newbery, [about 1781].
9.5 cm. [3], iv–ix, 10–112, 115–126 p. (Incomplete: H_1, H_8, *and ?* I_1–$_8$ *wanting.)*
Roscoe J369 (2A).
Elisabeth Ball Collection.

The title of this work expresses very well the threatening nature of the children's books known as Cautionary Tales. Ominous little woodcuts illustrate chapters in which Master Jack Idle is turned into a donkey, Miss Dorothy Chatter-fast becomes a magpie, Master Stephen Churl a little cur, Master Anthony Greedy-Guts a pig, and so on. A single copy is recorded of the first edition of this book, which was published about 1774. The next known edition is the one shown here, of which this copy is the only one recorded.

127 THE HISTORY OF LITTLE KING PIPPIN; WITH AN ACCOUNT OF THE MELANCHOLY DEATH OF FOUR NAUGHTY BOYS, WHO WERE DEVOURED BY WILD BEASTS. . . .

London: E. Newbery, 1783.
10 cm. [3], 5–62, [1] p. Dutch flowered wrappers.
Roscoe J168.
Elisabeth Ball Collection.

Through English translations of the mediaeval French romance *Valentin et Orson*, the monarch Pippin (i.e., Pépin) entered English children's literature. The hero of the cautionary tale shown here, illustrated with woodcuts and published by Elizabeth Newbery, is Peter Pippin, King of the Good Boys. Peter attends faithfully to his studies and devotions and rises inexorably in the world until it is recommended to the King of England that he be made governor of an important island. Allowing himself a cynical thought here, the anonymous author says: "Though virtue is generally a poor recommendation at court, in this instance it succeeded, and King Pippin was immediately appointed." At the same time some less virtuous friends of the young hero, having desecrated birds' nests and neglected school and their prayers, come to dreadful ends. This is the sole recorded copy of the earliest known edition of the book.

128 [William Darton]

THE FIRST CHAPTER OF ACCIDENTS AND REMARKABLE EVENTS: CONTAINING CAUTION AND INSTRUCTION FOR CHILDREN.

London: Darton and Harvey, 1801.
12 cm. [26] f. Blue-gray wrappers.

[William Darton]

THE SECOND CHAPTER OF ACCIDENTS....

London: Darton and Harvey, 1801.
12 cm. [21] f. Blue-gray wrappers.
Osborne, p. 115.

[William Darton]

THE THIRD CHAPTER OF ACCIDENTS....

London: Darton and Harvey, 1801.
12 cm. [26] f. Blue-gray wrappers.

Elisabeth Ball Collection.

Darton's *First Chapter of Accidents*, together with the *Second* and *Third* chapters, all appearing in the same year, contained an appalling recital of the physical hazards lying in wait for the disobedient, overinquisitive, or merely incautious child. The author of these books was not only their publisher as well, but he also executed the engravings in the three volumes. All three are first editions.

129 [Elizabeth Turner]

THE DAISY; OR, CAUTIONARY STORIES IN VERSE. ADAPTED TO THE IDEAS OF CHILDREN FROM FOUR TO EIGHT YEARS OLD.

London: J. Harris, 1807.
13 cm. [36] f.
NBL 337. Darton, p. 193.
Elisabeth Ball Collection.

The rare first edition of a classic English cautionary work of the early nineteenth century. It was intended for rather young children. Although the rhymes by Elizabeth Turner are not notable as specimens of light-hearted humor, most of them are fortunately less menacing than this one about Giddy Helen.

130 LE CHIEN DE M. CROQUE

Paris: P. Blanchard, [about 1820].
10 cm. [6] f.
Gumuchian 1702.
Elisabeth Ball Collection.

This small, rather savage French cautionary volume is directed at very young children. It concerns a mustachioed, whip-brandishing character named Monsieur Croque and his huge dog, Terrible, whom he sends out to seize and drag back to him various naughty children. The crime of the unfortunate child depicted here was disobedience; other wrongdoers are hauled off for such sins as overeating and laziness. The artist responsible for these colored engravings, no doubt the source of many a nightmare, has not been identified.

131 [Heinrich Hoffmann-Donner]

THE ENGLISH STRUWWELPETER OR PRETTY STORIES AND FUNNY PICTURES.

[? Leipzig: ? 1848.]
23.5 cm. 24 f. Blue ribbed cloth gilt.
Schatzki 129.
Loaned by Miss Julia P. Wightman.

The most famous of all cautionary tales, *Struwwelpeter* (*Shock-Headed Peter*, or *Slovenly Peter*) is also the most controversial. It was written in 1844 by a German physician who had despaired of finding in bookstores a suitable picture-book for his three-year-old son. Dr. Heinrich Hoffmann-Donner (1809–1894) of Frankfurt-am-Main was accustomed to distracting his very young patients by drawing pictures and telling them stories; he merely extended this technique to produce a picture-book for his own child. *Struwwelpeter* proved to be one of the most popular books ever written for children, going into more than a hundred editions in German and being translated from German into numbers of other languages. Millions of copies have been sold, and it is still in print today. Some of the punishments meted out to the misbehaving children who people the Frankfurt physician's book are violent in the extreme. Many adults have interpreted as sadistic the depictions of children being burned alive or having their thumbs snipped off, whereas other adults have felt that the pictures and situations are so clearly unrealistic that children do not take them seriously. And the controversy shows little sign of abating today. Whatever psychological wounds *Struwwelpeter* may or may not inflict on children, the popularity of the book with them is undeniable. The reasons for this popularity have always been somewhat mysterious, and the matter has attracted many learned investigators, Sigmund Freud among them. (He is said to have come to no conclusion.) The fifth German edition was the first to include all the characters and verses that have since formed the "standard" version. The first edition in English, translated from the sixth German edition, appeared in 1848. Its rarity is legendary and its bibliographical difficulties considerable. The copy illustrated here is a very early English edition, possibly the first.

Vice in its proper Shape. 83

CHAP. VI.

The diſmal Tranſmigration of Maſter TOMMY FILCH, *into the Body of a Wolf.*

AS ſoon as he had lifted up the latch to enter into the

F 2 next

126

THE HISTORY OF LITTLE KING PIPPIN;

WITH AN

Account of the melancholy DEATH of four naughty Boys, who were devoured by WILD BEASTS.

AND THE

Wonderful Delivery of MASTER HARRY HARMLESS, by a LITTLE WHITE HORSE.

LONDON:
Printed for E. NEWBERY, at the Corner of St. Paul's Church Yard. 1783.

[Price Two-pence.]

127

36 KING PIPPIN.

from the paws of the lions, could protect him from every other danger, he mounted on his back, and he was

no ſooner ſeated, but the pretty little thing gallopped away with him as faſt as he could run, and never ſtopt till he brought him within a little diſtance of his home; when, dropping down again on his knees, in the ſame manner as when he took him up, Harry imagining it to be the ſignal for him to diſmount, immediately alighted, and letting go the

127

W.Darton & J.Harvey London Feb.y 27th 1801.

Henry was a very lively boy, and the ſon of a tradeſman in a large manufacturing town, in the neighbourhood of which, as many accidents had happened to youth, and others, by horſes, his parents had repeatedly cautioned him not to ride any horſe without their know-

128

Never turn haſtily round the corner of a ſtreet, by this ſome have been greatly hurt. One young woman, in ſo doing, ran againſt a porter's load, and nearly loſt one of her eyes by the blow ſhe received: but this was partly owing to the porter not being in his proper place, for

CHAP. II. D

128

ever, ſlipped, and he fell down and lay ſenſeleſs on the ground for ſome time, being quite ſtunned by the fall.

FINIS.

Darton and Harvey, Printers, Gracechurch ſtreet, London.

128

V.

The giddy Girl.

Miss Helen was always too giddy to heed
  What her mother had told her to shun;
For frequently over the street, in full speed,
  She would cross where the carriages run.

And out she would go, to a very deep well,
  To look at the water below;
How naughty! to run to a dangerous well,
  Where her mother forbade her to go!

One morning, intending to take but one peep,
  Her foot slipp'd away from the ground;
Unhappy misfortune! the water was deep,
  And giddy Miss Helen was drown'd.

A 7

129

A Paris, chez P. Blanchard Lib. Galerie Montesquieu, N.° 15 et 16, et chez Lecerf, Grav.r Quai des Augustins, N.° 25.

Ecoute, Terrible, écoute, mon chien: je te charge de m'amener tous les petits mauvais sujets que tu rencontreras.

130

2.

Le chien de Mr. Croque emporte chez son maître un petit désobéissant.

130

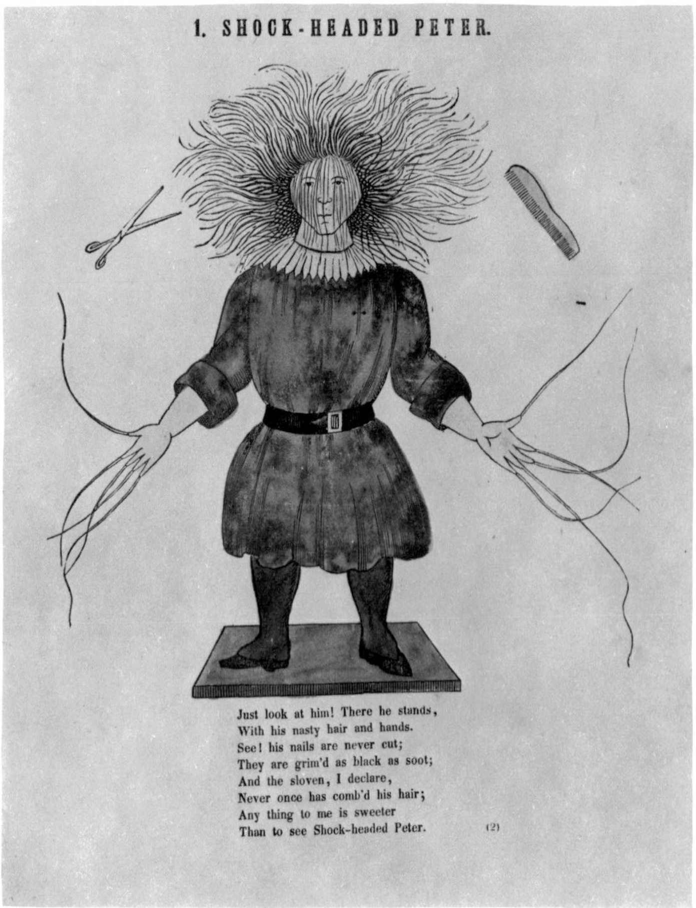

1. SHOCK-HEADED PETER.

Just look at him! There he stands,
With his nasty hair and hands.
See! his nails are never cut;
They are grim'd as black as soot;
And the sloven, I declare,
Never once has comb'd his hair;
Any thing to me is sweeter
Than to see Shock-headed Peter.

(2)

131

The door flew open, in he ran,
The great, long, red-legg'd scissar-man.
Oh! children, see! the tailor's come
And caught out little Suck-a-Thumb.
Snip! Snap! Snip! the scissars go;
And Conrad cries out—Oh! Oh! Oh!
Snip! Snap! Snip! They go so fast;
That both his thumbs are off at last.

Mamma comes home; there Conrad stands,
And looks quite sad, and shows his hands;—
"Ah!" said Mamma, "I knew he'd come
To naughty little Suck-a-Thumb."

(16)

131

Robinson Crusoe and Robinsonnades

Few books written in English are more famous than *Robinson Crusoe.* Daniel Defoe's remarkable work is an exciting, romantic tale of a hero's lonely but triumphant survival on a desert island. The appeal of the theme has proven to be universal, and the book has maintained its popularity, particularly with children, for more than two and a half centuries. *Robinson Crusoe* was not written specifically for children, but beyond any doubt children have been the principal readers of the many editions—at least a thousand—in which it has appeared throughout the world. The American bibliographer Clarence Brigham called it "the most widely read, published, translated, adapted, and imitated, of any romance ever written in the English language." New editions—most, but by no means all, of them for children—are still being published every year.

Daniel Defoe (1660–1731) was an immensely prolific writer, the greater part of whose productions fell into the category of political journalism. He modeled *Robinson Crusoe* on journalistic narratives of the period, and he based it on a real event. In 1704 a Scottish seaman named Alexander Selkirk had become embroiled in a shipboard quarrel and as a result was put ashore on an uninhabited island (Más a Tierra, in the Juan Fernández group). He survived there, alone, for more than four years, living on such things as fish and the meat of wild goats. He was rescued by an English captain, Woodes Rogers, in 1709, and in 1711 he returned to England, where his story became widely known. He later took ship again, and he died at sea in 1723. It is not known whether Daniel Defoe ever talked with Alexander Selkirk, although scholars have debated the question for a long time. But several accounts of Selkirk's experience were published in the years immediately after 1711, and these were all available to Defoe.

132 Richard Steele

THE ENGLISHMAN: BEING THE SEQUEL OF THE GUARDIAN.

London: Sam. Buckley, 1714.
22.5 cm. [3], ii–vi, [1], 2–410, [14] p.
Gumuchian 5437.
Elisabeth Ball Collection.

The Englishman was a periodical, largely political in content, that Sir Richard Steele (1672–1729) conducted beginning in 1713, about a year after his joint editing and writing, with Joseph Addison, of the celebrated periodical *The Spectator*. In the intervening year Steele had produced another periodical, *The Guardian*, to which *The Englishman* was a "sequel." Addison contributed fifty-one papers to *The Guardian*, but Steele conducted *The Englishman* alone, writing much of its content. The marooned mariner Alexander Selkirk returned to England in October of 1711; the story of his experience brought him some fame, and Steele met and "frequently conversed with him." Steele's account of this appeared in *The Englishman* on 3 December 1713, as paper Number 26.

133 [Daniel Defoe]

THE LIFE AND STRANGE SURPRIZING ADVENTURES OF ROBINSON CRUSOE OF YORK, MARINER.

London: W. Taylor, 1719.
19.5 cm. [5], 2–364, [4] p. + frontispiece.
Hutchins.

When he wrote *Robinson Crusoe*, Daniel Defoe was sixty years old and in the prime of his creative life. In the next five years he would produce half a dozen novels and other long works, including *Moll Flanders*, *Roxana*, *Captain Singleton*, and *A Journal of the Plague Year*, in addition to a voluminous flow of pamphlets and journalism. He clothed *Robinson Crusoe* in a convincing guise of journalism, endowing it with an apparent verisimilitude down to the smallest, but always vivid, detail. *The Travels and Strange Surprizing Adventures of Robinson Crusoe of York, Mariner* was published by William Taylor in London on 25 April 1719. It was an instantaneous best-seller and was reprinted at once, a second edition appearing on May 12, a third on June 6, and a fourth on August 8, all in the year 1719. Meanwhile, Defoe's busy pen was turning out a sequel. This was entitled *The Farther Adventures of Robinson Crusoe*, and it was published in August of 1719. The demand for more about his hero continuing, Defoe produced a third and last volume, which appeared in 1720 under the title *Serious Reflections during the Life and Surprising Adventures of Robinson Crusoe*. The second and third volumes have been frequently included with the first to make a "complete" set, and they have found their way into many abridgments of the whole; but the first volume is a work complete in itself, and it is that work, *The Life and Strange Surprizing Adventures . . .*, which is Robinson Crusoe to the world. On it the fame of Daniel Defoe's creation rests. The first issue of the first edition of that volume is shown here. The frontispiece is a copperplate engraving by Clark & Pine. Its portrayal of the shipwrecked mariner in furs and conical hat has left its mark on virtually every subsequent attempt to illustrate the book.

134 [Daniel Defoe]

LA VIE ET LES AVANTURES SURPRENANTES DE ROBINSON CRUSOE.

Amsterdam: L'Honoré & Chatelain, 1720–1721.
15.5 cm. 3 vols.: [3], ii–xii, [1], 2–629, [1] + frontispiece + 6 plates + fold-out map; [3], ii–viii, [1], 2–588 + frontispiece + 6 plates + fold-out map; [3], iv–xxxiv, [3], 2–632 + frontispiece + 6 plates + fold-out map.
Brunet, II, 566; Supplément I, 356. Gumuchian 4794.
Elisabeth Ball Collection.

The first edition of the first translation of *Robinson Crusoe* into French. It was published in Amsterdam in three volumes, comprising all three parts of Defoe's work. The illustrators were Hyacinthe Cordonnier, called Saint Hyacinthe (1684–1746), and Juste van Effen (1684–1735). This first French edition of *Robinson Crusoe* is the earliest version of the work to be illustrated with more than a frontispiece and maps. It contains, in addition to large maps, twenty-one illustrations engraved on copper by Bernard Picard (1673–1733).

135 [Daniel Defoe]

THE WONDERFUL LIFE AND MOST SURPRISING ADVENTURES OF ROBINSON CRUSOE, OF YORK, MARINER.

London: J. Fuller, [about 1750].
15 cm. [7], 8–82, [1], 84–144 p.

No book as popular as *Robinson Crusoe* could long be overlooked by the printers and purveyors of chapbooks, the "street literature" of the eighteenth century. This chapbook edition of *Robinson Crusoe* was probably published no later than 1750. It describes itself on the title page as being "faithfully epitomized from the three volumes, and adorned with cuts suited to the most remarkable stories." It is indeed plentifully illustrated with woodcuts, most of which show signs of long use.

136 [Daniel Defoe]

HISTORY OF ROBINSON CRUSOE.

Windsor, Vermont: Jesse Cochran, 1815.
10.5 cm. [2], 4–31 p. (First and last leaves are pastedowns.) Buff printed wrappers.
Brigham 88. Welch 260.81.
Elisabeth Ball Collection.

The frontispiece portrayal of Crusoe in this rare provincial American chapbook for children is directly in the tradition established in 1719, except for the shipwrecked mariner's headgear. His conical straw sunshade has become a conventional hat, with a wide brim and a round crown. Besides this frontispiece, the thirty-one-page book is illustrated with ten woodcuts—at least some of which appear to have been made specifically for the story. This is one of two recorded copies of this New England chapbook.

137 [Daniel Defoe]

THE LIFE AND ADVENTURES OF ROBINSON CRUSOE OF YORK, MARINER.

London: William Darton, 1823.
8.5 cm. [12] f. Red wrappers (bound in).
Elisabeth Ball Collection.

Each page of this early nineteenth-century picture-book version of *Robinson Crusoe* is a copperplate engraving, colored by hand, with engraved text. The volume is an attractive production characteristic of the books issued by the Darton firm, one of the most important publishers of books for children in the nineteenth century in England.

138 Daniel Defoe

THE LIFE AND SURPRISING ADVENTURES OF ROBINSON CRUSOE OF YORK, MARINER.

London: John Major, 1831.
20.5 cm. 2 vols.: [7], ii–xv, [2], 2–434 p. + frontispiece; [5], 2–406, [2] p. + frontispiece.
Layard. Cohn 229.
Loaned by Gordon N. Ray.

The superb illustrations produced by George Cruikshank for *Robinson Crusoe*, which appeared in this edition of 1831, are considered to be among the very finest ever to adorn that much-illustrated book. The publisher was John Major, and the printing was done by W. Nicol, the able successor at the Shakespeare Press to the famous printer William Bulmer. The two volumes contain thirty-seven text illustrations and two frontispieces, all engraved on wood by Fox and Raddon after Cruikshank's designs. For the originals of the frontispieces Cruikshank did two paintings in oil, which he rated as his best efforts in that medium. Printer, illustrator, and engravers combined to produce a most harmonious and altogether admirable result. The large-paper issue of the first edition is shown here.

Robinsonnades

Robinson Crusoe was not only reprinted, abridged, and adapted throughout the eighteenth century, but it also was the stimulus for a vast flock of imitations. So plentiful are these imitations, in fact, that a word has been coined to describe them: Robinsonnades. Some of the more famous and important of the Robinsonnades are shown here.

139 [Joachim Heinrich Campe]

THE NEW ROBINSON CRUSOE; AN INSTRUCTIVE AND ENTERTAINING HISTORY, FOR THE USE OF CHILDREN OF BOTH SEXES.

London: John Stockdale, 1788.
16.5 cm. 4 vols. bound in 2.
Gumuchian 4876.
Elisabeth Ball Collection.

In 1779, in Hamburg, the German educator and writer Joachim Heinrich Campe (1746–1818) produced the first important Robinsonnade. It was entitled *Robinson der Jüngere* (*Robinson the Younger*), it was clearly intended for children, and it was inspired not only by Defoe but also by Jean-Jacques Rousseau and the concepts of the "noble savage" and the ideal or "natural" education of youth. (Rousseau's *Émile* had appeared in 1762, and the moral tale was soon to be in full spate.) The young Robinson Crusoe of Campe is cast away not on a desert island but on a similarly desolate stretch of South American coast. His achievements in his lonely plight are even more striking—and more educational—than those of Defoe's hero, for he is neither so experienced nor so well equipped (he has no nearby wreck to ransack for supplies) as his English model. The narrative, in which a father recounts the story to his children, allows for much lecturing by the author, who was of course a teacher by profession. Campe's book was popular over the Continent, and he himself translated it into French (1779) and English (1781). But the most famous and influential English translation of *Robinson der Jüngere* was that published in London in 1788 by Stockdale. This was the first English edition of Campe's book to be published in England. Translated anonymously into English from the French version of the German original, it was entitled *The New Robinson Crusoe*. The work was illustrated with thirty-two wood-engravings by John Bewick. The first edition of the book is shown here. It has been described as the rarest of all the books illustrated by John Bewick.

140 Johann Rudolf Wyss

THE FAMILY ROBINSON CRUSOE. TRANSLATED FROM THE GERMAN OF M. WISS.

London: M. J. Godwin and Co., 1814.
18 cm. [7], viii–xix, [2], xxii–xxiv, [1], 2–346, [3], 2–12 p. + frontispiece + 3 plates.
Gumuchian 4907.
Elisabeth Ball Collection.

This is the best-known of all Robinsonnades, and the one that has been unquestionably the most popular in the English-speaking world. It was composed by Johann David Wyss, a clergyman in Berne, Switzerland, for the amusement and edification of his four sons. One of these sons, Johann Rudolf Wyss (1781–1830), edited and published it, in 1812–1813, in Zurich. He entitled it *Der Schweizerische Robinson* (*The Swiss Robinson*). The story is about a family of six—father, mother, and four sons—shipwrecked on a remote island. It is an uninhabited but scarcely a desert island, for it teems with vegetation and animal life enough to provide material for dozens upon dozens of little excursions into natural history. The story is full of didacticism and piety and wild improbabilities of nature (which grew even more bizarre as other hands expanded the book in later decades). But its appeal for the young was magical from the first, and it has been one of the best-loved of all children's books—loved especially, but by no means exclusively, by boys. The first edition of the first translation into English, a book of great rarity, is shown here. It is probable that the translator was none other than William Godwin. (He was also the publisher, together with his wife.) This was the book's first appearance in English, but other publishers subsequently brought out many other versions, some of them very much augmented, throughout the nineteenth century. A second Godwin edition, published in 1818, was considerably enlarged and bore the title under which the book was to become a favorite with generations of children—*The Swiss Family Robinson.*

141 Frederick Marryat

MASTERMAN READY; OR, THE WRECK OF THE PACIFIC. WRITTEN FOR YOUNG PEOPLE.

London: Longman, Orme, Brown, Green, & Longmans, 1841–1842.
17 cm. 3 vols.: [5], vi–viii, [1], 2–287, [2], 2–12 p.; [1], 2–16, [1], 2–16, [5], 2–269, [3] p.; [5], 2–225, [4], 2–16, [1], 18–32 p.
Gumuchian 3970. Sadleir 1583.
Elisabeth Ball Collection.

Captain Frederick Marryat (1792–1848) was a naval officer who experienced much action and adventure during a long career in the British navy of the Napoleonic and post-Napoleonic eras. When his children asked that he write them a sequel to *The Swiss Family Robinson*, he resolved to produce a work of fiction that would be based on solid probability and fact—unlike the Wyss book, which he found deplorable in maritime matters as well as in geography and natural history. In *Masterman Ready*, a knowledgeable old seaman helps a shipwrecked English family cope very successfully with life as castaways (and all the facts are presumably correct). Marryat's book is full of preaching, but he was a fine storyteller (who wrote a number of other narratives of adventure). His Robinsonnade survives as one of the most successful of the genre, in both its quality as fiction and its appeal for the young. The copy shown here is the rare first issue of the first edition.

168 *The* ENGLISHMAN. N° 26.

'great Thankfulneſs and Alacrity, were I not 'obliged to the nauſeous Addreſſes, Compli'ments and Oglings of every Fopling that lays 'out Two-Pence at my Houſe. It is not to be 'imagin'd the Pain I ſuffer from the lewd Inti'mations of their Looks and Geſtures, when 'they oppreſs me almoſt to Tears with their 'odious Mirth and Raillery; that too is turned 'to a ſtupid Interpretation their own way. Be 'pleaſed, Sir, to inform theſe Men, that they 'have no Right, from my way of Livelihood, 'to uſe me with this Familiarity. If that will 'not reform them, I ſhall hereafter ſend you 'Word for Word what they ſay to me; that 'they may ſee what could not bear a Repetiti'on even to thoſe that ſpoke it, muſt be much 'more diſagreeable to the Perſon to whom it 'was directed. Give me Leave to call my ſelf,

Your moſt obedient Cup-bearer,

Rachel Bohea.

[N° 26. Dec. 3.]

Talia monſtrabat relegens errata retrorſum. Virg.

UNDER the Title of this Paper, I do not think it foreign to my Deſign, to ſpeak of a Man born in Her Majeſty's Dominions, and relate an Adventure in his Life ſo uncommon, that it's doubtful whether the like has happen'd to any of human Race. The Perſon I ſpeak of is *Alexander Selkirk*, whoſe Name is familiar to Men of Curioſity, from the Fame of his having lived four Years and four Months alone

N° 26. *The* ENGLISHMAN. 169

alone in the Iſland of *Juan Fernandez*. I had the pleaſure frequently to converſe with the Man ſoon after his Arrival in *England*, in the Year 1711. It was matter of great Curioſity to hear him, as he is a Man of good Senſe, give an Account of the different Revolutions in his own Mind in that long Solitude. When we conſider how painful Abſence from Company for the ſpace of but one Evening, is to the generality of Mankind, we may have a ſenſe how painful this neceſſary and conſtant Solitude was to a Man bred a Sailor, and ever accuſtomed to enjoy and ſuffer, eat, drink, and ſleep, and perform all Offices of Life, in Fellowſhip and Company. He was put aſhore from a leaky Veſſel, with the Captain of which he had had an irreconcileable difference; and he choſe rather to take his Fate in this place, than in a crazy Veſſel, under a diſagreeable Commander. His Portion were a Sea Cheſt, his wearing Cloaths and Bedding, a Firelock, a Pound of Gun-powder, a large quantity of Bullets, a Flint and Steel, a few Pounds of Tobacco, an Hatchet, a Knife, a Kettle, a Bible, and other Books of Devotion, together with Pieces that concerned Navigation, and his Mathematical Inſtruments. Reſentment againſt his Officer, who had ill uſed him, made him look forward on this Change of Life, as the more eligible one, till the Inſtant in which he ſaw the Veſſel put off; at which moment, his Heart yearned within him, and melted at the parting with his Comrades and all Human Society at once. He had in Proviſions for the Suſtenance of Life but the quantity of two Meals, the Iſland abound-

132

Clark & Pine sc.

THE

LIFE

AND

STRANGE SURPRIZING

ADVENTURES

OF

ROBINSON CRUSOE,

Of *YORK*, MARINER:

Who lived Eight and Twenty Years, all alone in an un-inhabited Iſland on the Coaſt of AMERICA, near the Mouth of the Great River of OROONOQUE;

Having been caſt on Shore by Shipwreck, wherein all the Men periſhed but himſelf.

WITH

An Account how he was at laſt as ſtrangely deliver'd by PYRATES.

Written by Himſelf.

LONDON:

Printed for W. TAYLOR at the *Ship* in *Pater-Noſter-Row*. MDCCXIX.

133

Page 434.
Le Sauvage apres sa delivrance se prosterne aux pieds de Robinson.

134

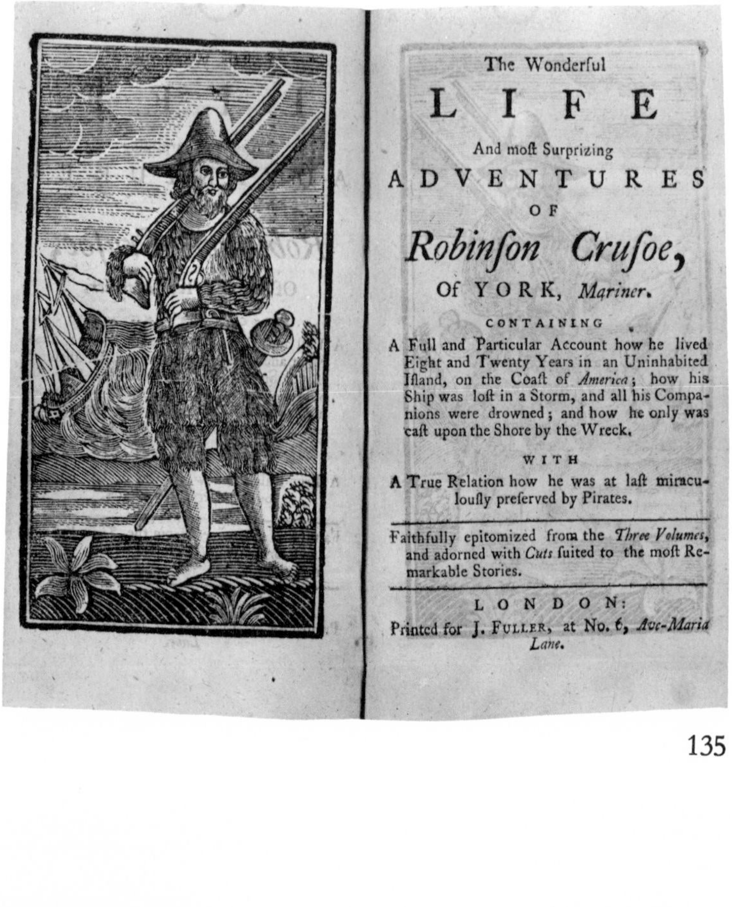

The Wonderful

LIFE

And most Surprizing

ADVENTURES

OF

Robinson Crusoe,

OF YORK, *Mariner.*

CONTAINING

A Full and Particular Account how he lived Eight and Twenty Years in an Uninhabited Island, on the Coast of *America*; how his Ship was lost in a Storm, and all his Companions were drowned; and how he only was cast upon the Shore by the Wreck.

WITH

A True Relation how he was at last miraculously preserved by Pirates.

Faithfully epitomized from the *Three Volumes*, and adorned with *Cuts* suited to the most Remarkable Stories.

LONDON:

Printed for J. FULLER, at No. 6, *Ave-Maria Lane.*

135

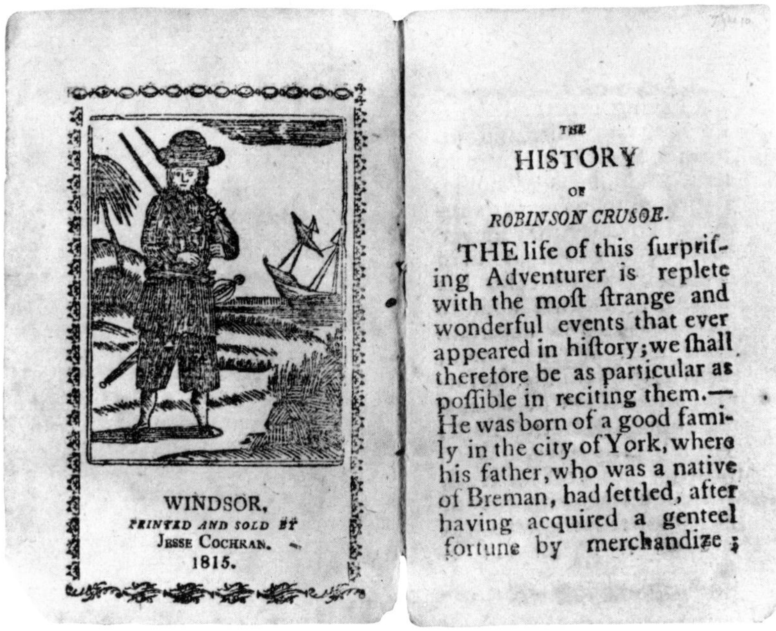
WINDSOR,
PRINTED AND SOLD BY
JESSE COCHRAN.
1815.
THE
HISTORY
OF
ROBINSON CRUSOE.
THE life of this surpris-
ing Adventurer is replete
with the most strange and
wonderful events that ever
appeared in history; we shall
therefore be as particular as
possible in reciting them.—
He was born of a good family in the city of York, where
his father, who was a native
of Breman, had settled, after
having acquired a genteel
fortune by merchandize;

136

Discovers the corn.
To my great amazement, I found about ten or twelve ears of green barley appeared the very same shape and make as that in England.
Discovers the print of a man's foot.
One day it happened, that, going to my boat, I saw the print of a man's naked foot on the shore.

137

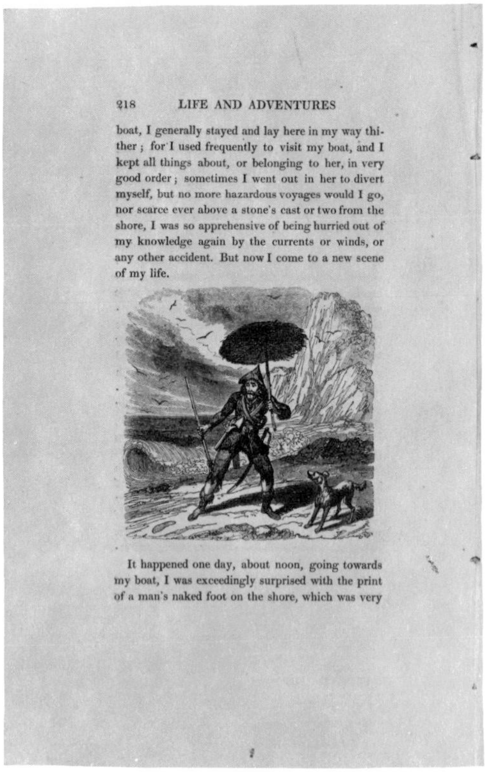

218 LIFE AND ADVENTURES

boat, I generally stayed and lay here in my way thither; for I used frequently to visit my boat, and I kept all things about, or belonging to her, in very good order; sometimes I went out in her to divert myself, but no more hazardous voyages would I go, nor scarce ever above a stone's cast or two from the shore, I was so apprehensive of being hurried out of my knowledge again by the currents or winds, or any other accident. But now I come to a new scene of my life.

It happened one day, about noon, going towards my boat, I was exceedingly surprised with the print of a man's naked foot on the shore, which was very

138

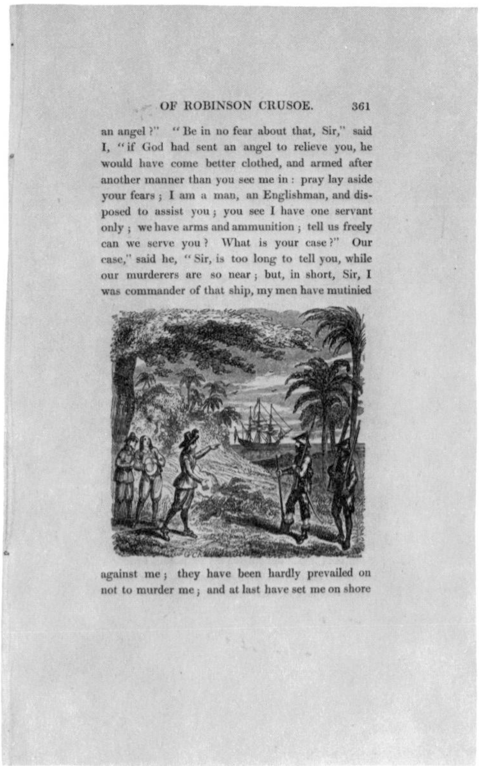

OF ROBINSON CRUSOE. 361

an angel?" "Be in no fear about that, Sir," said I, "if God had sent an angel to relieve you, he would have come better clothed, and armed after another manner than you see me in: pray lay aside your fears; I am a man, an Englishman, and disposed to assist you; you see I have one servant only; we have arms and ammunition; tell us freely can we serve you? What is your case?" Our case," said he, "Sir, is too long to tell you, while our murderers are so near; but, in short, Sir, I was commander of that ship, my men have mutinied

against me; they have been hardly prevailed on not to murder me; and at last have set me on shore

138

139

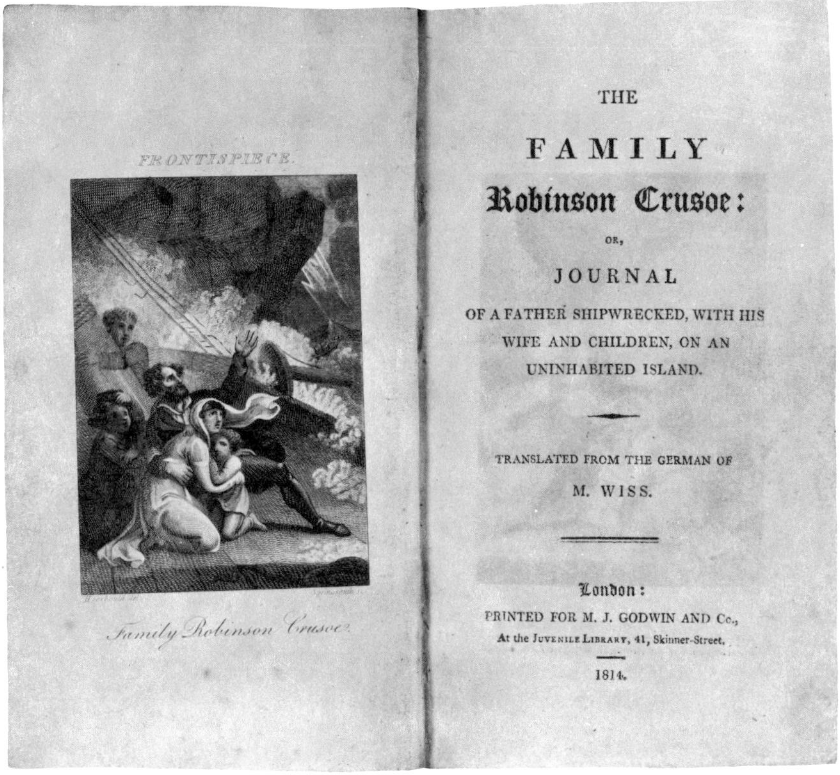
FRONTISPIECE.

Family Robinson Crusoe.

THE

FAMILY

Robinson Crusoe:

OR,

JOURNAL

OF A FATHER SHIPWRECKED, WITH HIS WIFE AND CHILDREN, ON AN UNINHABITED ISLAND.

TRANSLATED FROM THE GERMAN OF

M. WISS.

London:

PRINTED FOR M. J. GODWIN AND Co.,
At the JUVENILE LIBRARY, 41, Skinner-Street.

1814.

140

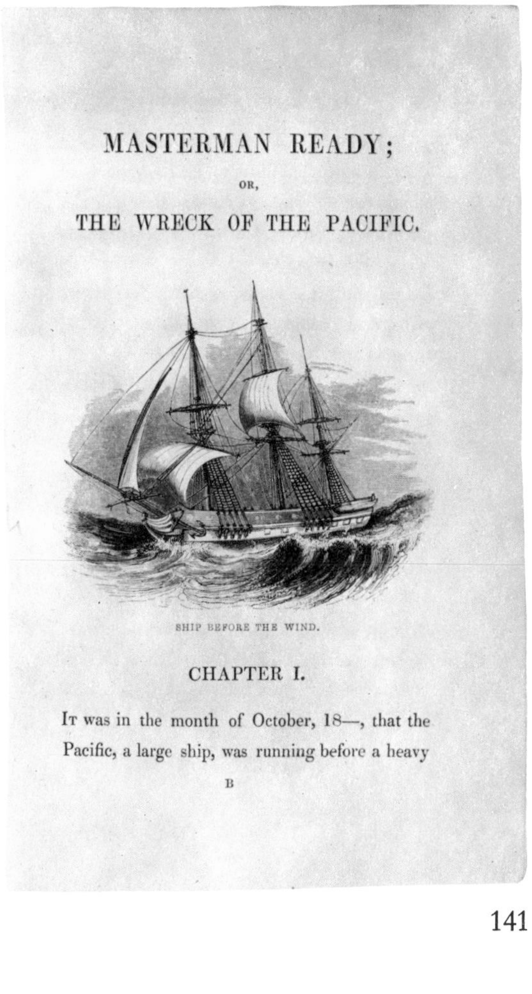
MASTERMAN READY;

OR,

THE WRECK OF THE PACIFIC.

SHIP BEFORE THE WIND.

CHAPTER I.

It was in the month of October, 18—, that the Pacific, a large ship, was running before a heavy

B

141

Gulliver's Travels

142 Lemuel Gulliver [i.e., Jonathan Swift]

TRAVELS INTO SEVERAL REMOTE NATIONS OF THE WORLD. IN FOUR PARTS. BY LEMUEL GULLIVER, FIRST A SURGEON, AND THEN A CAPTAIN OF SEVERAL SHIPS.

London: Benj. Motte, 1726.
22 cm. 2 vols.: [5], vi–ix, [4], xiv–xvi, [1], 2–148, [7], 2–164 p. + frontispiece + 2 plates; [9], 2–155, [10], 2–199, [1] p. + 2 plates.
Teerink 289A.

The first edition of one of the greatest examples in the history of children's books of an "adopted" classic—a book that was not originally intended for children but that nevertheless became a children's favorite (and incidentally a favorite with illustrators of books for children). In the diminutive world of Lilliput, and the colossal one of Brobdingnag, children have found settings of endless enchantment. Swift's acid satire and profound misanthropy have in the main passed over their heads. The discovery of these elements in the book usually startles adults who return to it long after their reading of it in childhood; but their shock is probably no greater than the shock Jonathan Swift would feel at knowing that his often savage work is best known today as a children's book. This is the large-paper issue of the first edition; it has been shown to be the first printing of the work. The portrait of Lemuel Gulliver is in the first state, with the inscription beneath, not within, the oval frame.

154

154

SALUTATION
Ho! why dost thou ſhiver and ſhake,
Gaffer-Gray!
And why doth thy nose look so blue?

158

The Absence of Beauty Lamented.

109

I hope you do not imagine that there was any impro
priety in the Prince and Princess walking together in
the palace Garden, and because Giglio kissed Ange
lica's hand in a polite manner. In the first place
they are cousins. next, the Queen is walking in the
Garden too (you cannot see her for that cactus in the
flower pot;) and her Majesty always wished that
Angelica and Giglio should marry. So did Giglio:
so did Angelica sometimes for she thought her
cousin very handsome brave and good natured;
but then you know she was so clever and knew so
many things, and poor Giglio knew nothing &
had no conversation! When they looked at the
stars what did Giglio know of the heavenly
bodies? Once when, on a sweet night in
a balcony where they were standing when
Angelica said "There is the Bear". "Where?" says
Giglio. "Dont be afraid Angelica! if a dozen
bears come I will kill them rather than they shall hurt you.
'O you silly creature!' says she 'You are very good but you are not very wise.
When they looked at the flowers Giglio was utterly unacquainted with
botany and had never heard of Linnaeus. When the butter
flies passed Giglio knew nothing about
them, being as ignorant of
Entomology as I am of
Algebra. So you see
Angelica though she liked
Giglio pretty well, rather
despised him on account
of his ignorance. I think
she probably valued her
own learning rather too
much: but to think too
well of one's self is the
fault of people of all
ages and both sexes.
Finally when nobody else
was there Angelica liked
her cousin well enough.

111

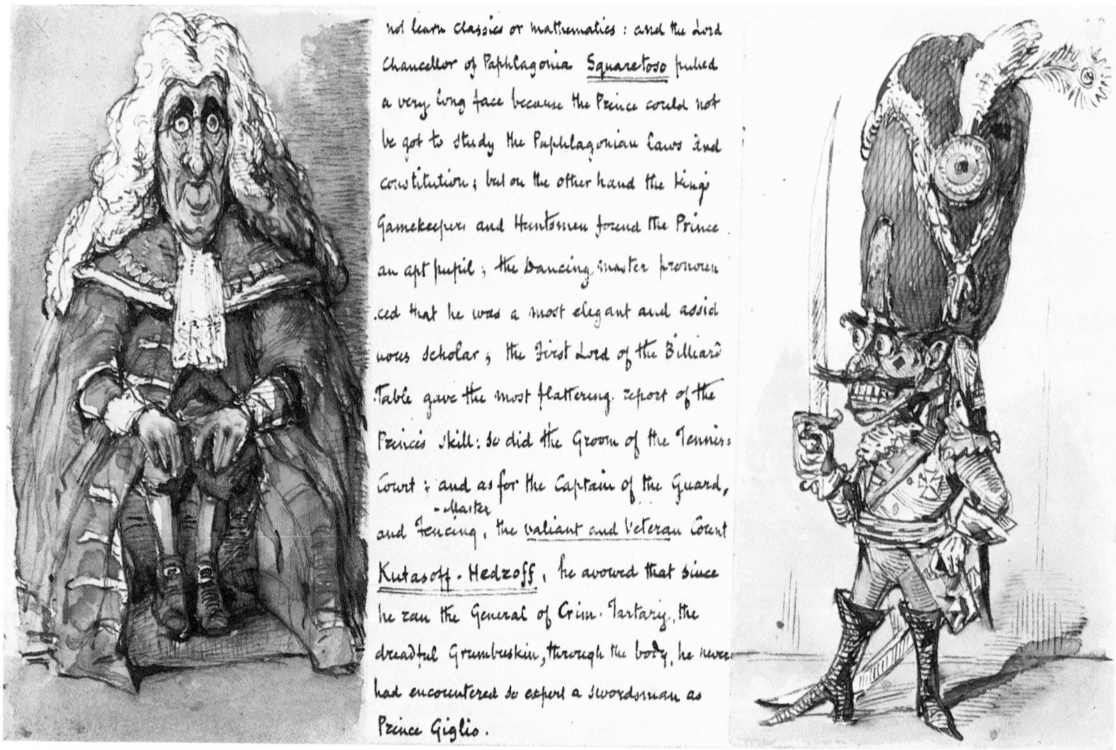

not learn classics or mathematics: and the Lord
Chancellor of Paphlagonia Squaretoso pulled
a very long face because the Prince could not
be got to study the Paphlagonian laws and
constitution; but on the other hand the King's
Gamekeepers and Huntsmen found the Prince
an apt pupil; the Dancing master pronoun
ced that he was a most elegant and assid
uous scholar; the First Lord of the Billiard
Table gave the most flattering report of the
Prince's skill: so did the Groom of the Tennis
Court; and as for the Captain of the Guard,
and Fencing-Master, the valiant and Veteran Count
Kutasoff-Hedzoff, he avowed that since
he ran the General of Crim-Tartary, the
dreadful Grumbuskin, through the body, he never
had encountered so expert a swordsman as
Prince Giglio.

111

143 [Jonathan Swift]

THE TRAVELS AND ADVENTURES OF CAPT. LEMUEL GULLIVER, SHEWING HOW HE WAS CAST UPON AN UNKNOWN LAND, WHERE THE INHABITANTS WERE BUT SIX INCHES HIGH; THE C[U]STOMS OF THE COUNTRY, COURT, KING, &C. AND THE AUTHOR'S EXPLOITS, AND SURPRIZING RETURN.

London: Printed and Sold in Aldermary Church Yard, [about 1750].
15 cm. [1], 2–24 p.

This twenty-four-page abridgment of Gulliver's Travels was produced in Aldermary Churchyard, a center of the chapbook trade in the mid-eighteenth century. Gulliver was one of the most popular items in the chapman's stock, and the Voyage to Lilliput, which this little pamphlet presents, was probably the section of Swift's book that was most frequently reprinted. The crude woodcuts show signs of repeated use, evidence of the story's popularity.

144 ❧ Jonathan Swift

VOYAGES DE GULLIVER DANS DES CONTRÉES LOINTAINES PAR SWIFT. ÉDITION ILLUSTRÉE PAR GRANDVILLE. TRADUCTION NOUVELLE.

Paris: Furne et Cie, H. Fournier Aîné, 1838.
20 cm. 2 vols.: [7], vi–lxix, [4], 4–279, [1]; [7], 4–319, [1] p.
Carteret, III, 578–579.
Purchased for the Elisabeth Ball Collection.

The first edition of a French translation of Gulliver's Travels illustrated by the French artist Jean-Ignace Isidore Gérard (1803–1847), who worked under the pseudonym of Grandville. He made his reputation as a political caricaturist with a bizarre imagination and great artistic endowments. The Grandville Gulliver is one of the most notable Continental efforts at illustrating Swift's great book. The pictures were used for a London edition in 1840; Grandville, however, never achieved the popularity in England that he enjoyed in France. The engraved illustrations in this copy are hand-colored. Four extra India-paper proofs are laid in, along with thirteen of Grandville's original pen-and-ink drawings for the illustrations.

TRAVELS

INTO SEVERAL

Remote NATIONS

OF THE

WORLD.

In FOUR PARTS.

By *LEMUEL GULLIVER*, First a SURGEON, and then a CAPTAIN of several SHIPS.

VOL. I.

LONDON:

Printed for BENJ. MOTTE, *at the Middle* Temple-Gate *in* Fleet-street. MDCCXXVI.

142

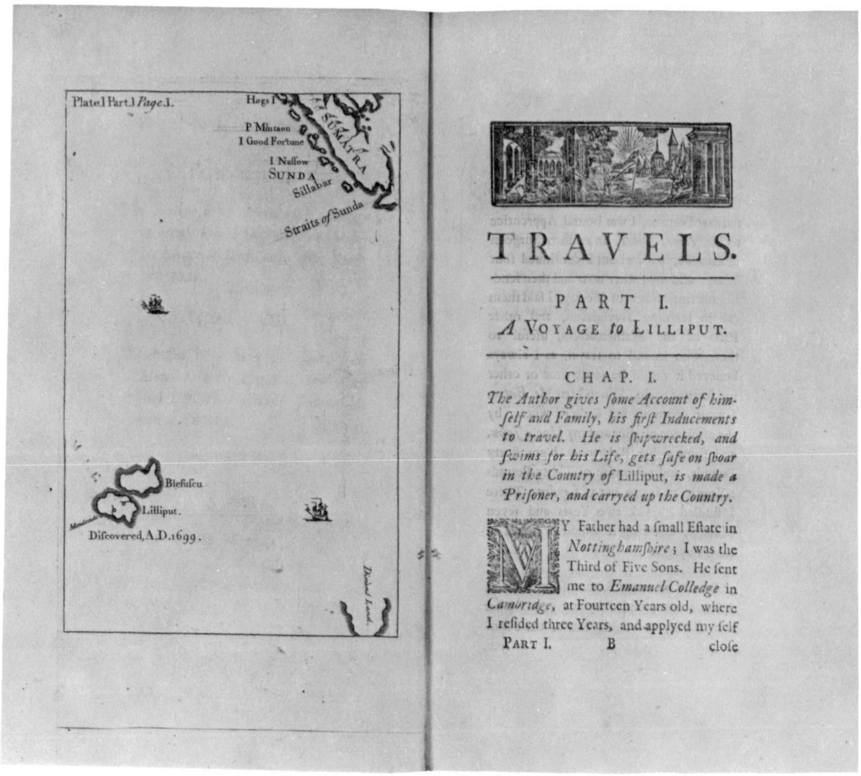

TRAVELS.

PART I.

A VOYAGE *to* LILLIPUT.

CHAP. I.

The Author gives some Account of himself and Family, his first Inducements to travel. He is shipwrecked, and swims for his Life, gets safe on shoar in the Country of Lilliput, *is made a Prisoner, and carryed up the Country.*

MY Father had a small Estate in *Nottinghamshire*; I was the Third of Five Sons. He sent me to *Emanuel Colledge* in *Cambridge*, at Fourteen Years old, where I resided three Years, and applyed my self

PART I. B close

142

THE

Travels and Adventures

OF

Capt. LEMUEL GULLIVER,

SHEWING

How he was caſt upon an unknown Land, where the Inhabitants were but ſix Inches high; the C ſtoms of the Country, Court, King, &c. and the Author's Exploits, and ſurprizing Return.

Printed and Sold in Aldermary Church Yard, London. Bow-Lane,

143

CHAP. II.

The Emperor of Lillipur attended by his Nobility, come to ſee the Author in his Confinement.

WHEN I found myſelf on my feet, I looked about me, and ſaw trees about ſeven feet high, and a town upon my left hand like the painted ſcenes at a play houſe.

The Emperor advanced to me on horſeback, when the beaſt unuſed to ſuch a ſight, reared up on his hinder feet; but the prince being a good horſeman, kept his ſeat, while ſome of his attendance ran in, and held him, while his Majeſty diſ-

Hymns

145 Isaac Watts

DIVINE SONGS ATTEMPTED IN EASY LANGUAGE FOR THE USE OF CHILDREN.

London: M. Lawrence, 1715.
15.5 cm. [*21*], *2–49*, [*3*] *p.* + *frontispiece* (*inserted*).
Pafford.

The first edition of the best-known group of hymns, and some of the most influential poetry, ever written for children. Dr. Isaac Watts (1674–1748), an English clergyman, was among the first to think of his young audience as really children and not miniature adults. He brought gentleness and some thought of entertainment into the stern Puritan religious verse that had been the customary diet of English children. Watts' intentions were educational and religious, but he was a gifted poet and his work had a profound effect on much of the poetry that would henceforth be written for children. During the writing of these verses, Watts was the house guest of Sir Thomas Abney in Hertfordshire, and he dedicated his book to the young Abney daughters, Sarah, Mary, and Elizabeth. The first edition of *Divine Songs* is a book of very great rarity; the Morgan Library copy is one of perhaps two known perfect copies. It has an inserted frontispiece portrait of Watts engraved by George Vertue. This is the author's presentation copy, inscribed by Watts to Elizabeth Abney.

146 Isaac Watts

DR. WATTS'S CELEBRATED CRADLE HYMN, ILLUSTRATED WITH APPROPRIATE ENGRAVINGS.

London: J. Harris, 1 August 1812.
13 cm. [*16*] *f.* *Buff printed wrappers* (*bound in*).
Pafford B6.
Elisabeth Ball Collection

Isaac Watts' "A Cradle Hymn," which would be crooned lovingly over so many young children in years to come, did not appear in the first edition of *Divine Songs* in 1715. It was added not later than 1727, when it was printed in the eighth edition. "A Cradle Hymn" quickly became a favorite, and it was frequently issued in separate form. The volume shown here is the first edition of a version published by John Harris; each quatrain is illustrated with a stipple engraving.

147 [Christopher Smart]

HYMNS, FOR THE AMUSEMENT OF CHILDREN.

Dublin: T. Walker, [? about 1772].
12.5 cm. [6], vii–viii, 104 p.
Minnick. Sherbo.
Purchased for the Elisabeth Ball Collection.

This is the sole known copy of a hitherto unrecorded edition of a famous book of hymns written for children by the English poet Christopher Smart (1722–1771). The unfortunate author, who was twice confined in an insane asylum during his relatively short life, was married to a stepdaughter of the publisher John Newbery. Smart published this book anonymously while he was being held in prison for debt; it is probable that he wrote most, if not all, of it in prison. It was his last work. There is some scholarly controversy over the exact date of the first English edition of *Hymns for the Amusement of Children*, but in all likelihood it was first published in London in 1771, by Thomas Carnan, John Newbery's stepson. (One of the two or three known copies of that first English edition is in Miss Elisabeth Ball's collection.) The unique T. Walker, Dublin, copy illustrated here bears a frontispiece copied from the frontispiece in the first English edition. It is a portrait of Prince Frederick, Bishop of Osnabrug, at the age of six. The portrait is engraved after a painting by Benjamin West.

148 Christopher Smart

HYMNS FOR THE AMUSEMENT OF CHILDREN . . . TO WHICH ARE ADDED, WATTS'S DIVINE SONGS FOR CHILDREN.

Philadelphia: William Spotswood, 1791.
12.5 cm. [2], iii–iv, 92 p. Dutch flowered paper over wooden boards.
Welch 1087.
Purchased for the Elisabeth Ball Collection.

One of the two known copies of the first American edition of Christopher Smart's *Hymns for the Amusement of Children*. An interesting feature of this Philadelphia edition is that the woodcut illustrations appear to be printed from many of the same blocks that were used in the unrecorded T. Walker edition, which was issued in Dublin probably some twenty years earlier.

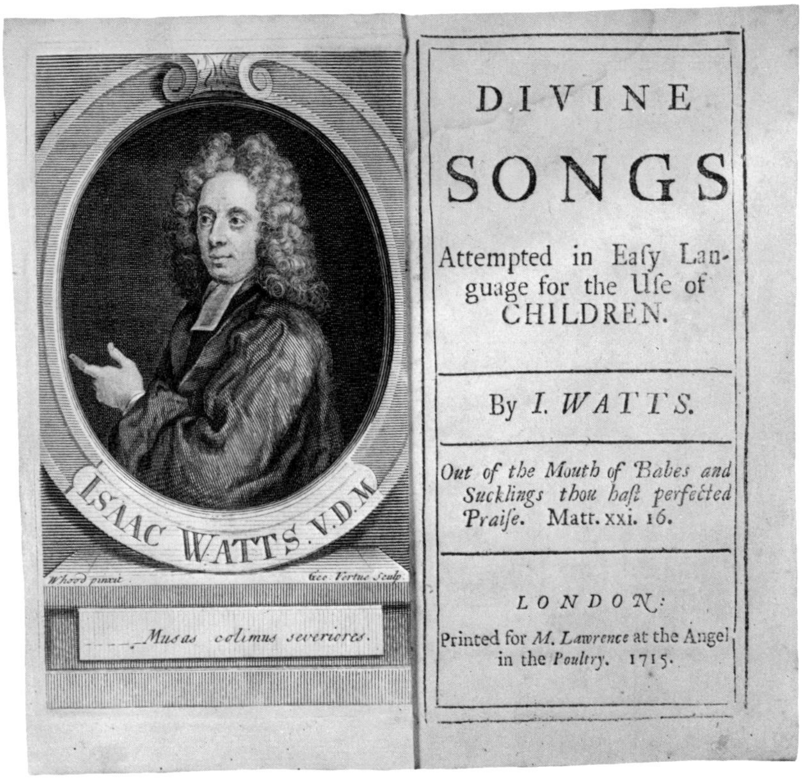

DIVINE
SONGS
Attempted in Easy Language for the Use of CHILDREN.
By I. WATTS.
Out of the Mouth of Babes and Sucklings thou hast perfected Praise. Matt. xxi. 16.
LONDON:
Printed for *M. Lawrence* at the Angel in the *Poultry*. 1715.

145

DR. WATTS'S
CELEBRATED
CRADLE HYMN
ILLUSTRATED WITH
APPROPRIATE ENGRAVINGS.
LONDON:
PRINTED FOR J. HARRIS,
CORNER OF ST. PAUL'S.

146

HUSH! my dear.

HUSH! my dear, lie still, and slumber,
Holy angels guard thy bed!
Heavenly blessings without number
Gently falling on thy head.

146

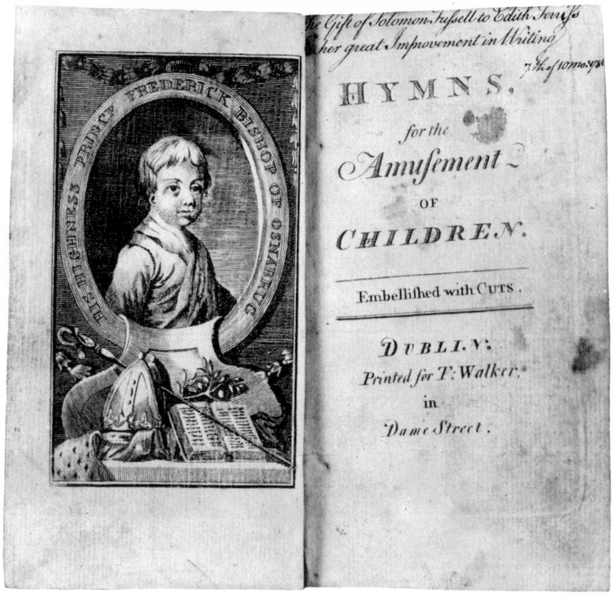

HIS HIGHNESS PRINCE FREDERICK BISHOP OF OSNABRUG

he Gift of Solomon Fussell to Edith
her great Improvement in Writing
7th of 10mo.

HYMNS,
for the
Amusement
OF
CHILDREN.

Embellished with CUTS.

DUBLIN:
Printed for T. Walker.
in
Dame Street.

147

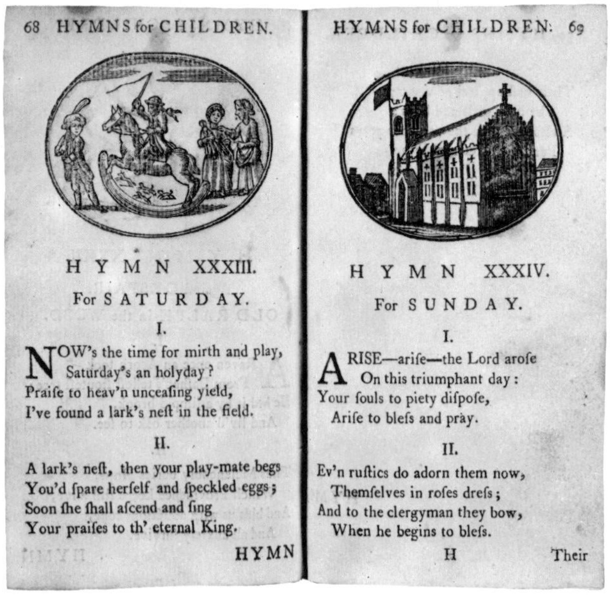

68 HYMNS for CHILDREN.

HYMN XXXIII.

For SATURDAY.

I.

NOW's the time for mirth and play,
Saturday's an holyday?
Praise to heav'n unceasing yield,
I've found a lark's nest in the field.

II.

A lark's nest, then your play-mate begs
You'd spare herself and speckled eggs;
Soon she shall ascend and sing
Your praises to th' eternal King.

HYMN

HYMNS for CHILDREN. 69

HYMN XXXIV.

For SUNDAY.

I.

ARISE—arise—the Lord arose
On this triumphant day:
Your souls to piety dispose,
Arise to bless and pray.

II.

Ev'n rustics do adorn them now,
Themselves in roses dress;
And to the clergyman they bow,
When he begins to bless.

H Their

147

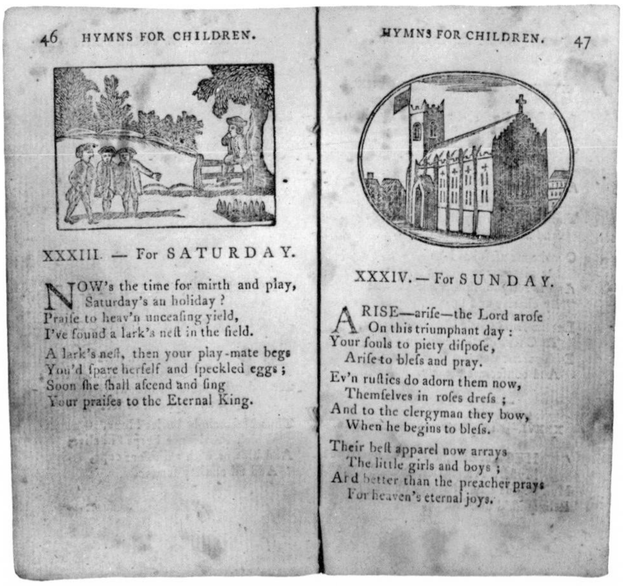

46 HYMNS FOR CHILDREN.

XXXIII. — For SATURDAY.

NOW's the time for mirth and play,
Saturday's an holiday?
Praise to heav'n unceasing yield,
I've found a lark's nest in the field.

A lark's nest, then your play-mate begs
You'd spare herself and speckled eggs;
Soon she shall ascend and sing
Your praises to the Eternal King.

HYMNS FOR CHILDREN. 47

XXXIV. — For SUNDAY.

ARISE—arise—the Lord arose
On this triumphant day:
Your souls to piety dispose,
Arise to bless and pray.

Ev'n rustics do adorn them now,
Themselves in roses dress;
And to the clergyman they bow,
When he begins to bless.

Their best apparel now arrays
The little girls and boys;
And better than the preacher prays
For heaven's eternal joys.

148

149 [Marcellus Lauron ("Old Laroon")]

THE CRYES OF THE CITY OF LONDON DRAWNE AFTER THE LIFE.

[London:] P. Tempest, [between 1689 and 1709].
35.5 cm. [74] f.
Raines, p. 13–17, 95–99.
Gift of Benjamin Sonnenberg.

A rare copy of an early and influential book of London street cries. The theme was a popular one from the seventeenth century on, and books of cries, illustrated with woodcuts or engravings, became part of the stock in trade of booksellers in London and provincial towns. Chapmen, the "running stationers," hawked them through the countryside. The fact that the title page and the captions of *The Cryes of the City of London* are in French and Italian as well as English may indicate that the publisher was also trying to appeal to buyers on the Continent, where books of cries had appeared somewhat earlier. The artist, Marcellus Lauron (1653–1702), also known as "Old Laroon," appears to be depicting realistically many characters who were commonly seen on the streets of London; it has been remarked that in this he anticipates William Hogarth, who worked nearly half a century later.

Books of cries for children began to appear in England in the mid-eighteenth century, and they took their inspiration directly from early examples—sometimes from very early examples indeed, as the next item shows.

150 THE CRIES OF LONDON; OR, CHILD'S MORAL INSTRUCTOR: FOR THE USE OF SCHOOLS, PRIVATE FAMILIES, GOVERNESSES, TUTORS, &C. . . . VOL. II.

London: Edward Ryland, [? about 1760].
10.5 cm. [3], 2–56 p. + frontispiece + 29 (of ?32) plates. (Incomplete: leaves B_2,E_{5-8} wanting.)
Purchased as the gift of the Viscount Astor.

This eighteenth-century book of London cries may be among the earliest addressed specifically to children, but it is notable for another reason as well. Of its twenty-nine plates (originally probably thirty-two, but three have been lost—a routine occurrence in the surviving copies of early children's books), all but five are clearly, sometimes slavishly, copied from the plates in the Marcellus Lauron *Cryes of the City of London*, first published three quarters of a century earlier. In both the examples shown here, background scenes have been added, and in the Singing Glasses plate the figure has been reversed; but it is still quite obvious that the engraver was copying Lauron. It is interesting to note that the seventeenth-century clothing of the singing-glasses vendor has been brought up to date. The costumes have been modernized this way in most of the plates in the book. The copy shown here is the second volume (the first volume apparently having not survived) of a hitherto unrecorded work.

151 THE UNCLE'S PRESENT, A NEW BATTLEDOOR.

Philadelphia: Jacob Johnson, [about 1810].
16 cm. [3] f.
Rosenbach 428. Hamilton 1014.
Elisabeth Ball Collection.

This American battledore features an alphabet of English cries. They are probably cries of Newcastle or York, and they may have been modeled on an early set of cries engraved by Thomas Bewick. One cover of the battledore bears a wood-engraving by one of the more famous successors of Bewick, the American engraver Alexander Anderson.

152 THE CRIES OF LONDON.

New York: Samuel Wood and Sons, 1818.
10 cm. [6], 6–29 p. (First and last leaves are pastedowns.) Buff flowered wrappers.
Purchased as the gift of the Viscount Astor.

The children of the young United States were fascinated by the colorful street cries of London, and many chapbook editions of the cries were published in New York, Boston, Philadelphia, and other American cities. This tiny woodcut-illustrated pamphlet of London cries was brought out by Samuel Wood, a prolific early American publisher of children's books. It is a hitherto unrecorded edition.

149

150

149

150

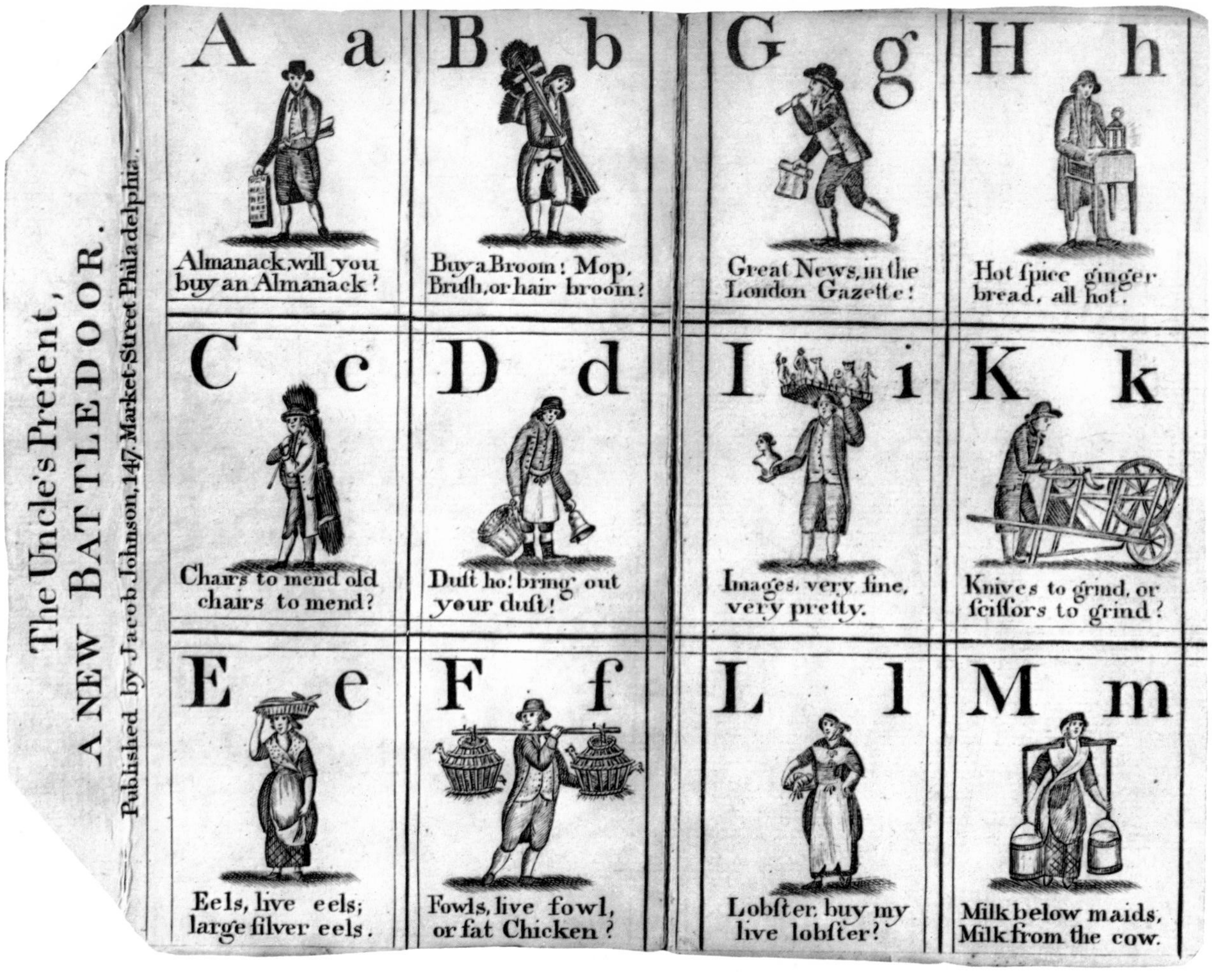
The Uncle's Prefent,
A NEW BATTLEDOOR.
Published by Jacob Johnson, 147. Market-Street Philadelphia.
A a
Almanack, will you buy an Almanack?
B b
Buy a Broom: Mop, Brufh, or hair broom?
G g
Great News, in the London Gazette!
H h
Hot fpice ginger bread, all hot.
C c
Chairs to mend old chairs to mend?
D d
Duft ho! bring out your duft!
I i
Images, very fine, very pretty.
K k
Knives to grind, or fciffors to grind?
E e
Eels, live eels; large filver eels.
F f
Fowls, live fowl, or fat Chicken?
L l
Lobfter, buy my live lobfter?
M m
Milk below maids, Milk from the cow.

151

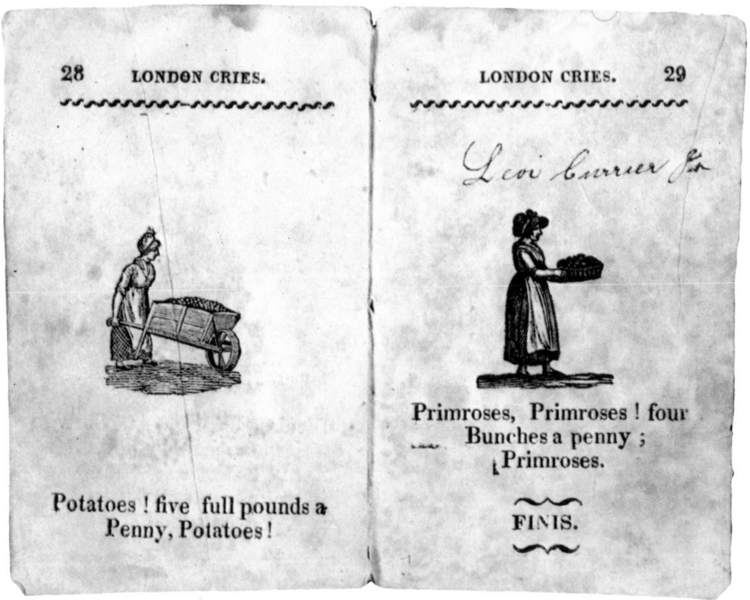
28 LONDON CRIES.
Potatoes! five full pounds a Penny, Potatoes!
LONDON CRIES. 29
Primroses, Primroses! four Bunches a penny; Primroses.
FINIS.

152

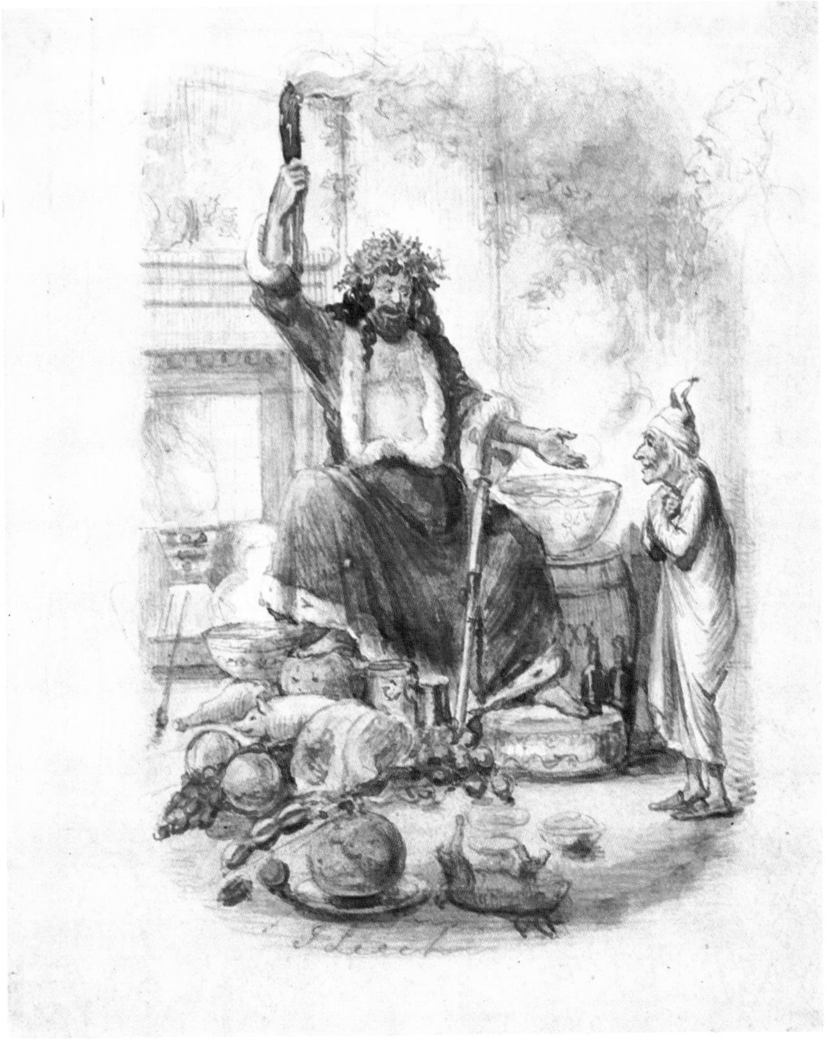

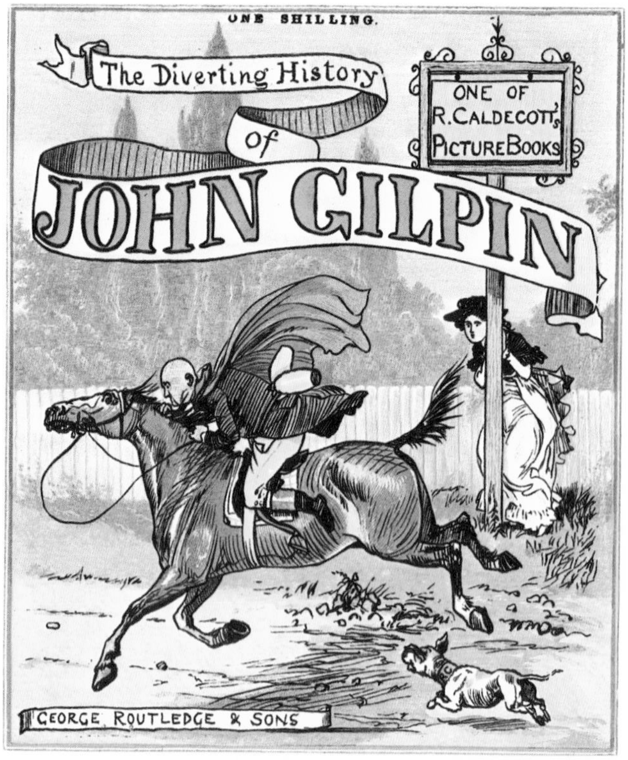
ONE SHILLING.
The Diverting History
of
JOHN GILPIN
ONE OF
R. CALDECOTT'S
PICTURE BOOKS
GEORGE ROUTLEDGE & SONS

171

·KING·COLE·

170

Nursery Rhymes and Poetry

153 THE BARTHOLOMEW-TIDE FAIRING: BEING A COLLECTION OF SIXTEEN MERRY POETICAL TALES. . . . TO EXCITE THE INFANT MIND TO VIRTUE, IN THE PATH OF PLEASURE.

London: E. Ryland, [about 1760].
10.5 cm. 32 p. + frontispiece + engraved title page + 16 plates.
Elisabeth Ball Collection.

A fairing was a children's book sold or given away at a fair. *The Bartholomew-Tide Fairing*, with its engraved plates and its rather carefully printed text, is a more elaborate production than the usual eighteenth-century fairing. It is typical of its period, however, in that its "Sixteen merry poetical Tales, each Tale decorated with an elegant Copper Plate" are in fact far less merry than they are moralistic. The book is really a series of verses on moralized themes taken from accompanying engravings, much in the manner of the emblem books. As the title page proclaims: "The Intention of this little Work, is to excite the Infant mind to Virtue, in the Path of Pleasure." This is the first edition.

154 ❧ William Blake
SONGS OF INNOCENCE.

[London:] William Blake, 1789.
16.5 cm. [17] f.
Keynes and Wolf D.
The bequest of Miss Tessie Jones in memory of her father, Herschel V. Jones.

With the production of his *Songs of Innocence* in 1789, the mystic genius William Blake sounded a new, visionary note in poetry for children. Blake wrote less to inform than to quicken and inspire, and his verses transmitted a feeling of intense joy in the workings of the imagination. In his own time Blake's poetry was little read by children, and perhaps not much more by writers for children, but to those writers who could see it the message was there. Reason was no longer to be the sole avenue through which children might develop, and through which they might be reached by those writing for them. The Romantic movement was beginning, an era when—in the words of one historian of children's literature (Mary Thwaite)—"The child, at last, was put at the centre, and his need to wonder and laugh and dream and to live in a world of his own making was recognised." The values did not change, nor the aim of children's literature, which was still to inculcate virtue and morality. But the approach would be different; the imagination would be played upon and encouraged to flower.

Songs of Innocence was a truly personal production in every way. Its creator wanted it to be an "Illuminated Book" in which his words would blend with his pictures to bring about the effect he sought. Blake was an accomplished engraver who earned much of his living by executing engraved book-illustrations from the designs of other artists (usually artists both more conventional and more successful than himself). For *Songs of Innocence* he devised a method of producing an etched copper plate combining his written text with pictures. He printed this plate using various colored inks, and he usually worked over the resulting prints with watercolors. The process was slow, laborious, and unique. It grew more complex as he worked at it; the earlier copies of *Songs of Innocence* are less elaborate than the later ones. The copy illustrated here is relatively early in the series.

155 [Sarah Catherine Martin]

THE COMIC ADVENTURES OF OLD MOTHER HUBBARD AND HER DOG.

London: J. Harris, 1 June 1805.
12 cm. [16] f. Yellow printed wrappers (bound in).
ODNR 365.
Elisabeth Ball Collection.

Few nursery rhymes are more famous than this one about Old Mother Hubbard and her talented dog. The antiquity of its origins and the authorship of the version shown here continue to exercise scholars. It seems probable, however, that Miss Sarah Catherine Martin (1768–1826) in about 1804 took a traditional character, Mother Hubbard, and put her in these verses—which may or may not be copied from a slightly earlier poem about Old Dame Trot. *The Comic Adventures of Old Mother Hubbard and Her Dog* was published by John Harris in 1805, and it became an immediate best-seller in an era when most children's books were still in the somber clutch of the moral tale. The copy shown here, illustrated with handsomely colored copperplate engravings, is the first edition. The dedication is signed SMC, a mistaken transcription of Miss Martin's initials; this was corrected in a subsequent issue of the book.

156 [Charles Lamb]

THE KING AND QUEEN OF HEARTS: WITH THE ROGUERIES OF THE KNAVE WHO STOLE THE QUEEN'S PIES.

London: M. J. Godwin, 1806.
14 cm. [16] f. Pink printed wrappers.
Muir, p. 130. Thomson 18.

This anonymous poem is the first of Charles Lamb's published writings for children. It is a book of very great rarity. The fact that it was written by Lamb was not discovered until the twentieth century, when there was brought to light, in a letter of Charles Lamb's dated 1 February 1806, a passage acknowledging his authorship. The book was first published in 1805; a single copy is known bearing an 1805 date on the front wrapper. It was issued the next year in wrappers dated 1806. A copy of this edition is shown here. The publisher was the writer and revolutionary political thinker William Godwin, who with his second wife, Mary, had just begun a bookselling and publishing business. Godwin had an inflammatory reputation at the time, and the couple deemed it prudent to publish under the name of the firm's manager, Thomas Hodgkins. The copperplate engravings illustrating the book are after drawings by William Mulready.

157

WILL WANDER'S WALK, WITH BOTH HIS COMPANIONS AND ALL OF THEIR TALK.

London: J. Aldis, 9 August 1806.
11 cm. [12] f.
Elisabeth Ball Collection.

Not a moralistic note is heard in this cheery little entertainment. It is one of the earliest glimmerings of levity to appear in a world in which children's books were still blanketed by the moral tale. (Some of the engravings have been colored, evidently by a child.) This is the first edition; its text, which is engraved, contains some misspellings that were corrected in a later issue.

158 ❧ [?William Godwin]

GAFFER GRAY: OR, THE MISFORTUNES OF POVERTY. A CHRISTMAS DITTY, VERY FIT TO BE CHANTED AT MIDSUMMER.

London: Thomas Hodgkins, 1806.
11.5 cm. [16] f. Pink printed wrappers.
Darton, Note, *p. 98. James, p. 43.*
Elisabeth Ball Collection.

The publishers of these amusing, albeit fairly bitter, verses were William and Mary Godwin, who concealed the Godwin name behind that of the firm's manager, Thomas Hodgkins. The copperplate engravings, hand-colored in this copy, are after original drawings believed to have been made by William Mulready. It is known that William Godwin wrote children's books for the firm, usually under the pseudonyms "Theophilus Marcliffe" and "Edward Baldwin"; he may well have been the author of *Gaffer Gray*. This is the first edition.

159 [William Roscoe]

THE BUTTERFLY'S BALL, AND THE GRASSHOPPER'S FEAST.

London: J. Harris, 1 January 1807.
12.5 cm. [16] f.
Darton, p. 205. Muir, p. 100. Osborne, p. 76.
Loaned by Miss Julia P. Wightman.

The first issue of the first edition of a little book that has often been credited with ushering in a new era in children's books, an era in which the moral tale was no longer dominant and levity—fun for fun's sake—came into its own. William Roscoe (1753–1831), a historian and a Member of Parliament, wrote these sprightly verses about a gay soirée attended by butterflies and beetles and snails and moles to amuse his young son. The poem was first printed in *The Gentleman's Magazine* for November 1806. The John Harris book, with copperplate engravings after drawings by William Mulready, was published almost immediately afterward, in January of the next year. *The Butterfly's Ball* was not the first light-hearted, non-didactic, non-moralistic book for children—others had already rebelled against the tyranny of the moral tale—but it was the first of a special kind of airy revel in children's books. Roscoe (whose work inspired a flood of imitators) had tapped a vein that would lead ultimately to the fantasies of Lewis Carroll and the elfin world of Richard Doyle.

160 [Oliver Goldsmith]

AN ELEGY ON THAT GLORY OF HER SEX MRS. MARY BLAIZE. [In *The Bee*, No. IV, 27 October 1759.]

London: J. Wilkie, 1759.
17 cm. [5], *2–252 p.*
NCBEL 1195. Scott, p. 58.

The first publication in book form of a sardonic little poem by Oliver Goldsmith which was later to become a great favorite with children, appearing in many different illustrated editions throughout the nineteenth century. *The Bee*, a periodical edited and probably entirely written by Goldsmith, had but a brief existence, wholly within 1759. The poem on Mrs. Blaize—not originally intended for children—appeared in the number for 27 October 1759. *The Bee* ran as a periodical from 6 October to 24 November; on 15 December the eight numbers were collected and issued in the form shown here.

161 [Oliver Goldsmith]

DR. GOLDSMITH'S CELEBRATED ELEGY ON THAT GLORY OF HER SEX, MRS. MARY BLAIZE.

London: I. Harris, 1 November 1808.
12 cm. [13] *f.*

Half a century after the first appearance of Goldsmith's *Elegy on that Glory of Her Sex Mrs. Mary Blaize*, an astute publisher of books for the young, John Harris, perceived its delightful possibilities as a children's book. Harris commissioned an artist—probably William Mulready—to do the watercolor drawings on which the book's copperplate engravings are based. The Morgan Library copy, which is the first edition, has black-and-white engravings; the book was apparently also issued with engravings colored by hand.

162 ❧ [?William Mulready]

Watercolor drawings for Oliver Goldsmith's ELEGY ON THAT GLORY OF HER SEX, MRS. MARY BLAIZE.

10×9 cm.; 10×8 cm.

Two of the original watercolor drawings for the copperplate engravings illustrating the John Harris children's edition (1808) of Goldsmith's *Mary Blaize*. The artist is believed to have been William Mulready. (The objects attached to the shoes of Mrs. Blaize as she walks abroad are pattens, devices used in the eighteenth century to keep one's feet up out of the mud.)

163 ❧ [Oliver Goldsmith]

AN ELEGY ON THE GLORY OF HER SEX MRS MARY BLAIZE.

London & New York: Frederick Warne & Co., [?1885].
20× 24 cm. 3–22 p. Yellow printed wrappers.
Muir, Victorian, *p. 168.*
Loaned by Miss Julia P. Wightman.

An interpretation of Goldsmith's *Mary Blaize* by one of the greatest Victorian illustrators of children's books, Randolph Caldecott. The color printing is by the celebrated Edmund Evans. This book was part of the Randolph Caldecott Toy-Books series, which began in 1878 and was greeted with overwhelming success from the appearance of the first volume. Caldecott and Evans collaborated on two new titles in the series each year until Caldecott's death in 1886.

164 MOTHER GOOSE'S MELODY, OR SONNETS FOR THE CRADLE.

Boston: N. Coverl[y] Jun., 1812.
10 cm. [8] f.
Welch 825.6.
Elisabeth Ball Collection.

This tiny booklet of nursery rhymes is notable for its rarity and for the rather brash ingenuity of its printer, who made capital of the fact that he happened to be well supplied with small woodcuts of birds. The book's verses are illustrated with thirteen woodcuts, and eleven are of birds. The resourceful printer simply altered the traditional rhymes to make his bird pictures fit.

165 THE HISTORY OF AN OLD WOMAN; WHO HAD THREE SONS JERRY, JAMES, AND JOHN, TOGETHER WITH WHAT BECAME OF THEM, HER PROPERTY, AND LAST OF ALL HERSELF.

London: J. Harris, 25 June 1815.
13 cm. [16] f. Buff printed wrappers.
ODNR 541.
Elisabeth Ball Collection.

The origin of these nursery verses can be traced back to a model nearly two hundred years earlier than this 1815 John Harris chapbook. A broadside ballad entitled *Choice of Inuentions, Or Seuerall sorts of the figure of three* was entered in the Stationers' Register on 2 January 1632 (a copy is at the British Museum). It contained the lines:

There was a man had three sonnes,
Ieffery, Iames and Iacke,
The one was hang'd, the other drown'd,
The third was lost and never found,
The old man he fell in a sownd,
come fill vs a cup of Sacke.

Harris' nursery adaptation is illustrated with fine stipple engravings, by an unknown artist. This is the first edition.

166 THE DANDIES' BALL; OR, HIGH LIFE IN THE CITY.

London: John Marshall, 1819.
18 cm. [16] f. Buff wrappers.
Gumuchian 2044. NBL 366.
Elisabeth Ball Collection.

In the spirit of fun and frolic that enlivened children's books in the early nineteenth century, the Regency dandy came in for much ridicule. This anonymous *Dandies' Ball* was probably the first of its kind; it was followed by many books on dandies' weddings and other vicissitudes. The copy shown here, with illustrations by Robert Cruikshank, is the extremely rare first edition.

167 [William Wordsworth]

THE LITTLE MAID AND THE GENTLEMAN; OR, WE ARE SEVEN.

York: J. Kendrew, [about 1820].
9.5 cm. [5], 6–15, [1] p. Yellow printed wrappers.
Healey 57.
Elisabeth Ball Collection.

Surprising things sometimes are found in early chapbooks for children. This little sixteen-page booklet published in York about 1820 presents, anonymously, a poem by William Wordsworth. Composed in 1798 and published later that same year in Wordsworth and Coleridge's *Lyrical Ballads*, the verses treat of a child's inability to comprehend the fact of death. This is one of a handful of surviving copies of the chapbook.

168 Richard Doyle

IN FAIRYLAND. A SERIES OF PICTURES FROM THE ELF-WORLD. BY RICHARD DOYLE. WITH A POEM, BY WILLIAM ALLINGHAM.

London: Longmans, Green, Reader, & Dyer, 1870 [i.e., 1869].
38 cm. [7], 3–31 f. Green cloth gilt.
Muir, Victorian, *p. 102.*
Loaned by Miss Julia P. Wightman.

It is generally felt that Richard Doyle rose to his greatest heights with the graceful clusters of humanized and sentimentalized but endearing little elves he created for *In Fairyland.* In the case of this book the pictures preceded the text, a situation not uncommon in the history of illustrated children's books. The Irish poet William Allingham wrote verses to accompany Doyle's colorful fantasies. Edmund Evans produced the colored engravings; they are among the very finest examples of his work. The Doyle illustrations for *In Fairyland* were used again, in 1884, to illustrate *Princess Nobody,* an original fairy tale for children by Andrew Lang. This is the first edition of *In Fairyland.*

169 Christina G. Rossetti

SING-SONG.

London: George Routledge and Sons, 1872.
18 cm. [7], viii–x, [2], 130, [2] p. Blue cloth gilt.
Darton, p. 282.
Gift of Miss Jane Douglass in memory of Mrs. Walter Edge.

The first edition of a book of poems for children by the poet Christina Rossetti. The volume was produced in England during an era that saw the flowering of the illustrated book—and especially the illustrated children's book. In his simple, eloquent pictures (they are considered some of his best work) Arthur Hughes matched superbly the grace and the gravity of Christina Rossetti's poems. The note of sadness in the verses illustrated here is characteristic of the poet, who in these poems—for all their beauty—is never far from thoughts of the grave.

170 Walter Crane

THE BABY'S OPERA. A BOOK OF OLD RHYMES WITH NEW DRESSES BY WALTER CRANE. THE MUSIC BY THE EARLIEST MASTERS.

London: Frederick Warne and Co., [1877].
18 cm. [8], 9–56 p. Brown printed boards.
Doyle, p. 321. Engen, p. 98. Massé, p. 30.
Loaned by Gordon N. Ray.

A book of nursery rhymes, together with music for singing, all presented in the stately, decorative manner characteristic of the art of Walter Crane. The book was printed by Edmund Evans, the superlative Victorian color-printer. It was perhaps the most satisfactory of all the children's books illustrated by Crane and printed in color by Evans.

171 [William Cowper]

Color proof sheets for THE DIVERTING HISTORY OF JOHN GILPIN. ONE OF R. CALDECOTT'S PICTURE BOOKS.

[London:] George Routledge & Sons, [1878].
21.5 cm.
Muir, Victorian, *p. 165.*
Purchased as the gift of the Viscount Astor.

The gentle wit of the poet William Cowper and the good humor and sense of fun of the artist Randolph Caldecott blend perfectly in this famous version of John Gilpin's ride. The printer of this colored picture-book was Edmund Evans; Caldecott's *Gilpin* was published as one of the initial pair in the long and greatly successful series of Caldecott Picture Books. Two of these appeared every year from 1878 through 1885, beginning with *The House That Jack Built* and *John Gilpin*. The Caldecott-Evans collaboration resulted in a series of books every one of which has a fine, often superb, quality of entertainment and artistic excellence. Shown here is Edmund Evans' color proof of the cover for the first printing of *John Gilpin*. The Morgan Library possesses Evans' proof sheets for the first printings of both *John Gilpin* and *The House That Jack Built*.

172 ❧ Kate Greenaway

Watercolor drawing for THE PIED PIPER OF HAMELIN, by Robert Browning.

25 × 22 cm.
Spielmann and Layard, p. 171.
Gift of Mrs. George Nichols.

Kate Greenaway's thirty-five watercolors for the Routledge children's edition of Browning's poem, *The Pied Piper of Hamelin*, are among her finest work. They were certainly among the best-received; praise was heaped upon the artist, and one approving reader in America wrote, "You have more followers in the States than ever the Pied Piper of Hamelin had." Miss Greenaway was in the habit of making careful use of models—professional as well as amateur—for her drawings of children and adults. In this book she used her nephew, "Eddie," who had been a favorite model of hers since at least 1878. John Ruskin, Kate Greenaway's great friend, mentor, and sometime severe critic, wrote to her (23 February 1888) after seeing the book: "It is all as good and nice as it can be, and you really have got through your rats with credit—and the Piper is sublime—and the children lovely. But I am more disappointed in the 'Paradise' than I expected to be—a *real* view of Hampstead ponds in spring would have been more celestial to me than this customary flat of yours with the trees stuck into it at regular distances—And not a Peacock!—nor a flying horse!!"

(For a color reproduction of this drawing, see the Frontispiece.)

Lads and Laſses blith and gay, | Merry Work will there be done,
Now to Smithfield haſte away; | Punch ſhall charm us with his Fun.

THE

BARTHOLOMEW - TIDE FAIRING:

Being a Collection of Sixteen *merry po-etical* Tales, *each Tale decorated with an elegant* Copper Plate.

The Intention of this little Work, *is to ex-cite the* Infant *mind to* Virtue, *in the Path of* Pleaſure.

Each Boy thats good, and ev'ry Miſs
Shou'd have a Fairing, *ſuch as this.*

LONDON.

Printed for E. Ryland, *at* No. 67, *in the* Old Bailey, *and ſold by all Bookſellers in Town and Country.*

Price Sixpence Plain. One Shilling Colour'd.

153

V

A Monkey Piping.

And here's another:—very true,
He plays as many Monkeys do.

(9)

TALE V.

A Monkey piping.

OFT' in a public houſe we ſee
These *Monkeys* piping hot;
This brings a drum, a fiddle that,
A tabor, and what not?

Then up they ſtrike ſome wretched ſtrain,
Quite out of time and tune,
The ſilly company to pleaſe,
As wiſe as this baboon;

And

153

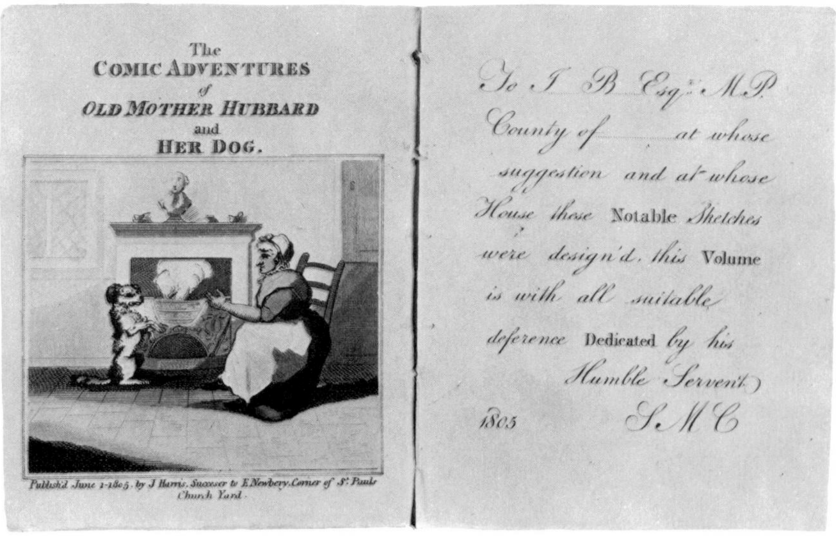
The
COMIC ADVENTURES
of
OLD MOTHER HUBBARD
and
HER DOG.
Publish'd June 1-1805. by J Harris, Successor to E Newbery, Corner of St Pauls Church Yard.
To I B Esqr. M.P.
County of ______ at whose
suggestion and at whose
House these Notable Sketches
were design'd. this Volume
is with all suitable
deference Dedicated by his
Humble Servant
1805 S M C

155

Old Mother Hubbard
Went to the Cupboard,
To give the poor dog a bone.
When ſhe came there
The Cupboard was bare,
And so the poor dog had none.
She went to the Bakers
To buy him ſome bread;
When ſhe came back
The Dog was dead!

155

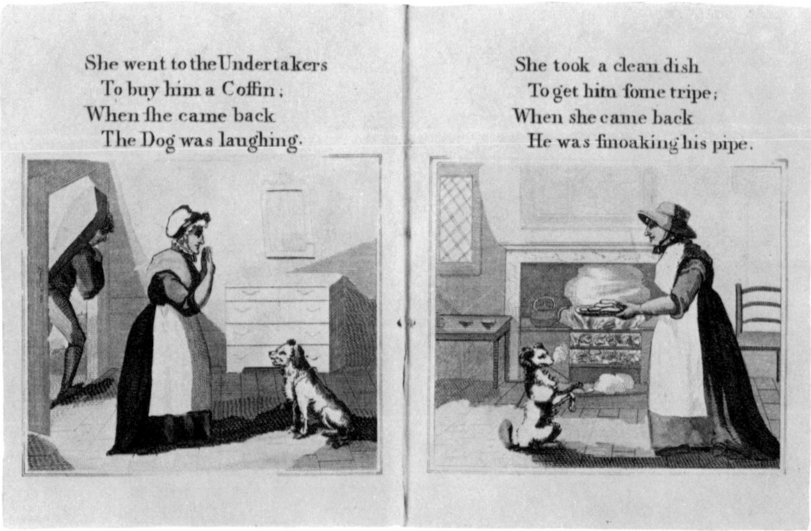
She went to the Undertakers
To buy him a Coffin;
When ſhe came back
The Dog was laughing.
She took a clean dish
To get him ſome tripe;
When she came back
He was ſmoaking his pipe.

155

THE KING
and
QUEEN of HEARTS

Showing how notably
the Queen made her Tarts,
(and how scurvily
the Knave stole them away:
with other particulars belonging thereun

Printed for Thos. Hodgkins, Hanway Street, Novr. 18. 1805.

156

The Queen of Hearts

High on a Throne of ſtate is seen
She whom all Hearts own for their Queen.
Three Pages are in waiting by;
He with the umbrella is her Spy,
To ſpy out rogueries in the dark,
And smell a rat, as you ſhall mark.

156

WILL WANDER's WALK,
With both his Companions
And all of their Talk.

Says Will to his Sister
My Dog here proposes,
To take a nice Walk
And just follow our noses.

London Publishd by J.Aldis, No. 9, Pavement, Moorfields, August 9, 1806.

157

Will Wander got tiered
And dropped in the Fields,
So they carryed him home
By his head and his heels.

157

Come take up your Hats, and away let us haſte,
To the Butterfly's Ball, and the Graſshopper's feaſt.

THE

BUTTERFLY'S BALL,

and the

GRASSHOPPER'S FEAST.

Said to be written for the Use of his Children
By Mr. Roscoe.

LONDON:

Printed for J. Harris, corner of
St. Paul's Church Yard,
Jan.y 1st 1807.

159

The Trumpeter Gad-Fly has ſummon'd the crew,
And the Revels are now only waiting for you.

On the ſmooth-ſhaven Graſs by the ſide of a Wood,
Beneath a broad Oak which for ages had ſtood,
See the Children of earth, and the tenants of Air,
To an evening's amusement together repair.

159

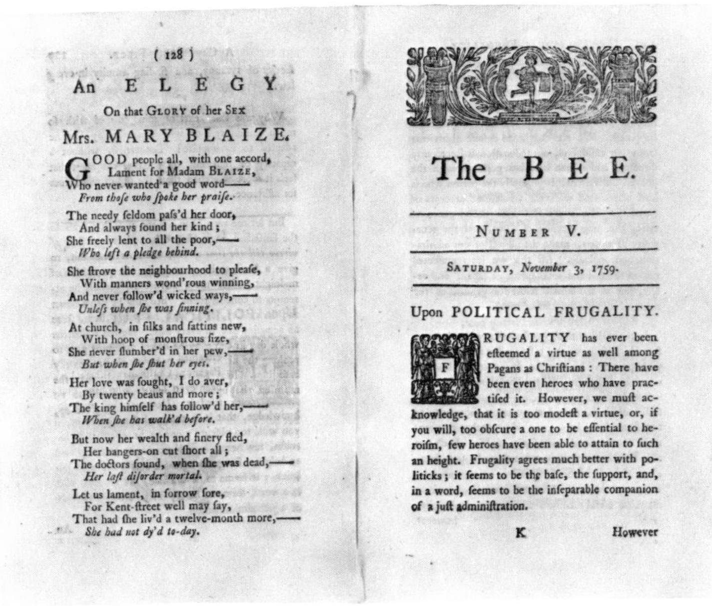
(128)

An ELEGY

On that GLORY of her SEX

Mrs. MARY BLAIZE.

GOOD people all, with one accord,
Lament for Madam BLAIZE,
Who never wanted a good word——
From thoſe who ſpoke her praiſe.

The needy ſeldom paſs'd her door,
And always found her kind;
She freely lent to all the poor,——
Who left a pledge behind.

She ſtrove the neighbourhood to pleaſe,
With manners wond'rous winning,
And never follow'd wicked ways,——
Unleſs when ſhe was ſinning.

At church, in ſilks and ſattins new,
With hoop of monſtrous ſize,
She never ſlumber'd in her pew,——
But when ſhe ſhut her eyes.

Her love was ſought, I do aver,
By twenty beaus and more;
The king himſelf has follow'd her,——
When ſhe has walk'd before.

But now her wealth and finery fled,
Her hangers-on cut ſhort all;
The doctors found, when ſhe was dead,——
Her laſt diſorder mortal.

Let us lament, in ſorrow ſore,
For Kent-ſtreet well may ſay,
That had ſhe liv'd a twelve-month more,——
She had not dy'd to-day.

The BEE.

NUMBER V.

SATURDAY, *November* 3, 1759.

Upon POLITICAL FRUGALITY.

FRUGALITY has ever been eſteemed a virtue as well among Pagans as Chriſtians: There have been even heroes who have practiſed it. However, we muſt acknowledge, that it is too modeſt a virtue, or, if you will, too obſcure a one to be eſſential to heroiſm, few heroes have been able to attain to ſuch an height. Frugality agrees much better with politicks; it ſeems to be the baſe, the ſupport, and, in a word, ſeems to be the inſeparable companion of a juſt adminiſtration.

K However

160

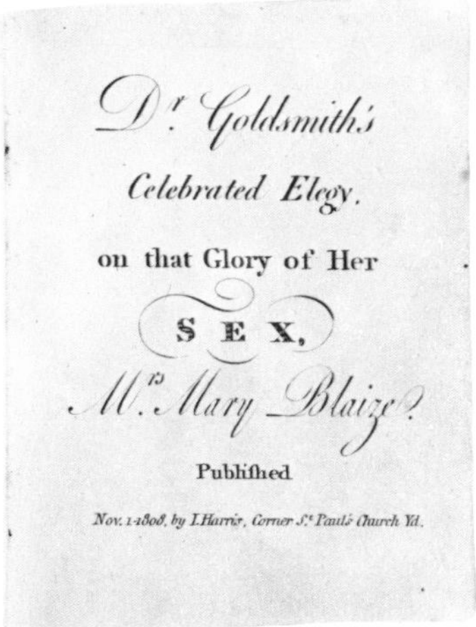
Dr. Goldsmith's

Celebrated Elegy,

on that Glory of Her

SEX,

Mrs. Mary Blaize.

Publiſhed

Nov. 1.1808, by I. Harris, Corner St. Paul's Church Yd.

161

161

161

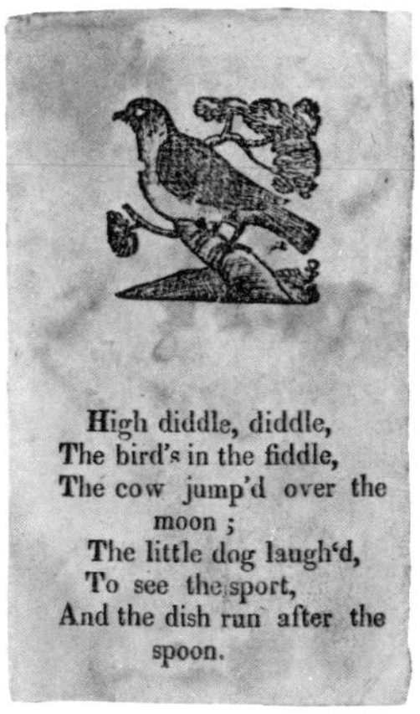

High diddle, diddle,
The bird's in the fiddle,
The cow jump'd over the moon;
The little dog laugh'd,
To see the sport,
And the dish run after the spoon.

164

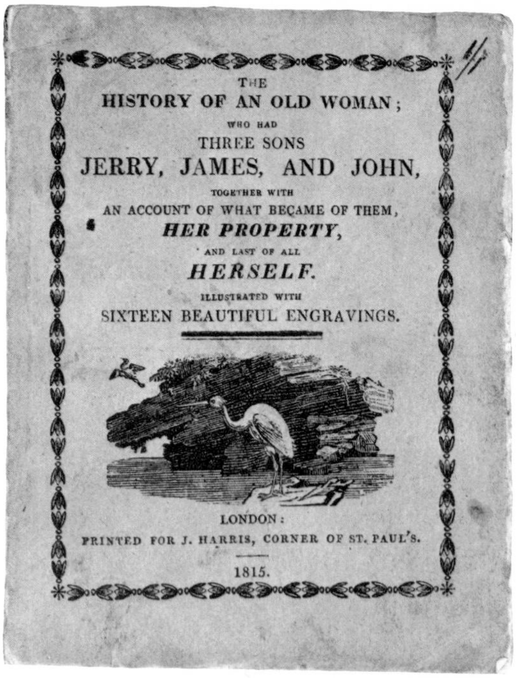

THE
HISTORY OF AN OLD WOMAN;
WHO HAD
THREE SONS
JERRY, JAMES, AND JOHN,
TOGETHER WITH
AN ACCOUNT OF WHAT BECAME OF THEM,
HER PROPERTY,
AND LAST OF ALL
HERSELF.
ILLUSTRATED WITH
SIXTEEN BEAUTIFUL ENGRAVINGS.

LONDON:
PRINTED FOR J. HARRIS, CORNER OF ST. PAUL'S.
1815.

165

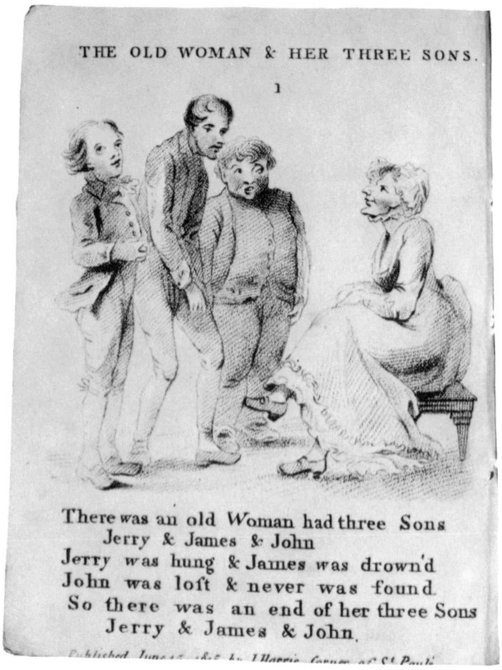

THE OLD WOMAN & HER THREE SONS.

1

There was an old Woman had three Sons
Jerry & James & John
Jerry was hung & James was drown'd
John was loft & never was found
So there was an end of her three Sons
Jerry & James & John.

165

15

This famous Old Woman had three Rings
Diamond & Silver & Gold
The Silver lost, she the Diamond gave me
And she swallow'd the Gold in a Cup of Bohea
So there was an end of her three Rings
Diamond & Silver & Gold.

16

This famous Old Woman took three Drams
Hollands & Brandy & Rum
Alas in her stomach they made such a strife
That they stopped up her breath, & that ended her life
So she came to her death by her three Drams
Hollands & Brandy & Rum.

165

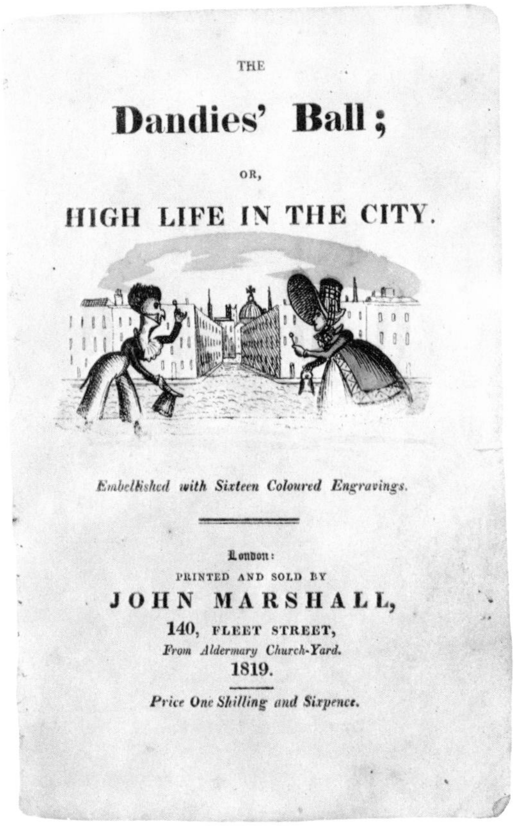

THE

Dandies' Ball;

OR,

HIGH LIFE IN THE CITY.

Embellished with Sixteen Coloured Engravings.

London:
PRINTED AND SOLD BY
JOHN MARSHALL,
140, FLEET STREET,
From Aldermary Church-Yard.
1819.

Price One Shilling and Sixpence.

166

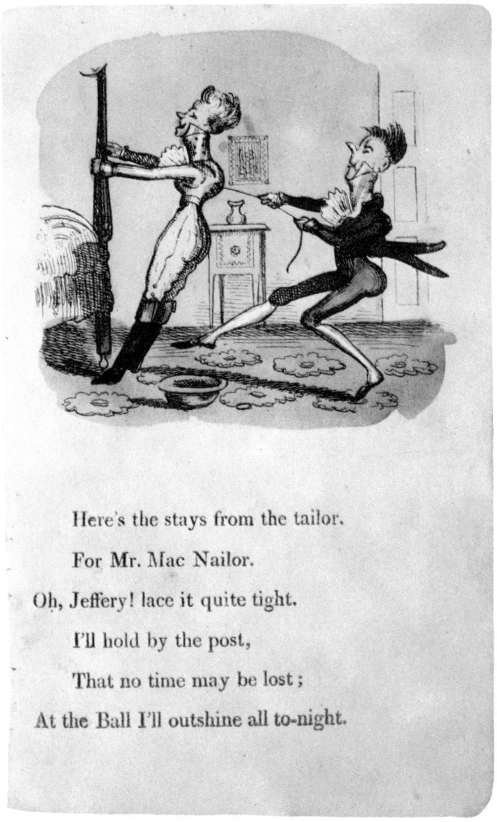

Here's the stays from the tailor.
For Mr. Mac Nailor.
Oh, Jeffery! lace it quite tight.
I'll hold by the post,
That no time may be lost;
At the Ball I'll outshine all to-night.

166

8

"Two of us in the church-yard lie,
"My sister and my brother,
"And in the church-yard cottage, I
"Dwell near them with my mother.

"You say that two at Conway dwell,
"And two are gone to sea,
"Yet you are seven: I pray you tell,
"Sweet maid, how this may be."

9

Then did the little maid reply,
"Seven boys and girls are we;
"Two of us in the church-yard lie,
"Beneath the church-yard tree."

"You run about my pretty maid,
"Your limbs they are alive:
"If two are in the church-yard laid,
"Then you are only five."

167

H. Mills July 1919.

SING-SONG.

A NURSERY RHYME BOOK.

By CHRISTINA G. ROSSETTI.

WITH ONE HUNDRED AND TWENTY ILLUSTRATIONS
By ARTHUR HUGHES.
ENGRAVED BY THE BROTHERS DALZIEL.

LONDON:
GEORGE ROUTLEDGE AND SONS,
THE BROADWAY, LUDGATE.
1872.

169

Sing me a song—
  What shall I sing?—
Three merry sisters
  Dancing in a ring,
Light and fleet upon their feet
  As birds upon the wing.

Tell me a tale—
  What shall I tell?—
Two mournful sisters,
  And a tolling knell,
Tolling ding and tolling dong,
  Ding dong bell.

73   10

169

Thomas Boreman

173 [Thomas Boreman]

THE GIGANTICK HISTORY, VOLUME THE SECOND: WHICH COMPLETES THE HISTORY OF GUILDHALL, LONDON. WITH OTHER CURIOUS MATTERS.

London: Tho. Boreman, 1740.
6 cm. [5], vi–xxiv, [1], 26–128 p.
Stone, p. 12, 37.
Loaned by Miss Elisabeth Ball.

This is the first edition of one of the early volumes in the Gigantick Histories, a series of miniature children's books issued from 1740 to 1742 by Thomas Boreman, who may with justice be described as the first English publisher of books for children. Others before him had of course brought out volumes intended for children—John Weever's doggerel New Testament, the *Agnus Dei* of 1601, is an example—but Boreman was the first to make, however briefly, a business out of publishing children's books. Although the format of Boreman's diminutive books seems to have been inspired by the *Agnus Dei* and the Thumb Bibles of the seventeenth and early eighteenth century, in other ways this vigorous, imaginative publisher was a considerable innovator. He developed subscriber lists, which he printed in his books—a device common enough in publishing, but one never before used for children. Boreman was also the first publisher of children's books to indulge in the practice, later so assiduously (and successfully) followed by John Newbery and Isaiah Thomas, of weaving bits of self-advertising into his texts.

There can be little doubt that Thomas Boreman himself wrote the books he published for children. And one cannot look through these books without perceiving how deeply convinced Boreman was that any instruction of children should be accompanied by diversion and entertainment. "During the Infant-Age," he writes, "ever busy and always inquiring, there is no fixing the attention of the mind, but by amusing it." In this book Boreman also gives the reasons for his almost invariable practice of issuing his Gigantick Histories in two-volume sets. If he were to put the two parts of a work into a single volume, he explains, "such a huge volume would come too dear for children, and be too heavy to carry in one pocket; it was therefore better to have two; one for each, which would balance them so equally, there would be no fear of their growing lopsided, from the weight of such a gigantick work."

174 [Thomas Boreman]

THE HISTORY AND DESCRIPTION OF THE FAMOUS CATHEDRAL OF ST. PAUL'S, LONDON.

London: Tho. Boreman, 1741.
6 cm. [4], vi–xxxvii, [2], 40–125, [3] p. (Frontispiece is a pastedown.) Dutch flowered boards.
Stone, p. 21, 39.
Loaned by Miss Elisabeth Ball.

The first edition of another title in Thomas Boreman's Gigantick History series. This volume is notable in that Boreman's list of juvenile subscribers, printed in the book as was his custom, includes a number of children from the British colonies in America. Among these are Master Sammy Mather, grandson of Cotton Mather, and Miss Polly Oliver, daughter of Andrew Oliver, sometime lieutenant governor of the province of Massachusetts Bay. Thomas Hutchinson of Boston, who later would be governor of the Massachusetts Bay province, visited England in the fall of 1740; he subscribed for the books in the names of his young compatriots, and by the time he embarked for New England, late in 1741, the books had been published and he could bring them home with him.

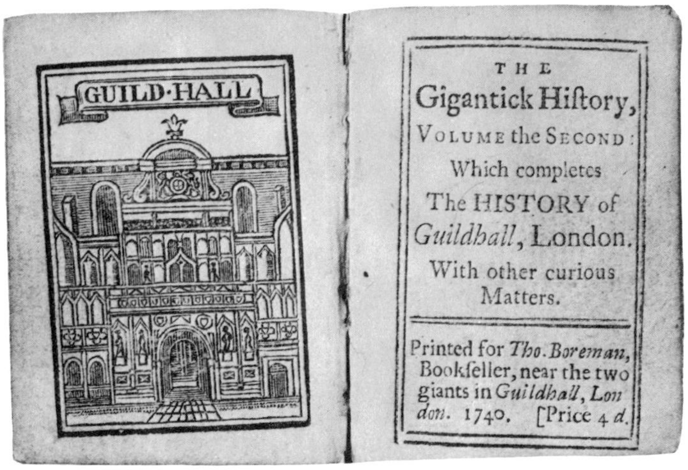
GUILD·HALL
THE
Gigantick Hiſtory,
VOLUME the SECOND:
Which completes
The HISTORY of
Guildhall, London.
With other curious
Matters.
Printed for Tho. Boreman,
Bookſeller, near the two
giants in Guildhall, London. 1740. [Price 4 d.

173

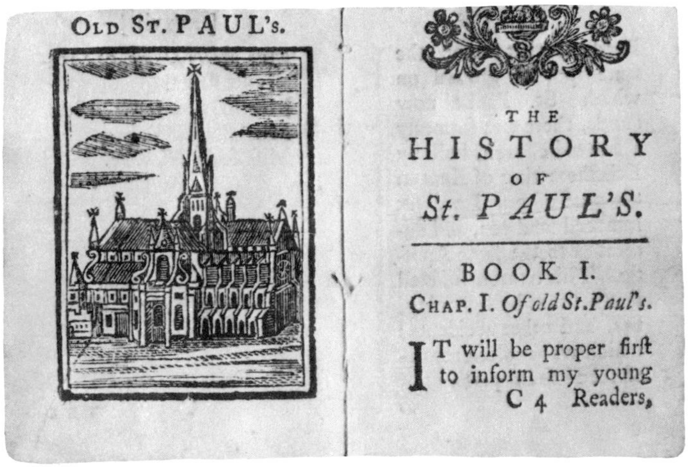
OLD ST. PAUL's.
THE
HISTORY
OF
St. PAUL'S.
BOOK I.
CHAP. I. Of old St. Paul's.
IT will be proper firſt
to inform my young
C 4 Readers,

174

Almanacs and Albums

175 YOUTH'S ENTERTAINING AND INSTRUCTIVE CALENDAR FOR THE JUBILEE YEAR 1750.

London: W. Owen, [1749].
15 cm. [81] f. Brown flowered boards.
Elisabeth Ball Collection.

At the price of a shilling (not insignificant in the mid-eighteenth century), this sturdy little volume offers its young owners a wealth of useful information both religious and secular. An added feature is a selection of tales, fables, and precepts, all heavy with moralizing, in the manner of eighteenth-century children's books. The copperplate-engraved frontispiece, on the other hand, has an elegance not usually found in children's books of this era.

176 PRENTJES ALMANACH, VOOR KINDEREN; VOOR HET JAAR 1799.

Amsterdam: W. Houtgraaff, [1798].
10 cm. [20], 28 p. + 15 plates. Green printed wrappers (bound in).
Elisabeth Ball Collection.

A Dutch children's almanac for the year 1799. The copperplate engravings, delicately colored by hand, are typical of the fine illustrations in Dutch children's books of this period.

177 Kate Greenaway

ALMANACK FOR 1883.

London: George Routledge and Sons, [1882].
10 cm. [12] f.
Spielmann and Layard, p. 122.
Loaned by Miss Julia P. Wightman.

In 1883 the first of Kate Greenaway's diminutive almanacs for children was published. The almanac had been a popular form of children's book since at least the middle of the eighteenth century; Miss Greenaway's little volume, printed in color by Edmund Evans, now breathed new life into the tradition. It was printed in English, French, and German, and nearly 100,000 copies were sold in Europe and America. This gratifying success encouraged artist, printer, and publisher to embark on a regular yearly series, and a Kate Greenaway almanac was thenceforward published by the firm of George Routledge every year through 1895. A copy of the first almanac in the series is shown here. It is one of a special clothbound issue, the ordinary issue being bound in glazed paper boards.

178 Kate Greenaway

KATE GREENAWAY'S ALMANACK & DIARY FOR 1897.

London: J. M. Dent & Co., [1896].
10.5 cm. [32] f. Gray-green leather gilt.
Spielmann and Layard, p. 210.
Loaned by Miss Julia P. Wightman.

The firm of George Routledge brought out its last Kate Greenaway almanac in 1895. No almanac for 1896 was published, but for 1897 the firm of J. M. Dent brought out one more (it would be the final almanac in the series). A copy is illustrated here; bound in leather, it encompasses a small diary as well as an almanac. This is the rarest of all Kate Greenaway's almanacs.

179 Kate Greenaway

KATE GREENAWAY'S ALBUM.

London: George Routledge & Sons, [1888].
8.5 cm. [25] f. Green printed boards.
Loaned by Arthur A. Houghton, Jr.

This exceedingly rare book by Kate Greenaway is a survivor of a project that was abandoned, for reasons that are unclear today. Only eight copies were printed, and the book was never published. The reason may have been that the color work of Miss Greenaway's printer, Edmund Evans, did not come up to her standards in this instance. The book contains 192 separate pictures. A number of the original watercolor drawings for these are preserved with the *Album*; some of them show that the colors were changed for the printed version, in which each picture was set in a gold frame.

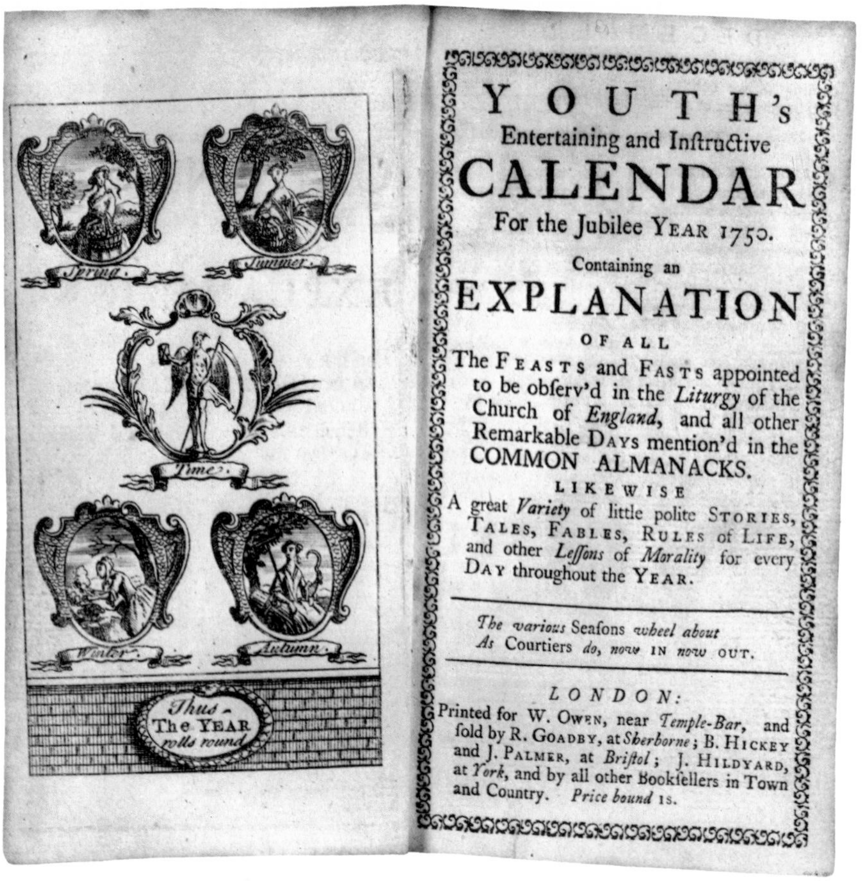
Spring
Summer
Time
Winter
Autumn
Thus The YEAR rolls round
YOUTH's
Entertaining and Instructive
CALENDAR
For the Jubilee YEAR 1750.
Containing an
EXPLANATION
OF ALL
The FEASTS and FASTS appointed to be observ'd in the Liturgy of the Church of England, and all other Remarkable DAYS mention'd in the COMMON ALMANACKS.
LIKEWISE
A great Variety of little polite STORIES, TALES, FABLES, RULES of LIFE, and other Lessons of Morality for every DAY throughout the YEAR.
The various Seasons wheel about
As Courtiers do, now IN now OUT.
LONDON:
Printed for W. OWEN, near Temple-Bar, and sold by R. GOADBY, at Sherborne; B. HICKEY and J. PALMER, at Bristol; J. HILDYARD, at York, and by all other Booksellers in Town and Country. Price bound 1s.

175

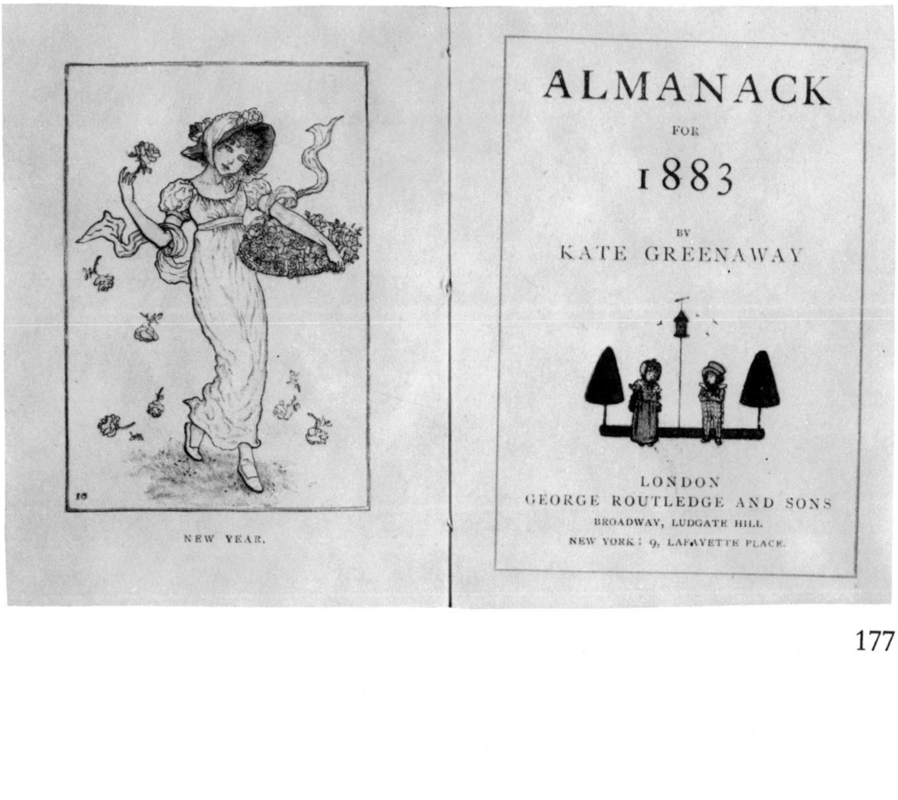
NEW YEAR.
ALMANACK
FOR
1883
BY
KATE GREENAWAY
LONDON
GEORGE ROUTLEDGE AND SONS
BROADWAY, LUDGATE HILL.
NEW YORK: 9, LAFAYETTE PLACE.

177

KATE
GREENAWAY'S
ALMANACK
& DIARY for
·1897·
J·M·DENT & CO:
·67··ST JAMES'S ST: LONDON

178

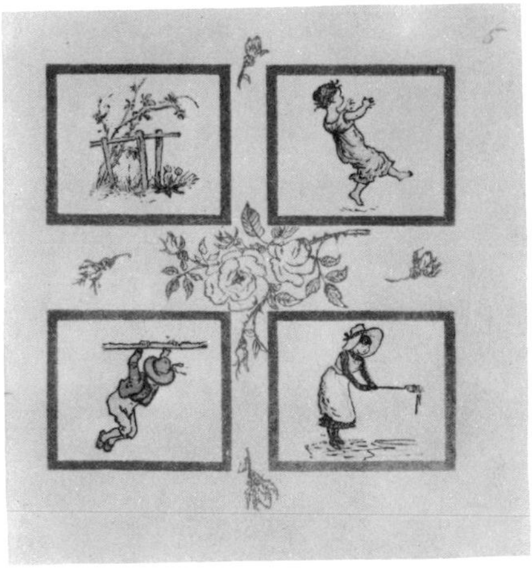

179

179

Books of Knowledge and Instruction

180 A MUSEUM FOR YOUNG GENTLEMEN AND LADIES.

London: J. Hodges; J. Newbery; B. Collins, [1750 or earlier].
11 cm. [2], iii–vi, 226 p. Dutch flowered boards.
Roscoe J253(1). NBL 250. McKell 1620.
Elisabeth Ball Collection.

This is the rare first edition of one of John Newbery's earliest publications for children. The exhaustive title page gives an indication of the ambitious scope of the book, which is virtually a miniature encyclopedia—and a courtesy book, story book, and elocution guide as well. The book has a shrewd, brisk, multifarious, no-nonsense, yet kindly approach; all these were attributes of Newbery himself, and he may indeed have been the author. Only three other perfect copies are recorded.

181 Tom Telescope [i.e., ?Oliver Goldsmith ?John Newbery].
THE NEWTONIAN SYSTEM OF PHILOSOPHY.

London: J. Newbery, 1761.
11.5 cm. [4], 140 p. Marbled boards.
Roscoe J348(1).
Elisabeth Ball Collection.

The scientific principles of Sir Isaac Newton and the philosophic approach of John Locke inform this cheery little series of lectures, covering an astonishing variety of topics from optics and natural history to ethics and theology. A well-written and well-received book, it is thought to have had a wide influence on children of the day. The authorship of the book has been attributed to either Oliver Goldsmith or John Newbery; both possibilities are reasonable. This is the first edition.

182 [William Darton]

LITTLE TRUTHS BETTER THAN GREAT FABLES: IN VARIETY OF INSTRUCTION FOR CHILDREN FROM FOUR TO EIGHT YEARS OLD.

London: William Darton, 1787.
10 cm. [4], iii–vi, 7–84 p. Marbled wrappers.
McKell 701.
Elisabeth Ball Collection.

This is a book of kindly instruction in natural history and various other matters, including papermaking, the habits of blind persons, and the necessity of charity. It is all presented in the form of an amiable but relentlessly moralistic discourse by a tutor to his very young charges. The author and illustrator are in all likelihood the same person—the book's publisher, William Darton. *Little Truths* was one of his earliest productions. The copy illustrated here is the first edition; it is extremely rare.

183 PAUL PENNYLOVE'S POETICAL PARAPHRASE, OF THE PENCE TABLE.

London: E. Wallis, [about 1814].
12.5 cm. [16] f. Gray printed wrappers (bound in).
James, p. 58.
Elisabeth Ball Collection.

An extremely rare early-nineteenth-century "numerator," or guide to calculations. The hand-colored engravings are accompanied by verses—often rather forced verses—that are supposed to help children master the complexities of English currency.

184 Maurice Boutet de Monvel

JEANNE D'ARC.

Paris: E. Plon, Nourrit & Cie, [1896].
24×31.5 cm. [2], 3–47, [1] p.
Thwaite, p. 254. Mahony, p. 132.
Purchased for the Elisabeth Ball Collection.

The children's-book illustrations of the French artist Maurice Boutet de Monvel (1850–1913) are characterized by delicate but precise line drawing and flat colorings of great subtlety. His work marked a high point in the illustration of French children's books at the close of the nineteenth century, and it influenced enormously the picture-book for children in the twentieth century, not only in France but in England and elsewhere. Boutet de Monvel's illustrations in *Jeanne d'Arc*, for which he also wrote the text, are considered his finest and most important work. Shown here is the first edition.

A *MUSEUM*

FOR

Young GENTLEMEN and LADIES:

OR, A

Private TUTOR for little *Masters* and *Misses*.

Containing a Variety of *useful Subjects*, and in particular,

1. Directions for Reading with Elegance and Propriety.
2. The ancient and present State of *Great Britain*; with a compendious History of *England*.
3. An Account of the Solar System.
4. Historical and Geographical Description of the several Countries in the World: With the Manners, Customs, and Habits of the People.
5. An Account of the Arts and Sciences.
6. Rules for Behaviour.
7. Advice to young Persons on their entering upon the World; with short Rules of Religion and Morality.
8. Tables of Weights and Measures.
9. Explanation of Abreviations used in Words and Dates.
10. The Seven Wonders of the World.
11. Prospect and Description of the Burning Mountains.
12. Dying Words and Behaviour of great Men, when just quitting the Stage of Life: With many other useful Particulars, all in a plain familiar Way for Youth of both Sexes.

Interspersed with LETTERS, TALES, and FABLES for Amusement and Instruction, and illustrated with CUTTS.

(Being a Second Volume to the *Pretty Book* for *Children*.)

LONDON:

Printed for J. HODGES, on the *Bridge*; J. NEWBERY, in St. *Paul's-Church Yard*; and B. COLLINS, in *Salisbury*.

[Price One Shilling, neatly bound.]

180

(101)

A *Chinese* Man and Woman in their proper Habits.

An Account of China.

THE Empire of *China* is a great and spacious Country on the East of *Asia*, much fam'd for its Fruitfulness, Wealth, Beautifulness of Towns, and incredible Number of Inhabitants. It is divided into seventeen Kingdoms, which contain 160 large Cities, 240 lesser, and 1200 Towns, the Chief of all is *Peking*. The Air is pure and serene, and the Inhabitants live to a great Age. Their Riches

H 3 consist

180

Elinor Rendel. 11th March/90

THE

NEWTONIAN SYSTEM

OF

PHILOSOPHY

Adapted to the Capacities of young GENTLEMEN and LADIES, and familiarized and made entertaining by Objects with which they are intimately acquainted:

BEING

The Substance of SIX LECTURES read to the LILLIPUTIAN SOCIETY,

By TOM TELESCOPE, A.M.

And collected and methodized for the Benefit of the Youth of these Kingdoms,

By their old Friend Mr. NEWBERY, in *St. Paul's Church Yard*;

Who has also added Variety of Copper-Plate Cuts, to illustrate and confirm the Doctrines advanced.

O Lord, how manifold are thy Works! In Wisdom hast thou made them all, the Earth is full of thy Riches.

Young Men and Maidens, Old Men and Children, praise the Lord. PSALMS.

LONDON,

Printed for J. NEWBERY, at the BIBLE and SUN, in *St. Paul's Church Yard*. 1761.

181

p.115

Chariot fired by Motion

181

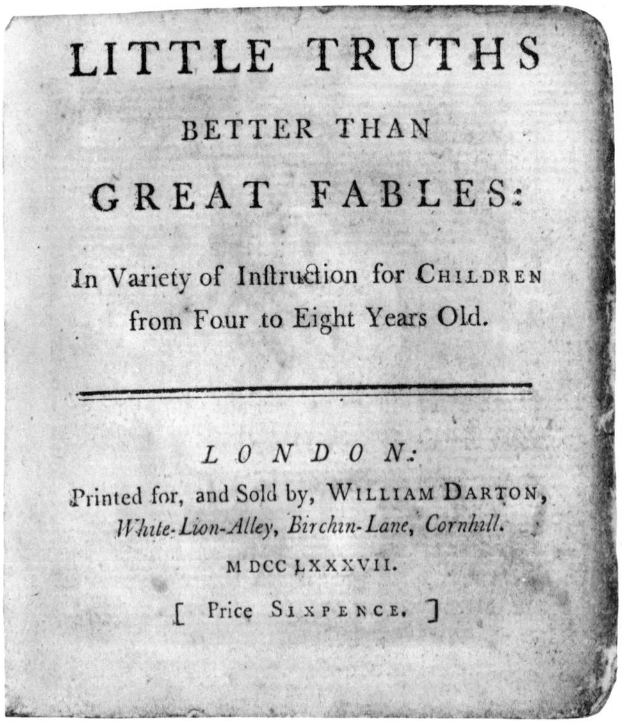

LITTLE TRUTHS
BETTER THAN
GREAT FABLES:
In Variety of Inſtruction for CHILDREN
from Four to Eight Years Old.

LONDON:
Printed for, and Sold by, WILLIAM DARTON,
White-Lion-Alley, Birchin-Lane, Cornhill.
MDCCLXXXVII.
[Price SIXPENCE.]

182

I have ſeen a Dog lead a blind man, and pull him from a poſt, or round the corner of a ſtreet.

182

Two Great Novelists

185 Samuel Richardson

CLARISSA, OR THE HISTORY OF A YOUNG LADY . . . ABRIDGED FROM THE WORKS OF SAMUEL RICHARDSON, ESQ.

London: E. Newbery, [about 1780].
11.5 cm. [3], 4–176, [4] p. + frontispiece + plates. Dutch flowered boards.
Roscoe J315(4).
Elisabeth Ball Collection.

Samuel Richardson's monumental novel about Clarissa Harlowe and her tormentor Robert Lovelace ran to more than a million words in its original (1747–1748) edition. The abridgment shown here was published for children by Elizabeth Newbery about 1780. This version, in addition to being drastically shortened, alters the original from a novel told in letters to a conventional narrative; in this form it was widely read by children. The copy shown here, with illustrations colored by hand, is one of the few surviving copies of any early Newbery edition of *Clarissa.*

186 Henry Fielding

THE HISTORY OF TOM JONES, A FOUNDLING. ABRIDGED FROM THE WORKS OF HENRY FIELDING, ESQ.

London: E. Newbery, 1784.
11.5 cm. [7], 2–194, [13] p. + frontispiece + plates. Dutch flowered boards.
Roscoe J132(2).
Elisabeth Ball Collection.

Henry Fielding's great novel—often called the greatest in the English language—as it was first abridged for children. From advertisements in the *London Chronicle* in 1768 it is known that this version was first brought out in that year, or the next, in an edition by Francis Newbery, John Newbery's nephew and one of the heirs to his business. The copy illustrated here is from an edition published in 1784 by Elizabeth Newbery, the widow of Francis. This is the earliest surviving edition. The Morgan Library copy is one of perhaps two known perfect copies.

Frontispiece
Lovelace forces Clarissa to leave her Fathers House

185

THE

HISTORY

OF

TOM JONES,

A

FOUNDLING.

Abridged from the Works of

HENRY FIELDING, Esq.

LONDON:

Printed for E. NEWBERY, the Corner
of St. Paul's Church Yard.

MDCCLXXXIV.

186

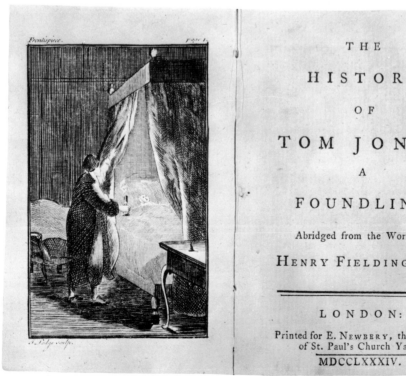

Baron Munchausen

187 [Rudolf Eric Raspe]

GULLIVER RESSUSCITÉ, OU LES VOYAGES, CAMPAGNES ET AVENTURES EXTRAORDINAIRES DU BARON DE MUNIKHOUSON.

Paris: Royez, 1787, 1786.
18.5 cm. [5], *vi–viii*, [1], *2–34*, [3], *38–75*, [1] *p.* + *3 plates. Buff printed wrappers.*
Gumuchian (Catalogue 15) 86. Wackermann 4.1.
Elisabeth Ball Collection.

Baron Munchausen, the hero of the most famous "tall tales" known, was given to the world by an unprincipled rogue whose talents, brashness, and improbable exploits were almost comparable to those of Munchausen himself. Rudolf Eric Raspe (1737–1794) was a German scholar, scientist, poet, teacher, mineralogist, translator, librarian, and journalist (to name no more of his many virtuosities). He was also a swindler, fraud, and thief, who sold for his own pocket valuable coins from a collection entrusted to his care by a German nobleman. Absconding, he was captured by the police. But he escaped and made his way to England, where earlier, on the strength of his scientific writings, he had been elected an honorary fellow of the Royal Society. Fluent in English, he supported himself in England by his pen, bringing out translations and writings on a wide variety of subjects. These included an essay on the origin of oil painting which so impressed Horace Walpole that he helped Raspe publish it. At the end of 1785 Raspe brought out anonymously (the publisher was Smith, in London) a forty-nine-page pamphlet entitled *Baron Munchausen's Narrative of his marvellous Travels and Campaigns in Russia.* This was a collection of incredible exploits recounted in a straightforward, apparently precise manner for comic effect. Baron Munchausen was a real person, an old soldier Raspe had known in Germany who was fond of relating unbelievable anecdotes as if they were the exact truth.

The 1785 first edition (which sold for one shilling) of Raspe's *Munchausen* is believed to have been a very small printing; no copy is known to survive. A second edition appeared in 1786, with a slightly different title but the same text. The printer, Smith, then sold the rights to another printer, Kearsley, who engaged a writer to augment considerably the five chapters of Raspe's original text. This writer, whose identity is unknown but who was certainly inferior to Raspe in originality, added fifteen chapters, one at the beginning and fourteen at the end. The new material was borrowed from various sources, including the ancient Roman writer Lucian, and it also contained many allusions to such current events as Montgolfier's balloon ascents. Raspe's original now occupied Chapters II through VI, the place it has held in all subsequent versions. Kearsley added some engraved illustrations and published the work, at a price of two shillings, in 1786. It was an immediate success, and other editions followed rapidly. The first French edition, which is illustrated here, was probably published in 1786, the same year as Kearsley's first English edition. This French edition is a book of extreme rarity, especially when containing the engraved plates, as this copy does. (The plates were not ready in time, and some copies were issued without them.) The plate reproduced depicts Munchausen severing his horse's bridle with a pistol shot, releasing the animal from the church steeple to which he had tethered it the previous night. (There had been a great snowfall, and the Baron mistook the steeple for the stump of a little tree. But by morning the snow had thawed. . . .) What may well be a typical Munchausen touch occurs in the dating of this edition; the two parts are paged continuously, but the first part is dated 1787 and the second 1786.

188 Baron Munchausen [i.e., Rudolf Eric Raspe]

GULLIVER REVIVED: OR, THE VICE OF LYING PROPERLY EXPOSED.

London: G. Kearsley, 1789.
15.5 cm. [4], v–xxiii, [1], 25–252, [10] p. + 20 plates.
Wackermann 3.7.
Purchased for the Elisabeth Ball Collection.

This is the sixth Kearsley edition of *Munchausen*. It is the first edition to contain the supplementary voyage in which the Baron, on the back of a cooperative eagle, travels to America. Only two other copies of this edition are recorded.

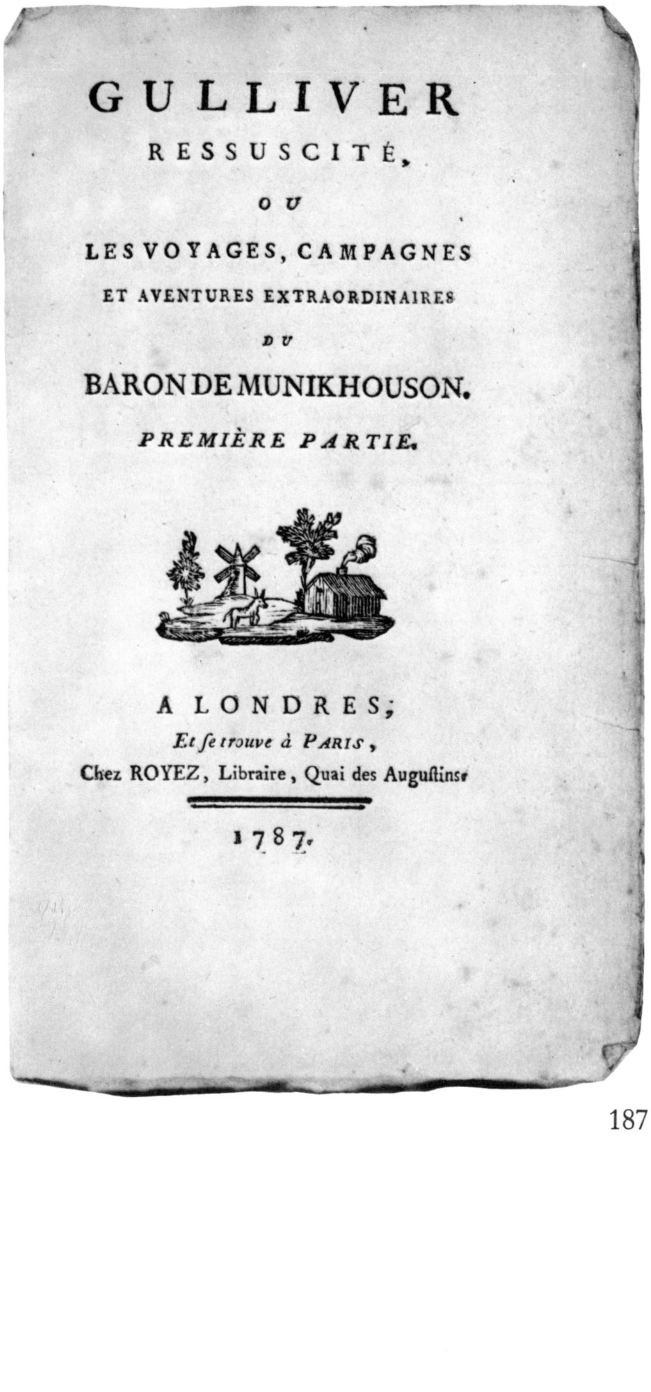

GULLIVER
RESSUSCITÉ,
OU
LES VOYAGES, CAMPAGNES
ET AVENTURES EXTRAORDINAIRES
DU
BARON DE MUNIKHOUSON.
PREMIÈRE PARTIE.

A LONDRES;
Et se trouve à PARIS,
Chez ROYEZ, Libraire, Quai des Augustins.

1787.

187

187

188

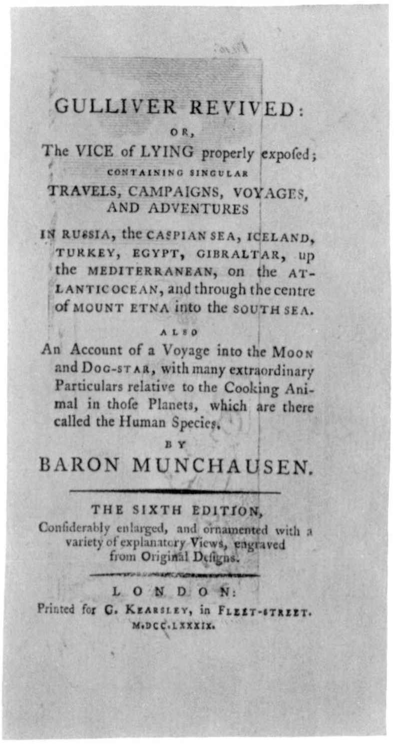

GULLIVER REVIVED:
OR,
The VICE of LYING properly exposed;
CONTAINING SINGULAR
TRAVELS, CAMPAIGNS, VOYAGES,
AND ADVENTURES
IN RUSSIA, the CASPIAN SEA, ICELAND, TURKEY, EGYPT, GIBRALTAR, up the MEDITERRANEAN, on the ATLANTIC OCEAN, and through the centre of MOUNT ETNA into the SOUTH SEA.
ALSO
An Account of a Voyage into the MOON and DOG-STAR, with many extraordinary Particulars relative to the Cooking Animal in those Planets, which are there called the Human Species.
BY
BARON MUNCHAUSEN.

THE SIXTH EDITION,
Considerably enlarged, and ornamented with a variety of explanatory Views, engraved from Original Designs.

LONDON:
Printed for G. KEARSLEY, in FLEET-STREET.
M.DCC.LXXXIX.

188

188

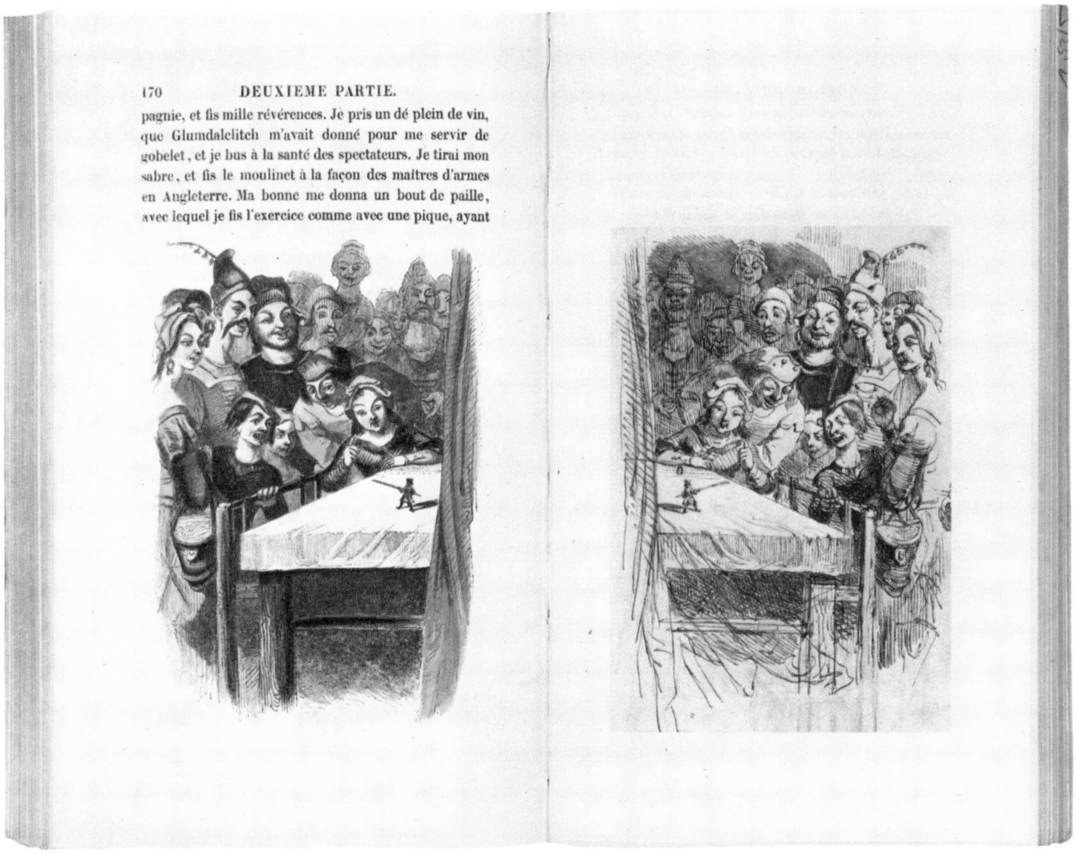

170 DEUXIEME PARTIE.

pagnie, et fis mille révérences. Je pris un dé plein de vin, que Glumdalclitch m'avait donné pour me servir de gobelet, et je bus à la santé des spectateurs. Je tirai mon sabre, et fis le moulinet à la façon des maitres d'armes en Angleterre. Ma bonne me donna un bout de paille, avec lequel je fis l'exercice comme avec une pique, ayant

144

168

But yet its simple tone's preserved in *use*,
Nursery verses, and shameful *abuse*.
In *Viscount* and *island*, *isle* and *demesne*,
'Tis mute as though S ne'er in them had been.

T

Three sounds hath T, which may be called its own ;
The first we find in *tinker*, *last*, *taught*, *tone;*
The next in *creature*, where a *tche* is heard,
SH we find in *nation* for the third.
TH hath tones, to name them still we fear,
Practice alone perfects them to the ear.
Oft mute the H, as in the verb to *rhyme*,
T sounds alone in *asthma*, *Thames*, and *thyme*.

E 2 35

Puzzles, Riddles, and Jests

189 SIX-PENNYWORTH OF WIT; OR, LITTLE STORIES FOR LITTLE FOLKS, OF ALL DENOMINATIONS.

London: Carnan and Newbery, [about 1769].
9.5 cm. [4], 3–126, [2] p.
Roscoe J336(2A).
Elisabeth Ball Collection.

This merry compendium of puzzles, poetry, and anecdotes is a typical John Newbery publication. Bubbling with entertainment, good humor, and assiduous self-advertisement, it manages to promote two other Newbery books on the title page alone. The copy shown here is one of two recorded from this edition, which is probably the second. It was brought out by two of Newbery's immediate successors, his stepson Thomas Carnan and his son Francis Newbery, not long after John Newbery's death in 1767.

190 THE PUZZLING CAP: A CHOICE COLLECTION OF RIDDLES, IN FAMILIAR VERSE.

London: E. Newbery, 1786.
10 cm. [5], 8–95 p. Pink gilt wrappers.
Roscoe J312(2).
Elisabeth Ball Collection.

This charming assemblage of riddles presents the conundrums and their solutions on facing pages. The woodcuts, which are rather good for a children's book of this period, may show the influence of the Bewicks. The answer to Riddle Number One is the book itself, and the last riddle in the collection is the venerable poem beginning "I saw a Peacock with a fiery tail," which goes back at least to the mid-seventeenth century and first appeared in a children's book about 1705 (in *A Little Book for Little Children*, by the unidentified "T.W."). *The Puzzling Cap* was advertised in 1771, but the Morgan Library copy is the earliest known. It would appear to be unique.

191 Benjamin Franklin

THE ART OF MAKING MONEY PLENTY, IN EVERY MAN'S POCKET. BY DR. FRANKLIN.

London: Darton, Harvey and Darton, 1817.
11.5 cm. [8] f.
NBL 730.
Elisabeth Ball Collection.

An early nineteenth-century rebus-book for children, published in England, expressing Benjamin Franklin's well-known philosophy of thrift and honest toil. Both the pictures and the text are engraved.

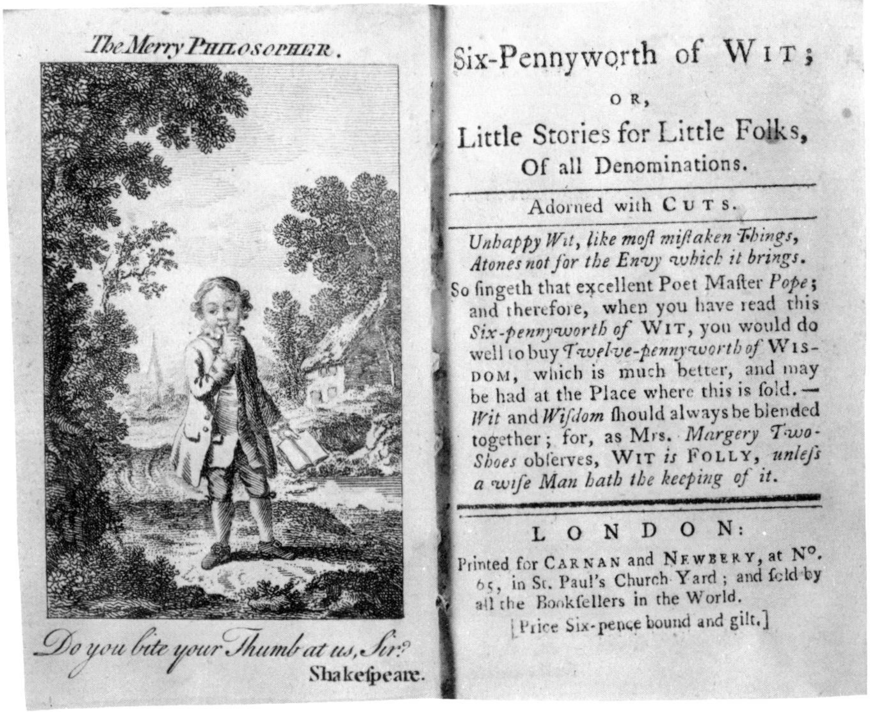
The Merry PHILOSOPHER.

Do you bite your Thumb at us, Sir?
Shakespeare.

Six-Pennyworth of WIT;

OR,

Little Stories for Little Folks,
Of all Denominations.

Adorned with CUTS.

Unhappy Wit, like most mistaken Things,
Atones not for the Envy which it brings.

So singeth that excellent Poet Master *Pope*; and therefore, when you have read this *Six-pennyworth of* WIT, you would do well to buy *Twelve-pennyworth of* WISDOM, which is much better, and may be had at the Place where this is sold.—*Wit* and *Wisdom* should always be blended together; for, as Mrs. *Margery Two-Shoes* observes, WIT *is* FOLLY, *unless a wise Man hath the keeping of it.*

LONDON:
Printed for CARNAN and NEWBERY, at N°. 65, in St. Paul's Church Yard; and sold by all the Booksellers in the World.
[Price Six-pence bound and gilt.]

189

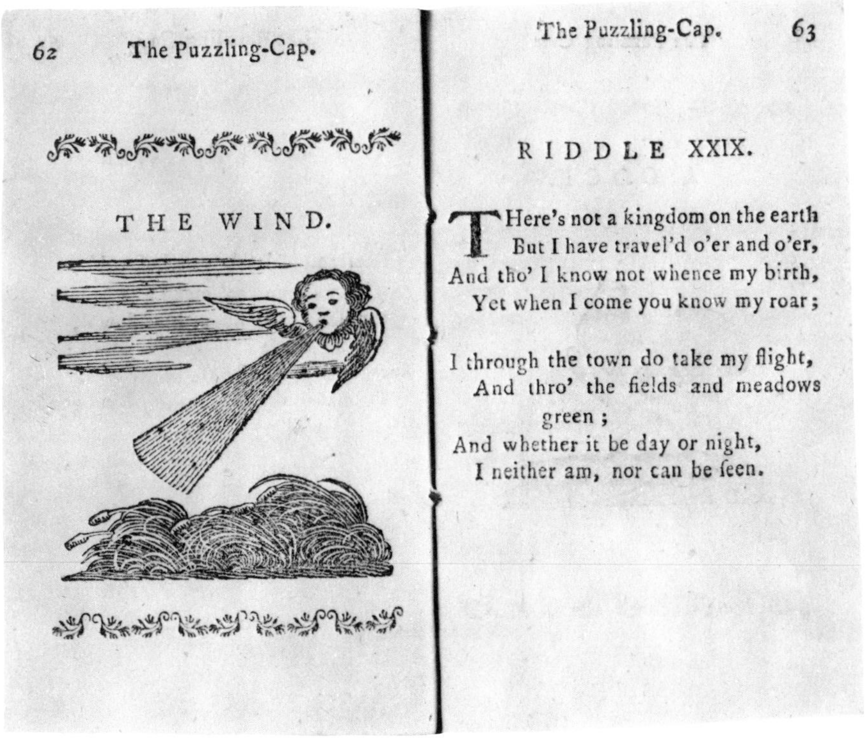
62 The Puzzling-Cap.

THE WIND.

The Puzzling-Cap. 63

RIDDLE XXIX.

THere's not a kingdom on the earth
But I have travel'd o'er and o'er,
And tho' I know not whence my birth,
Yet when I come you know my roar;

I through the town do take my flight,
And thro' the fields and meadows green;
And whether it be day or night,
I neither am, nor can be seen.

190

4
keep them ways . Two simple
d w ll do the
bus nefs. 1st Let ho y
and thy const
keep them always full. Two simple rules, well observed; will do the businefs. 1st Let honesty and industry
be thy constant
5
2d S d one
every day, lefs than thy cl gains,
T sh thy
soon gin to thr ve;
companions: 2d Spend one shilling every day, lefs
than thy clear gains, Then shall thy pockets soon
begin to thrive;

Sports and Games

192 Jacques Stella

LES IEUX ET PLAISRIS [*sic*] DE L'ENFANCE.

Paris: Aux Galleries du Louvre chez la ditte Stella, 1657.
18.5×24.5 cm. [4], 50 f.
Gumuchian 3413.
Purchased on the Lathrop C. Harper Fund.

The first edition of one of the most noteworthy of all books devoted to children's games. The fifty plates illustrating the work, each accompanied by six lines of verse, depict fifty games, sports, and amusements, from tops and kites to leap-frog and blind-man's bluff. The plates are by the French engraver Claudine Bouzonnet Stella (1636–1697) after designs by her uncle, the painter Jacques Stella, some of whose works are in the Louvre. These prints are among the best work of Claudine Bouzonnet Stella, who engraved many highly regarded plates after Jacques Stella and Nicholas Poussin. *Les Jeux et Plaisirs de l'Enfance* was produced for, and dedicated to, children, but it has an additional significance today: it is an important contemporary visual source for knowledge of Continental children's games in the seventeenth century. The attitudes of the children's bodies, which seem strangely unjuvenile to us, are of course an indication of the era's conception of children as miniature adults.

193 Master Michael Angelo [i.e., Richard Johnson]

JUVENILE SPORTS AND PASTIMES.

London: T. Carnan, 1780.
11 cm. [5], 6–108 p. Buff printed boards.
Gumuchian 2764. Roscoe J16(3).
Elisabeth Ball Collection.

A cheerful little eighteenth-century treatise on such sports and pastimes as cricket, hockey, archery, and marbles. This was for a long time attributed to Oliver Goldsmith, but it is now believed to be the work of Richard Johnson. The Morgan Library copy is one of two recorded copies of this edition, which is probably the third. Only one earlier copy is recorded; it is a second edition in the Bodleian Library, Oxford. No copy of the first edition is known to survive.

194 C. G. Salzmann [i.e., J. C. F. Guthsmuths]

GYMNASTICS FOR YOUTH: OR A PRACTICAL GUIDE TO HEALTHFUL AND AMUSING EXERCISES FOR THE USE OF SCHOOLS.

London: J. Johnson, 1800.
21 cm. [3], iv–v, [2], viii–x, [1], xii–xvi, [1], 2–433, [1] p. + plates.
Gumuchian 5093. Schatzki 149. Bentley and Nurmi 403.

The first English edition of an important work on physical training for the young. The translator was Mary Wollstonecraft, who earlier had translated Salzmann's *Elements of Morality* from the German. The author of *Gymnastics for Youth* was J. F. C. Guthsmuths, whose name is on the title page of the original German edition of 1793. The success of the English version of Salzmann's *Elements of Morality*, however, apparently induced the publisher to substitute Salzmann's name for that of the real author of *Gymnastics for Youth*. The book has been considered a foundation treatise of modern gymnastics, but this first English edition is of interest for another reason as well. Its copperplate-engraved illustrations are believed to be the work of William Blake.

195 [Mary Belson Elliott]

A NOSEGAY, FOR THE TROUBLE OF CULLING, OR, SPORTS OF CHILDHOOD.

London: W. Darton, Jun., 1813.
16.5 cm. [4], 5–48 p. Blue-green printed wrappers.
Gumuchian 4290.
Elisabeth Ball Collection.

The first edition of an attractive book on sports and games for children. The author, Mary Belson Elliott, was a prolific writer of humorless moral tales, and her verses and text here, though they are undeniably well written, are in her accustomed vein. The activities she presents include hoop-rolling, standing on the head, riding in a wheelbarrow, doll-dressing (for girls), hopping, blowing soap-bubbles, leap-frog, and (as a pretext for a moral lesson) robbing birds' nests. The remarkably fine engravings are by John Thurston, who had a distinguished career as a book-illustrator and engraver.

196 R. Stennett

ALDIBORONTIPHOSKYPHORNIOSTIKOS; A ROUND GAME, FOR MERRY PARTIES: WITH RULES FOR PLAYING THE GAME.

London: A. K. Newman & Co., [about 1822].
17.5 cm. 35 p.
James, p. 78. Osborne, p. 226.
Elisabeth Ball Collection.

"Rapidity of utterance, and gesticulation, are essential," announce the instructions to this improbable but lively "round game," designed for parties (and preferably, according to the instructions, for sixteen participants). Each child was required to read aloud from a series of tongue-twisting passages of happy nonsense. The author-artist is the same R. Stennett to whom have been attributed the engravings in the early editions of *Dame Trot* and *Dame Wiggins of Lee*. This is the first edition.

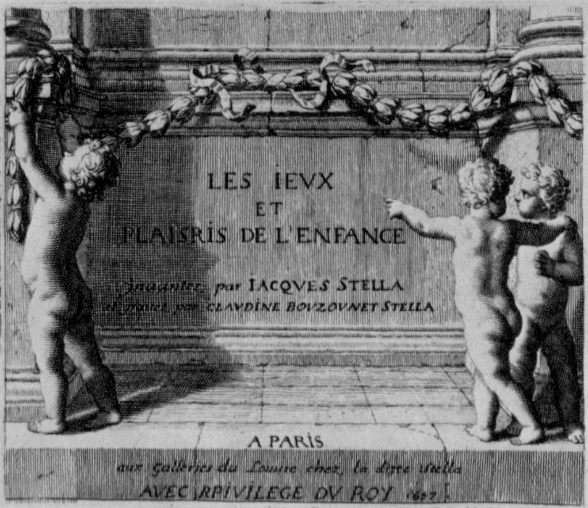
LES IEVX
ET
PLAISRIS DE L'ENFANCE
Inuantez par IACQVES STELLA
par CLAVDINE BOVZOVNET STELLA
A PARIS
aux Galleries du Louure chez la ditte Stella
AVEC RPIVILEGE DV ROY

192

LES BOUTEILLES DE SAVON
Ceux cy se gourment tout de bon
pour ces Bouteilles de Savon
Comme si cestoit des Pistoles;
Mais souvent parmy les grans
on voit naistre des differens
pour milles choses plus frivoles 8

192

LA FOSSETTE

Ce mignon, pour trouver lieu
d'atteindre à celle du milieu,
vse d'adresse et d'artifice ;

Il pouroit bien estre pourtant
que l'Estoeuf, par belle malice,
ne fera pas ce qu'il pretend.

14

192

LA CVLEBVTE

A voir leurs Soubresauts bouffons
qui ne diroit que ces Poupons
auroient bon besoin d'Ellebore ;

Leurs corps est pourtant bien dressé
Si, Selon que dit Pythagore,
l'homme est vn arbre renversé.

24

JUVENILE SPORTS

AND

PASTIMES.

TO WHICH ARE PREFIXED,

MEMOIRS of the AUTHOR:

INCLUDING A NEW MODE OF

INFANT EDUCATION.

By MASTER MICHEL ANGELO,

AUTHOR OF

The DRAWING-SCHOOL for LITTLE MASTERS and MISSES.

LONDON,

Printed for T. CARNAN, at Number 65, in St. Paul's Church-yard. Price Six-pence.

MDCCLXXX.

of; and am ſorry to find it dwindled even to ſo low an ebb, as to become the paſtime of little children only. Can any thing look more manly than this little fellow, who is ſhooting at a bird perched on a tree? and, from the manner in which he holds his bow and arrow, I will lay fifty marbles that he brings it down.

The reaſon why the bow and arrow are ſo much neglected is, as I apprehend, the want of knowing where to buy them, or how to make them. For my part, I would not give a penny for a hundred of thoſe ſold in the ſhops: they are indeed well enough

Pl. 3. p. 218.

The Leap in Length, with & without a Pole.

Publish'd by J. Johnson in St. Pauls Church Yard London Feb. 1, 1800.

to the whole frame. For our place of exerciſe we chooſe ſoft ground, ſomewhat moiſt, and well-covered with graſs, or a ſandy ſoil. We mark the place of the riſe (*terminus a quo*) by a white rod, or ſome other conſpicuous object; and the diſtance to be attained (*terminus ad quem*), by another. The maſter ſettles how far they ſhall be apart, which at firſt may be five feet. He places the leapers at firſt a few ſteps from the neareſt rod, gradually increaſing the length of the preparatory run as far as fifteen ſteps. The pupils leap one after another, till they have all cleared the rods. The maſter then places the farther rod a foot or two more diſtant, the leap is repeated, and thus they go on. When the pupils have carried this leap as far as they can, which is commonly to three times the length of the leaper, within half a foot, or a foot *, the ſame exerciſe may be repeated with the leaping-pole. The proceeding here is exactly the ſame as in the high leap with the pole, only the arc deſcribed is made as long as poſſible.

To render this leap more ſerious, we ſometimes repair to the brook, that winds through

* An expert youth, five feet high, uſually leaped fourteen feet and half, or fifteen feet.

Q 2 our

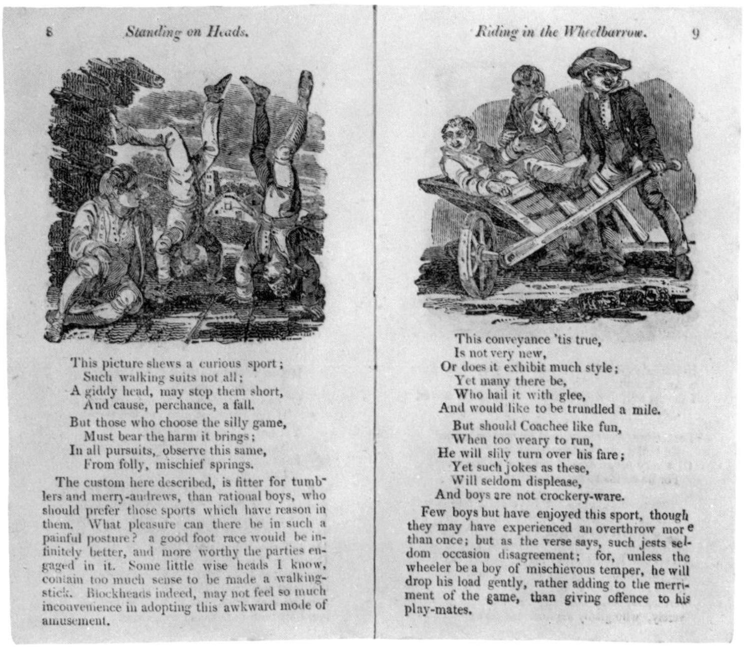

8 *Standing on Heads.*

This picture shews a curious sport;
Such walking suits not all;
A giddy head, may stop them short,
And cause, perchance, a fall.

But those who choose the silly game,
Must bear the harm it brings;
In all pursuits, observe this same,
From folly, mischief springs.

The custom here described, is fitter for tumblers and merry-andrews, than rational boys, who should prefer those sports which have reason in them. What pleasure can there be in such a painful posture? a good foot race would be infinitely better, and more worthy the parties engaged in it. Some little wise heads I know, contain too much sense to be made a walking-stick. Blockheads indeed, may not feel so much inconvenience in adopting this awkward mode of amusement.

Riding in the Wheelbarrow. 9

This conveyance 'tis true,
Is not very new,
Or does it exhibit much style;
Yet many there be,
Who hail it with glee,
And would like to be trundled a mile.

But should Coachee like fun,
When too weary to run,
He will slily turn over his fare;
Yet such jokes as these,
Will seldom displease,
And boys are not crockery-ware.

Few boys but have enjoyed this sport, though they may have experienced an overthrow more than once; but as the verse says, such jests seldom occasion disagreement; for, unless the wheeler be a boy of mischievous temper, he will drop his load gently, rather adding to the merriment of the game, than giving offence to his play-mates.

195

Aldiborontiphoskyphorniostikos.

A ROUND GAME,

FOR

MERRY PARTIES.

LONDON:
A. K. NEWMAN & Co. LEADENHALL-STREET.

Price One-Shilling.

196

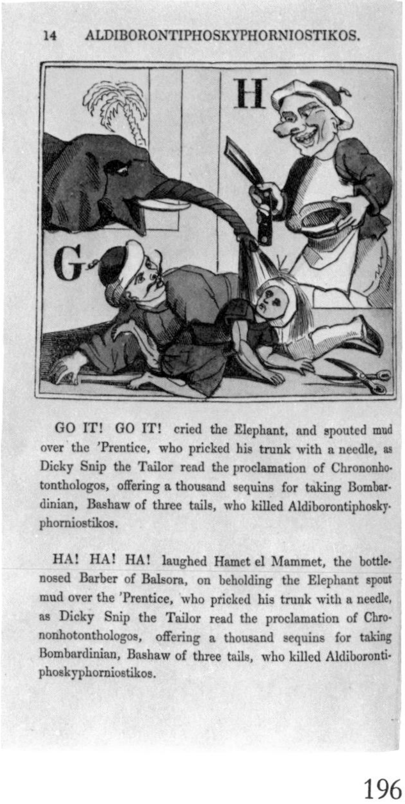

14 ALDIBORONTIPHOSKYPHORNIOSTIKOS.

GO IT! GO IT! cried the Elephant, and spouted mud over the 'Prentice, who pricked his trunk with a needle, as Dicky Snip the Tailor read the proclamation of Chrononhotonthologos, offering a thousand sequins for taking Bombardinian, Bashaw of three tails, who killed Aldiborontiphoskyphorniostikos.

HA! HA! HA! laughed Hamet el Mammet, the bottle-nosed Barber of Balsora, on beholding the Elephant spout mud over the 'Prentice, who pricked his trunk with a needle, as Dicky Snip the Tailor read the proclamation of Chrononhotonthologos, offering a thousand sequins for taking Bombardinian, Bashaw of three tails, who killed Aldiborontiphoskyphorniostikos.

196

The Brothers Grimm

197 Jacob and Wilhelm Grimm

GERMAN POPULAR STORIES, TRANSLATED FROM THE KINDER UND HAUS MÄRCHEN, COLLECTED BY M. M. GRIMM, FROM ORAL TRADITION.

London: C. Baldwyn, 1823; James Robins & Co., 1826.
17.5 cm. 2 vols.: [3], iv–xii, [1], 2–240 p. + frontispiece + plates + extra impressions of etched plates; [3], iv, [1], 2–256, [2] p. + frontispiece + plates.
Cohn 369 (second issue).
Loaned by Gordon N. Ray.

The stories that we know today as Grimm's Fairy Tales were collected from oral tradition by the brothers Jacob and Wilhelm Grimm, philologists and pioneer folklorists. They began to publish the results of their work in 1812, in Germany, under the title *Kinder- und Haus-Märchen.* The tales first appeared in English in 1823, with the publication of the first volume of *German Popular Stories.* The translator was Edgar Taylor, and the book's publication was an auspicious event for at least two reasons. It launched an era in which folklore and the fairy tale would stimulate writers to produce an increasingly imaginative literature for children. And *German Popular Stories* also put before the public the remarkable illustrations—perhaps his best work—of George Cruikshank. The illustrations evoke wonderfully the grotesque, awesome, yet matter-of-fact qualities of witch and goblin, of Frog Prince, Rapunzel, Rumpelstiltskin, and all the other characters that people the tales. As illustrations to these fairy tales Cruikshank's etchings have never been surpassed. This is the second issue of the first edition.

210

221

221

Un jour, Stafford et Warwick vinrent la voir avec Jean de Luxembourg. Et comme celui-ci, en raillant, lui disait qu'il venait la racheter si elle promettait de ne plus s'armer contre l'Angleterre : « En nom Dieu, répondit-elle, vous vous moquez de moi, car je sais bien que vous n'en avez ni le vouloir, ni le pouvoir; je sais bien que les Anglais me feront mourir, croyant, après ma mort, gagner le royaume de France; mais quand ils seraient cent mille de plus, ils n'auront pas le royaume. » Furieux, le comte de Stafford se jeta sur elle. Il l'aurait tuée sans l'intervention des assistants.

198 Jacob and Wilhelm Grimm

HOUSEHOLD STORIES, FROM THE COLLECTION OF THE BROS. GRIMM: TRANSLATED FROM THE GERMAN BY LUCY CRANE; AND DONE INTO PICTURES BY WALTER CRANE.

London: Macmillan Co., 1882.
25 cm. [*7*], *viii–x*, [*1*], *2–269*, [*1*] *p.* + *frontispiece* + *10 plates.*
Massé, p. 33. Hardie, p. 270.
Loaned by Gordon N. Ray.

The first edition of a collection of the fairy tales of the Brothers Grimm illustrated by Walter Crane and translated by his sister Lucy. The stylized, decorative pictures—eleven full-page plates and 108 head- and tail-pieces—of Walter Crane represent an approach vastly different from the cloudy melodrama of George Cruikshank, but Crane's version of the tales is romantic and effective. It is a fine example of his early work, which has been somewhat eclipsed by his later efforts, so many of which were in color.

GERMAN POPULAR STORIES,
Translated from the
Kinder und Haus Märchen,
COLLECTED BY
M. M. GRIMM,
From Oral Tradition.

Published by C. Baldwyn Newgate Street.
LONDON,
1823.

197

197

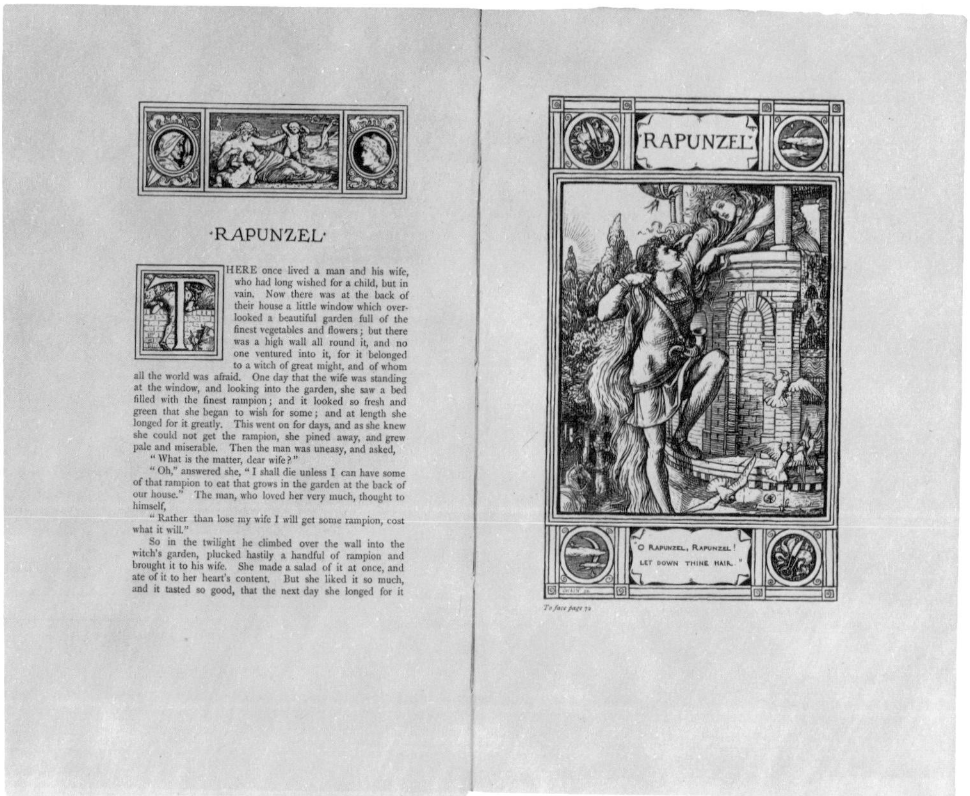
·RAPUNZEL·

THERE once lived a man and his wife, who had long wished for a child, but in vain. Now there was at the back of their house a little window which overlooked a beautiful garden full of the finest vegetables and flowers; but there was a high wall all round it, and no one ventured into it, for it belonged to a witch of great might, and of whom all the world was afraid. One day that the wife was standing at the window, and looking into the garden, she saw a bed filled with the finest rampion; and it looked so fresh and green that she began to wish for some; and at length she longed for it greatly. This went on for days, and as she knew she could not get the rampion, she pined away, and grew pale and miserable. Then the man was uneasy, and asked,

"What is the matter, dear wife?"

"Oh," answered she, "I shall die unless I can have some of that rampion to eat that grows in the garden at the back of our house." The man, who loved her very much, thought to himself,

"Rather than lose my wife I will get some rampion, cost what it will."

So in the twilight he climbed over the wall into the witch's garden, plucked hastily a handful of rampion and brought it to his wife. She made a salad of it at once, and ate of it to her heart's content. But she liked it so much, and it tasted so good, that the next day she longed for it

RAPUNZEL
O Rapunzel, Rapunzel!
Let down thine hair.

198

Hans Christian Andersen

199 Hans Christian Andersen

EVENTYR, FORTALTE FOR BØRN.

Copenhagen: C. A. Reitzel, 1835.
12 cm. [6], 1–61, [1] p.
Hersholt. NBL Andersen 10.

The first edition of the first collection of fairy tales by Hans Christian Andersen. It includes the tales known in English as *The Tinderbox*, *Little Claus and Big Claus*, *The Princess on the Pea*, and *Little Ida's Flowers*. Andersen was thirty years old in 1835. He had already won fame as a writer for adults, having produced poetry, plays, and a novel. The idea of writing children's fairy tales had been with him for some time; at the end of his *Poems*, published in 1830, there had appeared a story entitled "The Ghost, a Fairy Tale from Fünen." (The first edition of *Poems* is at the Morgan Library.) Five years later, on 10 February 1835, he wrote to a friend: "I have started some 'Fairy Tales Told for Children' and believe I have succeeded. I have told a couple of tales which I as a child was happy about, and which I do not believe are known, and have written them in such a way as I would tell them to a child." Andersen used his creative gifts to refashion folktales in a new and profoundly imaginative way. In this he anticipated the best of later fantasies for children. The pamphlet shown here was published on 8 May 1835; today only a very few copies of it are known to exist.

200 Hans Christian Andersen

A DANISH STORY-BOOK. TRANSLATED BY CHARLES BONER.

London: Joseph Cundall, 1846.
17 cm. [172] f. + frontispiece + 3 plates.
NBL Andersen 35.

The first appearance of Andersen's fairy tales in English was in 1846, when several collections, by different translators, were published in London. The collection shown here, published in February 1846, was the first to be illustrated. The translator, Charles Boner, did not use the original Danish text but instead made his translations from German versions of the tales. The illustrations by the Count Pocci are aquatints and woodcuts. These were the first children's-book illustrations to be done by Pocci, a highly regarded artist. His pictures were given the benefit of excellent reproduction in this Cundall edition, and they are considered among the most successful of the early illustrations for Andersen's fairy tales. Among the tales appearing in this edition for the first time in English are *The Ugly Duckling* (here called *The Ugly Duck*) and *The Little Mermaid.*

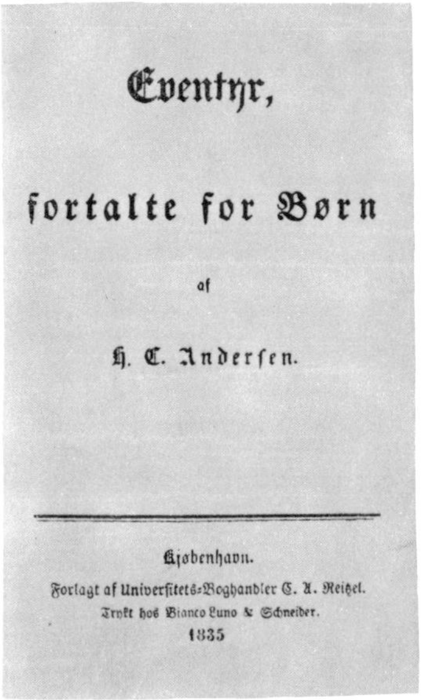

Eventyr,

fortalte for Børn

af

H. C. Andersen.

Kjøbenhavn.

Forlagt af Universitets-Boghandler C. A. Reitzel.

Trykt hos Bianco Luno & Schneider.

1835

199

THE TINDER-BOX.

NCE upon a time, a soldier came marching along on the highway. He had his knapsack upon his back, and his sword by his side; for he came from the wars, and was going home. Presently an old witch met him; she was a loathsome-looking creature; for her under-lip hung down over her chin.

"Good evening, soldier!" said she. "What

K 2

200

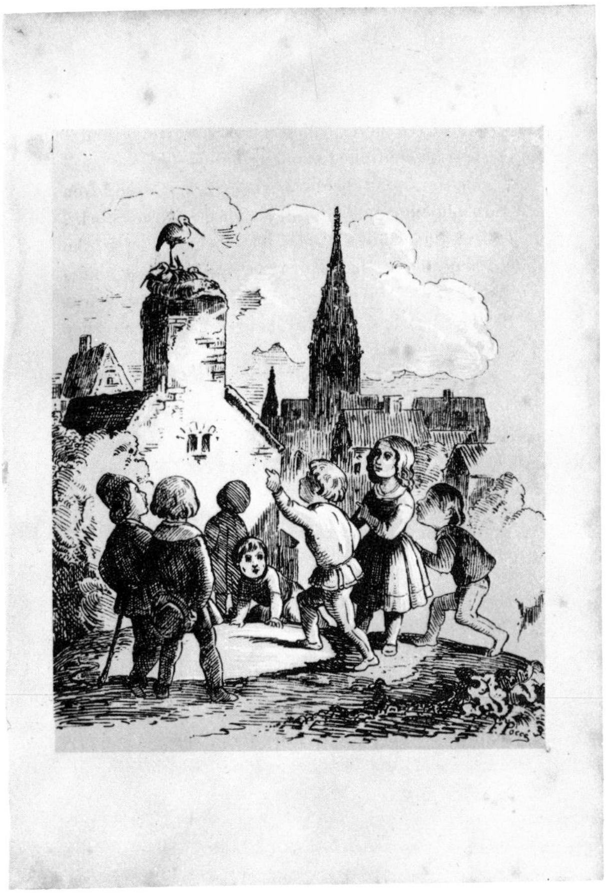

200

A Christmas Carol

201 Charles Dickens

Autograph manuscript, signed on the title page and dated December 1843, of A CHRISTMAS CAROL IN PROSE: BEING A GHOST STORY OF CHRISTMAS.

22.5 cm. 68 f.

The immortality of Charles Dickens rests as much on this brief story as on anything he ever wrote. By 1843 Dickens had enjoyed a decade of great success as a writer, but he now found himself in need of money. His newest novel, *Martin Chuzzlewit*, was not selling up to expectations and he could not cope with his expenses, which had grown steadily along with his fame. In mid-October, in the hope of relieving his financial pressures, he began to write—in some haste, for it would have to be published in December—a Christmas story. Dickens wrote the story confidently and with considerable speed, using a plot he had constructed seven years earlier for a tale incorporated into *Pickwick*. He finished *A Christmas Carol* before the end of November. The autograph manuscript reflects—despite the rapidity with which Dickens worked—its author's constant and painstaking perfectionism. Dickens wrote *A Christmas Carol* as more a family story than a children's tale, but children have of course made it their own long since. Certainly there must be very few English-speaking persons who in childhood did not meet Bob Cratchit and Tiny Tim and the memorable Scrooge.

202 Charles Dickens

A CHRISTMAS CAROL. IN PROSE. BEING A GHOST STORY OF CHRISTMAS.

London: Chapman & Hall, 1843.
16.5 cm. [9], 2–166, [2] p. + 4 plates. Pink cloth gilt.
Eckel, p. 110. Calhoun and Heaney. Gimbel.

On the title page of the manuscript of *A Christmas Carol* Charles Dickens wrote "My own, and only, MS of the book," and signed his name. The busy intricacies of his handwritten pages must have presented the printers with something of a challenge, but they performed well. The first edition, first issue of *A Christmas Carol* is shown here, as it was published by Chapman & Hall on 19 December 1843. Two days earlier, this copy was inscribed by the author and presented to his friend Albany Fonblanque, Esquire. Dickens himself supervised the production of the book, which was rather lavish. It had eight illustrations by John Leech, then the principal artist for the magazine *Punch*. Four of the illustrations were reproduced as vignette wood-engravings by W. J. Linton after Leech's drawings, and four were reproduced as full-page hand-colored etchings.

Six thousand copies of the book were ordered for the first edition. After the printing was under way, Dickens raised objections to various features, including the color of the endpapers and of the inks used on the title page. Changes were made, and made again, and yet again. The printing of the first edition was not completed until Christmas day. Dickens now apparently had books the appearance of which pleased him—and scholars ever since have had a confusing series of issues and states to analyze. The presentation copy shown here is probably the second state of the first issue, but bibliographical investigation continues—as does controversy.

203 John Leech

Watercolor drawing for A CHRISTMAS CAROL, by Charles Dickens.

14 × 11.5 cm.

The original watercolor drawing by John Leech for one of the full-page hand-colored etchings illustrating Dickens' *A Christmas Carol*. It depicts Scrooge beholding the Ghost of Christmas Present, and it is faithful to Dickens' richly detailed description of that memorable confrontation.

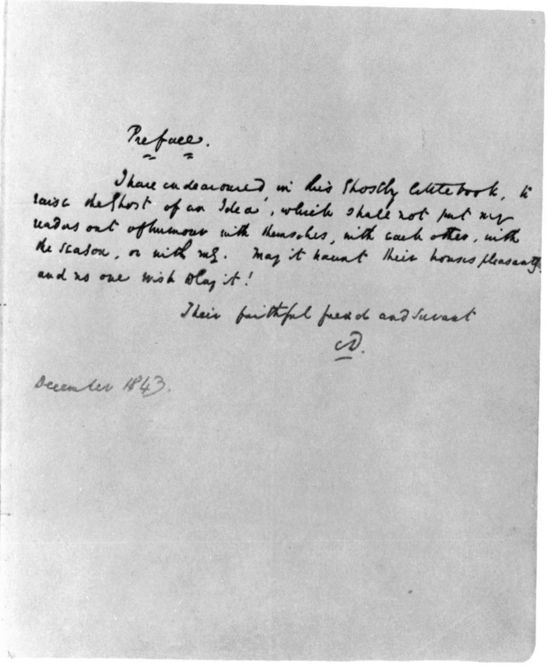

Preface.

I have endeavoured, in this Ghostly little book, to raise the Ghost of an Idea, which shall not put my readers out of humour with themselves, with each other, with the season, or with me. May it haunt their houses pleasantly, and no one wish to lay it!

Their faithful Friend and Servant
C.D.

December 1843.

201

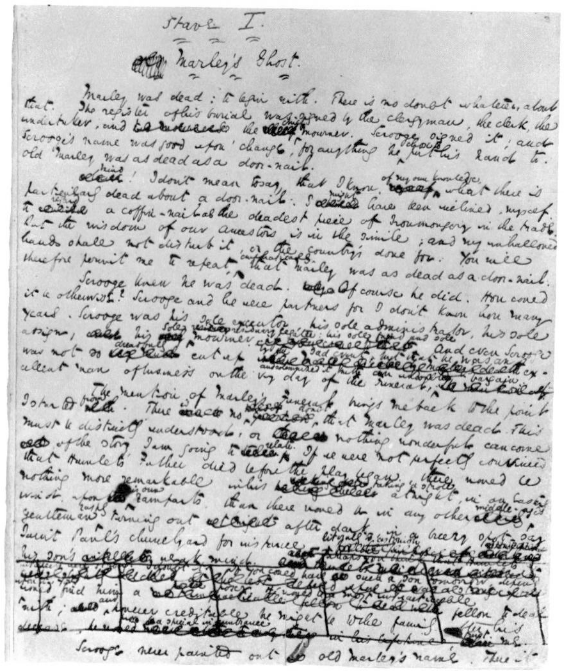

Stave I.

Marley's Ghost.

Marley was dead: to begin with. There is no doubt whatever about that. The register of his burial was signed by the clergyman, the clerk, the undertaker, and the chief mourner. Scrooge signed it; and Scrooge's name was good upon 'Change, for anything he put his hand to. Old Marley was as dead as a door-nail.

201

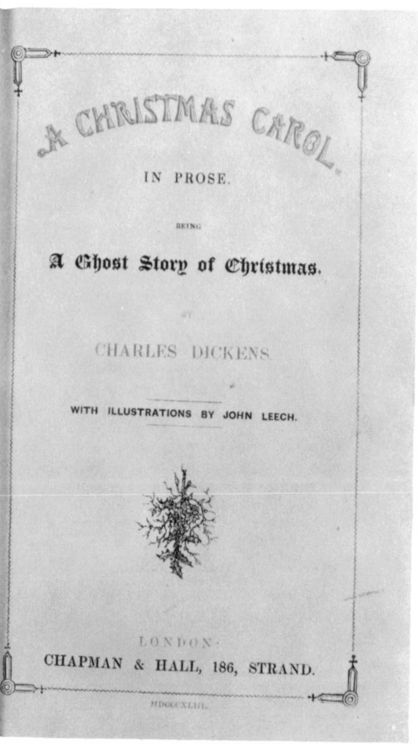

A CHRISTMAS CAROL.

IN PROSE.

BEING

A Ghost Story of Christmas.

BY

CHARLES DICKENS.

WITH ILLUSTRATIONS BY JOHN LEECH.

LONDON:
CHAPMAN & HALL, 186, STRAND.

MDCCCXLIII.

202

Later Fiction

204 Sir Walter Scott

IVANHOE; A ROMANCE.

Edinburgh: James Ballantyne and Co., 1820 [i.e., 1819].
20 cm. 3 vols.: [8], 9–298; [7], 4–327, [1]; [7], 4–371, [2], 2–3, [1] p.
Van Antwerp, p. 109. Worthington, p. 84.
William C. Van Antwerp Collection.

Much of the historical fiction written for children since the mid-nineteenth century, whether adventure story or romance, can be said to owe a debt to Sir Walter Scott. One of the principal figures of English literature in the early nineteenth century, Scott has been credited with originating the historical romance. He wrote novels set in past eras, with dramatic and colorful associations, and containing all the trappings of strange, often exotic backgrounds. Scott wrote very little specifically for children, but the young read many of his works in his day and still read many of them now. More significantly, however, Scott's writing exerted a powerful influence on the children's books of the future. The form he created, the concept of using history as source and setting, would become increasingly attractive to the writers of fiction for children. Scott's *Ivanhoe*, which was immediately and lastingly popular with adults, has been read by generations of children —often, alas, under duress as a school assignment. The first issue of the first edition is shown here.

205 Sir Walter Scott

Autograph manuscript of IVANHOE.

27 cm. 113 f.

Sir Walter Scott's autograph manuscript for parts of Volumes II and III of *Ivanhoe*. These are the only portions of the original manuscript which are known to survive. A leaf from Volume III is shown here.

206 Robert Louis Stevenson

TREASURE ISLAND.

London: Cassell & Company, 1883.
19 cm. [7], viii, [1], 2–292, 1–8 p. + frontispiece map. Gray-green cloth gilt.
Beinecke 241.

The first edition of an immortal among adventure stories. The endlessly exciting narrative of a quest for a mysterious pirate hoard, it has taken an honored place in English literature. This is the initial appearance of Stevenson's tale in book form; it had originally been published as a serial in the children's periodical *Young Folks,* where it appeared in installments from October 1881 to January 1882. Stevenson wrote the serial under a *nom-de-plume* (Captain George North), and in its periodical appearance the story also had a different title: *The Sea Cook.* It was not Stevenson but an inspired editor who changed the title to *Treasure Island.*

207 Rudyard Kipling

CAPTAINS COURAGEOUS, A STORY OF THE GRAND BANKS.

London: Macmillan and Co., 1897.
18.5 cm. [7], viii, [1], 2–245, [3] p.
Stewart-Yeats 163.

The first edition of the only Kipling story to have an American setting. It takes place in Atlantic fishing grounds off the Newfoundland coast, and its protagonist is an American millionaire's spoiled son, Harvey Cheyne, who is unexpectedly brought up against some of the grimmer realities of life. This is the first edition in book form, published in October 1897, with illustrations by I. W. Taber; the story was serialized in *McClure's Magazine* from December 1896 to May 1897.

208 Rudyard Kipling

Autograph manuscript, signed, of HARVEY CHEYNE —BANKER.

28 cm. 74 f.

Rudyard Kipling's original manuscript, completed in 1896, for the story he later entitled *Captains Courageous.* In writing this tale of adventure and regeneration, Kipling made use of background material given him by an American friend, a doctor from Vermont.

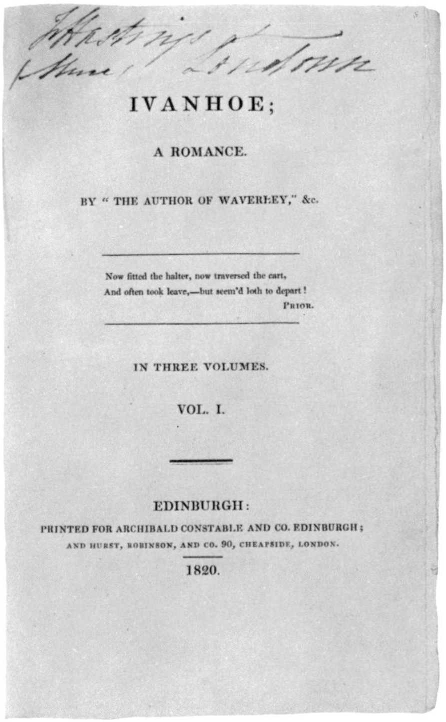
Hastings of Lowdoun

IVANHOE;

A ROMANCE.

BY " THE AUTHOR OF WAVERLEY," &c.

Now fitted the halter, now traversed the cart,
And often took leave,—but seem'd loth to depart!
PRIOR.

IN THREE VOLUMES.

VOL. I.

EDINBURGH:
PRINTED FOR ARCHIBALD CONSTABLE AND CO. EDINBURGH;
AND HURST, ROBINSON, AND CO. 90, CHEAPSIDE, LONDON.
1820.

204

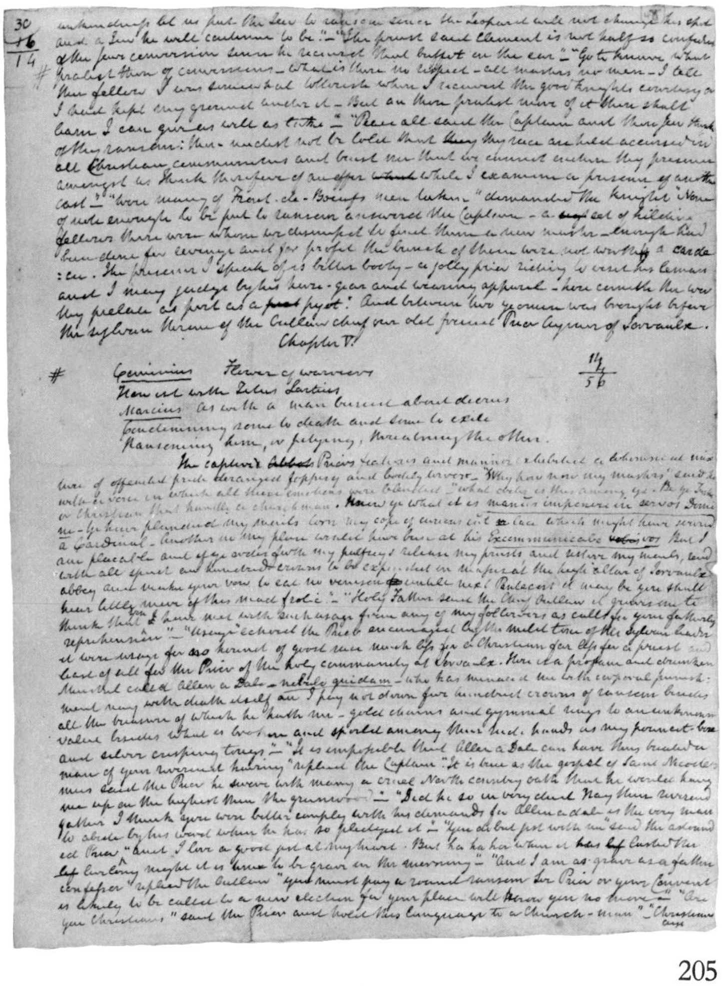

205

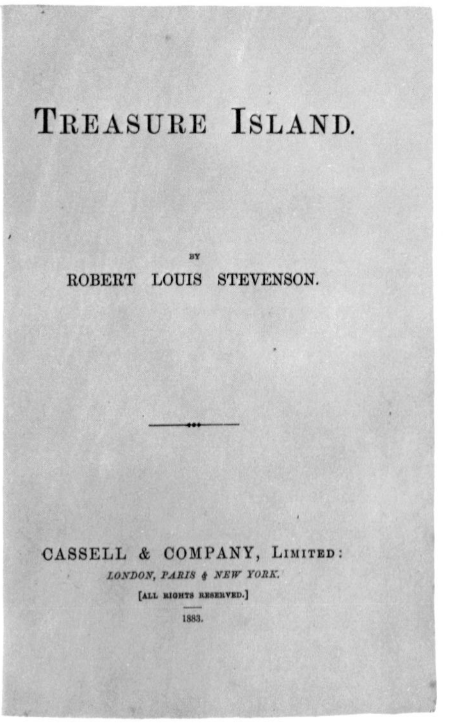

TREASURE ISLAND.

BY

ROBERT LOUIS STEVENSON.

CASSELL & COMPANY, LIMITED:
LONDON, PARIS & NEW YORK.
[ALL RIGHTS RESERVED.]
1883.

206

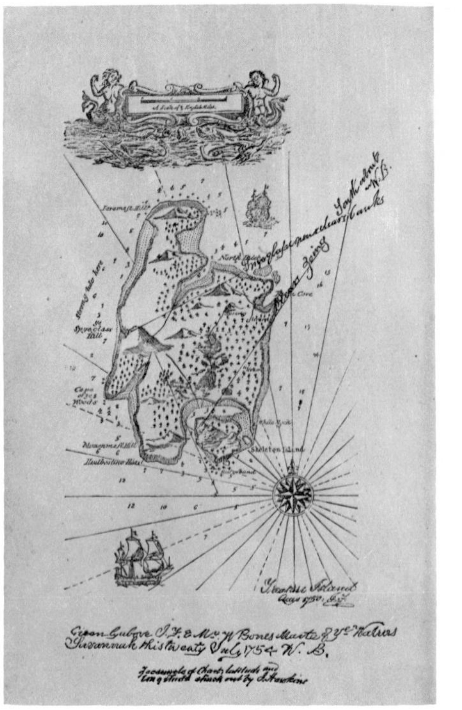

206

FOR AN HOUR LONG JACK WALKED HIS PREY UP AND DOWN, TEACHING, AS HE SAID, 'THINGS . . . EVRY MAN MUST KNOW, BLIND, DHRUNK, OR ASLEEP.'

207

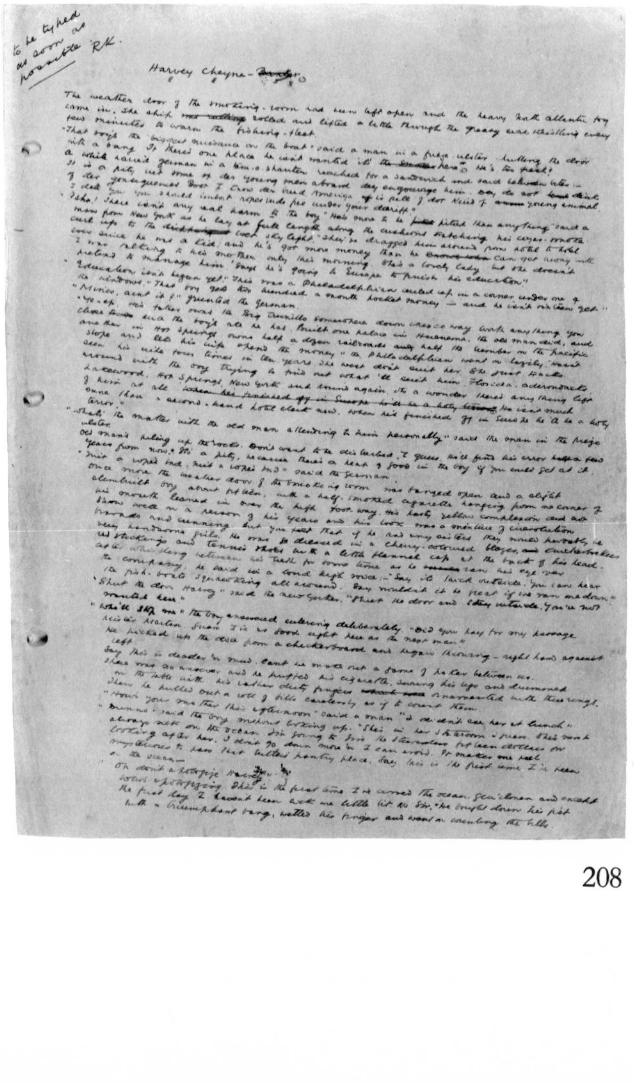

to be typed as soon as possible RK.

Harvey Cheyne

The weather door of the smoking-room had been left open and the heavy North Atlantic fog came in. The ship rolled and lifted a little through the greasy seas, whistling every few minutes to warn the fishing-fleet.

"That boy's the biggest nuisance on the boat" said a man in a frieze ulster, hulling the door with a bang.

208

Fantasy

209 Lewis Carroll [i.e., Charles Lutwidge Dodgson]

ALICE'S ADVENTURES IN WONDERLAND.

London: Macmillan and Co., 1865.
20 cm. [13], 2–192 p.
Williams-Madan-Green 42. Weaver 8.
Loaned by Mr. and Mrs. Francis Kettaneh.

"Began writing fairy tale for Alice, which I told them July 4, going to Godstow—I hope to finish it by Christmas," reads the entry for 13 November 1862 in the diary of Charles Lutwidge Dodgson, a lecturer in mathematics at Oxford University. The "fairy tale" was of course *Alice's Adventures under Ground*, which Dodgson first told as an extemporaneous story to entertain three small girls at a picnic on the river. The girls, one of whom was named Alice, were the daughters of Dean Liddell of Christ Church, Oxford. It was to please Alice Liddell that Dodgson later wrote the story down. The mathematician's inspired fantasy was published in 1865 as *Alice's Adventures in Wonderland*, with Dodgson using the *nom-de-plume* of Lewis Carroll. To claim the very least for Lewis Carroll's *Alice*, it occupies a peak in sustained free imagination in children's literature—a peak from which it has never been dislodged. A copy of the first issue of the first edition of *Alice's Adventures in Wonderland* is shown here. It exists in fewer than two dozen copies, all richly prized by collectors.

The genius who created—who enriched English literature with—the Mad Hatter and the Cheshire Cat was a tense perfectionist when it came to illustrations for his book. He insisted that the artist he had chosen, John Tenniel, conform in every detail to the exact vision of the characters and settings in the author's mind. (Carroll was subsidizing the illustrator's work, as well as the publisher's costs, out of his own pocket.) "Lewis Carroll is impossible . . . ," Tenniel later wrote to the artist Harry Furniss, who was about to illustrate one of Carroll's books: "I'll give you a week, old chap; *you* will never put up with that fellow a day longer."

The first printing of *Alice*—it comprised two thousand copies—was ready in the latter part of June 1865. The events thereafter have become legendary. Tenniel was dissatisfied with the printing of his illustrations, and he wished them to be done over. Carroll agreed that the book should be reprinted. Accordingly, the entire edition was withdrawn before publication and disposed of, in a different form, in America. A new, improved edition was published, with which both Tenniel and Carroll found favor this time. But a small number of the books from the original, unsatisfactory issue had been distributed as presentation copies; some of these were recovered by Carroll and others were not. At the present writing, nineteen or twenty copies of the first issue of *Alice's Adventures in Wonderland* are known to survive. The copy shown here is one of them. In all likelihood, this was Carroll's own copy. It contains a large number of markings, all of them in the purple ink Carroll is known to have used. These markings appear to indicate necessary improvements for the new, corrected printing of the book. This copy of the "suppressed" *Alice* also contains ten of the original drawings for the illustrations, together with a penciled note: "The pencil drawings in the book are the original sketches done by me, John Tenniel."

210 ❧ John Tenniel

Watercolor drawing for ALICE'S ADVENTURES IN WONDERLAND, by Lewis Carroll.

13×9.5 cm.
Williams-Madan-Green, p. 28.
Loaned by Mr. and Mrs. Francis Kettaneh.

This is the original watercolor drawing made by John Tenniel for the illustration "Alice and the White Rabbit" in *Alice's Adventures in Wonderland.* When Lewis Carroll approached him about illustrating *Alice,* Tenniel was busy with work for the famous satirical magazine *Punch.* But he had illustrated books before—among them a highly regarded Aesop—and he had a predilection for drawing animals, so he agreed to illustrate Carroll's book.

211 Lewis Carroll [i.e., Charles Lutwidge Dodgson]

THROUGH THE LOOKING-GLASS, AND WHAT ALICE FOUND THERE.

London: Macmillan and Co., 1872.
18.5 cm. [*13*], *2–224,* [*4*] *p. Red cloth gilt.*
Williams-Madan-Green 84.

On 24 August 1866, some nine months after the successful publication of *Alice's Adventures in Wonderland*, Lewis Carroll wrote to his publishers: "It will probably be some time before I again indulge in paper and print. I have, however, a floating idea of writing a sort of sequel to 'Alice', and if it ever comes to anything, I intend to consult you. . . ." The author of *Alice* finally did begin, in June of 1868, to write "a sort of sequel." His working title for the new book was *Looking-Glass House*, and probably the key inspiration came from a meeting, in August 1868, between Lewis Carroll and a young cousin named Alice Raikes. This second little girl named Alice stood with Carroll before a large mirror and wondered what it would be like to be on the other side of the glass. *Through the Looking-Glass* was completed by early January of 1871. Tweedledum and Tweedledee, the Jabberwock, and the Walrus and the Carpenter were soon to join the glorious creations of the first book. Children forever after would read both "Alice" books with equal delight—and later find it difficult to distinguish between them. The first edition of *Through the Looking-Glass* is illustrated here.

212

John Tenniel

Pencil drawing for THROUGH THE LOOKING-GLASS, by Lewis Carroll.

15.5×12.5 cm. Hudson, p. 179.
Loaned by Arthur A. Houghton, Jr.

John Tenniel had found Lewis Carroll such a troublesome overseer of his illustrations for *Alice's Adventures in Wonderland* that he declined Carroll's invitation to illustrate the sequel. Carroll made attempts to interest other artists in the project. He approached Richard Doyle, J. Noel Paton, and W. S. Gilbert, but for one reason or another nothing could be worked out. Tenniel, however, finally changed his mind and agreed to illustrate the book after all. He may have come to rue his decision, for after this second experience with Carroll was over he wrote: ". . . with *Through the Looking-Glass* the faculty of making drawings for book illustration departed from me . . . I have done nothing in that direction since." Shown here is Tenniel's original pencil drawing of Alice's first encounter with the looking-glass.

213 Carlo Collodi [i.e., Carlo Lorenzini]

"*LA STORIA DI UN BURRATINO.*" ["THE STORY OF A PUPPET."] [In: *Giornale per i Bambini*, Vol. I, Nos. 1, 2, 5, 7, 10, 11, 16, 17.]

Rome: 1881–1883.
30 cm.
Doyle, p. 56.
Purchased for the Elisabeth Ball Collection.

The first appearance—in a children's newspaper, *Giornale per i Bambini*—of Italy's most famous contribution to children's literature, the engaging wooden puppet Pinocchio. He is the hero of an inventive tale in which his nose grows longer whenever he tells a lie and returns to normal size when he tells the truth. The story ran as a serial from July 1881 to January 1883. In the first installments its title was *La Storia di un Burratino* (*The Story of a Puppet*), but before the serial ended this had been changed to *Le Avventure di Pinocchio* (*The Adventures of Pinocchio*). It was published in book form under this title in 1883. The author, Carlo Lorenzini (1826–1890), took the name Collodi from his mother's native village in Tuscany.

214 L[yman] Frank Baum

THE WONDERFUL WIZARD OF OZ.

Chicago and New York: Geo. M. Hill Co., 1900.
22 cm. [11], 12–259, [3] p. Green pictorial cloth.
PPP, p. 111.
Purchased for the Elisabeth Ball Collection.

The adventures of Dorothy, a little farm girl who is swept up by a Kansas cyclone and deposited in the Land of Oz, where she is befriended by a Scarecrow, a Lion, and a Tin Woodman, among others. This homespun American fantasy has remained popular with children for three quarters of a century. The first of its many adaptations for stage or screen was made in 1902 by Baum himself; it was a musical extravaganza that ran for eighteen months on the stage in New York. Baum meanwhile was writing other sorts of books for children. None, however, matched this in popularity, so in 1904 he returned to Oz for a sequel, *The Marvellous Land of Oz*. In all, Baum wrote fourteen Oz books before he died in 1919. The success of these stimulated other writers, in the years after Baum's death, to produce for his publishers no less than twenty-six more Oz books, or nearly twice as many as Baum had written. The edition shown here is the first (the various states of the first edition present a bibliographical complexity that is notorious). It is the only edition illustrated by W. W. Denslow.

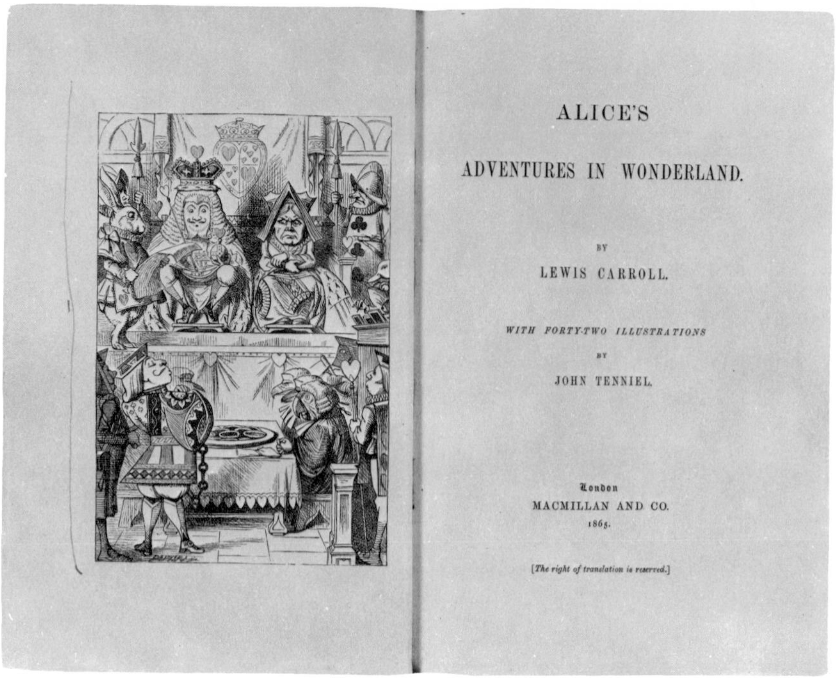

ALICE'S

ADVENTURES IN WONDERLAND.

BY

LEWIS CARROLL.

WITH FORTY-TWO ILLUSTRATIONS

BY

JOHN TENNIEL.

London

MACMILLAN AND CO.

1865.

[*The right of translation is reserved.*]

209

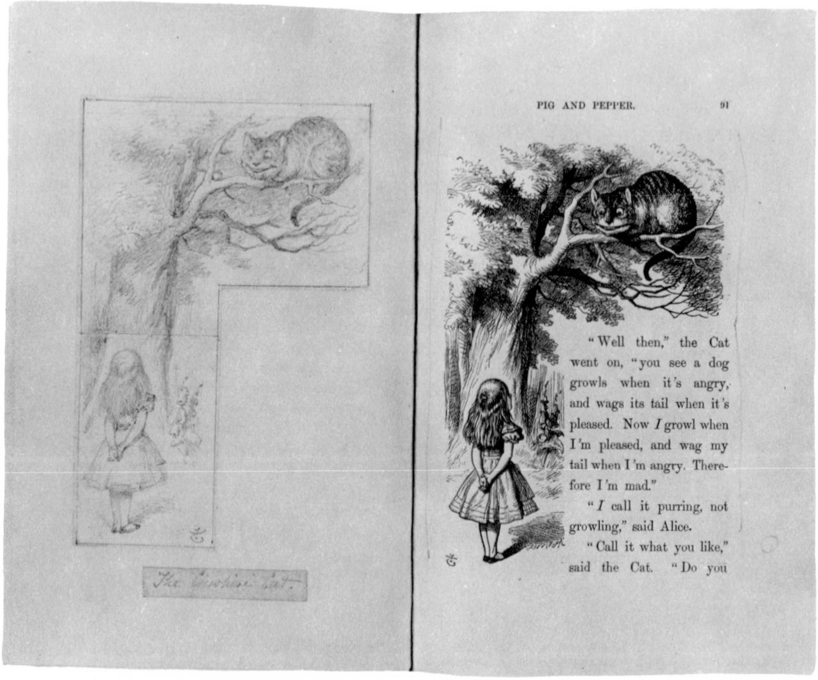

PIG AND PEPPER. 91

"Well then," the Cat went on, "you see a dog growls when it's angry, and wags its tail when it's pleased. Now *I* growl when I'm pleased, and wag my tail when I'm angry. Therefore I'm mad."

"*I* call it purring, not growling," said Alice.

"Call it what you like," said the Cat. "Do you

209

12 LOOKING-GLASS HOUSE.

glass, and had jumped lightly down into the Looking-glass room. The very first thing she did was to look whether there was a fire in the

211

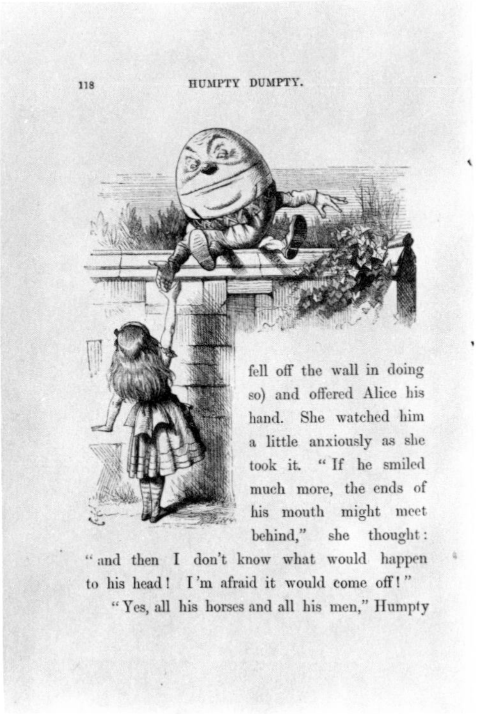
118 HUMPTY DUMPTY.

fell off the wall in doing so) and offered Alice his hand. She watched him a little anxiously as she took it. "If he smiled much more, the ends of his mouth might meet behind," she thought: "and then I don't know what would happen to his head! I'm afraid it would come off!"

"Yes, all his horses and all his men," Humpty

211

212

GIORNALE PER I BAMBINI

ANNO I. - N. 5. FERDINANDO MARTINI direttore *Roma, 4 Agosto 1881.*

ABBONAMENTI.	SI PUBBLICA OGNI GIOVEDÌ	AVVERTENZE.
Un anno { per l'Italia. . . . . L. 12 / per l'estero (Unione Postale) » 15 Un Numero separato Centesimi 25.	DIREZIONE E AMMINISTRAZIONE Roma, Piazza Montecitorio N.° 130.	Non si restituiscono i manoscritti. Dirigere lettere e vaglia all'Amministrazione del *Giornale per i Bambini*.

Sommario

LA STORIA DI UN BURATTINO.(*)

IV.

Vi dirò dunque, ragazzi, che nel mentre che il povero Geppetto era condotto senza sua colpa in prigione, quel monello di Pinocchio, rimasto libero dalle grinfie del carabiniere, se la dava a gambe giù attraverso ai campi per far più presto a tornarsene a casa; e nella gran furia del correre saltava greppi altissimi, siepi di pruni e fossi pieni d'acqua, tale e quale comé avrebbe potuto fare un capretto o un leprottino inseguito dai cacciatori.

Giunto dinanzi a casa, trovò l'uscio di strada socchiuso. Lo spinse, entrò dentro, e appena ebbe messo tanto di paletto, si gettò a sedere per terra, lasciando andare un gran sospirone di contentezza.

(*) Continuazione V. N. 2.

Ma quella contentezza durò poco, perchè sentì nella stanza qualcuno che fece:

— Cri-cri-cri!

— Chi è che mi chiama? - disse Pinocchio tutto impaurito.

— Sono io?

Pinocchio si voltò e vide un grosso grillo che saliva lentamente su su per il muro.

— Dimmi, Grillo: e tu chi sei?

— Io sono il Grillo-parlante, ed abito in questa stanza da più di cent' anni.

— Oggi però questa stanza è mia, disse il burattino, e se vuoi farmi un piacere, vattene subito, senza nemmeno voltarti indietro.

— Io non me ne anderò di qui, rispose il Grillo, se prima non ti avrò detto una gran verità.

— Dimmela e spicciati.

— Guai a quei ragazzi che si ribellano ai loro genitori e che abbandonano capricciosamente la casa paterna. Non avranno mai bene in questo mondo; e prima o poi dovranno pentirsene amaramente.

— Canta pure, Grillo mio, come ti pare e piace: ma io so che domani, all'alba, voglio andarmene di qui, perchè se rimango qui, accadrà a me quel che accade a tutti gli altri ragazzi, vale a dire mi manderanno a scuola e per amore o per forza mi toccherà a studiare, e io, a dirtela in confidenza, di studiare non ne ho punto voglia e mi diverto più a correre dietro alle farfalle e a salire su per gli alberi a prendere gli uccellini di nido.

— Povero grullerello! Ma non sai che, facendo così, diventerai da grande un bellissimo somaro e che tutti si piglieranno gioco di te?

— Chetati, Grillaccio del mal'augurio! - gridò Pinocchio.

Ma il grillo, che era paziente e filosofo, invece di aversi a male di questa impertinenza, continuò con lo stesso tono di voce:

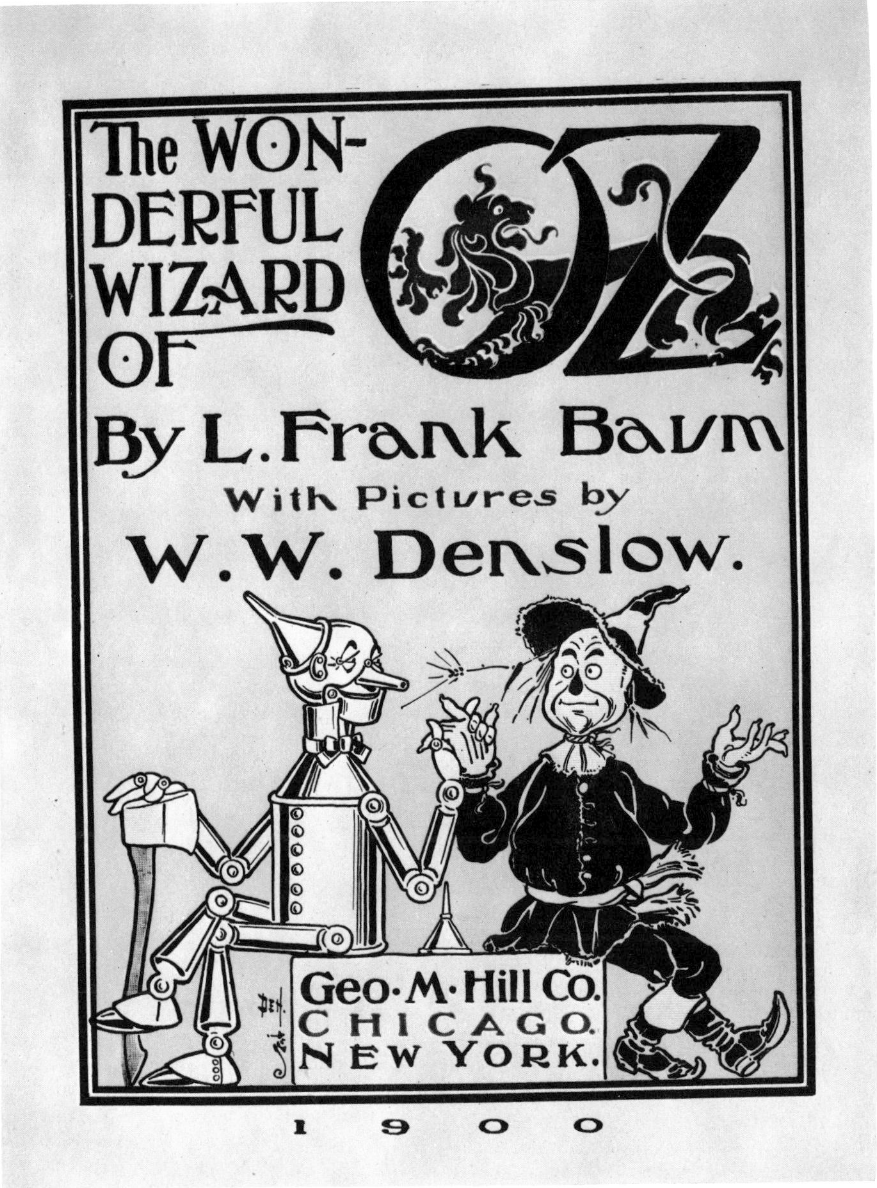
The WONDERFUL WIZARD OF OZ
By L. Frank Baum
With Pictures by
W. W. Denslow.
Geo · M · Hill Co.
CHICAGO
NEW YORK.
1900

Edward Lear

215 [Edward Lear]

A BOOK OF NONSENSE. BY DERRY DOWN DERRY. PART 1. . . . [PART 2.].

London: Thos. McLean, 10 February 1846.
14×21 cm. 2 vols.: [37]; [37] f. Gray printed boards (rebacked).
Opie, NBL, 774. Noakes.
Loaned by Arthur A. Houghton, Jr.

Inspired, delightful nonsense for children—nonsense cheerfully acknowledged as such, and as such gleefully seized upon by the young ever since the first appearance of this book. Edward Lear (1812–1888) was an accomplished landscape artist and animal painter, and a constant traveler. In 1832 he went to stay with the Earl of Derby at Knowsley near Liverpool, on assignment to paint the animals in the private menagerie at Knowsley Hall. There, to entertain the grandchildren and great-grandchildren of the Earl, he produced the nonsense verses and pictures on which he later based his *Book of Nonsense*. Lear's drawings are purely his own, but the limerick form he later admitted to having seen in a book of his childhood, *Anecdotes and Adventures of Fifteen Gentlemen*. Why are these verses called limericks? No one really knows, though scholars continue to form hypotheses, both related and unrelated to the County of Limerick in Ireland. The first edition of *A Book of Nonsense* is shown here. It is in two volumes, with lithographed pictures and text. It is a book of the very greatest rarity. Some scholars feel that its bibliographical complexities are almost as mysterious as the origins of the limerick. The book was first issued in a somewhat unorthodox binding, in which separate leaves were held together by an adhesive backing. The poor quality of the adhesive encouraged the leaves to depart easily, and when they were re-inserted their sequence seems to have been inevitably changed. The resultant confusion is formidable. But investigation has shown that the leaves in this copy are in their original, or close to their original, order. This first edition would thus appear to be one of the finest extant two-volume sets of a book that is known to survive in but a very few copies, and those usually with leaves in jumbled order.

216 Edward Lear

Autograph manuscript, with 49 pen-and-ink drawings, of
A BOOK OF NONSENSE.

1855–1860.
13.5×21.5 cm. 49 f.
Noakes, p. 188.
Loaned by Arthur A. Houghton, Jr.

Edward Lear's original pen-and-ink drawings and hand-lettered text for *A Book of Nonsense.* It is believed that Lear prepared this manuscript for the third edition of the book, which was published in 1861. In the first two editions (1846 and 1856) Lear's drawings had been reproduced by lithography. For this third edition, wood-engraving was used instead, the work being done by the Dalziel Brothers.

217 [?Richard Scrafton Sharpe]

ANECDOTES AND ADVENTURES OF FIFTEEN GENTLEMEN.

London: E. Marshall, [?1823].
18 cm. [16] f.
Opie, NBL, 761.
Elisabeth Ball Collection.

This is the book, and this is the limerick—"There was a sick man of Tobago"—that Edward Lear described as the inspiration for his verses in *A Book of Nonsense.* The authorship of *Anecdotes and Adventures of Fifteen Gentlemen* is attributed to Richard Scrafton Sharpe, and the illustrations are believed to be the work of Robert Cruikshank. What Lear did not know (or at least did not say) is that limericks had appeared in an earlier book, *The History of Sixteen Wonderful Old Women* (see the next item). The copy of *Anecdotes and Adventures* shown here is a very early edition. The first edition is thought to have been issued about 1821; this copy bears an 1823 watermark.

218 ❧ THE HISTORY OF SIXTEEN WONDERFUL OLD WOMEN, ILLUSTRATED BY AS MANY ENGRAVINGS, EXHIBITING THEIR PRINCIPAL ECCENTRICITIES AND AMUSEMENTS.

London: John Harris, [?1827].
17.5 cm. 16 f. Buff printed wrappers (bound in).
Opie, NBL, 760.
Elisabeth Ball Collection.

As far as is known, this is the very first appearance of the verses called limericks. No reference to this book is found in any of Lear's writings, but it seems unlikely that he would not have known of such a book's existence. Perhaps the author of "The Owl and the Pussy Cat went to sea / In a beautiful pea-green boat" forgot that he had once seen this limerick about an old woman named Towl who went out to sea with her owl. (In this stipple engraving, which is hand-colored, the boat is painted pea-green.) *The History of Sixteen Wonderful Old Women* was first published in 1820; the copy shown here uses the plates, dated 1820, of the first edition, but the paper is watermarked 1827.

(Another page from the book is reproduced as color illustration 218.)

PART I.

There was an old Derry down Derry,
Who loved to see little folks merry:
So he made them a Book,
And with laughter they shook,
At the fun of that Derry down Derry!

215

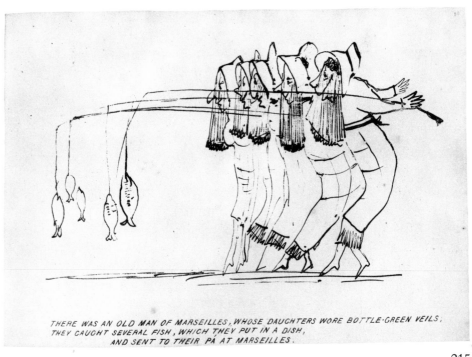

THERE WAS AN OLD MAN OF MARSEILLES, WHOSE DAUGHTERS WORE BOTTLE-GREEN VEILS;
THEY CAUGHT SEVERAL FISH, WHICH THEY PUT IN A DISH,
AND SENT TO THEIR PÁ AT MARSEILLES.

215

There was an Old Man with a beard, who said, "It is just as I feared !—
Two Owls and a Hen, four Larks and a Wren,
Have all built their nests in my beard.

216

1

MISTRESS TOWL.

There was an Old Woman named Towl,
Who went out to Sea with her Owl,
But the Owl was Sea-sick,
And scream'd for Physic;
Which sadly annoy'd Mistress Towl.

218

Beatrix Potter

219 Beatrix Potter

[AUTOGRAPH LETTER, SIGNED, TO NOËL MOORE. 4 February 1895.]

18 × 23 cm.
Linder.
Gift of David McCandless McKell.

Beatrix Potter wrote this illustrated letter early in February 1895 to Noël Moore, the seven-year-old son of her former governess, Annie Carter Moore. It is one of eleven letters in the Morgan Library written by Beatrix Potter to Noël Moore. The theme of rabbits, her pet rabbit Peter among them, was not a new one in Miss Potter's letters to young Noël; as early as September 1893, in a letter written when the five-year-old Noël was ill, she told and illustrated a little adventure of the rabbit named Peter. The idea of making the tale into a book did not come to Miss Potter until a few years later. She then wrote to Noël, asked for the return of her letter (which was fortunately still extant!), and used it as the basis for a manuscript called "The Tale of Peter Rabbit and Mr. McGregor's Garden, by H. B. Potter." She sent the manuscript to at least six publishers without success. Finally, in 1901, she decided to have the book privately printed, at her own expense.

220 Beatrix Potter

THE TALE OF PETER RABBIT.

[London: Privately printed, 1901.]
13.5 cm. [42] f. + frontispiece. Gray-green printed boards; flat back.
Linder, p. 420.
Loaned by Miss Julia P. Wightman.

This is the first issue of the privately printed edition of Beatrix Potter's *The Tale of Peter Rabbit*. The printing was done by the London firm of Strangeways & Sons. Except for a colored frontispiece, all the illustrations are in black and white. The first issue comprised

250 copies; they are distinguished by a flat-backed binding of gray-green boards, printed with a black-line drawing. The books were ready on 16 December and Miss Potter began giving them away to selected friends and relatives and selling them to others at one shilling two pence each. By this time, however, Beatrix Potter's career had already been given its first impetus, for the publisher Frederick Warne & Co. had agreed to accept the book for publication in a regular trade edition. But in February 1902, before the trade edition was ready, Miss Potter ordered another 200 copies to be printed of her private edition; this second issue had a rather better binding, with a rounded back and darker printed boards. In October 1902 the Warne commercial edition was published. The first printing of 6000 copies was sold out before publication, and *The Tale of Peter Rabbit* has been in print ever since, together with the long list of books Beatrix Potter subsequently produced. It is perhaps worth a smile today to learn that on 18 December 1901, in a letter to Frederick Warne & Co., she wrote: ". . . I am aware that these little books don't last long, even if they are a success."

221 ❧ Beatrix Potter

THE TAILOR OF GLOUCESTER.

[London: Privately printed], 1902.
13 cm. [32] f. + 16 plates. Pink printed boards; rounded back.
Linder, p. 420.
Loaned by Miss Julia P. Wightman.

Beatrix Potter wrote *The Tailor of Gloucester* for another of the young Moore children, Freda, and sent it to her as a Christmas present in December of 1901. The story was based on a tale Miss Potter heard about a strange occurrence in the shop of a Gloucester tailor, who one Saturday left on his work table the cut-out parts for a fancy waistcoat he was making, and came back on Monday to find the waistcoat finished—except for one buttonhole, which had pinned beside it a note reading, "No more twist" (meaning silk twist, the thread used for buttonholes). Beatrix Potter later wrote that she "had the story from Miss Caroline Hutton, who had it of Miss Lucy, of Gloucester, who had it of the tailor." Enchanted by the story's possibilities, Miss Potter threw herself into research for it. She made careful sketches of Gloucester streets, of an archway beside the cathedral, of Gloucester houses both inside and out. She tore a button from her coat and went into a tailor's shop to have it sewn on again, so that she might observe the tailor and his workbench and later sketch them.

Her privately printed edition of *Peter Rabbit* having enjoyed some success, Beatrix Potter decided to have this next work brought out in the same manner. The copy shown here is the first edition of the privately printed *Tailor of Gloucester.* It has a format similar to the privately printed *Peter Rabbit,* but with a binding of pink printed boards and a rounded back instead of a flat one. Miss Potter ordered 500 copies printed; they were ready by the middle of December 1902. "I find," she wrote later, "that children of the right age—12—like it best." *The Tailor of Gloucester* was Beatrix Potter's favorite among all her books. Her research, incidentally, seems to have been very accurate, for the British tailoring trade journal, *The Tailor & Cutter,* noticed the book and gave it what Miss Potter described as "a beautiful review!"

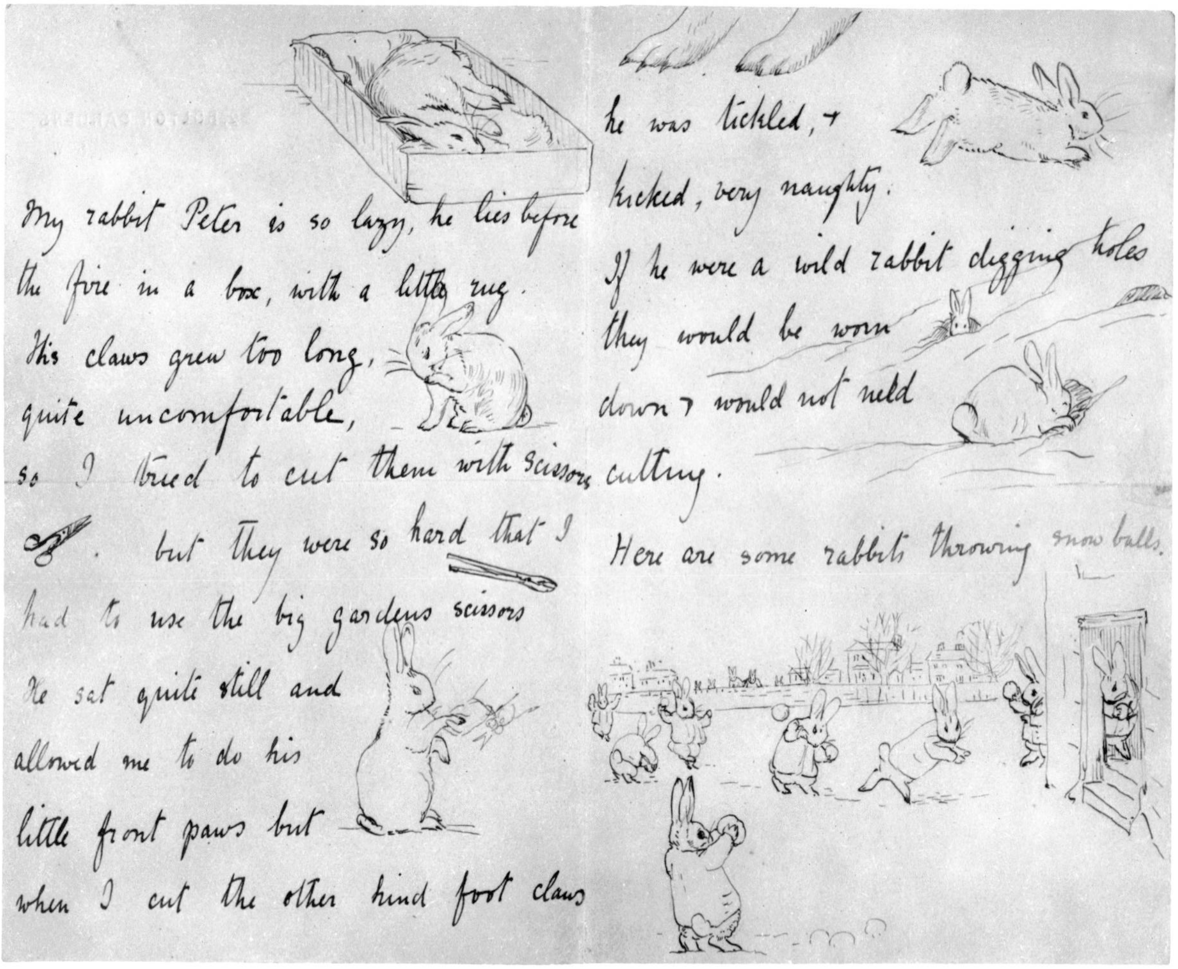

My rabbit Peter is so lazy, he lies before
the fire in a box, with a little rug.
His claws grew too long,
quite uncomfortable,
so I tried to cut them with scissors
but they were so hard that I
had to use the big gardens scissors
He sat quite still and
allowed me to do his
little front paws but
when I cut the other hind foot claws
he was tickled, &
kicked, very naughty.
If he were a wild rabbit digging holes
they would be worn
down & would not need
cutting.
Here are some rabbits throwing snow balls.

219

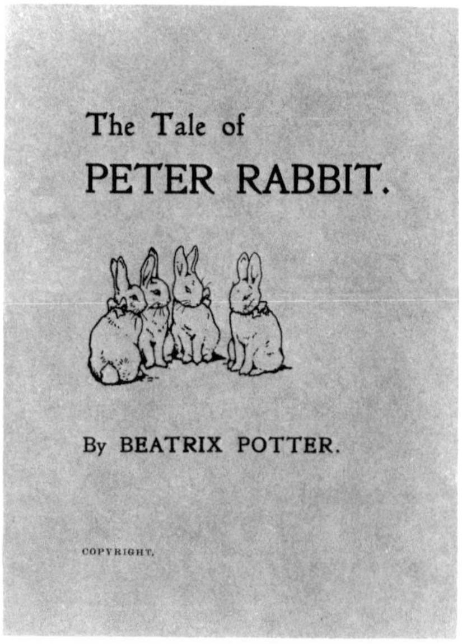

220

220

Coda

222 Munro Leaf

THE STORY OF FERDINAND.

New York: Viking Press, 1936.
20.5 cm. [36] f.
Doyle, p. 174.
(Copyright 1936 by Munro Leaf and Robert Lawson. Copyright © 1964 by Munro Leaf and John W. Boyd. Reprinted by permission of The Viking Press, Inc.)
Gift of the Mary Flagler Cary Charitable Trust.

The first edition of Munro Leaf's *The Story of Ferdinand.* This is perhaps one of the finest twentieth-century examples of the inspired wedding of a text and illustrations to make a children's book that as a whole is even greater than the sum of its parts—which are in themselves very fine indeed. The simple, delightful Leaf story about a Spanish bull who prefers the fragrance of flowers to the roar of the bull-ring is lovingly illustrated by Robert Lawson. The overworked word "classic" is well deserved here. Children have adored *The Story of Ferdinand* ever since the book was published, more than a generation ago now. This copy is signed by Robert Lawson.

223 Robert Lawson

Drawing for the illustration to THE STORY OF FERDINAND, by Munro Leaf.

23.5 × 20 cm.
Mahony, p. 331. Jones.
Gift of the Mary Flagler Cary Charitable Trust.

A preparatory pen-and-ink drawing by Robert Lawson (1893–1957) for one of his illustrations to Munro Leaf's *The Story of Ferdinand.* Lawson's superb sense of design and visual wit combined marvelously well with Leaf's quiet little tale. All the artist's drawings for the book are at the Morgan Library.

224 Antoine de Saint-Exupéry

THE LITTLE PRINCE. [*Translated from the French by Katherine Woods.*]

New York: Reynal & Hitchcock, [1943].
22.5 cm. [8], 7–91, [3] p.
Hürlimann, p. 93.
Gift of Mrs. Eugène Reynal.

Antoine de Saint-Exupéry, a French writer-aviator who was lost over the Mediterranean in 1944, left the world some sensitive writing about the experience of flying in an airplane, but his name probably endures more because of a rather strange little book he wrote just before he died. *Le Petit Prince* (*The Little Prince*) is a fantasy about an aviator who is forced down in the Sahara desert and is befriended there by a child-prince, the sole denizen of a distant asteroid, who is on a visit to Earth. Whether Saint-Exupéry wrote it really for children or slyly for adults is not entirely clear. Figuratively speaking, the tale has something of Hans Christian Andersen in it, something of Lewis Carroll, and even, it may perhaps be said, a bit of John Bunyan. It is often lyrical, too often coy, sometimes profound. Children have enjoyed and loved it, for it frequently expresses their own special vision; adults have read it both as an amusing fantasy and as a satiric allegory. However it is classified, *The Little Prince* has entered children's literature, in the manner of quite a few other such hard-to-define works in the preceding centuries. Saint-Exupéry's book was originally published in both French and English; copy B, signed by the author, of the first edition in English is illustrated here.

225 Antoine de Saint-Exupéry

Autograph manuscript, with illustrations by the author, of LE PETIT PRINCE.

About 1943.
28×22 cm. 172 f.
Purchased for the Elisabeth Ball Collection.

The original manuscript, written in pencil and illustrated with the author's sketches, of Antoine de Saint-Exupéry's *Le Petit Prince* (*The Little Prince*). Included with the manuscript are some pages that were discarded by the author in favor of the final versions. The first page of the manuscript is shown here. It bears Saint-Exupéry's drawing which adults saw as a hat but the Little Prince recognized as a picture of a boa constrictor that had just swallowed an elephant.

As the years went by Ferdinand grew and grew until he was very big and strong.

222

223

"I believe that for his escape he took advantage of the migration of a flock of wild birds."
The Little Prince
WRITTEN AND DRAWN BY
ANTOINE DE SAINT-EXUPÉRY
TRANSLATED FROM THE FRENCH BY KATHERINE WOODS
REYNAL & HITCHCOCK · NEW YORK

224

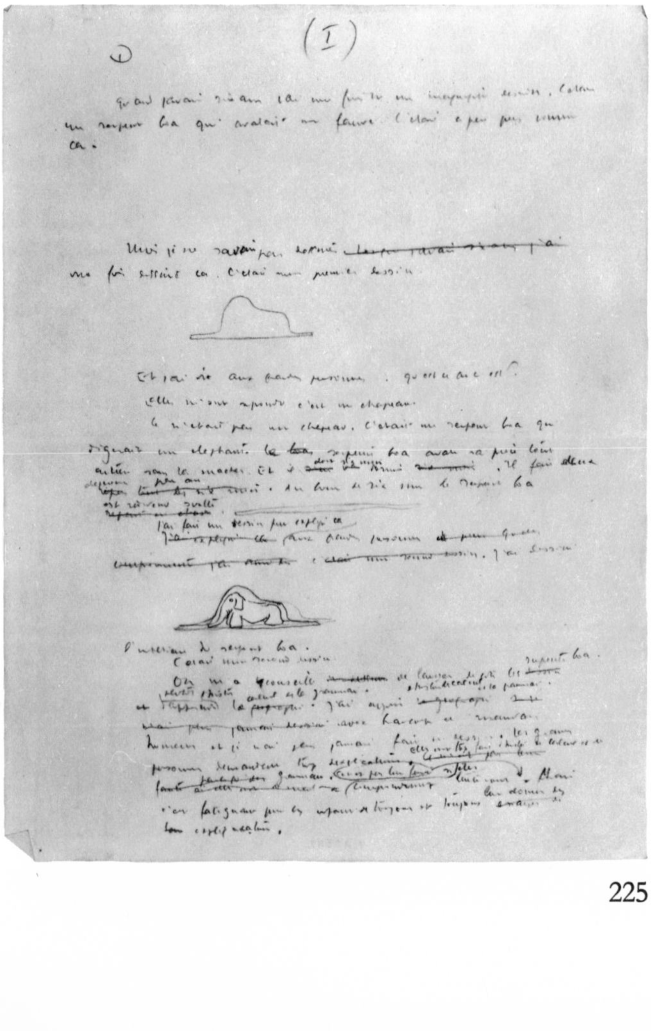
(I)

225

Bibliography

Beinecke: George McKay, compiler. *A Stevenson library . . . formed by Edwin J. Beinecke.* New Haven, 1951–1964.

Bell: Dora M. Bell. *L'idéal éthique de la royauté en France au moyen age d'après quelques moralistes de ce temps.* Geneva, 1962.

Bentley and Nurmi: G. E. Bentley, Jr., and Martin K. Nurmi. *A Blake bibliography.* Minneapolis, [1964].

Brigham: Clarence S. Brigham. "Bibliography of American editions of Robinson Crusoe to 1830." *Proceedings of the American Antiquarian Society*, October 1957.

Brunet: Jacques-Charles Brunet. *Manuel du libraire et de l'amateur de livres.* Fifth edition. Paris, 1860–1865.

Bühler: Curt F. Bühler, editor. *The history of Tom Thumbe [by] R.I.* Evanston, Illinois, 1965.

Butterworth: Charles C. Butterworth. "Early primers for the use of children." *Papers of the Bibliographical Society of America*, Fourth quarter, 1949.

Calhoun and Heaney: Philo Calhoun and Howell J. Heaney. "Dickens' *Christmas Carol* after a hundred years: a study in bibliographical evidence." *Papers of the Bibliographical Society of America*, Fourth quarter, 1945.

Carteret: Léopold Carteret. *Le trésor du bibliophile.* Paris, 1946–1948.

Catalogue J. de Rothschild: *Catalogue des livres composant la bibliothèque de feu M. le baron James de Rothschild.* 5 vols. Paris, 1884–1920.

Cohn: Albert M. Cohn. *George Cruikshank: a catalogue raisonné.* London, 1924.

Cutt: M. Nancy Cutt. *Mrs. Sherwood and her books for children.* London, 1974.

Darton: F. J. Harvey Darton. *Children's books in England.* Second edition. Cambridge, 1966.

Darton, Note: F. J. Harvey Darton. *A note on old children's books. (The Harvey Darton collection.)* Ann Arbor, [1960].

De Ricci, Census: Seymour De Ricci. *Census of medieval and renaissance manuscripts in the United States and Canada.* New York, 1935–1940.

Dickson: Arthur Dickson. *Valentine and Orson: a study in late medieval romance.* New York, 1929.

DNB: Leslie Stephen and Sidney Lee, editors. *Dictionary of national biography.* London, 1885–1901.

Doyle: Brian Doyle, compiler and editor. *The who's who of children's literature.* London, 1968.

Eckel: John C. Eckel. *The first editions of the writings of Charles Dickens.* Revised and enlarged. New York and London, 1932.

Engen: Rodney K. Engen. *Walter Crane as a book illustrator.* London, 1975.

Esdaile: Arundell Esdaile. *A list of English tales and prose romances printed before 1740.* London, 1912.

Evans: Charles Evans. *American bibliography.* Chicago, 1903–1959.

Freeman: Rosemary Freeman. *English emblem books.* London, 1948.

Gaskell: Philip Gaskell. *John Baskerville: a bibliography.* Cambridge, 1959.

Gimbel: Richard Gimbel. *Charles Dickens'* A Christmas Carol. *Three states of the first edition.* [New Haven, 1956].

Goff: Frederick R. Goff. *Incunabula in American libraries.* New York, 1964.

Graesse: J. G. T. Graesse. *Trésor de livres rares et précieux*. Dresden, 1859–1869.
Green: Henry Green, editor. *Andreae Alciati emblematum fontes quatuor*. Manchester, 1870.
Gumuchian: Gumuchian et Cie. *Les livres de l'enfance du XVe au XIXe siècle*. 2 vols. Paris, 1930.
Gumuchian (Catalogue 15): Gumuchian & Co. *100 noteworthy firsts in juvenile literature. Catalogue XV*. Paris, 1932.
GW: *Gesamtkatalog der Wiegendrucke*. Leipzig, 1925–1940.
Hamilton: Sinclair Hamilton. *Early American book illustrators and wood engravers 1670–1870*. 2 vols. Princeton, 1958, 1968.
Hardie: Martin Hardie. *English coloured books*. New York, 1906.
Harrsen: Meta Harrsen, compiler. *Central European manuscripts in the Pierpont Morgan Library*. New York, 1958.
Healey: George H. Healey. *The Cornell Wordsworth collection*. Ithaca, 1957.
Heartman: Charles F. Heartman. *The New-England primer issued prior to 1830*. New York, 1934.
Heartman, Non-New England Primers: Charles F. Heartman. *American primers, Indian primers, royal primers and thirty-seven other types of non-New-England primers issued prior to 1830*. Highland Park, New Jersey, 1935.
Heath: A. R. Heath. *Catalogue 22: children's books and chapbooks*. Bristol, 1972.
Hersholt: Jean Hersholt. *Catalog of the Jean Hersholt collection of Hans Christian Andersen*. Washington, 1954.
Hofer: Philip Hofer. *Francis Barlow's Aesop*. Harvard Library Bulletin, II (1948), 289.
Hofer-Mortimer: Harvard College Library Department of Printing and Graphic Arts. *Catalogue of books and manuscripts . . . French sixteenth century books*. Compiled by Ruth Mortimer under the supervision of Philip Hofer and William A. Jackson. Cambridge, Massachusetts, 1964.
Hoskins: Edgar Hoskins. *Horae Beatae Mariae Virginis, or Sarum and York primers, with kindred books, and primers of the reformed Roman use*. London, 1901.
Hudson: Derek Hudson. *Arthur Rackham*. New York, 1975.
Hudson, Carroll: Derek Hudson. *Lewis Carroll*. London, [1954].
Hugo: Thomas Hugo. *The Bewick collector: a descriptive catalogue of the works of Thomas and John Bewick*. London, 1866.
Hürlimann: Bettina Hürlimann. *Three centuries of children's books in Europe*. London, 1967.
Hutchins: Henry Clinton Hutchins. Robinson Crusoe *and its printing, 1719–1731: a bibliographical study*. New York, 1925.
James: Philip James. *Children's books of yesterday*. (*The Studio*, special autumn number.) London, 1933.
James, Roxburghe: M. R. James, editor. *The bestiary*. Oxford, 1928.
Jones: Helen L. Jones. *Robert Lawson, illustrator*. Boston, 1972.
Kauffmann: C. M. Kauffmann. *A survey of manuscripts illuminated in the British Isles*. Vol. 3. *Romanesque manuscripts 1066–1190*. London, 1975.
Keynes and Wolf: G. L. Keynes and Edwin Wolf II. *William Blake's illuminated books: a census*. New York, 1953.
Landwehr: John Landwehr. *Emblem books in the Low Countries, 1554–1949*. Utrecht, 1970.
Layard: George Somes Layard. "*Robinson Crusoe* and its illustrators." *Bibliographica*, 1896. Vol. II, pp. 181–203.
Linder: Leslie Linder. *A history of the writings of Beatrix Potter*. London and New York, 1971.
Mahony: Bertha E. Mahony, Louise Payson Latimer, and Beulah Folmsbee, compilers. *Illustrators of children's books, 1744–1945*. Boston, 1947.
Massé: Gertrude C. E. Massé. *A bibliography of first editions of books illustrated by Walter Crane*. London, 1923.

McCulloch: Florence McCulloch. *Mediaeval Latin and French bestiaries.* Chapel Hill, 1960.
McKell: Frank B. Fieler, assisted by John A. Zamonski and Kenneth W. Haas, Jr. *The David McCandless McKell Collection.* Boston, 1973.
McLean: Ruari McLean. *Victorian book design and color printing.* Second edition. London, 1972.
Merritt: Percival Merritt. "The royal primer." In *Bibliographical essays:* a tribute to Wilberforce Eames. Cambridge, Massachusetts, 1924.
Minnick: Thomas L. Minnick, editor. *Christopher Smart. Hymns for the amusement of children. 1772.* London, 1973.
Muir: Percy Muir. *English children's books, 1600 to 1900.* London, 1954.
Muir, Victorian: Percy Muir. *Victorian illustrated books.* London, 1971.
NBL: National Book League. *Children's books of yesterday.* Compiled by P. H. Muir. London, [1946].
NBL Andersen: National Book League. *Hans Christian Andersen 1805—2nd April—1955: catalogue of a jubilee exhibition.* London, 1955.
NCBEL: George Watson, editor. *The new Cambridge bibliography of English literature.* Cambridge, England, 1974.
Newberry, Amherst: Percy E. Newberry. *The Amherst papyri.* London, 1899.
NGA, Dürer: National Gallery. *Dürer in America.* Charles W. Talbot, editor; notes by Gaillard F. Ravenel and Jay A. Levenson. Washington, 1971.
Noakes: Vivien Noakes. *Edward Lear: the life of a wanderer.* London, 1968.
ODNR: Iona and Peter Opie, editors. *The Oxford dictionary of nursery rhymes.* Oxford, 1952.
Opie, Classic: Iona and Peter Opie. *The classic fairy tales.* London, 1974.
Opie, NBL: Iona and Peter Opie. *Three centuries of nursery rhymes and poetry for children: an exhibition held at the National Book League, May 1973.* London, [1973].
Osborne: Judith St. John. *The Osborne collection of early children's books, 1566–1910: a catalogue.* Toronto, 1958.
Pafford: J. H. P. Pafford, editor. *Isaac Watts: divine songs attempted in easy language for the use of children.* London, 1971.
Panofsky: Erwin Panofsky. *Albrecht Dürer.* Princeton, New Jersey, 1943.
Perry, Aesopica: Ben Edwin Perry. *Aesopica.* Urbana, Illinois, 1952.
Perry, Loeb: Ben Edwin Perry. *Babrius and Phaedrus.* (Loeb Classical Library.) Cambridge, Massachusetts, 1965.
PPP: Jacob Blanck. *Peter Parley to Penrod.* New York, 1956.
Praz: Mario Praz. *Studies in seventeenth-century imagery.* 2 vols. London, 1939, 1947.
Quayle: Eric Quayle. *The collector's book of children's books.* London, 1971.
Raines: Robert Raines. *Marcellus Laroon.* London, 1967.
Roscoe: S. Roscoe. *John Newbery and his successors, 1740–1814: a bibliography.* Wormley, Hertfordshire, 1973.
Roscoe, Bewick: S. Roscoe. *Thomas Bewick: a bibliography raisonné.* London, 1953.
Roscoe, Bibles: S. Roscoe. "Early English, Scottish and Irish thumb Bibles." *The Book Collector,* Summer, 1973.
Rosenbach: A. S. W. Rosenbach. *Early American children's books.* Portland, Maine, 1933.
Rothschild: *The Rothschild Library: a catalogue of the collection of eighteenth century books and manuscripts formed by Lord Rothschild.* Cambridge, 1954.
Sabin: Joseph Sabin. *Bibliotheca Americana: a dictionary of books relating to America.* Begun by Joseph Sabin, continued by Wilberforce Eames and completed by R. W. G. Vail. New York, 1868–1936.
Sadleir: Michael Sadleir. *XIX century fiction.* London and Los Angeles, [1951].

Sadler: John E. Sadler, editor. *John Amos Comenius: Orbis Pictus*. London, 1968.
Schatzki: Walter Schatzki. *Old and rare children's books: catalogue number one*. [New York, 1941.]
Scott: Temple Scott. *Oliver Goldsmith bibliographically and biographically considered*. New York, 1928.
Shepherd: Richard Herne Shepherd. *The bibliography of Thackeray*. London, 1880.
Sherbo: Arthur Sherbo. *Christopher Smart: scholar of the university*. East Lansing, 1967.
Simpson: Claude M. Simpson. *The British broadside ballad and its music*. New Brunswick, New Jersey, [1966].
Sloane: William Sloane. *Children's books in England & America in the seventeenth century*. New York, 1955.
Spielmann: Percy Edwin Spielmann. *Catalogue of the library of miniature books collected by Percy Edwin Spielmann*. London, 1961.
Spielmann and Layard: M. H. Spielmann and G. S. Layard. *Kate Greenaway*. London, 1905.
STC: A. W. Pollard and G. R. Redgrave. *A short-title catalogue of books printed in England, Scotland & Ireland and of English books printed abroad, 1475–1640*. London, 1926.
Stewart-Yeats: James McG. Stewart. *Rudyard Kipling: a bibliographical catalogue*. Edited by A. W. Yeats. Toronto, 1959.
Stone: Wilbur Macey Stone. *The gigantick histories of Thomas Boreman*. Portland, Maine, 1933.
Storer: Mary Elizabeth Storer. *Un épisode littéraire de la fin du XVIIe siècle: la mode des contes de fées (1685–1700)*. (Réimpression de l'édition de Paris, 1928.) Geneva, 1972.
Tchemerzine: Avenir Tchemerzine. *Bibliographie d'éditions originales et rares d'auteurs français des XVe, XVIe, XVIIe, et XVIIIe siècles*. Paris, 1927–[1934].
Teerink: Herman Teerink. *A bibliography of the writings of Jonathan Swift*. Second edition. Edited by Arthur H. Scouten. Philadelphia, [1963].
Thomson: J. C. Thomson. *Bibliography of the writings of Charles and Mary Lamb*. Hull, 1908.
Thwaite: Mary F. Thwaite. *From primer to pleasure in reading*. Boston, 1972.
Van Antwerp: William C. Van Antwerp. *A collector's comment on his first editions of the works of Sir Walter Scott*. San Francisco, 1932.
Wackermann: Erwin Wackermann. *Münchhausiana*. Stuttgart, 1969.
Weaver: Warren Weaver. "The first edition of *Alice's Adventures in Wonderland*: a census." *Papers of the Bibliographical Society of America*, First quarter, 1971.
Weekley: Montague Weekley. *Thomas Bewick*. London, 1953.
Welch: d'Alté A. Welch. "A bibliography of American children's books printed prior to 1821." *Proceedings of the American Antiquarian Society*, April 1963, October 1963, October 1964, October 1965, April 1967, October 1967.
Wharey: James Blanton Wharey, editor. *John Bunyan. The pilgrim's progress*. Oxford, 1928.
Wheatley: Henry B. Wheatley, editor. *The history of Sir Richard Whittington. By T.H.* London, 1885.
Williams-Madan-Green: S. H. Williams, Falconer Madan, and Roger L. Green. *The Lewis Carroll handbook*. London, 1962.
Wing: Donald G. Wing. *A short-title catalogue . . . 1641–1700*. New York, 1945–1951.
Worthington: Greville Worthington. *A bibliography of the Waverley novels*. London, [1931].

Index

In this index, which is selective, numbers refer to items rather than pages.

D

E

F

G

H

I

J

K

L

M

N

O

P

R

S

PRODUCED BY
THE STINEHOUR PRESS
AND
THE MERIDEN GRAVURE COMPANY